AN INTRODUCTION TO
Anthropology's Four Fields
Culture, Biology, Language, and Archaeology

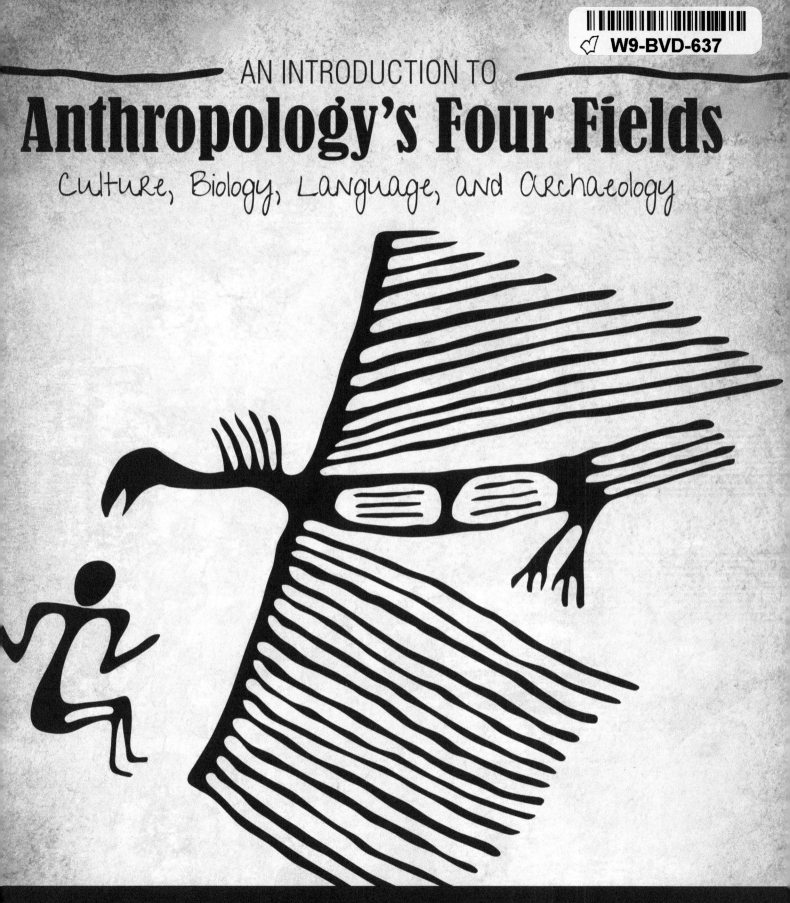

LIAM KILMURRAY

Carleton University

Kendall Hunt
publishing company

Cover image © Shutterstock.com

Chapters 7, 10, and 11 are written by Liam Kilmurray.

*Denotes original material from the author.

www.kendallhunt.com
Send all inquiries to:
4050 Westmark Drive
Dubuque, IA 52004-1840

Table of Contents

Introduction

We can reproduce within our own minds the way that the world is put together for other people. This is the extraordinary privilege and adventure of anthropology.

Marshall Sahlins

What is the purpose of an anthropology textbook? Firstly, it is to inform, to educate, to provide the reader with an understanding of the basic tenets of anthropological history, research, and theory. This text will ensure that the essential signposts are clearly marked and explained to the student of anthropology. It will also provide the reader with opportunities to be captivated by anthropology's gaze over its vast subject matter. The reader will be challenged, engaged, perplexed, and enlightened by this journey through the various domains of anthropological thinking. We will examine the fascinating process of human evolution, the wonderful complexities of early and modern civilizations, and we will examine in detail how anthropologists specialize in various fields in order to understand the past thoroughly, from a holistic perspective.

Anthropologists ask interesting questions and produce fascinating answers. For instance, why do Dani women sometimes cut off their fingertips at funerary rituals, and why do some people believe that poisoning chickens will reveal witchcraft, or hitting the ice-hockey goalposts in warm-up will keep out the puck? We will employ the intricate theoretical constructs that anthropologists have created in order to interpret, understand, and describe such actions. In order to address the theories in anthropology, there will be no "downpour of Latin tags"; rather, the language used will be succinct and descriptive, and plainly explained. We will point the reader in the direction of more nuanced analyses of theoretical, biological, and many other fields of anthropology. When we speak of linguistics, or archaeology, we will provide the introductory information on the history of the subfield, its practices, problems, and theories. We will examine certain areas in detail, providing examples of cultural diversity and anthropological research through specific case studies.

In anthropology, a holistic approach is taken: all aspects of society are analyzed not in isolation but rather as contributory parts to a unique whole. The goal is a complex understanding of human physical, social, and cultural adaptations. Anthropology, with its various domains and subfields, is well suited to this task—the task of attempting to understand all facets of society, and how they are linked. The complex web of human practices and adaptations is analyzed against the canvas of the past, which is frequently opaque and neglected. The past is a potent force in human societies, and it is this past that anthropology includes in its examination of cultures.

Anthropology intersects with many other programs of study. Within the areas typically studied in an anthropology undergraduate degree are geology, language, biology, environmental sciences, ecology, economics, sociology, critical theory, culture studies, indigenous studies, and many more. This diversity is undoubtedly a strength, as students of anthropology gain exposure to so many different fields of research and their associated professions. It is therefore an excellent undergraduate degree as it opens the students to many possible pathways in learning and career choices.

Most introductory anthropology textbooks focus on cultural anthropology. They pay little attention to the other fields in anthropology, such as physical anthropology or archaeology. This is not surprising, given that the majority of North American university programs focus on cultural anthropology. This book, however, incorporates all four fields of anthropology. Cultural anthropology is a vibrant and essential component of anthropology, and we address the standard topics within this subfield such as kinship, economy, marriage, religion, and other key cultural institutions. Yet the four-field approach incorporates linguistics, physical anthropology, and archaeology as well as cultural anthropology.

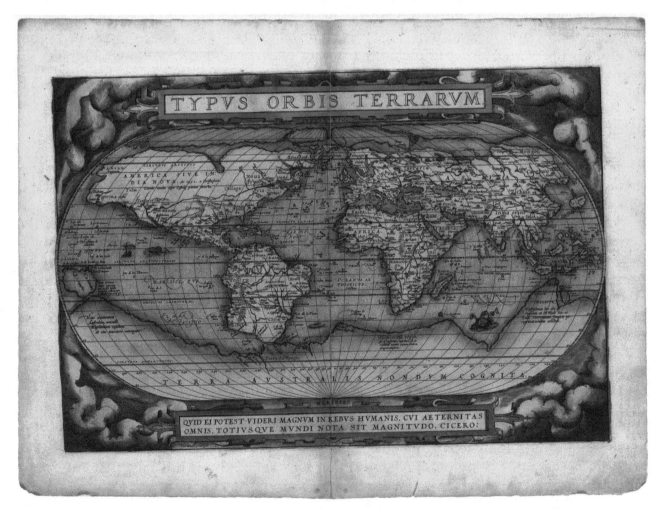

Theatrum Orbis Terrarum (Latin: "Theatre of the World") is considered the first modern atlas. Written by Abraham Ortelius and originally printed on May 20, 1570, in Antwerp, Belgium.

Source: Library of Congress

Therefore, this text also addresses these three other key subfields. We include chapters largely omitted from many cultural anthropology texts, such as applied anthropology, archaeology, evolutionary studies, and ethnography. In a broad and lengthy teaching career, we have found that students, both undergraduate and graduate, are excited to learn not only about the field of cultural anthropology but also areas that incorporate the archaeology of the past, the evolution of humanity and of its languages, and the history of ethnographic research.

Archaeology and prehistory are essential aspects of anthropology.

We also examine the emergence of anthropology from a variety of sources: sociology, the natural sciences, and geology. This enables the text to incorporate a variety of fascinating topics such as the emergence of a prehistory through the works of Charles Darwin, Alfred Wallace, Charles Lyell, and others. We also examine the evolution of the genus *Homo* and the adaptations that enabled us to dominate today's planet, for better or worse. We turn to ethnographic studies to learn how the first anthropologists travelled the globe in search of difference and similarity, and in so doing began the process of developing anthropological theory. In all, this book offers a well-rounded view of the diverse fields of anthropology. It is hoped that by the end of this text the reader will have a good appreciation of the complexity and of the excitement of the anthropologist's world.

Chapter 1: What is anthropology?

We begin by answering this fundamental question: anthropology is clearly defined, and its subject matter—culture—is explained and expanded upon. We learn how anthropology is a four-fielded science that consists of the following: cultural anthropology, physical anthropology, linguistic anthropology, and archaeology. Chapter 1 details the nuances of each field and explains how they are combined to form the holistic approach that is the hallmark of anthropology. We discuss how anthropology is both a science and yet retains elements of the humanities. We distinguish between anthropology and other social sciences such as sociology, history, and economics, offering the reader a clear view of just how anthropology situates itself as that field which combines many elements of other soft and hard sciences, yet emerges as a unique field of research and practice. Next, we talk of the guiding principles of anthropology, those ideas, constructs, and theories that shape the view of the discipline. We raise issues such as cultural relativism, ethnocentrism, holism, and the biocultural and comparative perspectives. These are important terms and issues that will be revisited throughout the book. It is important to have an appreciation of the structured and detailed nature of the anthropological approach before reading further in the text, and Chapter 1 ensures that the reader will be knowledgeable about all of these terms and issues before diving into the body of the book. This introductory chapter concludes by answering another question: why is anthropology important? Because it provides us with a unique view on the human experience and it equips us to understand, analyze, and appreciate this view.

Chapter 2: Evolutionary theory

Evolutionary studies have been around for a long time and are well established in many fields other than anthropology. The facts of evolution by means of natural selection as outlined by Wallace and Darwin have never had an easy ride in either the public domain or in some branches of academia. Within anthropology, specifically physical anthropology, evolution is a matter of great importance and one that is central to the reconstruction of hominid evolutionary patterns and the construction of paleoanthropological chronologies. In some parts of the world evolution is much disputed, rejected, passionately defended, or opposed. In the United States, for example, only 12% of people believe that humans evolved from another physical form. For anthropologists, following Darwinian principles, evolution is *what* happened, and natural selection, mutation, and drift are *how* it happened. In Chapter 2, we detail the slow emergence of evolutionary thinking, beginning with the Dark Ages, moving on to the Enlightenment, and the Age of Discovery before settling into the great developments of the nineteenth century with the advent of Wallace's and Darwin's theories of natural selection. Along the way, we will learn how geologists such as Charles Lyell and James Hutton enabled curious knowledge-seekers to understand the sheer longevity of the time it took the Earth to form its valleys, rivers, and canyons. We will learn how amateur archaeologists discovered strange-looking fossils and ancient tools. In doing this work, and allied with philosophical and theoretical developments from scholars such as Thomas Malthus and Georges Cuvier, these people and events paved the way for Charles Darwin to formulate his evolutionary theories. We present a detailed analysis of the component parts of Darwinian evolutionary theory, such as natural selection, migration, drift, and mutation. Understanding evolutionary forces and the history of the adaptations our species has undergone, and continues to undergo, is essential. It is crucial to the anthropological project of understanding humanity in all its manifestations and histories. It is also essential to an understanding of just how we became the bipedal, large-brained, and communicative animals that we are today.

Chapter 3: And then there was one: Modern humans

In Chapter 3, we focus on the evolutionary history of anatomically modern humans. Set in the evolutionary theatre of Africa, we examine the earliest known members of our species, various contemporary hominids, and those who lived in earlier times. Paleoanthropology is a subject that has very professional jargon, dates, names, and techniques which sometimes seem designed to confuse the reader. However, in this chapter we explain the terminology, we delve into the dating techniques and we explain the role of DNA in reconstructing the human lineage. In tracing the footsteps of our earliest ancestors, we examine various archaeological sites that have yielded fascinating human remains. We analyze the findings from sites such as Kebara, Tabun, and Qafzeh in Israel, and the famed sites of Border Cave and Klasies River Mouth in southern Africa. As we look back roughly 120,000 years ago, we will see how Neanderthals and early humans lived in the same regions of northern Africa and the Middle East for tens of thousands of years, often in very close proximity. The principal focus is placed upon the developments in the period known as the Upper Paleolithic, when in Europe the Neanderthals died out and were replaced by *homo sapiens*, the last surviving member of the genus *Homo*. The road from quadrupedal (four-footed) arboreal ancestors runs through a sometimes bewildering variety of species—*Ardipithecus, Australopithecus*, and so on, before it arrives in North Africa and Europe during the Upper Paleolithic. This was a period of intense cultural development that witnessed the beginnings of true art, and the establishment of complex and beautiful tool technologies. The road taken and the archaeological effort to retrace it are well illuminated in this chapter.

Chapter 4: The meaning of culture

Culture is the cumulative repository of the knowledge, beliefs, values, materials, attitudes, and stories of a particular people. As such, it is central to anthropological analysis. In this chapter, we define culture and explain why it is of such importance to all fields of anthropology. We examine the various definitions of culture, the ways in which different anthropologists through the years have approached its study, and we speak to its continued importance in all human social life. By citing numerous examples, we discuss the endless varieties of human cultural behavior, the attempts by anthropologists to understand them and contribute to an overall comprehension of the importance of culture. We discuss culture in its various manifestations, such as language, ideology, and mental culture. We consider the importance of concepts such as the sacred and the secular, taboos and restrictions. We explore laws, norms, folkways, mores, and taboos. In order to convey the central importance of culture to social identity and social memory, we cite examples of particular practices from particular groups around the world and discuss some anthropological interpretations of these practices. We also attempt to convey how anthropology has constructed specific terms and theories in order to discuss cultural practices. Topics addressed include acculturation, enculturation, and integration. This chapter also raises the issue of primates using technology and other cultural practices. We discuss racism and culture, tackling biological differences and their supposed relationship with culture, we also unpack various issues that are important to the discussion of race and racism in regard to culture, such as hypodescent, blood quantums, so-called IQ tests, and brain sizes. Finally, we touch upon important areas of the relationship between society and culture. The goal is to explain the many different usages of the term "culture," its manifestations in society and how anthropologists view this in a distinctly different way than other social scientists.

Chapter 5: Kinship, marriage, and family

In Chapter 5, we undertake an anthropological examination of the variety of human social approaches to sex, kinship, and marriage. We begin by addressing some of the different cultural practices regarding sexual relations, such as polygamy and monogamy. We discuss understandings of masculinity, femininity, third genders, and the different approaches that societies may take in regulating, tolerating, or banning certain sexual relations. Throughout this chapter we call upon evidence collected by anthropologists such as Margaret Mead, Franz Boas, and Bronislaw Malinowski regarding different forms of marriage, postmarriage residency rules, and gift and dowry giving. We see the fascinating diversity in how people construct their kinship structures, and comment upon the impact of such patterns on daily life. We review the various descent systems that anthropologists have named and studied over the centuries, provide examples of these systems and look at how they are not just naming systems but in fact have an impact on all other aspects of social life. This chapter reveals how sex, kinship, and descent are crucial structuring principles of society, and how they operate is of great interest to anthropologists.

Chapter 6: Expressive culture: Language and symbols

In Chapter 6, we present a detailed examination of the field of anthropology that deals with language—linguistic anthropology. This field is different from the study of language itself—philology. Rather than studying language for its own sake, linguistic anthropology examines the social and cultural aspects of language and language usage. This includes communication in forms other than the spoken word. Chapter 6 explores how linguistic anthropology is concerned with forms of communication such as the written word, gestures, facial expressions, clothing, bodily stance, and bodily ornamentation—known collectively as *para langue*. Anthropologists consider language one of *the* hallmarks of what it means to be human. Its study in anthropology includes physical anthropologists examining the brain patterns and vocal tracts of early hominids to determine whether they had the ability to communicate in a complex manner. Primatological research studies communication among chimpanzees, bonobos, and other primates. For the anthropological linguist, language is a product of the brain, and speech a product of the vocal tract. Both of these aspects are examined to fill in the picture of the emergence of spoken human language. Historical linguists in anthropology seek to trace the emergence, development, and bifurcation (splitting off) of languages from a parent language. For example, the superfamily known as the Indo European language family gave rise to hundreds of different languages. Historical linguists trace this process, seeking to determine, for example, under what conditions Latin gave rise to Portuguese, French, Spanish, Italian, Provencal, and other languages. They seek the conditions necessary for languages to spread and be altered, adapted, abandoned, or persist. Was there a demographic or ideational reason for language development and change, or was it a colonial, economic, or religious process that gave rise to various languages and their offspring?

Chapter 6 asks whether culture has a symbolic basis. We examine the relationship between signs and objects and discuss iconic and indexical meaning as anthropologists understand these terms. An overriding issues for anthropological linguistics is how exactly culture shapes the way we communicate. To understand this we discuss movement, gesture, body posture, and many other methods of communicating. Keeping to the anthropological approach of trying to grasp the long development of language and communication, we then examine the communicative abilities of early and contemporary nonhuman primates. We then investigate the structure of language, addressing phonemes, syntax, and morphemes of specific languages. Sociolinguistic approaches are also detailed, as we consider how language use and dialects can be linked to gender, class, or ethnicity. Finally, we tackle the issue of language change, of the conditions under which this happens, and we present data on evolving and disappearing languages. The chapter concludes with a discussion of linguistic determinism in anthropology, and the much-debated Sapir–Whorf hypothesis.

Chapter 7: Ethnographic studies

In Chapter 7, we discuss the field of anthropology known as ethnography, or participant-observation. This is where cultural anthropology had its beginnings, in the early to mid-nineteenth century. We trace the development of ethnography, from early traveller and "gentlemanly" inquiries to the more sophisticated and professional forms practiced today. We examine some of the most well-known ethnographers and their works, such as Bronislaw Malinowski, E. E. Evans-Prichard, Franz Boaz, and Clifford Geertz. We trace the development of ethnographic inquiry through the works of these pioneers of anthropology. We then detail the process of organizing an ethnographic enterprise. Beginning with site selection, paperwork, and other hurdles, we then examine the many challenges that the ethnographer may face in the field. Such challenges include culture shock, which we discuss in some detail. The challenges that ethnographers face in interpreting their data are also discussed. We analyze the impact of theory, as anthropologists sought to both standardize their research, and to apply a variety of theoretical approaches to studying and interpreting the data gathered form their immersion in various communities and cultures around the world. The chapter also includes an important discussion of postcolonial ethnography and how various revisionist phases in anthropology have impacted the field of ethnography. We conclude by envisioning the future of ethnography and its application in the virtual world and our more globalized world.

Chapter 8: Subsistence systems and material culture

Why are so many anthropologists focused on subsistence techniques? Chapter 8 answers this question in great detail. We explore the variety of ways in which people around the world secure a living from their environments. We examine the theoretical models that various anthropologists use to analyze and interpret subsistence practices. Cultural materialism—the idea that culture is shaped by technological and economic factors—is explained and explored. We examine cultural ecology, the view that the environment and energy are prominent in structuring societies' institutions and cultural values. We present an in-depth analysis of the many ways of life that humans have created and adapted to in terms of how they wrest a living from the earth. Foragers, hunters, horticulturalists, farmers, and pastoralists are each addressed. We will see how each adaptive mode, each "subsistence round," throws up particular social structures and ways of thinking. Cultural examples of each mode of adaptation are provided, as we examine the particularities of San bushmen, Mbuti pygmies, Yanomamo hunters, and Basseri pastoralists, to include just a few. Chapter 8 looks at the prehistory of each subsistence technique, examining particular archaeological sites. We trace the development of particular food producing or gathering strategies, using ethnographic data to paint a fuller picture of each example. Students will come to appreciate the fact that gathering, hunting, planting, or tending one's food supply is not just a matter of obtaining calories and energy. There are ritual associations, taboos, histories, and cultural preferences that must also be understood. Moreover, the manner in which food is procured impacts many of the structural components of societies. There are impacts on gender relations, kinship structures, and spiritual and religious institutions. Understanding what and how people eat, and how they share what they make or hunt, reveals to us many of the chief characteristics of a given society. Understanding subsistence systems is, for anthropologists, a matter of essential importance.

Chapter 9: Religion and culture

Chapter 9 begins with the long-studied relationship between religion and the maintenance of social and moral order. This question is central to both cultural anthropology and sociology and is analyzed through cross-cultural comparisons and theoretical constructs that have been used to explain religion's role in society. Linked to this is the issue of religious ideology, what it is, how it is defined, and what anthropologists have discovered over the years of researching this question. We trace the evolution of belief in supernatural beings and their power. We focus on the attempts of anthropologists to come to terms with what are often beliefs very different from their own, and we attempt to uncover how such beliefs have influenced a culture's world view and the social structures of their communities. In the history of anthropology, and more specifically of participant-observation, the study of early religious beliefs has figured prominently. We address animatism, mana, taboo, and provide a case-study on the sacred cows of India. We present the findings of early and current anthropological research on anthropomorphism—the attribution of human characteristics or behavior to a god, animal, or other object. The sources of religious symbolism and belief are of interest to anthropology as they reveal much of both the early religions and how they are still practiced today. The major religions of the world are analyzed, including those characterized by polytheism (many gods) and monotheism (a singular god). We also discuss shamanism and shamanic religions, both past and present. Analysis of religion through the anthropological lens also requires exploring the social organization of religion. This chapter uses the examples of communal religions and ecclesiastical religions. For the anthropologist studying religion and spirituality, one of the more interesting and important areas is that of ritual. It is through rituals that much of the social relevance of religious and spiritual beliefs are revealed. During rituals, whether of baptism, communion, or funerary rites, much of the social relevance of the belief system is on display. Our analysis is not confined to the major religions; we address areas such as magic, contagion, divination, witchcraft, and voodoo. We cite research into the psychology of religion, and what people hope to achieve through trances, what they take from near death experiences, and how some belief systems interpret and attempt to control dreams. We raise the vexing issue of religious extremism, seeking commonalties and motivations behind fundamentalism and violence, using the Christian Crusades as a case study of religious extremism. Finally, we present the anthropological views on religious change, such as those found in syncretism, secularization, and revitalization movements.

Chapter 10: Archaeology and prehistory

Archaeology, the field of anthropology that examines the material remains of past and present societies, is the subject of Chapter 10. We begin with a thorough examination of the earliest days of archaeology and how it developed. We trace the emergence of prehistory and the long battle to definitively establish a human past older than various creationist beliefs. We then take a tour of several major archaeological sites and their excavations. We discuss the importance of, for example, L'Anse aux Meadows in Canada, Çatalhöyük in Turkey, and Newgrange in Ireland. These sites provide a flavor of the importance of interpreting the contexts and crucial nature of specific moments in human prehistory as evidenced through material remains. We then discuss the role of theory in archaeology; how we interpret the findings from ancient archaeological sites. We address earlier theories such as culture-history, and we tackle the problems that are now recognized in such a school of thought that relied on an evolutionary framework to interpret and classify past societies. We move on to more recent approaches, such as processual archaeology, with its focus on empirical, data-driven interpretations. In contrast, postprocessual archaeologists seek to assert a more agency-centered past, one in which actors were knowledgeable and creative and which relies not only on interpreting hard data but also addresses symbol and meaning in the interpretation of archaeological remains. Archaeology has witnessed many technological innovations over the past few decades, and we discuss the application of LiDAR technology—noninvasive satellite and radar imagery of archaeological sites. We will see how such technologies have been applied recently in the discovery of archaeological sites in the Amazon jungle and how the use of such modern technologies raises debate among archaeologists. We then investigate ethnoarchaeological methods which allow archaeologists to use the present to understand the past. By examining the practices of living people as they go through their daily lives and how they thereby contribute to creating the archaeological record, archaeologists can better understand site formation processes, and this can provide a better view on past societies. Finally, we discuss the issue of environmental archaeology, and seek to demonstrate how archaeological knowledge can help us to understand the impact that people can have on their environment, for example, through the way they construct their villages and cities. We cite the demise of the Classic Mayan city-states of the eighth and ninth centuries AD, drawing parallels to some of current pressing issues of environmental degradation—how humans degrade their environments, but also how environmental issues like climate change affect archaeological remains.

Chapter 11: Applied anthropology

Chapter 11 focuses on the field of "applied" anthropology. This is anthropology performed outside of academic institutions. Applied anthropology is different from engaged-public anthropology, albeit with some overlap. We examine modern anthropologists working in human resources, medical anthropologists in the employ of NGOs, those involved in land-claims processes, and many other areas. We begin with definitions of applied anthropology, and then discuss the history and emergence of this subfield of anthropology. Titled "Anthropology at Work," Chapter 11 seeks to inform the reader and the student of anthropology about the many different fields of employment that exist outside of academic settings. We list these diverse fields and provide examples and case studies of several. For example, we look at forensic anthropology in the context of the awful Pickton Farm murders and subsequent investigation. We discuss how anthropologists employ indigenous knowledge in the context of business studies, and we examine the role anthropologists play in health issues through the case study of the Baby Bottle Formula scandal involving Nestle. There are particular challenges that the applied anthropologist faces, not least the cooption of their research by employers, such as the military or private corporations. We trace some of the more contentious issues and debates at the forefront of applied anthropology. These include the use of Human Terrain Systems (e.g., anthropologists working for the US military in Afghanistan and Iraq). We also examine the role the applied anthropologist can play in fields such as sustainability and development. This chapter will broaden appreciation for the areas in which anthropologists can gain employment and contribute to solving real world issues.

Chapter 12: Conclusion

Chapter 12 turns to the future of anthropology. We link this to a consideration of the future of humanity, for they are entwined in many ways. Anthropologists study culture, how it is transmitted, retained and impacts everything that we do and think. The rapid changes in the world have a tremendous impact on the field of anthropology. As cultures mingle, assimilate, adapt and are altered, anthropologists are there to observe the emergent patterns. The future of the planet, whether in regard to environmental issues, warfare, or over-population, is in the crosshairs of anthropological analysis. The book therefore concludes with a brief examination of how, as the world becomes more globalized, connected, polluted, and populated, anthropologists will adapt and persist in their studies of culture. We touch upon the Internet and how it has presented anthropology with newer yet more complex fields to plough. We finish by restating anthropology's age-old claim: to understand the myriad ways in which people live their lives and to document, predict, analyze, and appreciate these many ways of being human.

Chapter 1
Four Field Anthropology

Arnaud F. Lambert

Outline

"To the extent that we are all interested in people, in our fellow human beings, we are all anthropologists."

(Coleman and Watson 1990)

The term "**culture**" refers to the shared ideas and behavior patterns that characterize the way members of a society adapt to and utilize their environment, organize themselves, interact with other people, and express their ideas. In short, culture is what constitutes people's particular way of life. People today display a remarkable variety of cultural behaviors and customs. There are societies where warfare has been relatively unknown (Dentan 1979). Among some East African pastoralists (**Figure 1.1**), such as the Nuer (Evans-Pritchard 1940), cattle are exchanged in ways reminiscent of money. In India, there is a third gender of emasculated men (Nanda 1990). On some of the islands of Melanesia, such as Papua New Guinea, there are religious groups who await the arrival of their ancestors in planes filled with Western goods (Kilani 1983; Lawrence 1986; Worsley 1968). And so forth.

When we first hear about or encounter the customs of different cultures, it is easy to ignore them as "exotic" or "superstitious" behaviors. Perhaps, these traditions may even appear "backward" or "primitive" to you. You might even develop a strong moral disapproval for some of these behaviors depending on the value systems and beliefs with which you were raised in your own society. But anthropologists see these customs in a different light. Through anthropology we can learn about new and unexpected customs and come to realize that they are really not so different from our own taken-for-granted ways of life. Looking at cultures through the lens of anthropology, then, affords us the special opportunity to see both our similarities and our differences with the rest of humanity.

Cultural anthropology is the comparative study of human cultures based on information drawn from various societies all over the world. One of the goals of cultural anthropology is to show how the endless varieties of human cultural behavior—the unique customs and traditions that are often so puzzling to us at first glance (**Figure 1.2**)—can be explained as perfectly sensible solutions to the problems of human existence.

One of the great paradoxes of culture is that, as we learn to accept our own cultural beliefs and values, we unconsciously learn to reject those of other peoples. **Anthropology**,

© 2014 Dr_Flash. Used under license of Shutterstock, Inc.

Figure 1.1.   Maasai cattle herder from the Serengeti (Tanzania).

©2014 marcovarro. Used under license of Shutterstock, Inc.

Figure 1.2. Asaro Mudmen warriors (Goroka, Papua New Guinea).

by contrast, takes the view that other societies deserve to be studied and understood. This is not always easy. In life, you will encounter cultural behaviors that will frequently challenge your taken for-granted assumptions about what is right or wrong, good or bad, and beautiful or ugly. This relativistic approach may disturb some of you, but that is not the intent of this text or of anthropology as a discipline. Rather, one of the key roles of anthropology in today's increasingly global world is to help students broaden their perspectives and to become more sensitive to other ways of life. It is absolutely critical for understanding the multicultural perspectives, ethnic conflicts, and global human problems, which are characteristic of our contemporary world. Before we go further, however, we need to explore anthropology as a discipline in a little more detail.

1.1   What is anthropology?

The term "anthropology" is derived from two Greek words: *anthropos* (humans) and *logia* (study). In its broadest sense, then, anthropology refers to the study of human beings. This is an extremely broad topic. We are not just focusing on the workings of industrial societies or trying to model the human mind but we are attempting nothing less than to understand all human kind, all human societies, all human cultures, those that exist today and those that existed in the past. We are interested in the biological and cultural diversity of all human beings, the meaning of their customs, and the origins of their beliefs. We also seek to uncover the origins and evolution of the several thousand languages spoken in the world today. Although it might be tempting to focus on just examining and celebrating the human diversity present in the world, anthropology also reminds us that human beings belong to the same species. We share a common evolutionary heritage and more often than not, share many of the same social problems and day-to-day struggles.

In practice, the incredible breadth of anthropology has led to the creation of several sub-disciplines or sub-fields, each focusing on a distinct aspect of the human experience. These sub-fields include cultural anthropology, physical anthropology, archaeology, and anthropological linguistics (**Figure 1.3**). Over time, each of these sub-fields has developed its own theories and methodologies.

1. **Cultural anthropology** Sometimes called **social anthropology**, cultural anthropology deals with the description and analysis of human cultures and societies. It seeks to interpret and at times explain cultural differences and similarities. To accomplish this task, cultural anthropologists use a two-part methodology that relies on **ethnography** (participant-observation fieldwork) and **ethnology** (cross-cultural comparison).

   Ethnographic fieldwork allows anthropologists the opportunity to gather data about the cultural customs (**Figure 1.4**), settings, values, and beliefs of a society by spending an extended period of time living in a community, usually by focusing on a research problem or an issue of interest to the anthropologist (Bernard 1994; Wolcott 1995). This emphasis on small-scale social groups has historically given anthropologists a rather different point of view regarding human societies than someone focusing solely on large-scale systems or social organizations as is often done in political science and economics. The extended amount of time anthropologists spend in these communities has also allowed us to acknowledge the increasing amount of contact between cultures. Historically, such changes came about through the colonialism, independence movements in many parts of the world, and the subsequent rise of post-colonial states. Today, people in indigenous communities all around the world make use of Western commodities, participate in international organizations such as the United Nations, and communicate using the internet and cell phones. These cultural changes signify the increasingly global nature of human interaction and represent an important area of research in anthropology.

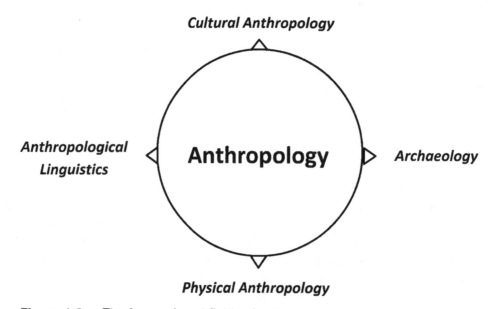

Figure 1.3. The four main subfields of anthropology.

Figure 1.4. Dani men (Indonesian New Guinea/Irian Jaya).

Once an anthropologist has gathered sufficient ethnographic information, ethnologists analyze, examine, and compare the results. The goal of ethnology is to make generalizations about how societies and cultures function and change. In turn, this permits anthropologists to reach a better understanding of cultural differences and similarities. Such data is also useful in other sub-fields such as physical anthropology and archaeology, where access to information from living peoples may be more problematic.

2. **Physical anthropology** Also known as **biological anthropology**, this sub-field is closely aligned with the natural sciences, especially human biology, anthropometrics, osteology, forensics, and genetics (Ice 2005; Leidy 1994; Relethford 2012). Although many physical anthropologists seek to understand the role that environmental factors such as nutrition, disease, and social variables play in the diversification, growth, and development of the human body (McElroy and Townsend 2008), others are primarily concerned with tracing the evolution of human beings and their hominid ancestors from the fossil record. This specialty of physical anthropology, known as **paleoanthropology**, shares many of the same methods with archaeology because researchers must uncover the **fossil remains** of our ancestors, especially their skulls, teeth, and long bones, and interpret their lifestyle from the contexts of these skeletal materials (Conroy and Pontzer 2012) (**Figure 1.5**). This requires careful excavation (removal) of the fossils to identify their relationships with other remains or artifacts and to determine their chronological placement.

Other physical anthropologists are interested in the relationship between human beings and their **primate** relatives such as chimpanzees, bonobos, gorillas, and orangutans (**Figures 1.6** and **1.7**). Sometimes called **primatology**, this branch of physical anthropology is closely related to zoology and examines the origins, anatomy, genetics, and behavior of non-human primates such as prosimians, monkeys, and apes in both their natural habitats and in captivity (Strier 2010; Sussman et al. 2013).

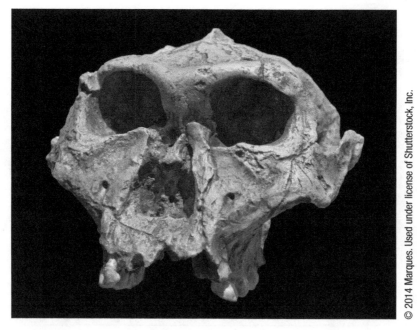

Figure 1.5. Skull of *Paranthropus robustus*, a hominid ancestor.

Figure 1.6. Chimpanzee (Uganda, East Africa).

3. **Archaeology** Archaeologists seek to make sense of the lifeways of past cultures (Renfrew and Bahn 1996). They examine how people in the past acquired food, traded with other communities, organized their societies, and made sense of the world through religion and ritual. To do this, archaeologists recover the material traces of these behaviors and customs in the form of artifacts, skeletal remains, and settlement patterns and meticulously record their contexts to reconstruct their original patterns of use. This methodology is known as **excavation** (**Figure 1.8**).

© 2014 Eric Gevaert. Used under license of Shutterstock, Inc.

Figure 1.7. Orangutan female and her offspring.

© 2014 Patricia Hofmeester. Used under license of Shutterstock, Inc.

Figure 1.8. Archaeological excavation of a Roman settlement known as "Vindolanda" (England).

Sometimes, archaeologists will rely on analogies with living peoples to make sense of these patterns but often they must interpret the **archaeological record** without much aid.

Although sometimes contrasted with **history**, archaeology does not just focus on the unwritten periods of human existence or **prehistory**. Many archaeologists use their skills at excavation and their focus on material remains to shed light on aspects of everyday life seldom recorded in official records. Sometimes referred to as **historical archaeology** (Insoll 2001; Moreland 2001; Orser and Fagan 1995), this specialty examines how people in medieval European households made a living, the first expressions of Buddhism in China and Southeast Asia (**Figure 1.9**), the life of a slave in the plantations of the American South, or the work habits of laborers in the industrial towns of the early nineteenth century to name a few.

4. **Anthropological linguistics**   Human **language** is such a complicated phenomenon that it deserves its own branch of study. Anthropological linguists describe and record the sounds and structures of many of the endangered languages of the world (Eastman 1990). They also attempt to trace the evolution of all known human languages and **language families** (Campbell 2000). Apart from these historical concerns, many linguists are also interested in how language is used within different cultural contexts to communicate different messages about a person's social position, values, and beliefs. This **ethnography of communication** is closely related to sociolinguistics and focuses on speech acts (Moerman 1988; Saville-Troike 2003) and how members of different speech communities interact by creating **pidgins** and **creole languages** (Bickerton 1976).

   Anthropological linguists also delve into deeper philosophical issues regarding the complex relationship between language, cognition and culture. To what degree is language a reflection of culture? And, to what extent does the language you speak influence the way you perceive the world? The answers to such problems may have major implications for cognitive science and the study of the human mind (Hickmann 2000; Lucy 1997).

© 2014 Twonix Studio. Used under license of Shutterstock, Inc.

Figure 1.9.   Angkor Thom (Cambodia).

1.2   Is anthropology a science?

Over its short history, there has been a strong emphasis on describing "anthropology" as the scientific study of humankind in the sense that it seeks to create generalizations about human societies and human behavior by drawing connections between **etic** (value-free and objective) observations of these phenomena (Harris 1979; Radcliffe-Brown 1965).

Certainly, anthropology as a whole is an empirically-grounded social science discipline. We base our interpretations of, and generalizations about, human behavior on observations, either as direct witnesses or by analyzing the material remains of the behavior. However, scientifically-minded anthropologists have sought to go beyond such **empiricism** and to create a **nomothetic** discipline in which customs are explained by finding statistically-significant correlations with other behaviors or environmental circumstances. While such approaches have been useful in the study of human adaptive strategies, particularly food-gathering strategies and economic systems, and to some degree the study of human organization (Ember and Ember 1997), they have been less able to adequately explain religious beliefs (Geertz 1973).

In addition, some of the sub-fields of anthropology, such as physical anthropology and archaeology, lend themselves more to hypothesis-testing and the search for general models of human behavior by virtue of the nature of their data. They focus on biological organisms and their evolution.

Other scholars have questioned our ability to adequately observe and model human behavior. Humans are so diverse and change so quickly, can we ever truly create general models of their behavior? These "**postmodern anthropologists**" also question the ability of ethnographers to dispassionately describe life in another culture (Clifford and Marcus 1986; Clifford 1988). If we are all products of our cultures, then how can we examine someone else's culture without any bias? This **emic** (culture-specific) perspective suggests that the only way to truly understand other cultures is to use terms that are meaningful only to members of those societies.

There is certainly a lot to be gained from trying to develop general models of human behavior, but perhaps one of the most important challenges of the postmodern critique has been to show us that we need to always be skeptical of the applicability of our models and of the adequacy of our observations. Rather than creating an impasse between scientifically-minded anthropologists and postmodern anthropologists, then, perhaps the best way forward would be to continue to hold the construction of cross-cultural generalizations and etic models of human behavior as the ultimate goal of anthropology while also understanding that the diversity of human cultures and lived experiences of people in other societies also deserve to be appreciated much like these aspects of the human experience are seen in the **humanities** (Peregrine et al. 2012).

1.3   How is anthropology different from other social science disciplines?

Anthropology is one of the youngest social sciences but it is also one of the most unique. Its breadth of scope and depth of coverage allow it to borrow freely from many other disciplines, especially sociology, history, and psychology. At the same time, there are some crucial differences between these social sciences. In this section, we will examine some of these differences.

1. **Sociology versus anthropology**   Both anthropology and sociology share many of the same founding figures such as Emile Durkheim and Karl Marx (Harris 1968). As a result, we also share many of the same terms regarding culture and society and have a common core vocabulary. In addition, both disciplines focus on understanding human behavior within its socio-cultural context. However, whereas sociology has historically examined both large and small groups in modern societies (usually whichever society the sociologist is from), anthropologists have generally had a much broader view of their subject and have examined the culture of small communities in any and every society (Wolcott 1995).

2. **Psychology versus anthropology**   Psychology is often characterized as the study of human behavior. This is usually accomplished by examining the human mind, psyche, or the brain depending on the orientation and training of the psychologist. Anthropology also has a long history of examining the relationship between the human mind and culture (e.g., Malinowski 1927; Mead 1930; Spiro 1993). However, like the new sub-discipline of **cultural psychology**, anthropologists are keenly aware of cultural differences in human behavior and the potential problems this diversity may bring in identifying abnormal behavior and defining ways of being an effective human (Fryberg 2012).

3. **History versus anthropology**   To study the human past, historians must rely on written records (e.g., census data, diaries, church records, hieroglyphic inscriptions, and the like). However, the earliest human records only go as far back as 5500 years ago (c. 3500 BC) in ancient Egypt and Mesopotamia (Robinson 1995) (**Figure 1.10**).

© 2014 Paul Vinten. Used under license of Shutterstock, Inc.

Figure 1.10.   Hieroglyphic carvings on the wall of an ancient temple (Luxor, Egypt).

The material record of human beings and their bipedal ancestors goes back at least seven million years (Brunet et al. 2002; Senut et al. 2001)! In other words, approximately 99.92% of human existence is outside the purview of history. By contrast, with its emphasis on excavation and the reconstruction of human behavior from material remains, archaeology is able to access these areas of unwritten human history.

4. **Economics versus anthropology** Economics offers a unique way to view human behavior as the rational product of human beings trying to maximize their finite resources. But from an anthropological perspective, it may be asked if such pragmatic views of human nature are applicable in all cultures. Take for example the Kwakiutl and the Tlingit from the Northwest Coast of North America. Periodically, the households and chiefs in these societies would participate in ceremonies known as potlatches (Boas 1966; Drucker 1965). During these ceremonies, a host chief would give away as much of their wealth as possible to the guests, sometimes competing chiefs! At first glance, such behavior does not seem to be economically or politically rational. However, on deeper inspection, it becomes clear that the host acquires a great deal of prestige from giving away their wealth.

   In many ways, then, the broad subject matter and theoretical orientations of anthropology complements the efforts of many of the other social sciences. It broadens the scope of sociology, it brings a cross-cultural perspective to psychology and economics, and greatly extends the reach of history.

1.4   What are the guiding principles of anthropology?

A key feature of anthropology is its ability to deal effectively with different human groups and their diverse customs. To accomplish this, anthropologists make use of a number of guiding principles to orient their work and research.

1. **Cultural relativism** Having been raised in our own cultures, we each have a tendency to view our own cultures as normal or even superior and to judge other people's beliefs and behavior based on those of our culture. Anthropologists call this tendency "**ethnocentrism.**" Ethnocentrism is all around us and is found in every culture. We hear it when people say, "The British drive on the wrong side of the road." And we experience it when other cultures such as the Xavante of central Brazil refer to us as non-humans because we are not members of their community (Maybury-Lewis 1965). The Semai people of Malaysia also highlight the difference between themselves and strangers. They use the word "maay" to refer to strangers (Dentan 1979:71; Dentan, Endicott, Gomes and Hooker 1997:35). To the Semai, people identified as "maay" are dangerous, aggressive, and unpredictable. They represent the complete opposite of the Semai ideals of peacefulness and non-violence.

   Although ethnocentrism is a natural consequence of socialization and enculturation, it can have many positive functions such as boosting group morale and fostering a sense of solidarity with fellow members of our social groups. It can also create problems for understanding other cultures. If you see a behavior that is different from what you are used to in your culture, your first reaction might be to view it as "strange" or "weird." But that initial reaction does not help you understand the custom.

A much more useful point of view is **cultural relativism**, the position that to understand a behavior you should examine it from the point of view of the culture in which it occurs. This perspective has sometimes been equated with the moral philosophy of relativism in which it is argued that the behavior of one culture should not be judged by the standards of another culture. Unfortunately, as a moral standard, relativism can be used to ignore or even legitimate cultural behaviors that cause human suffering such as the Holocaust or American slavery. However, most anthropologists do not use cultural relativism in this strong meta-ethical sense (Gellner 1990). Rather, they use it as a kind of epistemological strategy to help them override some of the initial ethnocentrism they may feel while conducting ethnographic fieldwork or when approaching a new cultural custom.

2. **Holism** Anthropologists have long recognized that cultures and societies are complex systems composed of multiple parts that work together. This perspective is very similar to the structural-functional view of society promulgated in both British

Learning Activity: Is it Ethnocentrism?

One of the biggest obstacles to learning about other cultures is ethnocentrism. While it can sometimes be easy to spot an ethnocentric comment or perspective, in many cases ethnocentrism is harder to spot. Ethnocentric ideas can be found in many of our taken-for-granted assumptions about the world and can be accepted as fact. Consider the following examples and statements. Can you identify which of these is ethnocentric?

1. *A tourist who visits a foreign country and says, "Look how dirty and smelly this country is! Why are they so backward?"*

2. *A world history book that focuses on the history of ancient Egypt, followed by Greece and Rome, and then Europe and the United States.*

3. *The Greenpeace campaign against the harvesting of seals for food and fur by people in the Arctic.*

4. *The assumption that Native North Americans are more susceptible to alcoholism than other groups of people.*

5. *The conviction that the Inuit kiss by rubbing their noses together.*

6. *The belief that indigenous people have a close spiritual relationship with the land and nature.*

7. *The view that Americans only care about money and material possessions, judging all things by their economic value.*

8. *The presumption that Asians are hardworking, studious, intelligent, and productive people.*

For the examples you identified as ethnocentric, how were you able to identify these as value judgements about different cultures? In what ways could these value judgements impact our ability to understand different cultures? And lastly, how might cultural relativism allow us to rethink and re-evaluate these ethnocentric perspectives?

social anthropology and in American sociology during the middle of the twentieth century (Bohannan and Glazer 1988; Turner, Beeghley, and Powers 1995). It asserts that social institutions such as economics, politics, and religion are interconnected with cultural customs such as marriage patterns, subsistence strategies, and shamanic ceremonies. Therefore, to understand one of these customs or institutions (i.e., a part of the culture), the anthropologist must be aware of all the other institutions and customs that may influence the way it works in the society (i.e., the whole culture).

3. **Bio-cultural perspective**   Just as the holistic perspective argues that to understand one aspect of a culture, anthropologists have to look at the whole culture, the bio-cultural perspective extends this point of view to include human biology (**Figure 1.11**). According to physical or biological anthropology, human beings are not simply cultural or social beings, they are also a biological species. As a result, to truly understand human behavior, anthropologists have to recognize how human biology shapes cultural institutions and behaviors and how our cultural customs can in turn influence our biological make-up. A good example of the former is the manner in which the technology and architecture of **pygmy** groups in Central Africa in which people do not grow taller than four feet reflects their small stature (Turnbull 1968) (**Figure 1.12**). Examples of the latter are more readily found in a number of cultural customs that alter the human body such as **cranial re-shaping** (deliberate modification of the head) (**Figure 1.13**), various forms of piercing, and other forms of body modification (Burton 2001:61–68). Even our diets can show to what extent cultural preferences and values impact our bodies on a nutritional level.

4. **Comparative perspective**   One of the joys of anthropology is the discovery that underlying so much of the cultural differences that we see around the world is a good deal of cross-cultural similarity. **Cross-cultural comparisons** allow anthropologists to identify these similarities and offer explanations as to why they occur among societies and not others (Ember and Ember 2001). At the same time, the comparative perspective can also aid in combating our own ethnocentrism. Rather than seeing our own ways of doing things and living as normal, comparing ourselves

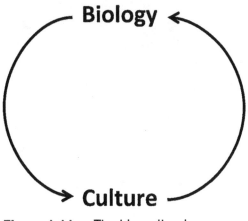

Figure 1.11.   The bio-cultural perspective in anthropology.

© 2014 Hector Conesa. Used under license of Shutterstock, Inc.

Figure 1.12. Pygmies at a dance (Kabale, Uganda).

© 2014 Dave Rock. Used under license of Shutterstock, Inc.

Figure 1.13. Human burial, showing evidence of cranial re-shaping, from the Cemetery de Chauchilla (Nazca, Peru).

to other cultures can serve to show just how out-of-place some of our own cultural customs are in a global context. As the old adage says, "Anthropology helps make the strange familiar and the familiar strange."

5. **Evolutionary perspective** Evolution is still a scary concept to many people. It should not be. Evolution simply means that things change over time. In anthropology, the evolutionary perspective has been applied in two distinct ways. In physical

or biological anthropology and archaeology, evolution is often used in a biological sense to refer to physical changes in a species over long periods of time that result in the creation of new species. Such changes are the result of a number of natural mechanisms such as natural selection, mutation, gene flow, and genetic drift.

Cultural anthropologists and archaeologists also use the concept of evolution to refer to cultural change. As in biological anthropology, we have to be very careful how we frame this kind of change. It is very easy to fall back to an ethnocentric point of view and to describe the change as "**progress**" or "**degeneration**" (e.g., Morgan 1985 [1877]; Tylor 1964 [1878]). Rather, it might be better to think about both **biological evolution** and **cultural evolution** as simply change. As species change and societies change, there are both advantages and disadvantages. No creature and no culture is perfect.

The evolutionary perspective also helps anthropologists to overcome a common ethnocentric point of view regarding non-Western cultures. In popular culture, it is often asserted that non-Western cultures (often labeled as "traditional," "tribal," or even "stone age" societies) have not changed or are somehow stuck in time. Even anthropologists have succumbed to this kind of thinking by relying on information from out-dated ethnographies. This is known as the **ethnographic present**. All cultures change and most change constantly. Many cultures are currently in **diaspora**; others are fighting to preserve some of their traditions and others are transforming in new and unexpected ways.

1.5   Why is anthropology important?

Anthropology has much to contribute to our understanding of human beings. Its global and comparative approach complement the perspectives of many of the other social sciences while extending the view of history far back into the ancient past. The bio-cultural and holistic perspectives of anthropology also provide us with a more well-rounded view of the human experience.

Because of its relativistic stance and evolutionary perspective, anthropology is not compatible with ethnocentric and biased views of human behavior. It does not view one society or group as inherently better or more evolved than another. Nor does anthropology favor a particular type of society or group as the origin point for all other cultures. Rather, anthropology fosters a greater sense of tolerance and critical thinking when it comes to our cherished notions about the "right" way to do things and our taken-for-granted views of the world.

Anthropologists also believe that it is possible to answer many of our most fundamental questions about being human. By exploring different cultures and recording their observations, anthropologists are bringing new data sets that will help us explain important issues such as the origins of social inequality, the evolution of different human populations, and how to solve world problems such as poverty, underdevelopment, and warfare.

Chapter Summary

Anthropology is the study of human beings, of their biological and cultural diversity and evolution, in both the past and present. It has four major sub-fields: cultural or social anthropology (the study of living cultures), physical or biological anthropology (the study of human beings as a biological species), archaeology (the study of past human societies), and anthropological linguistics (the study of human language). Although not everyone agrees on whether anthropology is a science, social science or one of the humanities, its unique point of view on the nature of the human experience is achieved through the application of five important guiding principles including cultural relativism, holism, the bio-cultural perspective, the evolutionary perspective, and the comparative perspective.

Key Terms

anthropological linguistics
anthropology
archaeological record
archaeology
bio-cultural perspective
biological anthropology
    (physical anthropology)
biological evolution
cranial re-shaping
creole languages
cross-cultural comparisons
cultural evolution (social
    anthropology)
cultural relativism

culture
degeneration
diaspora
emic
empiricism
ethnocentrism
ethnographic present
ethnography
ethnography of
    communication
ethnology
etic
excavation
fossil remains

historical archaeology
history
holism
humanities
language
nomothetic
paleoanthropology
pidgin
postmodern anthropology
prehistory
primates
primatology
progress
pygmy

Chapter 2
Evolutionary Theory

Conrad B. Quintyn

Outline

2.1 Middle Ages (Dark Ages or Medieval—10th Century to 15th Century)

In this cultural period, human beings believed in an unchanging world. All biological life on Earth had been present since the Creation, so nothing could be added (evolution) and nothing could be taken away (extinction). All aspects of life were fixed, which is referred to by some as the "**Fixity of Species**" (Jurmain and Nelson 1994). The general idea was that *God* was perfect, and *he* created a world in which everything was perfect. In essence, the concept of change was inconceivable because this would mean that *God* was imperfect. Moreover, all life was linked in a "great chain," which is commonly known as the **Great Chain of Being** or Aristotle's *scalae naturale* (Brace and Montagu 1977; Jurmain and Nelson 1994). This model went as far as proposing a hierarchy of life, which was roughly similar to the one listed below:

God
Angels
Humans
Animals
Inanimate objects

This hierarchy was fixed with everything, including human social organization, set nicely in its own place. The earth was seen as the center of the universe even though Nicolaus Copernicus (1473–1543) proposed a **heliocentric** solar system (Sakolsky 2005). At this time, hypotheses proposing environmental or biological change could not be formulated because there was no context for these ideas in a worldview of no change or **stasis**.

2.2 Age of Discovery (Renaissance—15th Century to 18th Century)

In this period of exploration, ship travel was the primary mode of transportation. Of course, this was not the first time ships were used for travel. What changed was that ships in this period were built for travel over vast oceans. As Europeans explored new continents, they began to realize that the world was not "fixed." In essence, they discovered new varieties of plants, animals, and, to their surprise, people. Also, Galileo Galilei (1564–1642) confirmed Copernicus's heliocentric solar system (Tyson 2005). Despite the fact that the worldview of the "fixity of species" was slowly unraveling, the Great Chain of Being remained as a resistant and powerful belief (Brace 1996; Gould 1994; Jurmain and Nelson 1994).

As in the Middle Ages, the answers to questions on human origins came from religion. The Church supported the notion of a young Earth—October 23, 4004 B.C.—based on the calculations of the Irish Archbishop James Ussher. Reverend John Lightfoot, working independently, confirmed Ussher's creation date (Campbell et al. 2006). Any fossilized marine or animal bones (associated with tools) that suggested life before Biblical creation was seen as heresy or remains of unfortunate animals drowned in Noah's flood.

But the growing collections of fossil fish, plants, and animals from explorations overseas and on the European continent continued to raise questions about the origin of life. Nicholaus Steno (1638–1686) and John Ray (1627–1705) were two of a handful of scholars who, while very religious, wanted to make sense of these fossils that contradicted the religious doctrine of the time. For instance, Steno recognized after dissection of a shark's head that the shark's teeth were very similar to fossil teeth found throughout Europe and Britain over the centuries (Wetherington 2012). Adding his knowledge of stratigraphy, Steno recognized the implication of older, deeper strata (layers) and younger, shallower strata—the law of superposition. Steno concluded that the earth was very, very old and some fossil deposits occurred before Noah's flood (Wetherington 2012).

The growing collections of fossils, while a problem for conventional wisdom of time, needed to be classified and John Ray was the first minister-naturalist to accomplish this task. He was the first person to recognize that groups of animals could be distinguished from other groups by their ability to mate with one another and produce offspring (Lewis et al. 2013). In short, Ray was the first person to develop the concept of species and placed reproductively isolated groups in the category *species*. Subsequently, he placed similar species into the category *genus*.

2.3　Age of Reason (Enlightenment—18th Century to 19th Century)

The scientific revolution did not happen all at once. It probably had roots going all the way back to the Renaissance. Nonetheless, a generation of "giants," for example, Francis Bacon, Isaac Newton, Galileo Galilei, and Johannes Kepler, led this revolution. They had an amazing way of balancing science and religion by making religion the primary impetus for the study of natural philosophy, which today is known as science. Other writers (Jurmain and Nelson 1994) have stated that these scientists studied the natural world to show the glory of God. But it was Carolus Linnaeus (1707–1778), using Aristotelian logic, who devised a system that he believed created "order" out of the chaos of organic life (Brace 2005, 25). Essentially, while John Ray devised a system of classification that revealed patterns in nature, Linnaeus created a taxonomy that organized those patterns in a hierarchical series from closer to more distant sharing of traits (Wetherington 2012).

Linnaeus was an Enlightenment figure who believed that the act of naming plants and animals was equated with showing the glory of God. This can be clearly seen in the words he used in the introduction to all the later editions of his *Systema Naturae*: "I saw the infinite, all-knowing and all-powerful God from behind as He went away and I grew dizzy. I followed his footsteps over nature's fields and saw everywhere an eternal wisdom and power, an inscrutable perfection" (Lindroth 1973, 380). In this respect, Linnaeus reflected the worldview of the medieval scholastics. He was also a complete Platonic essentialist and a classic creationist who believed that all biological species were fixed and mere imperfect reflections of their "true" underlying essences, and these true essences could only be found in the mind of God (Brace 2005, 27). According to this worldview, categories of species were not only treated in terms of similarity or difference, but were ranked based on the proximity or distance from the perfection of the divine. This arrangement was united with biblical assertions that human beings, as mentioned in the beginning of this chapter, were superior to all other forms of life and were given dominion over them by divine decree. This assertion, once more, is further emphasized in Psalms 8:4–9:

4 What is man that thou art mindful of him? And the son of man, that thou visitest him?

5 For thou hast made him *a little lower than the angels* [italics, my emphasis], and hast crowned him with glory and honour.

6 Thou madest him to have dominion over the works of thy hands; thou hast put all things under his feet:

7 All sheep and oxen, yea, and the beasts of the field;

8 The fowl of the air and the fish of the sea, and whatsoever passeth through the paths of the seas.

9 O LORD our Lord, how excellent is thy name in all the earth. (Baker Publishing Group 1995, 584)

The assumption that the world was ranked and fixed pervaded the medieval Christian worldview, and this worldview was inherited by Enlightenment thinkers. Linnaeus and his contemporaries simply took that general view and provided a more specific picture of all aspects of life arranged in a series of steps running from God at the top down through various entities of the living world to the inorganic—"base" metals—at the bottom (Brace 2005, 28). As Arthur O. Lovejoy (1961, 184) notes, "Next to the word 'Nature,' 'the Great Chain of Being' was the sacred phrase of the eighteenth century, playing a part somewhat analogous to that of the blessed word 'evolution' in the late nineteenth." In this Great Chain of Being anything closest to the divine had high status and embodied Plato's "Idea of Good." Plato is affirming, in what he says about the Idea of Good or *ens perfectissimum*, that a rational divine power exists and it is omnipotent (Lovejoy 1961, 40–42). For those who viewed the world as God-created, fixed, and perfect, ideas of variation, random change, or extinction were inconceivable. The loss of one of the steps in that Great Chain would mean that the world was not created perfectly or God was not all-powerful (Lovejoy 1961, 256–257). Of course, neither possibility was consistent with Enlightenment thinking: God was perfect, God did not make mistakes, and nothing occurred by chance.

Linnaeus recognized competition in nature but he interpreted it as God's way of weeding out unnecessary animals in order to maintain nature's balance. In his tenth edition of *Systema Naturae*, Linnaeus classified humans into the categories Kingdom, Animalia, Class, Vertebrata, Order, Primates, Genus, Homo, species, sapiens and recognized four human races (he labeled as 'varieties'), or subspecies of *Homo sapiens*: Americanus, Asiaticus, Africanus, and Europeanus (Wetherington 2012).

In the first quarter of the 1800s, Neanderthal (prehistoric human ancestor that lived from 130,000 years ago to 24,000 years ago in Europe, Asia, and the Middle East) bones were found with stone tools and animal bones. Since humans had no prehistoric ancestors, according to the creationist worldview, Neanderthals were associated with certain human populations deemed inferior, i.e. Southern and Eastern Europeans, Australian aborigines, and sub-Sahara Africans.

By the mid-1800s, the geologist and paleontologist Hugh Falconer (1808–1865) examined the collection of stone tools and was convinced that they were older than 4004 years ago based on examination of the geology of the Somme Valley. Giving additional support to this evidence was Sir Charles Lyell (1797–1875) who wrote a book titled *The Antiquity of Man* acknowledging a human prehistory. We see further unraveling of the young earth and the fixity of species beliefs.

2.4   Geology and the Ancient Formation of the Earth

In his book entitled *Histoire Naturelle* (1749), Comte de Buffon (1707–1788) suggested that the earth had been shaped over millions of years by natural processes, such as wind and soil erosion, volcanic activity, and earthquakes (Campbell et al. 2006). Buffon reasoned that the presence of fossil shells in respective horizontal strara indicated that slow, gradual natural processes were involved in Earth's formation which meant that the Earth was much older than Archbishop Ussher's date of 4004 BC. He was soon forced by the Catholic Church to recant his "heretical" notions of deep time or the ancient formation of the earth.

With advances in geology and the loosening grip of the Church over secular life, a new generation of scholars began to accept the theory of deep time. The layers and layers of sedimentary deposits seen on the sides of cliffs or on the sides of excavated trenches were too compelling to dismiss. James Hutton (1726–1797), a member of this new generation, described the earth as a decaying and self-renewing machine (Campbell et al. 2006; Larsen 2008). In his book entitled *Theory of the Earth* (1795), he wrote that terrestrial products such as soils and rocks decay through erosion and these products are carried into the sea. Subsequently, these erosional products are laid down as horizontal marine deposits, which eventually solidify into rocks. And later, these rocks are uplifted as continents by natural forces. Then the process repeats itself. But this was all speculation, albeit strong speculation. The proof for Hutton's hypothesis would come thirty years later.

In the meantime, the French paleontologist and comparative anatomist Georges Cuvier (1769–1832) was discovering the bones of long-extinct primates, dinosaurs, and mammoths in the rocks near Paris. He was able to show that at least 90% of the species he had recovered had become extinct (Campbell et al. 2006). Cuvier could not understand how such a massive loss of life could have occurred. In addition, he wondered why the bones of these prehistoric animals, particularly those of the dinosaurs, were so different from the bones of animals of the 18th and 19th centuries. "What destructive forces led to extinction of species, and what restorative forces controlled their replacement by later life forms?" (Campbell et al. 2006, 7).

Cuvier proposed his idea of **catastrophism** where global warming and cooling over time led to uplifting of the seafloor and caused sea levels to rise. Subsequently, there was a world-wide flood or "catastrophe" that wiped out many animal species over large areas. He believed that there were several of these sudden catastrophes. After the catastrophe, according to Cuvier, devastated areas were repopulated by different species of animals from other areas. And, to help with the repopulation, God created a few new species (Campbell et al. 2006; Larsen 2008). Cuvier never accepted the idea that the environment itself or needs of an animal can stimulate change. In essence, he rejected Jean Baptiste Lamarck's (1744–1829) evolutionary hypotheses. He also rejected the idea of slow, gradual geological change initially proposed by Buffon, adopted by Hutton, and expanded by Charles Lyell. In short, this catastrophism hypothesis competed with Lyell's uniformitarianism for acceptance. Nonetheless, Cuvier provided strong-evidence for the ancient formation of the earth, and he is associated with the idea of extinction.

Geoffroy Saint-Hilaire (1772–1844) disagreed with Cuvier on the nature of organic change. Cuvier believed in the fixity of species and replacement could only come through extinction and new creation. In contrast, Saint-Hilaire believed in evolution–change through time. In his 1831 report on the influence of the environment in changing animal forms, Saint-Hilaire foreshadows natural selection: "The external world is all-powerful in alteration of the form of organized [organic] bodies…these [modifications] are inherited, and they influence all the rest of the organization of the animal, because if these modifications lead to injurious effects, the animals which exhibit them perish and are replaced by others of a somewhat different form, a form changed so as to be adapted to the new environment" (as cited in Wetherington 2012, 71). Saint-Hilaire disagreed with Cuvier (and Lamarck) on the fact that form follows function. He believed in the now erroneous view that function followed form.

Building on the earlier work of Hutton, Sir Charles Lyell (1797–1875) proposed that the earth's geological history could be explained by such processes as erosion, volcanic eruptions, earthquakes, and floods, to name a few, that occur today. He concluded that these forces are *uniform*. His three-volume manuscript entitled *Principles of Geology*, published between 1830 and 1833, detailed the evidence for the ancient formation of the earth. William Whewell (1794–1866), a reviewer of *Principles of Geology*, coined the term *uniformitarianism* for Lyell's theory (Boaz and Almquist 2002). **Uniformitarianism** is the principle that processes that occur in the past are still occurring today. Specifically, Lyell proposed the following:

1. *Uniformity of law*: Through space and time, natural laws remain constant.

2. *Uniformity of process*: When possible, past phenomena should be explained as the results of processes now in operation.

3. *Uniformity of rate*: Change usually occurs slowly and steadily (unlike Cuvier's series of sudden catastrophic events).

4. *Uniformity of state*: Change, although continuous, is nondirectional and nonprogressive (Campbell et al. 2006; Gould 1987).

Lyell became one of the most influential geologists of the 19th century as he devoted most of his time writing about uniformitarianism and its implications for explaining Earth's history. And, his calculations of how long mountain-building took provided the proof that Earth was millions of years old (Larsen 2008). It is interesting that while Lyell provided the time for large-scale evolution to occur through his empirical geological work and in the process slowly came to accept the fact of evolution, he, ironically, rejected natural selection as the cause for the diversity of species. So, like Cuvier, he would reject Lamarck's evolutionary hypotheses of the early 19th century.

2.4.1 Erasmus Darwin

Eramus Darwin (1731–1802) proposed similar views as Jean Baptise Lamarck on how the environment influenced an animal's organs and behavior and views, like Saint-Hilaire, that foreshadowed his grandson's principle of natural selection. He states: "...from their first rudiment, or primordium, to the termination of their lives, all animals undergo per-petual transformations; which are in part produced by *their own exertions in consequence of their desires and aversions, of their pleasures and their pains, or of irritations, or of irritations, or of associations; and many of these acquired forms or propensities are transmitted to their pos-terity*" (as cited in Wetherington 2012, 59–60; italics added). On sexual selection, Erasmus Darwin writes: "A great want of one part of the animal world has consisted in the desire of the exclusive possession of the females; and these have acquired weapons to combat each other for this purpose, as the very thick, shield-like, horny skin on the shoulder of the boar is a defence only against animals of his own species" (as cited in Wetherington 2012, 60). On beaks and seeding strategies, he writes: "...some birds have acquired harder beaks to crack nuts, as the parrot. Others for the softer seeds of flowers, or the buds of trees, as the finches. Other birds have acquired long beaks to penetrate the moister soils in search of insects or roots, as woodcocks; and others broad ones to filtrate the water of lakes, and to retain aquatic insects, as ducks. All which seem to have been gradually produced during many generations by the perpetual endeavor of the creatures to supply the want of food, and to have been delivered to their posterity with constant improvement of them for the purposes required" (as cited in Wetherington 2012, 60).

2.4.2 Jean Baptiste Lamarck

The French naturalist Jean Baptiste Lamarck (1744–1829) was the first scientist who tried to explain how evolution worked. He believed, correctly, that there was a dynamic relation-ship between the organism and its environment. Furthermore, he believed in development and progression of animal organs. He states:

"Progress in complexity of organization exhibits anomalies here and there in the gen-eral series of animals, due to the influence of environment and of acquired habits" (as cited in Wetherington 2012, 62). In his book entitled *Philosophie Zoologique* (1809), Lamarck discussed his two propositions which complement each other to some respect: The first was the Law of **Use and Disuse**. According to Lamarck, a trait that is used frequently is enhanced over time. For instance, a monkey that leaps from tree to tree would develop stronger legs over time. In contrast, these same legs would grow weaker and wither away if the monkey remains sedentary. The second, more controversial law is the **Inheritance of Acquired Characteristics**. According to Lamarck, an organism will acquire a trait during its lifetime because of "need" and pass this newly acquired trait (at the specific stage of its development) to its offspring. Lamarck used this hypothesis to explain how the giraffe got its long neck. The original short-necked ancestor needed to reach the fruits on the top branches of tall trees. Consequently, this ancestor kept stretching its neck until the neck got progressively longer (Figure 2.1). In essence, the neck was used frequently and it was enhanced.

For much of the 19th and early 20th centuries, Lamarck's hypothesis was taken seri-ously at the expense of Darwinian evolution. But with the rediscovery of Mendel's work in 1900 and its synthesis with Darwinian evolution forming the Modern Synthesis and the discovery of DNA, Lamarckian evolution was proven wrong. Traits cannot be acquired during an organism's lifetime and then passed to its offspring. For a trait to be passed on to the offspring, it must be coded in the sex cells (egg and sperm).

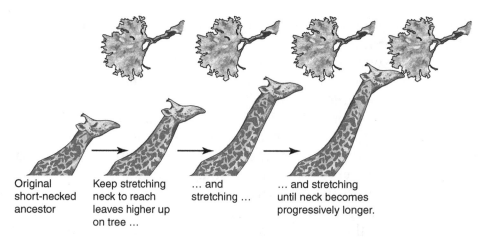

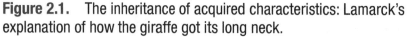

Original short-necked ancestor | Keep stretching neck to reach leaves higher up on tree ... | ... and stretching ... | ... and stretching until neck becomes progressively longer.

Figure 2.1. The inheritance of acquired characteristics: Lamarck's explanation of how the giraffe got its long neck.

2.4.3 Thomas Malthus

What Lamarck did not understand was that environmental competition, rather than an organism's need, could drive evolutionary change. Nonetheless, a British economist and demographer, Thomas Malthus (1766–1834), made the connection between competition and survival. Responding to both his father's views and those of Jean-Jacques Rousseau that with civilization man's social and moral future would be progressively improved and result in greater happiness, Malthus wrote *An Essay on the Principle of Population* (1798) where he observed that human populations increase geometrically whereas food supply increases only arithmetically (Wetherington 2012). Specifically, he stated that there is not enough food for everyone born, so population is limited by food supply. According to Malthus, overpopulation that comes with civilization leads to misery and despair as oppose to greater happiness. Those individuals who can compete successfully will be able to feed their offspring, and their offspring will survive to adulthood. Malthus noted that the positive and preventative checks on population, i.e., disease, famine, abortion, and birth control, were not always effective. You will see later how Darwin will apply this demographic model to his theory of natural selection.

2.4.4 Charles Darwin

The name Charles Darwin (1809–1882) (Figure 2.2) is celebrated by evolutionists and cursed by creationists. Some have even referred to his book *On the Origin of Species*, published in 1859, as "the evolutionist's bible." This would be an incorrect reference. To give students a more accurate understanding of Darwinian evolution, Darwin's early life must be explored to learn how he proposed his mechanism for evolution.

Darwin was born into the Age of Reason. At this time, a few European scholars had heretical notions of biological variation and change and the ancient formation of the earth—different from that written in the Book of Genesis in the Bible. Darwin would eventually use their writings to generate his theory of evolution.

As a student at Edinburgh University in 1825 (which he left after three years), and then Cambridge University in England in 1828, Darwin turned away from two of the most prestigious career paths for young men in the early 19th century: medicine and the priesthood. He was, however, passionately interested in natural history and in collecting insects, birds, flowers, and rocks. His circle of friends included men in the natural sciences: William Darwin Fox (1805–1880), a clergyman and entomologist; John Henslow (1796–1861), professor of minerology; Adam Sedgwick (1785–1873), professor of Geology; Joseph Dalton Hooker (1817–1911), botanist; Leonard Horner (1785–1864), geologist: and Charles Lyell, professor of geology. In effect, he was training to become a naturalist. Lyell and his uniformitarianism, more than anyone else, was responsible for shaping Darwin's view of nature. For instance, in a revealing letter to Horner, written in 1844, Darwin exclaimed: "I always feel as if my

Figure 2.2. Charles Darwin in later years.

© JupiterImages, Inc.

books came half out of Lyell's brains...for I have always thought that the great merit of the Principles [of Geology], was that it altered the whole tone of one's mind and therefore that when seeing a thing never seen by Lyell, one yet saw it partially through his eyes" (as cited in Wetherington 2012, 55).

For an upper-middle-class, 19th-century young Englishman, this nonpractical career was not a major problem because his family had enough money so that he could live in a certain level of comfort without working. Nonetheless, through the recommendation of Henslow, Darwin got the opportunity to sail as an unpaid naturalist aboard the survey ship HMS *Beagle* on a five-year journey around the world (see Figure 2.3).

This voyage was critical for Darwin because it enabled him to develop his theory of natural selection. Spending three-and-a-half years surveying and collecting along the coasts of South America, five weeks in the Galápagos Islands of Ecuador, and a year returning home via Tahiti, New Zealand, Australia, and South Africa enabled Darwin to see a tremendous amount of variation in most living species (Campbell et al. 2006; Relethford 2005). This variation was, in general, no different from what 15th- and 16th-century European explorers saw and wrote home about. Unlike these early explorers, Darwin would present this variation to the public in a scientific context.

Darwin observed that organisms seemed well adapted to their environments. For instance, he noted that organisms in cold climates have fur and birds in areas where seeds are hard have large beaks. One of the most important parts of the voyage for his understanding of **adaptation** was the visit to the **Galápagos Islands**. Darwin (1962 [1839]) wrote,

It was most striking to be surrounded by new birds, new reptiles, new shells, new Insects, new plants, and yet by innumerable trifling details of structure, and even by the tones of voice and plumage of the birds, to have the temperate plains of Patagonia, or the hot dry deserts of northern Chile, vividly brought before my eyes. (393)

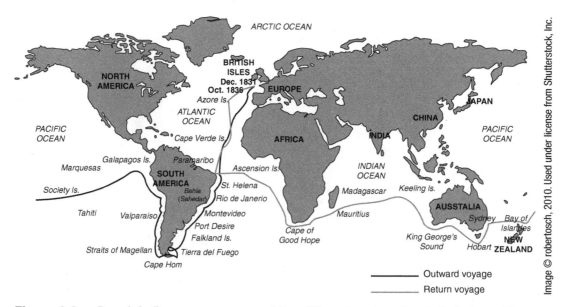

Figure 2.3. Darwin's five-year voyage and the different regions he visited aboard the HMS *Beagle* (from Relethford 2005).

The Galápagos animals were certainly different compared to the mainland species, but there were some similarities. In fact, Darwin believed that the finches on the islands originated from a common ancestor on the mainland. Due to unknown circumstances, some individuals got separated on the respective islands and over time became separate species as they adapted to their respective niches. For example, on island to island, the finches' beaks were strong and thick for cracking big nuts and seeds; smaller for catching insects; and elongated for feeding on flowers and fruit (Campbell et al. 2006). In the initial arrival on the islands many generations ago, the finches had found different foods on the islands. Over time, they adapted to better survive in their respective environments.

Darwin returned home in 1836 and devoted the remaining years of his life to the study of the data he had collected. It was fortunate that Darwin did not have to work for a living, because he had the time to think about the issues of variation, formation of new species, adaptation, and extinction and to read sources in geology, paleontology, taxonomy, demography, and evolutionary biology.

2.5   Darwin, Wallace, and the Theory of Natural Selection

Despite the fact that only "original" research is the criterion used for obtaining a Ph.D. or getting your work published in a scholarly journal, no work is really original. If you search deep enough, you will find that the so-called original work is based on the work of previous scholars. This was the same for Darwin. The context for Darwin, as mentioned earlier, was geology, paleontology, taxonomy, demography, and evolutionary biology. Geology in the form of Lyell's work gave Darwin the *time* he needed for evolution to work. According to Darwin, evolution needs time for gradual, slow change and the formation of new species: "Nothing at first can appear more difficult to believe than that the more complex organs and instincts should have been perfected, not by means superior to, though analogous with, human reason, but by the *accumulation of innumerable slight variations*, each good for the individual possessor" (Darwin 1964 [1859], 459; italics added). From paleontology or Cuvier's work, Darwin took away the idea of extinction. He believed that the fate of all species is extinction. Studying Linnaeus's taxonomy, Darwin noted the similarities in skeletal traits between apes and humans. He concluded that humans must be related in some way to these apes. Furthermore, reading Malthus's *Essay*, Darwin concluded that in an environment of competition, those individuals with favorable traits will survive and reproduce and those with unfavorable traits will die. Darwin states: "In October 1838, that is fifteen months after I had begun my systematic enquiry, I happened to read for amusement Malthus on Population, and being well prepared to appreciate the struggle for existence which everywhere goes on from long-continued observation of the habits of animals and plants, *it at once struck me that under these circumstances favourable variations would tend to be preserved, and unfavourable ones to be destroyed. The result of this would be the formation of new species*" (Barlow 1958, 119; italics added). Finally, he accepted Lamarck's conclusion that there was a dynamic relationship between the organism and its environment. However, Darwin believed that the environment itself stimulated change and not the organism's needs. Furthermore, he believed that variation in the population was necessary for change and survival. Alfred Russel Wallace (1823–1913) the co-founder of natural selection reached a similar conclusion stating: "Neither did the giraffe acquire its long neck by desiring to reach the foliage of the more lofty shrubs, and constantly stretching its neck for the purpose, but because any varieties which occurred among its antitypes with a longer neck than usual at once secured a fresh range of pasture over the same ground as their shorter-necked companions, and on the first scarcity of food were thereby enabled to outlive them" (quoted in Wetherington 2012, 102). In essence, Darwin's theory of evolution through natural selection is as follows: Individuals have more offspring than can survive. Because of this, there will be **struggle for existence**. Those individuals with favorable (adaptive) traits will survive and reproduce; those with unfavorable (nonadaptive) traits will die—**variation in fitness**. Those individuals who survive and reproduce will pass their traits on to the offspring—**inheritance of variation**. There will be a higher frequency of these traits in future generations. According to Darwin: "…can we doubt…individuals having any advantage, however slight, over others, would have the best chance of surviving and of procreating their kind? On the other hand, we may feel sure that any variation in the least degree injurious would be rigidly destroyed. This preservation of favourable variations and the rejection of injurious variations, I call Natural Selection" (Darwin 1859, 80–81). Darwin got the idea for using the words "natural selection" from animal breeders who were trying to obtain certain traits artificially by breeding male and female animals carrying those desired traits. He states: "I have called this principle, by which each slight variation, if useful, is preserved, by the term of Natural Selection, in order to mark its relation to *man's power of selection*" (Darwin 1964 [1859], 61; italics added).

After many years of thought and observation, Darwin published his revolutionary book *On the Origin of Species by Means of Natural Selection Or the Preservation of Favoured Races in the Struggle for Life* (1859), John Murray Publishers (Campbell et al. 2006). Darwin was hesitant in submitting his controversial work for publication. But he was encouraged to publish when Wallace (Figure 2.4) sent him a copy of his paper. Wallace, working independently, had come to similar conclusions. Wallace states: "The life of wild animals is a *struggle for existence*. The full exertion of all their faculties and all their energies is required to preserve their own existence and provide for that of their infant offspring" (as cited in Wetherington 2012, 99; italics added). Wallace, however, objected to the phrase "natural selection" because it suggested that nature had a consciousness, and strongly urged Darwin to use Herbert Spencer's "*survival of the fittest*" instead (Wetherington 2012). In his fifth edition (with a change in the book's title to The Origin of Species) Darwin compromised by changing the chapter heading to "Chapter IV: Natural Selection, or the Survival of the Fittest." Wallace studied species origins for five years in the interior of Brazil, and then he relocated to Indonesia where he studied the natural history of the islands in the Malay Archipelago (Boaz and Almquist 2002). He believed that selection acted on populations and not individuals as Darwin proposed. Nonetheless, while Darwin is generally recognized as the discoverer of the theory of natural selection, Wallace also gets some credit for contributing substantially to evolutionary theory (Larsen 2008). The First edition of *On the Origin of Species* was released on November 24, 1859 and sold, on the first day, according to John Murray Publishers, all

© Morphart Creation/Shutterstock.com

Figure 2.4. Alfred Russel Wallace, cofounder of the theory of natural selection.

1,170 copies (Wetherington 2012). The second edition was released on January 7, 1860 and sold 3,000 copies. The third and fourth editions in 1861 and 1866 were also success-ful reaching broader audiences.

It is ironic that Darwin, the defender of evolution, never used the term evolution in the first five editions of *Origin*; he used the term for the first time in his book *Descent of Man* 1871, and in the sixth edition of *Origin* in 1872 (Wetherington 2012).

Some important principles of evolution that were developed in the mid-20th century are as follows:

1. No trait is "good" or "bad." It depends on the specific environment.

2. Biological traits can change in different directions. For example, there was a steady *increase* in human cranial capacity from 1.0 million years to 100,000 years. Simultaneous, there was a *reduction* in the jaw and teeth.

3. Evolution does not occur in a vacuum. The environment provides the context.

4. Variation is critical in the evolutionary process.

Darwin knew much about variation and the fact that it is passed from the parent to offspring. But he did not know the sources of variation within each generation and the mechanism of inheritance. Interestingly, Gregor Mendel (1822–1884), an Augustinian monk living in a monastery in what is now Brno, Czech Republic, was addressing these problems. We can assume that due to the slow information system of the 19th century and the language barrier, Darwin was unaware of Mendel's work.

Summary of Key Ideas

1. Before Darwin proposed his theory of evolution, there was no context for variation and change because the worldview was stasis or the "fixity of species." God was perfect and God created a perfect Earth. Since religion was prominent in society at this time, ideas of variation and change implied that God was not perfect. This was heresy.

2. Aristotle's *scalae naturale* or Great Chain of Being was the dominant theme in the Medieval, Renaissance, and Enlightenment periods.

3. During the Enlightenment, the ancient formation of the earth (deep time), variation, and the dynamic relationship between the organism and the environment were established by naturalists who were willing to go against conventional wisdom of the day, such as Nicholas Steno, John Ray, Geoffroy Saint-Hilaire, Erasmus Darwin, and Comte de Buffon. Later, scientists in five scientific disciplines: geology (James Hutton and Charles Lyell), paleontology (Georges Cuvier), taxonomy (Carolus Linnaeus), demography (Thomas Malthus), and evolutionary biology (Jean Baptiste Lamarck) provided the context for Darwin to generate his theory of evolution.

4. Darwin's theory of evolution through natural selection states that in an environ-ment of competition, those individuals with favorable (adaptive) traits will survive and reproduce and pass their traits to the offspring. As time goes on, these traits will

increase in the population. Those individuals with unfavorable traits (nonadaptive) will die. Alfred Russel Wallace, working independently, proposed a theory of natural selection. However, he believed that the population is selected not individuals.

5. Important principles of evolution: (a) No trait is "good" or "bad." It depends on the specific environment. (b) Biological traits can change in different directions; for example, human brain size got larger while the teeth and jaw got smaller. Again, it depends on the environment. (c) Evolution does not occur in a vacuum—the environment provides the context. (d) Variation is critical in the evolutionary process.

6. Darwin did not know the following: (a) sources of variation within each generation; and (b) the mechanism of inheritance.

Key Terms

Adaptation
Catastrophism
Enlightenment
Evolution
Fixity of species
Galapagos Islands

Great Chain of Being
Heliocentric
Inheritance of Acquired
 Characteristics
Medieval
On the Origin of Species

Renaissance
Stasis
Uniformitarianism
Use and Disuse

Further Readings

Browne, J. 1995. *Charles Darwin: Voyaging*. New York: Knopf.

Gould, S. J. 1992. *Ever since Darwin: Reflections on natural history*. New York: Norton.

Moorehead, A. 1969. *Darwin and the Beagle*. New York: Penguin Books.

Repcheck, J. 2003. *The man who found time: James Hutton and the discovery of Earth's antiquity*. Cambridge, MA: Perseus Publishing.

Internet Resources

Pre-Darwinian Theories

http://anthro.palomar.edu/evolve/evolve_1.htm

This is the Anthropology Department at Palomar College's Web site on pre-Darwinian evolutionary hypotheses.

UCMP Exhibition Halls: Evolution

http://www.ucmp.berkeley.edu/history/evolution.html

This Web site provides biographical sketches of several scientists who contributed to theories about evolution and the ancient formation of the earth (deep time).

Victorian Science: An Overview

http://www.victorianweb.org/science/sciov.html

This Web site provides background information about Charles Darwin and other 19th-century scientists.

Chapter 2: Evolutionary Theory

Study guide: By knowing the material below you will be well prepared for the exam. Don't forget to read the chapter and study your notes (this includes the chapter worksheets).

1. Be able to discuss *blending inheritance*

2. Be able to name the scientists whose combine effort helped to learn the structure of DNA

3. Be able to name the first scientist who tried to explain evolutionary change

4. What was the context for Darwin to generate his theory of evolutionary change (natural selection)? In other words, his theory drew from many scientific disciplines. Name and discuss.

5. Why is Alfred Russell Wallace significant?

6. Be able to explain why Wallace did not like the words "natural selection."

7. Wallace and Darwin differed on the level of selection. What was this difference?

8. Why is Carolus Linnaeus significant?

9. Be able to compare and contrast Cuvier's and Hilaire's views on the nature of organic change.

10. *Uniformitarianism* is associated with a British geologist. Be able to name him and explain uniformitarianism.

11. Know why John Ray was important.

12. Know why Nicholas Steno is important.

13. The earth is a 'decaying and self-renewing machine.' Explain this proposal. Who is the naturalist responsible for this proposal?

14. Explain the "inheritance of acquired characteristics?" Who was responsible for this hypothesis?

15. What did the British demographer Malthus say about population and food supply?

16. Which scientist coined the term *Catastrophism*? Be able to explain *Catastrophism*

17. The controversial notion of extinction is associated with the following scientist named_____.

18. Be able to define mutation. It is the only source of_____.

19. What was the worldview about human origins before modern times?

20. Be able to explain natural selection.

21. Know why Erasmus Darwin was important.

22. According to Darwin's theory of natural selection, disadvantageous traits will disappear over time in a population. True/False?

23. When Darwin coined the term "natural selection" he was making an analogy to artificial selection. True/ False?

24. Variation in a population is the key to Darwin's idea of natural selection. True/ False?

25. What did Darwin not know about heredity?

26. "Fitness," in an evolutionary sense, refers to an individual's_____.

Chapter 2: Evolutionary Theory

Practice Exercises

The goal of the practice exercises is assess your knowledge of the concepts and ideas presented in the chapter.

Section 2.1: Pre-Darwinian Thought

1. A theory of evolution could not be proposed in the 10th to the 18th century. WHY?

2. Who was Carolus Linnaeus?

3. What important events during the Age of Reason set the foundation for a theory of evolution?

Section 2.2: Geology and Ancient Formation of the Earth

1. Compare and contrast Cuvier's and Hilaire's views on the nature of organic change.

2. Why was John Ray important?

3. Why was Nicholaus Steno important?

4. Discuss the development of the ancient earth hypothesis. What were the implications of this hypothesis on evolutionary theory?

5. Georges Cuvier and Charles Lyell had different ideas about the rate and state of geologic change. Compare Cuvier's Catastrophism with Lyell's theory of Uniformitarianism.

6. Who formulated the Inheritance of Acquired Characteristics? What did this naturalist propose? Can you use your own example to explain this hypothesis?

Section 2.3: Charles Darwin

1. What was the 'Voyage of the Beagle'? Why was this voyage critical to the development of the theory of natural selection? Discuss.

2. Explain why Wallace did not like the words 'natural selection'?

3. Wallace and Darwin differed on the level of selection. What was this difference?

Section 2.4: Darwin, Wallace, and the Theory of Natural Selection

1. What were some of the important sub-disciplines (and the work of respective scientists in these disciplines) Charles Darwin used to formulate his theory of natural selection?

2. Define natural selection. Explain how competition and natural selection are related in Charles Darwin's theory of evolution.

3. Charles Darwin and Jean Baptiste Lamarck had different ideas about evolutionary change. Compare Darwin's theory of natural selection with Lamarck's Inheritance of Acquired Characteristics.

Chapter 3

And Then There Was One: Modern Humans

Jeffrey Schwartz and Ian Tattersall

Outline

3.1   And Then There Was One

The quest to discover the evolutionary path of our species is one of the most profoundly important aspects of physical anthropology. One branch of this field, known as paleo-anthropology, seeks to understand the how, where, and when of hominid development. For over 150 years anthropologists have tried to piece together the fragmentary clues from the past. This task has not been an easy one, as prevailing opinion was often set harshly against *any* evidence that purported to demonstrate that modern humans evolved from earlier forms. When Darwin wrote that "man is descended from some less highly organized form" it marked a turning point. Since the mid Nineteenth century physical anthropologists have sought to understand how we modern humans evolved and under what circumstances. Often, criticisms and doubts sprang from within the field of anthropology itself. In 1924 when Raymond Dart discovered a skull in South Africa and designated it a new genus, Australopithecus africanus, he was roundly dismissed. Some of this criticism stemmed from professional jealousy within anthropology, but outside of the field itself, his claim to have identified an earlier genus, and species, of hominid was ridiculed. Similar reactions occurred when, in 1891, the Dutchman Eugene Dubois, working in Java, claimed to have discovered "a species in between humans and apes". The Twentieth century, however, has demonstrated that earlier claims were in fact correct, and slowly anthropologists began to fill in some of the blanks of human evolution. Human evolutionary story in Africa over the past million years has been an eventful one, although at present we can't at all clearly perceive what those events were. During this period new kinds of hominid continued to arise in Africa, almost certainly including the ancestors of the fossils now increasingly referred to as *Homo antecessor* and *H. heidelbergensis*—and, fatefully, the ancestor of *Homo sapiens*.

Africa declares itself paleontologically as the birthplace of our species for the most traditional of reasons: quite simply, that the earliest dates for potentially modern human fossils come from that continent.

Unfortunately, beyond this point the simplicity ceases, because the fossils in question tend either to be fragmentary or poorly dated, or sometimes both. For example, during the late 1960s, a braincase and a fragmentary skull were recovered from deposits of the Kibish Formation, in the Omo Basin of southern Ethiopia. The braincase is rather archaic in appearance but, once reconstructed, the other skull appeared to have all the attributes of modern *H. sapiens*. The problem was that nobody knew the age of these specimens: an uncertainty that continues to plague studies of them. One investigation suggested that the deposits in which the specimens were picked up were about 130 kyr old. However, both hominids were found lying on the surface, so it's hard to eliminate the possibility that one or both were washed down to where they were found from younger deposits above. This is a particularly frustrating situation, because if the more modern-looking specimen is indeed 130 kyr old, it is quite likely the earliest readily recognizable *H. sapiens* yet known from anywhere. Equally tantalizing is the new date of about 133 kyr recently derived for a specimen found in 1924 at Singa, in the Sudan. The daters are quite confident in their results, but the problem of interpretation lies with the fossil itself, which consists of a braincase that appears fairly modern in form but that may be distorted by pathology.

Almost rivaling Omo Kibish and Singa in age is the site of Klasies River Mouth, near the southern tip of Africa, where some human remains may date to as much as 120 kyr ago.

The dating methods used there are somewhat experimental, but several lines of evidence converge on this age. Unfortunately, the remains themselves are highly fragmentary, and have given rise to a great deal of debate over their modernity. They are quite *Homo sapiens*-like; but whether any or all of them actually represent our species still awaits definitive clarification. It has been quite convincingly argued that the charred and fragmentary nature of these fossils indicates that they represent victims of cannibalistic activities: if so, this is the earliest reliable case of such behaviors that has yet been reported. The Omo specimens are without archaeological context, but the Klasies hominids are clearly associated with a Middle Stone Age lithic industry: roughly speaking, the local version of the Mousterian. The site's excavator believes that he can discern some evidence for the organization of space that is so rare at Mousterian sites.

Another southern African locality that may yield very early *Homo sapiens* fossils is Border Cave, high in a cliff on the frontier between South Africa and Swaziland. It is believed that some unarguably anatomically modern specimens from Border Cave may be as much as 100 kyr old, or even considerably more; but unfortunately the stratigraphy in the cave was disrupted by early mining activity, and it's also possible that some apparently ancient burials may have been dug into earlier levels at a later time. [Figure 3.1] Nonetheless, taken together, the Klasies and Border Cave fossils do suggest that *H. sapiens* may well already have been present in southern Africa by 100–120 kyr ago.

The plausible early emergence of modern hominids in Africa did not, however, mean the immediate elimination of other members of the human family. The 120-kyr-old Ngaloba Beds of Laetoli, in Tanzania, have produced the braincase and partial face of a hominid with the relatively modest brain size of 1200 ml, and a suite of archaic features in the skull. [Figure 3.2]

Whatever species this individual may have belonged to, it was not the immediate ancestor of *Homo sapiens*. A much earlier partial skull from Guomde, in Kenya's Turkana Basin, looks more modern. This specimen has now been dated to at least 180 kyr ago, and may be older. In turn, the Guomde specimen contrasts strongly with a fossil face from Florisbad, in South Africa, that may be of around the same age. [Figure 3.3] The picture we gain from tantalizing glimpses such as these into Africa's paleoanthropological past is thus not only of the rather early emergence of anatomically modern humans in that continent. It is also the image of a complex set of morphologies in the period between 250–100 kyr ago, suggesting that the process of evolutionary experimentation among African hominids continued right into *H. sapiens* times. As the record expands, we can hope to figure out how many players there

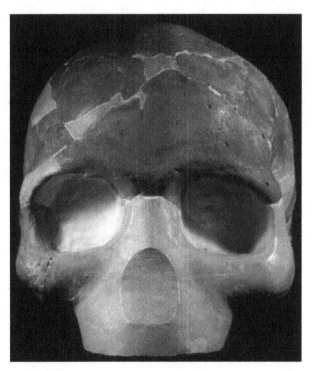

Figure 3.1. Front view of the Border Cave 1 cranium from South Africa. Lightly built and clearly modern in morphology, this specimen is of debatable antiquity but may be over 100 kyr old. Photograph by Jeffrey H. Schwartz.

were in the evolutionary theatre at this fateful juncture in the history of life that saw the emergence of our own species. For the present, however, it is already evident that the proto-*H. sapiens* was far from having had the stage to itself. Once again, we have to conclude that our species' current monopoly of hominid life on Earth is an unusual state of affairs.

3.1.1 African Eve

During the 1980s new techniques of molecular analysis began to have a significant impact on scenarios of modern human emergence. This was not because scientists had perfected techniques for extracting the molecule of heredity, DNA, from actual early *Homo sapiens* fossils. Indeed, the only successful example so far of this type of research is the very recent isolation of a short stretch of mitochondrial DNA (mtDNA) from the original Neanderthal fossil, which was hardly surprisingly shown thereby to lie well beyond the limits of all modern human populations combined. Rather, the new evidence on the geographic origin of modern humans came from the analysis of mtDNA variation in representative samples of living human populations from around the world. Before we follow up on this evidence, just what is mtDNA, and what makes it attractive to molecular systematists?

Human body cells contain not only the DNA that resides in their nuclei, and that furnishes the "blueprint" for the construction of each new individual. They also carry a small quantity of DNA in their mitochondria, the structures in the outer

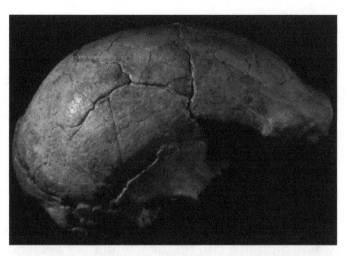

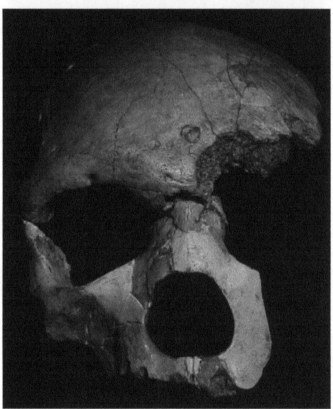

Figures 3.2. and 3.3. Two early near-modern African crania. Left: the LH 18 (Ngaloba) cranium from northern Tanzania; Right: the Florisbad face from South Africa. Photographs by Jeffrey H. Schwartz.

part of the cell that function as the "powerhouse" behind cell operations. This mtDNA has several qualities that make it particularly useful to those interested in what molecules can tell us about relationships. First, it lacks the elaborate self-repairing mechanisms of nuclear DNA, and thus accumulates mutations at a very high rate, giving molecular systematists lots of differences to look for even when they are studying quite closely related populations. Second, it is largely free of the "junk" (non-coding) DNA that composes so much of the nuclear DNA complement. Third, modern human mtDNA consists of about 16,500 nucleotides (the minimal units that are strung together to make up the DNA strand). This is in contrast with more than three billion nucleotides in the human nuclear DNA genome—obviously using mtDNA simplifies comparisons. Fourth, mtDNA is always transmitted between generations as a single unit, unlike the nuclear DNA which is carried on chromosomes that sometimes exchange material. And finally, and most interesting of all, everyone's mtDNA is often inherited only from their mother. This is because the mother's egg contains mitochondria but mitochondria are present only in the tail of the father's sperm. Usually only the head of a sperm cell penetrates the egg. But sometimes a piece of the tail also gets included. Most of the time, then, mtDNA avoids the mixing-up in every generation that accompnies the transmission of nuclear DNA, thereby avoiding the complicated consequences of sexual reproduction.

In a landmark study published in 1987, a group of molecular systematists at the University of California at Berkeley sampled mtDNA from representatives of a variety of human groups of different geographical origin. They used the data thus obtained to test the two major paleontological hypotheses of modern human origins and diversity that were current then (and still, in essence, are). On the one hand was the multiregional continuity idea, whereby the major geographical groups of modern humankind have roots very deep in the past. On the other was the "single origin" notion, whereby all modern human populations share a close common ancestry, probably in Africa, and have only diversified quite recently. The researchers found that their sample of Africans contained much more mtDNA diversity than did the representatives of other populations, suggesting that the African population had been accumulating mutations for much longer than either Europeans or Asians. Further, a "family tree" of mtDNA resemblance seemed to have its roots within the African sample, and from this the researchers derived the notion of "African Eve," the female founder of all surviving mtDNA lineages. Finally, assuming an average rate of change in mtDNA sequences of about twenty percent every million years (a big assumption, of course), they concluded that Eve had lived about 200 kyr ago. This rather short chronology seemed, however, to fit well with the observation of a very low mtDNA diversity in humans when compared with modern ape populations. The best explanation for this seems to be that humans went through a population "bottleneck" (dramatic shrinkage) in the fairly recent past. And, quite obviously, all of these findings conform much better to the "African Origin" paleontological model than to the multiregional idea, which predicts that mtDNA diversity should be roughly equally distributed among modern populations.

Early criticism of this research focused on the nature of the sample of modern humans that the Berkeley group had used (which included African Americans rather than individuals born in Africa). But later studies on larger samples obtained in diverse geographic regions, including Africa, came up with similar results. The work was also attacked on the grounds that the published family tree was not actually the best one that could be constructed on the basis of the available data sets. Again, however, there appears to be no getting away from the fact that the diversity data do seem to be telling us that humans have been diversifying longest in Africa, and that Asian and European populations appear to have been derived ultimately from emigrants from this older African population. The extrapolated dating of African Eve was also questioned, but studies incorporating later refinements continue to indicate a bottleneck in the period of about 150–200 kyr ago. Recent comparative studies of the human Y chromosome (uniquely passed along by men, presumably from an "African Adam") suggest a pattern similar to that suggested by the maternally derived mtDNA. Even more interesting is that in China, one hotbed of multi-regional thinking, a recent study of microsatellites (repeats of short nuclear DNA segments) has suggested a derivation of the Han Chinese from an ultimately African ancestry.

One important point to bear in mind here is that the postulated African Eve was not necessarily the first *Homo* sapiens. She was simply the mtDNA type from which our mtDNA lineage was descended. Such are the vagaries of the speciation process (which isolates one population from another but not population members from each other) that she might actually have been a member of an earlier species. In which case *H. sapiens* itself could have originated subsequent to Eve's tenure on Earth. Such quibbles aside, and especially when taken together with the minimal existing paleontological indications, the mtDNA data do provide us with quite a strong signal that our species emerged not only in Africa, but relatively recently.

Unfortunately, there is in Africa no equivalent of the "symbolic explosion" we find in Europe (albeit fairly late on) that announces the abrupt arrival of a fully formed modern human sensibility. There are, however, certain tantalizing hints in the archaeological record of "modern" behavior patterns in Africa at an unexpectedly early date. Earliest of all are recent findings that the manufacture of blade tools (the long, thin flakes typically made by the first *Homo sapiens* to enter Europe) at one site in eastern Africa dates to well over 200 kyr ago. Evidence of the hafting of projectile points is almost as old. Equally, recent reports have come from a Central African site of bone tools that may be as much as 80 kyr old. Africa also furnishes the earliest evidence of such "modern" activities as flint mining and the long-distance transport (trading?) of prized materials, as well as of efficient fishing in the form of abundant fish bones at living sites. What's more, there are also early inklings of overtly symbolic behaviors, such as the decorative or notational incising of ostrich eggshell fragments almost 50 kyr ago. And whereas even putting all this evidence together lacks the astonishing impact of the European symbolic record subsequent to about 40 kyr ago, it is hard to avoid the conclusion that important behavioral developments were afoot in Africa well before we see them so dramatically expressed in Europe.

On the other hand, even if Africa offers the earliest suggestions we have of both anatomical and behavioral modernity, it is clear that *Homo sapiens* did not make these twin acquisitions in lockstep. Indeed, the record we currently have leaves little doubt that modern anatomical form was achieved well before modern behavior found its fullest expression. Which, when you consider the matter, should come as no great surprise, for as we've already noted, there is only one place in which a new behavior can be acquired, and that is *within* a species. Any new behavior, after all, whether momentous or trivial, has to originate with a single individual. And that individual has to belong to a pre-existing species and can hardly differ too much from his or her parents or offspring. To find evidence that for all its unusual attributes *H. sapiens* is no exception to this pattern, we need look no farther afield than the Levant (specifically, Israel)—a region that, incidentally, many consider to be a biogeographic extension of the African continent.

3.1.2 The Levant

Tentative dating of the earliest levels of the site of Tabun, a huge cave in the western foothills of Israel's Mount Carmel, suggests that Mousterian tool technology was already established in the Levant by well over 200 kyr ago. A precursor industry from the site of

Zuttiyeh, a few dozen miles to the east, may be a good bit older. This industry is associated with a skull fragment that has traditionally been touted for its "archaic" characteristics, but that bears several strong Neanderthal resemblances. Exactly who made the earliest Mousterian implements at Tabun cannot at present be known for sure, but what is clear is that the two hominid finds at the cave, which come from deposits perhaps 125 kyr old or thereabouts, are fully formed Neanderthals. One of the specimens, assumed to represent a burial because much of the skeleton was present in articulation, is lightly built and thought to be female. The other specimen consists of an isolated and robust lower jaw that has numerous Neanderthal characteristics but which is often said to boast a chin, something normally associated with *Homo sapiens*. Our own examination of the fossil shows that although the area of the chin is broken, enough remains to demonstrate that no "inverted T" structure is present. Tabun thus offers a pretty strong association of the Mousterian with Neanderthals, as also do various other, much younger, Levantine sites. Among these are the cave of Kebara, which has yielded an extremely robust Neanderthal skeleton dated to about 60 kyr ago. Younger yet is another Israeli site, Amud, at which Neanderthal burials are also associated with Mousterian stone tools. An adult male burial is dated to about 45 kyr, and an infant skeleton is a little older, at between 50 and 60 kyr. Despite its tender age and incompleteness, this specimen shows distinctive Neanderthal morphologies.

So far so good; and it is of course no surprise to find Neanderthal bones associated with a Mousterian technology. But there are other Israeli sites at which the Mousterian is equally definitely associated with remains of anatomically modern humans. The clearest such association is found in the cave of Jebel Qafzeh, where the lithic industry is plainly Mousterian but where more than a dozen human burials, found in various parts of the cave, are rather oddly assorted. Of the two best preserved specimens, one looks just a little odd for a modern human, while the other (Qafzeh 9) is as representative a *Homo sapiens* as you could wish to find. This individual was laid to rest, arms folded and knees bent, in a shallow grave. And, because an infant was buried in the same grave, at the adult's feet, it has been generally assumed that here we have the skeleton of a female, buried with her child. However, our own observations show that if you apply the criteria generally used by anthropologists to sex modern skeletons to both skull and body skeleton, it is hard to avoid the conclusion that in fact these are the remains of a male. Even more remarkably, recent dating has shown that this Mousterian modern died well over 90 kyr ago. About the same age, or possibly even more ancient yet, is a series of burials from the site of Skhul, just a few minutes' stroll from Tabun. Ever since their excavation in the early 1930s these Mousterian remains have posed a puzzle to paleoanthropologists, appearing to be almost but not quite modern humans. Ironically, the stone tools found in some abundance along with the Skhul burials compare closely to those associated with both the Tabun and Qafzeh hominids. At its simplest, then, the Levantine record shows clearly that more or less indistinguishable Mousterian industries were produced both by Neanderthals and by *H. sapiens*; and the known fossils hint that the situation may have been more complex yet, at least on the biological side.

Neanderthals were thus quite likely already present in the Levant close to or even well over 200 kyr ago. And Neanderthals appear to have persisted in the region until 40–45 kyr ago. Anatomically modern humans appeared later, at a little under 100 kyr ago. Further, once arrived, moderns never left, at least for long. Obviously, then, there was a protracted period of coexistence between the two species, minimally from about 100 to 40 kyr ago. Exactly what form this coexistence took is a matter for speculation. On the basis of the supposed coldadaptedness of the Neanderthals, for example, it has been suggested that these now-extinct hominids moved south into this region when the climate cooled, and the "tropically adapted" (i.e., Africa-derived) moderns retreated toward the continent of their birth. The reverse, it is proposed, would have occurred in warmer times, as the Neanderthals sought the welcoming cool of the north. Well, perhaps, although rigid "time-sharing" of this kind seems a bit unlikely given what we know about the adaptability of both hominid species. But what does seem inescapable is that, after the arrival of the moderns, coexistence of some kind continued for almost exactly as long as both hominids shared a similar stoneworking technology (and whatever other behavioral patterns this implies). Unlike the situation in Europe, where the "Upper Paleolithic" technology of the first *Homo sapiens* was introduced by invaders from outside, in the Levantine region Upper Paleolithic stone tool making was initially an indigenous development, with Mousterian techniques being used at first to produce utensils of Upper Paleolithic form. We find the first evidence for this innovation at Israel's Boker Tachtit, a site that dates from about 47 kyr ago. We don't know what other behavioral advances might have accompanied this technological development. However, it is probably not coincidental that it was not long afterwards that Neanderthals disappeared from the Levantine record. Thus, for as long as *H. sapiens* and *Homo neanderthalensis* employed essentially similar technologies, it evidently remained possible for them to share the Near East landscape in some way. But, once their technologies diverged, coexistence was apparently doomed.

It is thus particularly regrettable that we have so little other evidence of the lifeways of Neanderthals and moderns in the Levant at this critical juncture in the human evolutionary story, especially because the key to the problem of coexistence seems to lie in what we might call "behavioral modernity." *H. sapiens* has at least intermittently existed as a distinctive anatomical entity in the Levant for at least a hundred thousand years, and in Africa quite probably for a lot more. But until we begin to pick up—unfortunately highly indirect—intimations of modern human behavior patterns, our species appears to have been capable of sharing its environment with a spectrum of relatives. *Homo sapiens*, in other words, was just another hominid. But once hints of modern human cognition appeared, everything changed. How it changed is without question incomparably best reflected in the archaeological record of Europe. Charges of Eurocentrism are often leveled at those who succumb to the fascination exerted by the astonishing archive left behind them by the first—both anatomically and behaviorally—modern Europeans. Yet even if this record is biased by the lack of comparable evidence elsewhere, it is also hugely compelling. We would be grievously wrong to ignore it, even as we recognize that Europe is and was merely a cul-de-sac tacked on to the western end of the Eurasian continent—and that, by the time the Upper Paleolithic record began there, the most momentous events of all in the history of the human species had already taken place somewhere else.

3.1.3 The First Modern Europeans

As we've seen, the first modern human invaders erupted into the (relatively) serene world of the European Neanderthals around 40 kyr ago, appearing more or less simultaneously in both the eastern and western extremes of the subcontinent. Whether eastern or western, these *Homo sapiens* brought with them a single distinctive Upper Paleolithic industry, known as the Aurignacian after a site in southern France. This new technology is quite distinct from the indigenous early Upper Paleolithic of the Levant, and nobody is sure exactly when or where it originated. Technologically, the Aurignacian is distinguished from the Mousterian by stone tools made from long, narrow blades struck successively from carefully shaped cylindrical "prismatic" stone cores, and by the widespread adoption of bone and antler as raw materials in toolmaking. These new materials were worked with an exquisite sensitivity to their mechanical properties: something that contrasts with the rather crude as well as rare Middle Paleolithic treatment of these substances. What's more, the relative monotony of the Mousterian was completely gone from early Upper Paleolithic tool assemblages: toolmakers from different sites apparently freely followed their own creative impulses, making the classification of the many local variants of the Aurignacian an enormous headache for archaeologists. At the same time, however, individual tool types become easier for modern humans to analyze because they were evidently made by people who saw the world and the interaction of its parts in the same way that we do. The categories that made sense to them are the categories that make sense to us. So, for the first time, we can have no doubt whatever that we are dealing with beings whose cognitive processes were essentially similar to our own.

But as impressive as the new technology may have been, it certainly does not furnish us with the most dramatic evidence for major cognitive innovation. For the most remarkable change in the archaeological record from the Middle to the Upper Paleolithic consisted not of a shift in the character of functional objects, but rather of the appearance of a wealth of symbolic or ceremonial artifacts. We have to look very hard at the Neanderthal record to discern anything at all that we can describe as symbolic with even the most modest confidence. In stark contrast, however, the Upper Paleolithic was drenched in symbol. Quite simply, if the archaeological record they bequeathed us means anything at all, it indicates that the Aurignacians were beings of an entirely different order from the Neanderthals who had preceded them. The best evidence we have of the arrival of this unprecedented sensibility comes from France and Germany, where the earliest Aurignacian sites have been dated to the period of 32–35 kyr ago.

Perhaps as good a place as any to start an account of this flowering is the lovely and tranquil little valley of the Lone River, in southern Germany: a place evidently as greatly favored by the Aurignacians during the last Ice Age as it is by ramblers today. Here, within a mile of each other, are two caves in the valley walls that were used for shelter by Aurignacians some 34 kyr ago. At one of them, Vogelherd, was found a whole series of animal figurines carved in mammoth ivory, among them a two-inch-long image of a horse that is still unrivaled today for its elegance and grace. Polished by long contact with someone's skin, this figurine was probably worn originally as a pendant. What is particularly interesting about it is that it is not in the least a straightforward representation of the stocky horses that roamed the steppes of Ice Age Europe. Rather, with its long arching neck and the exquisite line of its back, it is an evocation of the graceful essence of all horses. As simple representation and craftsmanship this figurine is already remarkable. But the abstraction of form that it embodies places it in the most refined category of art. What more could we ask for as proof of a fully formed modern sensibility? Well, how about an intriguing foot-high figure, also carved in mammoth ivory, from the nearby cave of Hohlenstein-Stadel? This piece is less impressive as art than the Vogelherd figurines, but it is more aggressively symbolic, consisting as it does of a man's standing body surmounted by a lion's head. We will never know exactly what the man/lion emblem represented to the individual who made this carving, or to the society to which he or she belonged. But nobody could ever doubt that this remarkable object was fashioned by someone possessing all the mysterious complexity of a fully modern human.

Impressive as such pieces of early "portable" art are, in the public mind the Aurignacians are more closely associated with the art they left on the walls of numerous caves that dot the limestone landscape of southern France and northern Spain. Until recently this was not technically the case, for it was generally believed that in Aurignacian times cave decoration (difficult or impossible to date directly) had been largely restricted to hand stencils and a few geometrical signs. The great period of deep cave art, it was thought, had began much later, maybe less than 20 kyr ago. But the astonishing discovery in late 1994 of the southern French cave of Chauvet has made it evident that extraordinary cave decoration, too, dates from the very beginning of the Upper Paleolithic in western Europe. An early estimate of the age of the art of Chauvet, based on its style and craftsmanship, had placed these images at about 18 kyr old. Imagine, then, the astonishment of scientists and art historians alike when direct dating of some of the images using new radiocarbon techniques revealed that some of them at least were painted as much as 32 kyr ago! At Chauvet a wealth of animal and abstract images, some 300 counted so far, cascade across the cave walls. Some are painted in red or black outline. Some are finger tracings in the soft coating of the cave walls. Some are represented by dots. And some gain their interior volume from shading, although others use the natural relief of the cave walls to achieve the same effect of bulk. Each of the most spectacular elements of the mammal fauna of the Ice Age Rhone valley is there: lions, woolly rhinos, mammoths, reindeer, horses, wild cattle, bears, ibexes, a leopard, and—most unusually—an owl. And all of them are depicted with the vitality, economy, and grace that have always marked the finest of graphic productions. It is interesting that some of the animal images of Chauvet were evidently "re-used" by the addition of body parts (horns, for example, or legs) to pre-existing images: a foreshadowing of later practices that emphasizes the functional as well as the aesthetic aspects of this art.

Just as do the masterpieces of portable art from the Lone valley, the Chauvet images announce the arrival of the modern human sensibility in an incomparably direct way. We don't have to understand what this art meant to its makers to know, viscerally, that it is not simple representation, but is rather a distillation of the artists' view of the natural world, and of their place in it. Clearly, these images have, or had to their makers, a symbolic significance that went far beyond the mere cataloguing of animal species. Perhaps it's odd, then, that very little Ice Age art is overtly narrative, at least in the way that we understand this term today. Indeed, of the thousands of Ice Age images known, only a handful are assembled in such a way as to suggest to modern eyes that a specific story is being recounted. The best such example, probably around 17 kyr old, is painted on the wall of a vertical shaft at the incomparable cave of Lascaux, in France. Here a very schematically represented bird-headed man falls backwards in front of a bison that has apparently been disemboweled by a spear. A woolly rhinoceros is beating a retreat behind the man, and the ensemble is completed by some dots and a staff bearing a bird symbol. Almost certainly significantly, the same scene seems to be enacted in simplified fashion (just the man and the bison) on the wall of the cave of Villars, not very far away from Lascaux. But that, literally, is about it for narrative in Ice Age art, at least in a form that we can readily recognize (if not interpret) today. In sensibility the Aurignacians were our equals, but their cultural traditions are, of course, lost in time. Thus most Ice Age animal images are juxtaposed with others, and it is obvious that such creations as the "parade" of polychrome animal images that tumbles across the wall of the Hall of Bulls at Lascaux—as powerful an ensemble as has ever been painted—are not simply random arrangements of the symbolic elements. But they are not evidently telling a sequential story, as in the case of the man and bison.

At one level this certainly seems curious, especially given how hard it is to escape the conclusion that the animal art of the Ice Age, and the geometric and other symbols associated with it, reflect a coherent, complex, and extensive body of knowledge, myth, and belief. At another level, it is easy enough to appreciate that the original Ice Age observers, inheritors of a rich and complex cultural tradition, would have responded readily to the symbolic references that the art embodied, including the juxtaposition of images that appears so mysterious to us. After all, to them this art was part of a living tradition. And even if, many thousands of years later and in an entirely different social milieu, we are in the end obliged to admit that for us the art of the Ice Age is art to be experienced rather than art to be understood, the power of this art to move us tens of millennia after its creation is as eloquent a testimony as could ever be found to the fact that its makers were people with whom we can identify at the most profound of levels.

Perhaps no more eloquent, though, than the arrival of music, another common denominator of modern human societies. From the site of Isturitz, in the French Pyrenees, comes a whole set of bone flutes, at least 32 kyr old. We will never know exactly what sounds echoed off the walls of the Isturitz cave during those long-ago Ice Age evenings; but in the hands of modern musicians, replicas of such wind instruments show remarkably complex sound capabilities. Music—even sophisticated music—is, it seems, inseparable from being human. And as if this were not enough, right from the beginning of the Aurignacian, at least 32 kyr old and possibly a good bit more, is a polished bone plaque from the site of the Abri Blanchard, in southwestern France.

This plaque bears a long, curving series of deliberate notations, and has been interpreted as a lunar calendar. Whether or not this interpretation is historically accurate, it is incontestable that this piece, and others like it of similar age, are testimony to recordkeeping of some kind. Aurignacians not only lived in a symbolically mediated world, but they kept accurate track of their experience. This fits in well with what we know, from the sites they left behind, of their social existence. On the basis of the relative complexity and size variations in their sites, we can conclude that Aurignacians lived in social groups that were much more complex and variable in size than any earlier groups. There is, indeed, good reason to believe that such "modern" socioeconomic features as division of labor and social stratification had already appeared in Aurignacian times.

Sculpture, engraving, painting, music, notation, elaborate burial, specialized social roles, recordkeeping, ever-evolving technology—it may seem remarkable that all of these quintessentially human activities are documented in Europe immediately upon the arrival of anatomically modern humans in this part of the world. But what the record appears to be suggesting very strongly is that the modern human sensibility—what has been called "the human capacity"—was acquired as a package, rather than bit by bit over the millennia. And this, as it happens, fits well with what we know about the evolutionary process itself. Of course, given the innate human urge to refine and improve, we should not be surprised to discover, as we do, that technological advances continued to be made throughout the Upper Paleolithic, even after the basic modern human behavior patterns had been established. Thus the "Gravettian" culture that replaced the Aurignacian introduced the eyed bone needle and, presumably, tailored clothing, by about 26 kyr ago. At around the same time we find the first ceramics, in the form of figurines baked at high temperatures in simple but remarkably effective kilns. Not too long after this, spear-throwers were introduced, devices that would have considerably improved hunting efficiency; and barbed harpoons announce advances in fishing techniques. Bows and arrows had become current by the end of the Ice Age, about 10 kyr ago, when the high cultures of the Upper Paleolithic were already on the wane. Throughout the Upper Paleolithic, in other words, technology continued to be refined and elaborated—as is, indeed, still happening today. But what is equally inescapable is that even at the very beginning of this period—right from the very earliest modern human occupation of Europe—all of the essential modern human characteristics were already established. What happened—or rather, what had happened—to create this new phenomenon? How did our ancestors come to buy this package? This is, of course, the mystery of mysteries, and there is probably no simple answer to it. But it's possible to make a few suggestions.

3.1.4 Becoming Human

Significant behavioral innovation has, as we've seen, been sporadic and quite rare in human evolution. Even as new species came and went, the general pattern over the eons was one of adding the occasional refinement to ancestral lifestyles, rather than of radical changes in ways of doing business. But with the advent on Earth of *Homo sapiens*—or at least, of *H. sapiens* with modern behavior patterns—this was emphatically no longer the case. Indeed, there has never been a more fateful arrival on the biological scene than that of our extraordinary species. On the other hand, however, there is absolutely no reason to believe that the rules of the evolutionary game had been even slightly bent in paving the way for our arrival. We can look nowhere else than at conventional processes of evolution in explaining the advent of our very unconventional selves. [Figure 3.4] Let's briefly look again at some of those processes.

It is often believed, if only implicitly, that natural selection is in itself a "creative" process that somehow "drives" evolution. But a moment's thought is enough to show that this cannot be the case. Any new structure must arise *before* it can assume a function, and thereby qualify as a target of natural selection. What's more, natural selection itself is a pretty blunt instrument. It can, after all, only vote up or down on the reproductive success of entire organisms, each one a complex bundle of characteristics. However convenient we may find it for analytical purposes to think in terms of the evolution of the brain, say, or of bipedalism, there is in fact no way in which natural selection can single out one particular trait to favor to or condemn. It's the whole individual whose reproductive success is at issue, just as at another level it is whole species that must succeed or fail. The story of evolution is thus much more than the simple sum of the direct results of natural selection alone. It is, instead, completed by the histories of entire organisms, populations, and species, all competing at their respective levels to make it in the ecological arena. And once (but not until) we understand that evolution cannot simply be a matter of fine-tuning of individual traits by natural selection, the way is open to comprehending in broad terms what might have happened to give rise to the extraordinary phenomenon of modern human cognition. Unfortunately, we are handicapped here by our ignorance of how human consciousness is generated in the brain. We know a lot about how the human brain is put together, and

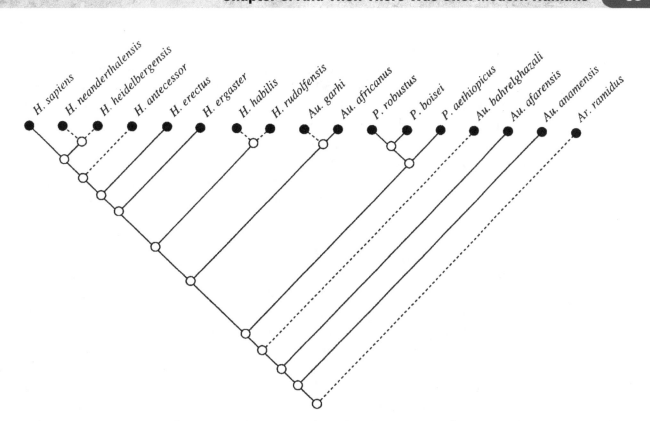

Figure 3.4. A cladogram showing suggested relationships among the various hominid species mentioned in this chapter. Many of these relationships (especially those indicated by dashed lines) are highly tentative, and await definitive testing. As it stands, this cladogram includes "paraphyletic" groups. This problem is only solvable by recognizing more genera. Courtesy of Ian Tattersall.

about how various parts of it are recruited in performing various specific functions. But, quite simply, we have as yet no idea whatever about how a mass of electrical and chemical discharges within the brain is converted into what we individually and subjectively experience as consciousness. To explain ourselves to ourselves completely, we shall ultimately have to achieve this knowledge. Fortunately, however, we do not need to command this level of detail to understand in principle what might have happened to bring our extraordinary consciousness about.

A routine phenomenon in the histories of organisms is what has been called "exaptation," whereby new characteristics arise in one functional context well before being recruited in another. Thus, for example, birds appear to have acquired feathers in the context of body temperature regulation long before these structures were recruited in the service of flight. Flight would ultimately not have been possible if feathers had not already been there, but feathers are not inherently flight-associated. For millions of years (as we can know only in retrospect), feathers were exaptations for flight, available to be co-opted in this new function when circumstances permitted, but already performing another essential role. In the case of human evolution, as good an example as any of exaptation is provided by the structures of the vocal tract that permit speech. The vocal tract itself is, of course, made of soft tissues that do not fossilize. But the roof of the tract is also the base of the skull, which sometimes does. And it turns out that a distinct downward flexion of the skull base is associated with the possession of a humanlike vocal tract capable of producing the sounds associated with language. What's more, this downward flexion can be traced all the way back to some members, at least, of *Homo heidelbergensis*—perhaps as much as 0.5 myr ago. Yet the archaeological record before about 50 kyr ago contains no evidence of the ability to manipulate symbols that almost certainly accompanied the advent of language. The modern vocal tract (which has a distinct downside—it makes it possible for its possessors to choke to death) must thus have been acquired in another context, possibly but not inevitably a respiratory one. In any event, the record is saying pretty clearly that our ancestors possessed an essentially modern vocal tract a very long time before we have any solid grounds for believing that they used it for linguistic purposes—something we'll return to in a moment.

The other concept that is useful to bear in mind as we seek the origins of the human capacity is that of the "emergent quality." Frequently, complex systems can add up to much more than the simple sum of their parts, and combining two or more unrelated elements can give rise to unexpected (emergent) results. The classic case of this is water, whose properties, so essential to life, are entirely unpredicted by those of its constituent atoms, hydrogen and oxygen. Perhaps the extraordinary phenomenon of modern consciousness is a quality of this kind, a chance combination of exaptations that were locked into place as an unexpected functioning whole by a final "keystone" acquisition that appeared, like all novelties, independently of any functional role. What that acquisition was in physical terms will have to await a more profound knowledge of the functioning of the human brain than anything we can lay claim to at present. But it does seem likely that, whatever it was, it lay fallow for a considerable period before being co-opted into its new role. For, as we've seen, modern anatomical structure considerably predated modern cognitive functioning. This is most clearly evident from the Levantine record, which shows Neanderthals and moderns behaving, as far as we can tell, in more or less indistinguishable ways for perhaps as much as 60 kyr.

What can we infer from this? Well, one possibility is that Neanderthals and early moderns initially possessed brains that were functionally identical, but that some radical biological reorganization eventually arose among the moderns that permitted them to express modern behavior patterns. This seems on the face of it a bit unlikely. For this scenario depends on the acquisition by anatomically modern *Homo sapiens* of a key heritable biological innovation at perhaps 50 kyr ago. Spreading such an innovation around the Old World would have involved the wholesale replacement throughout this vast region not only of osteologically and behaviorally archaic hominids (Neanderthal, Ngandong, and so forth), but of osteologically modern (but neurally archaic) populations. Not only is the time available for such an extraordinary replacement episode rather short, but (in an admittedly sketchy record) there is no evidence for it (such as might be furnished, for instance, by abrupt replacement, at individual sites, of behaviorally archaic moderns by behaviorally advanced moderns). The alternative is to conclude that the human capacity was born in potential by some "keystone" acquisition at or close to the birth of our species as an anatomical entity. This innovation then lay fallow, as an exaptation, until it was activated by some kind of behavioral invention in a particular local population. And, if that invention was highly advantageous, it's reasonable to expect that it would have spread rapidly by cultural contact among anatomically modern human populations, all over the Old World, that would already have possessed the biological potential to acquire it.

What could this innovation have been? There is no way at present of knowing for sure, but the obvious candidate is the invention of language. Language is not simply a refinement of earlier ways of communication, but is almost certainly integral to our reasoning abilities. Language and thought as we know them both involve forming and recombining mental symbols; and it is, indeed, virtually impossible for us to conceive of one in the absence of the other. Language is thus not simply the medium by which we communicate our thoughts to each other, but is rather basic to the thought process itself. And once we have symbolic thought we can live, not simply in the world as presented to us by Nature, but rather in the world as we reconstruct it in our minds: an ability that has had profound and fateful consequences. None of this means, of course, that many kinds of sophisticated understanding were not already possible before the advent of symbolic reasoning. Indeed, in their day the Neanderthals, whose record shows what remarkable achievements can be made on the basis of intuitive processes, clearly knew and understood their environment with unprecedented precision. Although they evidently had an advanced intuitive intelligence, there is no compelling evidence that the Neanderthals possessed symbolic reasoning. There is, indeed, some dispute over whether Neanderthals had the vocal equipment to produce speech.

Thus, it seems rational to conclude that the prosaic phenomenon of exaptation was what set the stage for the emergence of the astonishing and totally unprecedented human capacity. For whatever historical reasons, a set of neural and peripheral structures as in place early in the evolution of anatomically modern *Homo* that both permitted and capitalized on the invention of language by individuals of one local population, somewhere in the world. The resulting language need not have sprung forth full-blown, with all of the many subtleties and complexities that characterize languages worldwide today. Even a relatively simple language would have made the most profound of differences in the way in which our ancestors were able to view and interact with the world around them, simply by making it possible to create symbols in the mind, and to recombine them and ask questions such as "what if?"

Whatever the case, it is a related change in ways of interacting with the world around us that accounts for the fact that *H. sapiens* is the lone hominid on Earth today. The switch by our ancestors from intuitive to symbolic intelligence (or, more accurately, the grafting of symbolic onto intuitive intelligence) clearly made it impossible for our fossil relatives to coexist with us. Earlier in human evolutionary history, small differences in relative advantage doubtless led to the overall replacement of one hominid species by another over the long term. But typically such differences would have been sufficiently small that replacement was probably a fairly long-drawn-out process. What's more, the relative advantage would presumably have changed depending on local environments (that themselves oscillated), leading to a situation whereby various hominid species competed on different footings in different places. With the advent of symbolic reasoning, however, the behavioral advantage of *H. sapiens* became so overwhelming that other hominids could no longer compete under any ecological circumstances. And, once these closest relatives were gone, we turned our attention to a remoter group of relatives, the apes—and beyond.

In closing, it is worthwhile to point out that, as a model to explain the emergence of human beings and their remarkable attributes, the Great Chain of Being has once again let us down. There was nothing inevitable about how we got to where we are today, and in the truly unique and important aspects of our being we are not simply the result of steady improvement in a linear progression. The emergence of behaviorally modern *H. sapiens* was emphatically not just an extrapolation of earlier trends; and cognitively we are not merely a refinement of what went before. For reasons, and through mechanisms, that we still don't fully understand, something truly unprecedented happened in one of the terminal branches of our bushy family tree, and we are still learning how to live with the consequences.

Further Reading

The literature relating to human evolution is vast. Below are some recent popular titles that further explore some of the themes followed in this book. Most contain pointers to the primary literature.

Bahn, P. and J. Vertut. 1998. *Journey Through the Ice Age*. Berkeley, CA: University of California Press. A beautifully illustrated account of French and Spanish Paleolithic art, and its interpretation.

Byrne, R. 1995. *The Thinking Ape: Evolutionary Origins of Intelligence*. Oxford: Oxford University Press. A thoughtful and wide-ranging consideration of primate cognition and its evolution.

Darwin, C. 1871. *The Descent of Man, and Selection in Relation to Sex*. John Tyler Bonner (ed). Princeton, New Jersey: Princeton University Press. A classic and engaging account, if somewhat flawed by the assumptions of its times.

Deacon, T. 1997. *The Symbolic Species: The Co-evolution of Language and the Brain*. New York: W. W. Norton. Highly informative review of the function of the human brain and the potential pathways of its evolution, from a gradualist perspective.

Eldredge, N. 1998. *The Pattern of Evolution*. San Francisco: W. H. Freeman. A leading expert in evolutionary theory considers evolutionary mechanisms and the expected biotic patterns arising from them.

Huxley, T. 1864. *Man's Place in Nature and Other Anthropological Essays*. London: Macmillan. Periodically out-of-print, but well worth a trip to the library for this provocative and opinionated series of essays on the "question of questions."

Johanson, D., L. Johanson and B. Edgar. 1994. *Ancestors: In Search of Human Origins*. New York: Villard Books, 1994. Companion volume to a TV series, in which the discoverer of "Lucy" conducts an engaging and very personal tour of the human fossil record.

Johanson, D. and B. Edgar. 1996. *From Lucy to Language*. New York: A Peter N. Nevraumont Book, Simon and Schuster. A superbly illustrated and produced volume of human fossil images, structured around informative considerations of many of the most-frequently asked questions about human evolution.

Lieberman, P. 1998. *Eve Spoke: Human Language and Human Evolution*. New York: W. W. Norton. A distinguished linguistician provides his views on the evolution of language in an easily accessible form.

Pinker, S. 1994. *The Language Instinct: How the Mind Creates Language*. New York: William Morrow & Co. A leading cognitive psychologist and linguistician, and fluent writer, explains the intimate relationship between language and the functioning of the modern human brain.

Rudwick, M. 1985. *The Meaning of Fossils* (2nd ed.) Chicago: University of Chicago Press. An accessible and comprehensive account of paleontology from Renaissance times to Darwin.

Schwartz, J.H. 1993. *What the Bones Tell Us*. New York: Henry Holt. An osteologist and paleontologist provides a variety of perspectives on what we can learn from the study of bones—both fossil and modern.

Schwartz, J.H. 1995. *Skeleton Keys: an introduction to human skeletal morphology, development, and analysis*. New York: Oxford University Press. A detailed overview of the human skeletal with an eye toward distinguishing between features of the species and individual variation within the species.

Schwartz, J.H. 1999. *Sudden Origins: Fossils, Genes, and the Emergence of Species*. New York: John Wiley & Sons. A readable and informative account of a new theory of the evolutionary process, based on the latest advances in our understanding of genes and developmental processes.

Stanley, S. 1996. *Children of the Ice Age: How a Global Catastrophe Allowed Humans to Evolve*. New York: Harmony Books. A lively and readable account by a distinguished paleontologist of how the vagaries of climate have affected human evolutionary history.

Stringer, C. and R. McKie. 1996. *African Exodus: The Origins of Modern Humanity*. New York: Henry Holt. A prominent exponent of the "Out of Africa" model of modern human emergence provides a personal perspective on the later phases of human evolution.

Tattersall, I. 1995. *The Fossil Trail: How We Know What We Think We Know About Human Evolution*. New York: Oxford University Press. A history of human evolutionary thought and the human fossil record through the eyes of a practicing paleoanthropologist [2nd expanded edition, 2009].

Tattersall, I. 1998. *Becoming Human: Evolution and Human Uniqueness*. New York: Harcourt Brace. A personal investigation of what makes us different from the rest of the living world, and of how those differences came about.

Tattersall, I. 1999. *The Last Neanderthal: The Rise, Success, and Mysterious Extinction of Our Closest Human Relative* (Revised ed.). Boulder, CO: A Peter N. Nevraumont Book, Westview Press. A beautifully illustrated account of our closest well-documented extinct relatives, of their background, and of what may have befallen them.

Chapter 4
The Meaning of Culture

Arnaud F. Lambert

Outline

An infant had died in the night. The little corpse was flexed and wrapped in its mother's skirt. The infant's mother held onto the bundle and cried, repeatedly wiping her nose. A grave was being prepared in the middle of the house floor by a young man. When the grave had been dug as deep as the young man could reach with his arm, he gently took the bundle and placed it in one of the mother's cooking pots. The mother continued to cry intermittently for another week.

One week after the date of the burial, the grave was opened. The infant's father joined the mother in crying as the bundle was removed and placed in a new pot, at one point grabbing at the pot. The corpse was then cremated in the new pot. When the fire had burned for an hour, the charred ribs were removed and the rest of the body was burned for another hour or so. When all of the flesh had been burned away, the father stopped crying and began to talk with the other men. The mother placed the cremated remains and ashes back in the grave.

For several more days, the mother cried until her adult son came to make a new grinding trough for her. Into this trough she ground corn, added water, and made a gruel or thin porridge with the bone powder from the cremated infant. The mother continued to mourn the infant until she had consumed the entire mixture after which she stopped crying and her demeanor changed remarkably (Dole 1974:303–305).

According to Gertrude Dole (1974), proper treatment of deceased individuals among the Amahuaca people of eastern Peru involves two interrelated steps. First, the bereaved typically wail and cry over the burial and cremated remains of their loved one, often to the point that they must wipe the mucus from their noses. The more a person moans and cries, the better the deceased person's "shade" or "spirit" feels. It is also believed that the depth of one's sorrow is best measured by the amount of mucus running from one's nose. Second, it was not uncommon for the Amahuaca to consume the pulverized bones of their cremated loved ones as a way to banish the "shade" of the deceased from the places of the living.

How do we begin to make sense of these kinds of behaviors? Some disciplines, like biology and the medical sciences, might focus on searching for ecological explanations for these customs. They may, for instance, view **endo-cannibalism** as a way for people to supplement their poor diets. Psychologists and psychiatrists might view Amahuaca endo-cannibalism as aberrant or abnormal behavior emerging from several socio-psychological stressors such as the traumatic death of a family member. Still others might use the now discredited rubric of **"race"** to ethnocentrically refer to these customs as "primitive" and then go on to characterize the entire population as crafty and immoral. Anthropologists generally take a very different point of view. They use the concept of "culture" to explain human behavior.

4.1   What is Culture?

"Culture" refers to the shared ideas and behavior patterns that characterize the way members of a society adapt to and utilize their environment, organize themselves, interact with other people, and express their ideas. In short, culture is what constitutes a people's particular way of life.

Unfortunately, culture is such a broad topic that anthropologists have never agreed on a standard definition of culture (Freilich 1972). In the 1950s, Clyde Kluckhohn and Alfred Kroeber famously counted well over a hundred different definitions of culture in use by anthropologists at the time (Kroeber and Kluckhohn 1963). The situation has not improved.

In the nineteenth century, it was not uncommon for anthropologists to assert that culture represented a general mode of existence that could change or evolve over time (e.g., Morgan 1985 [1877]). In response to this approach, some anthropologists came to view culture as a strictly historical phenomenon and the result of numerous historical accidents rather than the product of a grand evolutionary scheme (Boas 1965).

Many anthropologists view culture as essentially a mental phenomenon that is composed primarily of beliefs, attitudes, and values passed on from one generation to the next (Geertz 1973). Others have narrowed this definition by arguing that culture is a reflection of specifically **elite** or **dominant ideologies** and belief systems (Marx and Engels 1979). Such symbolic approaches, then, ultimately view cultures as systems of meaning and sets of shared beliefs that can control human behavior. Still other anthropologists view culture in more materialistic terms as a set of practices and customs whose purpose is to aid human social groups to adapt to their various environments (Harris 1975, 1977, 1979). By establishing a common set of tools and patterns of behavior, cultures can be seen as one of our primary means of survival as a species. However, it would be an error to view all cultural practices as adaptive. Many can also be maladaptive, contributing to instances of environmental degradation, warfare and conflict, malnutrition and other social problems that can threaten the survival of a society (Edgerton 1992).

Despite the diversity of opinion regarding the nature of culture, anthropologists do seem to agree on some of the basic aspects of culture. Many rely on E.B. Tylor's (1958 [1871]) classic definition of culture from the first page of his book, *Primitive Culture*. Here he defines culture as "…that complex whole which includes knowledge, belief, arts, morals, law, custom, and any other capabilities and habits acquired by man as a member of society."

Although most anthropologists would agree in broad terms with E.B. Tylor regarding the elements that constitute a culture and many would applaud his prescient assertion of the intimate connection between human social groups and cultural customs, his definition still appears to us like a laundry list of traits. It does not truly account for the interrelationship of the different aspects of culture.

In this chapter, then, we will adopt a fairly simple but effective definition of culture that focuses on its holistic aspects but also pays homage to E.B. Tylor's classic definition:

Culture is everything we say, think, do, and make as members of a society.

Similar to the approach taken by other anthropologists (e.g., Ferraro 1992:18–19), this definition has the virtue of portraying culture as an all-encompassing aspect of human life (Figure 4.1)." It has both a mental side (i.e., everything we think) and a materialistic side (i.e., everything we make). Like E.B. Tylor's definition, it also points out that human cultures co-exist and are to some degree dependent on human social groups for their dissemination from one generation to another.

Let's examine the four major aspects of culture in more detail:

1. **Culture is everything we say** Culture consists of **language**, writing, sign language, and complex symbol systems—in other words, all of the various ways in which human beings communicate information. Language can be defined as a system for symbolic communication using verbal, graphic or gestural cues. It is the primary means by which cultural beliefs, values, and norms are passed from one person

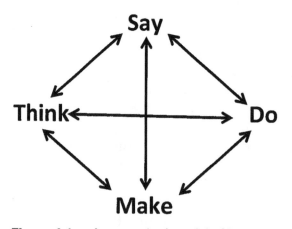

Figure 4.1. A conceptual model of human culture.

to another and from one generation to the next (Barrett 1991:55–57). Language can therefore be viewed as part of the symbolic dimension of culture. However, symbols can occur in many forms from various plastic arts (e.g., sculpture, painting, dress) to dance, theater, and music. Even the human body can serve as a potent symbol for cultural ideals of beauty, gender, purity, and sacredness.

Languages also vary in form and can even be converted into certain forms of music (i.e., talking drums). Human verbal language is an exceedingly complex tool that makes use of dozens of sounds ranging from basic consonants and vowels made with various parts of our mouths and throat to sounds consisting of clicks, whistles, trills, and nasals. Depending on the language, each of these distinctive elements is then capable of being used in a word to carry meaning.

2. **Culture is everything we think**   Sometimes referred to as "**mental culture,**" this dimension refers to the non-physical aspects of human culture such as our collective **beliefs** (what a person accepts as true) and **values** (the standards by which we decide what is good or bad) as members of particular social groups. These may change as we age and move from one group to another. Beliefs may involve religion or spirituality, political ideologies, broad philosophical points of view, and aesthetic principles of beauty. As such, they often inform the symbols of culture (Figure 4.2).

Together, our values and beliefs shape many of our behaviors through the rubric of **norms**, or a society's rules of right and wrong behavior. The rules or guidelines are almost innumerable, are often never written down (unless they become **laws**), and provide guidelines for every facet of our lives—from the kind of clothes we wear in a given situation to how we eat at a restaurant.

Not all norms are equal. Some norms are considered more important than others (Sumner 1979). For instance, **folkways** are very common but relatively weak norms. They govern small issues and behaviors like making sure to wear clothing with matching colors or holding the door for others. Many of us break or violate folkways and often do not realize it because our punishment is rarely more than a stare or a brief comment. **Mores** are generally more important and reflect the dominant values and beliefs of a culture. Often, mores will be transcribed into laws. As such they generally remind us not to commit acts that are seen as "wrong" such

Figure 4.2. Samburu woman (Samburu Park National Reserve, Kenya).

as stealing or assault. Failure to do carries a much heavier punishment such as fines or prison. Finally, **taboos** (or **tabus**) are the strongest norms and carry the strongest punishments. Taboos typically tell us in no uncertain terms to avoid certain restricted acts because they considered extremely heinous or especially wrong. In the United States, there are taboos against murder, cannibalism, necrophilia, and incest. What others can you think of?

Of course, if you think about it, it should not come as a surprise that different cultures have different norms guiding their customs. Even mores and taboos appear to be largely culture-specific.

For example, in India, it is taboo to eat beef in the Hindu religion, whereas Jews and Muslims are forbidden to eat pork. Likewise, in the United States we do not like to eat dogs or guinea pigs. But in parts of Peru and Bolivia, guinea pigs are seen as delicious treats. These taboos clearly reflect a culture's core beliefs and values (Harris 1975).

Learning Activity: The Incest Taboo

Although the incest taboo is universal in the sense that every culture forbids sexual relationships among family members, like food taboos, the incest taboo can vary from culture to culture. This is especially true of how cultures identify the relatives that are considered off-limits for sexual relationships or marriage. For example, consider the relatives listed below. Which relatives would you identify as off-limits according to your understanding of the incest taboo in your culture? Which relatives are not forbidden?

(Continued)

(Continued)

	Forbidden	Not Forbidden
Father	_____	_____
Mother	_____	_____
Brother	_____	_____
Sister	_____	_____
Twin siblings	_____	_____
Brother-in-law (i.e., sister's husband)	_____	_____
Sister-in-law (i.e., brother's wife)	_____	_____
Adopted siblings	_____	_____
Adoptive parents	_____	_____
Cross-cousins (i.e., the children of your father's sister or your mother's brother)	_____	_____
Parallel cousins (i.e., the children of your father's brother or mother's sister)	_____	_____
Maternal uncle (i.e., your mother's brother)	_____	_____
Maternal aunt (i.e., your mother' sister)	_____	_____
Paternal uncle (i.e., your father's brother)	_____	_____
Paternal aunt (i.e., your father's sister)	_____	_____
Wet nurse (not related by blood)	_____	_____

What might be some reasons that the relatives you identified as forbidden would be subject to the incest taboo? What about the relatives that you indicated were not forbidden?

3. **Culture is everything we do** Human behavior consists mainly of **cultural customs**—the daily activities, seasonal rituals, religious and political ceremonies, and household habits, which characterize human social life (Figures 4.3 and 4.4). These behaviors can be some of the most striking and among some of the most banal aspects of human life. They can range from various food-getting strategies and children's games to spectacular feasts and festivals. One useful way to think about customs from a cross-cultural comparative perspective is to divide them into **sacred** (i.e., religious) acts and **secular** (i.e., non-religious) acts. However, sometimes it is important to realize that this is an artificial division that can over-simplify human behavior. For example, there are many human activities that have both sacred and secular elements such as schooling.

Regardless of their sacred or secular nature, all cultural customs are guided by norms and are one of the most important ways for us to express our beliefs and

Figure 4.3.   Maasai warriors taking part in ritual jumping (Maasai Mara, Kenya).

Figure 4.4.   Chukchi folk dance (Siberia, Russia).

values. They also create opportunities for us to interact in a variety of ways and on many different levels.

4. **Culture is everything we make**   Human beings are creative beings. We make tools, monuments, and structures; we prepare food; and we invent new forms of clothing and art. And, with regard to the bio-cultural perspective, cultural norms and ideals play an important role in the ways we decorate and modify our bodies (Burton 2001; Robinson 1998). The material side of human life is so crucial to our definition of being human that anthropologists have used this observation historically to help

them define hominids as members of our genus *Homo*. The first recognized stone tool-making hominid was *Homo habilis* (the "handy man") (Leakey 1981).

Because much of what we make has a symbolic dimension, our tools, structures, dress, and art can communicate something about our social identities in terms of age, gender, occupation, ethnic background, and religion. Among the Toba Batak of Samo-sir Island in Indonesia, for instance, houses are more than just dwellings (Dawson and Gillow 1994). The houses mark the Toba Batak as a distinct group from their neighbors, the Karo Batak. Typical Toba Batak houses are characterized by steeply-pitched thatched roofs and a support structure of columns. Some of the columns terminate in carved singa heads, which represent protective spirits who are part-human and part water-buffalo (Figures 4.5 and 4.6).

By contrast, Karo Batak structures can be longhouses and feature hip roofs and water buffalo horn decorations. The outer walls are also decorated with braided designs consisting of geometric motifs, and a carved gecko carving protects the house from malevolent spirits (Dawson and Gillow 1994).

The symbolic dimension of human body decoration can likewise serve to highlight the cultural beliefs and values that underlie these practices. For instance, common forms of skin decoration such as tattooing, piercing, painting and scarification not only reflect ideals of beauty but can be used to highlight a person's status as an adult, their ethnic identity, or even their occupation and family ties (Burton 2001:51–68; Gregersen 1983:95–110; Robinson 1998:75–88). Elements of clothing and body ornamentation, from hairstyles and jewelry to the use of penis sheaths, can likewise express a person's gender identity in different societies. In other cases, such as the selective amputation of fingers among the Dani of western New Guinea (Irian Jaya), body modification may accompany specific rituals like funerals (Heider 1996).

© 2014 AHMAD FAIZAL YAHYA. Used under license of Shutterstock, Inc.

Figure 4.5.   Toba Batak house in Sam-osir Island, Lake Toba (North Sumatra, Indonesia).

Figure 4.6.   Toba Batak singa carving from Samosir Island, Lake Toba (North Sumatra, Indonesia).

Learning Activity: Body Modification Around the World

A recent survey of body decoration practices in sixty nonindustrial societies (Alford 1996) found several interesting patterns. In approximately 66% of these societies, men and women cover both their upper and lower bodies. In 20% of the societies, men cover only their lower body and in 33% of the societies, women do the same. Full-body nudity is comparably uncommon. Women wear no clothes in 7% of the societies, whereas men in 15% the societies wear no clothes.

In addition to clothing, other forms of body adornment are commonly used to denote social identity, gender, age, and ritual status in nonindustrial societies. These forms of decoration can include hairstyles, various forms of jewelry, as well as body painting.

People in many nonindustrial societies also permanently modify their bodies in a variety of ways. Tattooing is practiced among 45% of women and 32% of men. Forms of male circumcision have been recorded among 25% the societies, whereas different forms of female circumcision are found in 9% of nonindustrial societies. Scarification is found among 23% of both sexes and tends to be practiced on the head, arms, torso, and back. Tooth _ ling and removal is less common and is only found among 17% of men and women. The least common form of body modification is cranial reshaping. It is only documented among both sexes in 7% the societies surveyed.

As Alford's survey indicates, the choice of which parts of the body are to be decorated or modified in nonindustrial societies is not arbitrary, but reflects important social norms and cultural beliefs (Robinson 1998:74). Take a look at the following examples of more or less permanent forms of body adornment (Robinson 1998). Can you think of a potential rationale for these types of body modification? What might be their purpose or meaning?

(Continued)

(*Continued*)

Body Area	Form of Modification	Region	Purpose/Meaning
Forehead	Scarification	East Africa	_____
Face (male)	Tattooing	Polynesia	_____
Cheek	Piercing	Amazonia	_____
Cheek (female)	Tattooing/sewing	Arctic	_____
Chin (female)	Tattooing	Polynesia	_____
Chin	Piercing	Americas	_____
Lower lip	Ceramic plate insertion	Africa, Amazonia	_____
Teeth	Sharpening/filing	Central Africa	_____
Teeth	Blackening	Southeast Asia	_____
Neck	Elongation	Southeast Asia	_____
Back	Scarification	Papua New Guinea	_____
Breasts	Enlargement	Europe	_____
Abdomen	Scarification	Africa	_____
Fingers	Amputation	Papua New Guinea	_____
Waist (female)	Minimization	Europe	_____
Penis	Piercing/inserts	Borneo	_____
Penis	Lengthening with weights	East Africa	_____
Penis	Circumcision	Africa, Australia, Europe	_____
Penis	Subincision	Australia	_____
Penis	Superincision	Polynesia	_____
Labia minora	Lengthening with weights	Central Africa	_____
Clitoris	Removal (circumcision)	Africa	_____
Vulva	Infibulation (circumcision)	Africa	_____
Foot	Minimization/binding	China	_____

4.2 What are the Main Characteristics of Culture?

Tylor's definition of culture also points to other aspects of culture that require careful consideration. In particular, he mentions that culture is "acquired" and that it is found among members of a society. His definition suggests that in addition to the four dimensions of culture just discussed (i.e., culture is everything we say, think, do, and make), there are other characteristics of culture.

1. **Culture is learned** People are not born with culture but acquire it by growing up in a particular society. To some extent, our ability to learn culture (**enculturation**) is part of our biologically-based capacity to learn. Although this capacity to learn is universal (and it was sometimes been referred to as the "psychic unity of man" during the nineteenth century), what we learn is extremely diverse. In addition, unlike animals that may learn from experience, human beings can learn the beliefs, values, norms, and symbols of culture in a variety of ways.

   Culture can be passed on from person to person through direct instruction. This can occur in school settings, during religious rituals, but is also frequently invoked by our parents. By now, most of us are familiar with the phrase, "Do as I say, not as I do."

   Culture is also learned from observation and experience. We learn about gender roles by observing our parents, the media, and our peers. No one specifically tells how to act "masculine" or "feminine" but we learn what each of these labels entail through our observations of other people.

2. **Culture is shared** Culture is not the product of an individual but is a feature of life in a social group. The only way to learn culture is to be part of a community to observe, listen, experience, and ultimately, copy the interactions of its members. In a way, culture helps to unify people by providing a shared experience of the world and a shared way to communicate those beliefs and values.

   Many times, North Americans talk about the apparently stark difference between **individualistic cultures** that emphasize each person's right to make their own decisions and **collectivistic cultures**, which focus on the needs of the group before the individual. In actuality, however, our personal opinions and ideas are shared by many other members of our community and reflect a shared cultural background based on economic status, political power, belief systems, and ethnic background among other things. In other words, North Americans are not as individualistic as they might believe.

3. **Culture is integrated** Cultures are not simply random conglomerations of what we say, think, do, and make. These dimensions of culture not only co-exist but they also influence each other in a highly patterned way. If we think of culture as a system, then the various aspects of culture can be seen as integrated or working together within that larger whole. As one changes, the others will change as well. Our beliefs and values can shape our behaviors and may be expressed in our language and technology. But our technology can change our values and help introduce new terms into our languages as well. For instance, how many of us use the word "google" as a verb when we want to search for something online? The verb "to google" did not originate in Middle English and was never used by Shakespeare. It is a reflection of technological changes that occurred in the last few decades.

   There are many other examples. Among the Nuer, cattle are so important as a herd animal, as a source of milk and fertilizer, and as a form of wealth, that their herding way of life has influenced much of their culture. Nuer color terms reflect the coloration of cattle. Nuer children are named after their parent's favorite cows. Even criminal fines for wrongful acts ranging from theft to adultery and murder are paid via cattle (Evans-Pritchard 1940).

4. **Culture changes** Cultures are not stagnant systems. Human groups are constantly growing, moving, and interacting with each other. As a result, cultures always change. In the nineteenth century it was not unusual for anthropologists to refer to non-Western cultures as primitive, referring to their status as simpler societies possibly representing an earlier stage of Western culture. Today, we continue to hear reports of undiscovered tribes untouched by the "modern world" or of the discovery of "stone age" peoples. All of these perspectives imply that cultures, particularly Non-Western cultures, are stuck in a time warp in which nothing changes. The truth of the matter is that all cultures change. Many of the "stone age" people we hear about have an online presence such as *IndigiTUBE* (URL: http://www.indigitube.com.au/) and *Inuit Tapiriit Kanatami* (URL: https://www.itk.ca/). Others are currently in diaspora due to conflict or environmental destruction and are found in refugee communities all around the world. Many native cultures are also part of the world system and must struggle to make a living in industrializing market economies (Figure 4.7).

5. **Culture has many levels** Cultures are such complex systems that they work on different levels—subcultural, regional, national, and international. **Subcultures** refer to patterns of saying, thinking, doing things, and making things that are unique to small groups. Typically, these groups are differentiated from others within a larger society by a shared interest or occupation. However, subcultures can also be found among families and communities.

Figure 4.7. Maya women from Lake Atitlán (Sololá, Guatemala).

When several communities share a common history, certain ways of speaking and perhaps some common cultural customs such as favored sports or food items, then they form a **regional culture**. However, because the inhabitants of different regions may all be citizens of a particular country, they also share a certain number of beliefs, values, and laws (norms). They may also share a common language and participate in a number of similar institutions. These commonalities may be referred to as **national culture**.

Finally, because of the long history of culture contact initiated through colonialism, migration, and the world market, there are quite a few cultural traits and patterns of behavior that have a global scope. Examples of such an **international culture** include world religions such as Christianity and Islam, the familiar organization of supermarkets and airports around the world, the sharing of musical styles and TV programming across cultures, and the establishment of multinational sports such as World Cup soccer (football).

For anthropologists, then, culture is more than a grouping of tools or symbols. It is more than a set of beliefs and values. It is far more than a collection of customs and habits. Culture is an all-encompassing way of life

4.3 What is the Relationship between Culture and Society?

One of the most common mistakes both anthropologists and non-anthropologists make is to confuse culture and society. It is an easy mistake to make because these facets of human life are closely interconnected. Culture, as we have seen, refers to a shared and learned way of life (i.e., of thinking, speaking, doing things, and making things). What about society? A **society** is a group of people who interact regularly and often share the same area.

However, given the characteristics of culture we have just discussed, the distinction is hard to maintain. Cultures apparently cannot exist without societies and societies cannot exist without cultures. Cultures provide the norms and symbols through which people in social groups interact. But without people in social groups, there would be no way for humans to share and learn culture.

Perhaps, the best way to remember the difference between societies and cultures is to think of different customs, activities, beliefs, languages, and tools as "culture" and to refer to the people who carry or act out the culture (i.e., the group) as a "society."

4.4 Do (non-human) Animals have Culture?

Given the close relationship between human societies and human cultures, it is legitimate to ask whether non-human animals can also have cultures. After all, many animals live in organized communities such as herds, packs, and flocks. Social insects live in large colonies or hives and even appear to have **material culture** in the form of structures built to house these social groups.

However, there are some key differences between human cultures and the behaviors and of these non-human animals. To begin, it is not at all clear that all of the behavior of these animals is learned or shared. Some of their behavior may be instinctual. For instance, weaver finches are well-known for building intricately woven pendant nests (Dial 2003). Experiments have shown that weaver finches still have the ability to build nests even after many generations have passed because they were denied the materials to do so and well-after the original nest-building finches died curtailing any chance to learn the behavior (Walsh, Hansell, Borello, and Healy 2010) (Figure 4.8).

Although much of the behavior of pack and herd animals such as dogs and cetaceans (whales and dolphins) is learned and they appear to use a complex system of communication (Laland and Janik 2006), many elements of human culture appear to be absent. For example, with the exception of the bottlenose dolphins using sponges for foraging, many of these species lack material culture traditions and human-like symbolic systems such as language.

However, when we examine primates, much of the line that supposedly separates human beings from animals tends to dissipate. Primates have an impressively large repertoire of learned behaviors, many of which are group-specific within a species (Whiten et al. 1999). Examples include making tools such as termite fishing poles and nut crackers to sponges and stone tools among a variety of primates including chimpanzees, bonobos, orangutans, capuchin monkeys, and Japanese macaques (Boesch and Tomasello 1998; Canale et al. 2009; van Schaik et al. 2003) (Figures 4.9 and 4.10).

To be sure, some of these behaviors may be imitative of human beings (Kawai 1965) and humans have certainly experimented with a variety of great apes to see whether they too had the capacity to learn language (Patterson and Linden 1981). However, many primates are capable of developing complex symbolic cultures without human interference (Savage-Rumbaugh et al. 1986). Chimpanzees and bonobos have also learned to work cooperatively to hunt other primates such as the red colobus monkey (Boesch 1994).

© 2014 by kgb224. Used under license of Shutterstock, Inc.

Figure 4.8. A female weaver finch.

© 2014 Norma Cornes. Used under license of Shutterstock, Inc.

Figure 4.9. A female chimpanzee holding a tool.

© 2014 Luftikus. Used under license of Shutterstock, Inc.

Figure 4.10. Japanese macaque in Jigokudani (Nagano, Japan).

Given the cultural similarities between humans and primates and the apparent differences between human cultures and non-primate animals such as social insects, one has to wonder whether these patterns reflect actual differences in the lifeways of these creatures or represent a form of anthropocentric (human-based) interpretive bias on the part of researchers. In other words, are we looking for culture in general or human-like cultures? And might this bias be partly responsible for the seemingly "human" cultural aptitudes of the primates (Boesch 2010; Laland and Janik 2006)?

4.5 Is Cultural Variation Related to Biological Differences?

Although we know that culture is learned, not everyone agrees with this notion. Many people continue to interpret one another's behavior in terms of **race** or categories based on perceived differences between groups of people in terms of their physical characteristics. Often, these categories refer to some combination of skin pigmentation, other notable physical traits such as eye shape, blood type, hair color, and points of geographic origin (Klass and Hellman 1971).

However, "race" is a cultural labeling system. It varies significantly from culture to culture. It can also change within a culture over time. In Belize, for instance, people are referred variously as "ladino," "indio," "garifuna," "American," and "Mennonite." However, in Brazil, there can be over fifty distinctive racial labels, each signifying minute differences in skin tone and education level. And other cultures such as Britain have generally used simpler terminologies such as "white" and "colored." In the United States, by contrast, racial labels such as "African American," "White," "Asian," "Native American," and "Hispanic" are more commonly used.

One of the main problems with such cultural labeling systems is that they do not appear concerned with actual biological differences among populations. Many, including those of the United States, confuse "race" and **ethnicity** or a person's identification with a particular cultural group (i.e., their cultural background). For instance, the American label "Hispanic" refers to people from Latin America who speak Spanish but not people from Spain even though they speak Spanish. Spaniards are seen as "white." Similar conflations occur in Belize with the labels "American" and "Mennonite." As a result, cultural behaviors that are learned as part of someone's cultural background, such as language or religion, can sometimes be included under the rubric of "race" and be seen as in-born behaviors or even natural instincts.

Moreover, racial labels and categories also change over time. For example, the famous eighteenth-century taxonomist, Linnaeus, asserted that there were four racial groups based primarily on skin color. These categories included African, American, Asian and European varieties of Homo sapiens (Klass and Hellman 1971:24). Later American systems of racial classification focused on three groups - "whites," "negroes," and "Indians" (Banton 1998:2). Both of these classification systems were based on the notion that the biological differences between groups were distinctive and permanent. However, by shifting racial categories over time, they end up demonstrating just how inconstant these labeling systems can be from one period to another.

These patterns suggest that "race" is not an empirical reality but a socially constructed classification system. An example of how race is created by a culture is the notion of **hypodescent** (Harris and Kottak 1963). In Brazil, for example, the "race" of a child of parents from different racial groups will be considered the same as the parent belonging to the lowest status "race". In this way, "race" can be used to perpetuate social and economic inequalities between various groups of people. Another example would be the creation of **blood quantum laws**, introduced with the *Indian Reorganization Act of 1934*, which sought to allow or deny membership in Native American communities, such as the Navajo nation, on the basis of the percent of Native American "blood" or ancestry in a person's background (Spruhan 2008).

4.6   The Problem of Race and Scientific Racism

According to the *American Anthropological Association's Statement on "Race"* (URL: http://www.aaanet.org/stmts/racepp.htm) adopted in May 1998, most of the biological diversity (approximately 94%) observed among human beings occurs within so-called "races." As a result, racial classifications cannot be viewed as a biologically accurate way to classify people or explain their behavior.

Studies of genetic variation among different human populations have consistently shown that they display less variation than seen among subspecies (e.g., dog breeds) in non-human mammals (Templeton 1999:190). This suggests that enough gene flow (i.e., interbreeding) has occurred between these populations over the last 100,000 years to consider human beings as a single evolutionary lineage rather than a grouping of distinctive "races."

Other studies have shown that physical variations in any given trait tend to occur gradually rather than abruptly over geographic areas and because physical traits are inherited independently of one another, knowing the geographic distribution of one trait does not predict the range of other physical traits. For example, skin color has a **clinal distribution** that varies largely from light in the temperate areas in the north and south to dark in the tropical areas around the equator. This distribution is not related to hair color, hair texture, or eye shape (Cavalli-Sforza, Menozzi and Piazza 1994). These facts render any attempt to establish lines of division among biological populations in terms of "race" both arbitrary and subjective.

Given these observations, it is surprising that "race" continues to be used as an empirical and scientific means to differentiate between human groups. However, when such attempts are used to explain ethnocentric views about the superiority or inferiority of a particular group's customs, social norms, and cultural achievements, it is best to characterize these attempts as examples of **scientific racism**. A famous example of this approach is the r/K theory of "race" proposed by the late J. Philippe Rushton (2000).

Rushton argued that there are only three major racial groups – Asians, Caucasians, and Africans—based on an extensive list of behavioral and physical traits including brain size, genital size, IQ, promiscuity, mental health, and cultural achievements (Rushton 2000:9, Chart 1) (Table 4.1).

Rushton then claimed that the differences observed among these racial groups could be explained in evolutionary terms by using the rubric of reproductive strategies falling somewhere in the r and K scale. Groups with an r-selected strategy tend to have many offspring but do not extend a lot of effort nurturing these offspring. Groups with a K-selected strategy typically have fewer offspring and spend more time raising them. Although all humans display K-selected behavior, Rushton believes the "races" vary in the degree to which they exhibit that behavior. He asserted that people of African descent use a strategy more reminiscent of an r-selected strategy, whereas people of Asian descent use the K strategy and people of European descent (i.e., Caucasians) exhibit more intermediate tendencies (Rushton 2000:38).

He further suggested that people of European and Asian descent evolved more toward a K-selected reproductive strategy than people of African descent because such a strategy was more adaptive to the climates found in Europe and Asia, while environmental conditions in Africa appear to have promoted greater overall fertility and lack of parental care (Rushton 2000:12). Rushton then concluded that these reproductive strategies were

Table 4.1. Average Differences in Human Racial Groups, according to J. Philippe Rushton (2000).

	"Africans"	"Caucasians"	"Asians"
Brain Size	1,267 cc	1,347 cc	1,364 cc
IQ	85	100	106
Cultural Achievements	Low	High	High
Sex Traits	Larger	Intermediate	Smaller
Intercourse Frequencies	Higher	Intermediate	Lower
Aggressiveness	Higher	Intermediate	Lower
Skeletal/Motor Development	Earlier	Intermediate	Later
Lifespan	Shorter	Intermediate	Longer
Law Abidingness	Lower	Intermediate	Higher
Marital Stability	Lower	Intermediate	Higher
Mental Health	Lower	Intermediate	Higher

ultimately responsible for the differences in psychological attitudes, IQ scores, cultural norms, and other behaviors observed in these groups today and offered an explanation for their apparent unequal treatment as well. Anthropologists have critiqued Rushton's work on several different grounds. As is typical of many racial theories in the past, Rushton's approach to defining racial groups (as summarized in Table 4.1) confuses heritable traits such as skin pigmentation with cultural traits such as educational attainment and law abidingness. In doing so, he also ignores cultural influences on the fertility rates of different populations (Weizman et al. 1999:206–208).

Much of his work also mischaracterizes studies of brain size among various human groups by ignoring body size correlations (Weizman et al. 1999:210–211). And in terms of sex traits (i.e., genital size), much of his data is anecdotal and relies on non-representative samples from early twentieth century pseudo-anthropological texts.

Rushton's r/K theory and its critics raise many questions. How does his position compare to the *American Anthropological Association's Statement on "Race"*? Does he ultimately confuse "race" and "ethnicity"? Does Rushton inadvertently resort to using **racial stereotypes** to prove his theory of "race"? And most critically, if his theory does not properly explain cultural differences in terms of "race," what good is it to use "race" as a way of explaining human behavior?

In the final analysis, "race" seems to function more as a worldview than as a legitimate form of scientific or social scientific explanation. It distorts our ideas about human diversity and falsely links these to human cultural behaviors and cultural identities (ethnicities). Moreover, these racial myths and stereotypes do not bear any relationship to biological reality. Ultimately, it appears that "race" is a way for societies to divide and rank people within and outside their borders. As an ideology, "race" is used to justify social, economic, and political inequalities, thereby leading to acts of genocide and ethnocide, racial profiling, and other forms of **discrimination**.

4.7   Are there Cultural Universals?

As we have seen in the previous discussion on "race," anthropologists must be able to distinguish between unique cultural traits (**particularities**), general tendencies (cultural patterns found in most cultures), and **cultural universals** (cultural patterns found in every culture) to make sense of cross-cultural patterns.

Most cultural traits are unique to a specific nation, community, or region. These particularities consist of ways of thinking, speaking, acting, and making things that initially developed as historical accidents (i.e., a singular confluence of culture changes that resulted in a particular cultural pattern). A good example is the "pupusa"—a traditional dish from El Salvador that consists of a thick corn tortilla filled with cheese, refried beans, and a paste made from ground pork. This dish is not well known in neighboring countries such as Guatemala and appears to be unique to El Salvador.

Interestingly, these cultural particularities can be spread nationally or even internationally through trade and borrowing (**diffusion**). As we noted previously, some cultural traits can become global in scope although perhaps not universal. English, for example, has a global scope but its widespread distribution is a reflection of historical trends such as the colonial history of countries such as the United States, Canada, Australia, New Zealand, and South Africa.

Cultural universals are different. They are present in all human populations and distinguish human beings from other species. Some universals are biological in nature such as our capacity to learn language, our longer period of gestation and infant dependency, and our ability to habitually walk on two feet. It is an open question as to whether cultural universals are related to our biological make-up (Brown 1991). Many appear to reflect the organizational and structural necessities of human societies. For example, all human societies have some form of family life and food sharing (**reciprocity**). Every culture has a version of the incest taboo, although whether this applies to marriage or mating varies from culture to culture. Likewise, all cultures appear to have a prohibition against random homicide as well.

Chapter Summary

Culture is a fundamental part of being human. Culture has four major dimensions as a way of life. It consists of everything we say, think, do, and make as members of a society. Two of the most basic aspects of culture are material culture (what we make) and mental culture (what we think). Material culture consists of the physical products of human society, whereas mental culture refers to the intangible products of human society. Anthropologists often refer to nonmaterial culture as our values, beliefs, and norms. Values are the standards by which members of a society define what is good and bad, beliefs are cultural conventions that concern true or false assumptions, and norms are a society's rules of right and wrong behavior. Anthropologists recognize that humans throughout the world share some fundamental behavioral characteristics as well; these characteristics are known as cultural universals. Cultural universals consist of, among other things, mechanisms to care for children, ways of producing and distributing goods, and the ability to adapt to the physical environment. To avoid stereotypes and distortions about people in other societies, anthropologists do not overlook such basic similarities in human behavior and culture.

Key Terms

beliefs
blood quantum laws
clinal distribution
collectivistic cultures
cultural customs
cultural universals
culture
diffusion
discrimination
dominant ideology
endo-cannibalism

elite
ethnicity
folkway
hypodescent
individualistic cultures
language
material culture
mental culture
more
national culture
norm

race
racial stereotypes
reciprocity
regional culture
sacred
scientific racism
secular
society
subculture
taboo (tabu)
values

Chapter 5
Male and Female: Sex, Marriage, Family, and Kinship

Michael J. Simonton

Outline

More than just a system of naming people, the terms that people use to describe each other, such as mother or brother, carry with them a series of obligations, responsibilities and rewards. These terms carry histories, as individuals replicate being an uncle, a son, daughter and so forth, in a long line of ancestors. The system that governs who is considered a relative differs in many cultures. For instance, among the Haudenosaunee (Iroquois) peoples the brothers of a person's father, and the sisters of their mother, are referred to by the same parental kinship terms used for their father and mother. The Minangkbau of Western Sumatra practice matrilineal descent, Canadians have bilateral descent, others are patrilineal. In this chapter we discuss the various kinship and descent systems that anthropologists study. We will discuss sex roles, residency patterns, and family structures. Understanding kinship systems is essential from an anthropological perspective, specifically in ethnography. Kinship reveals many facets of society such as whom one can marry, who lives where after marriage, who inherits, who buries and grieves, who comes next in succession and who is in fact considered a relative.

5.1 Sex Roles

5.1.1 Margaret Mead

5.1.1.1 Sex and Temperament in Three Primitive Societies

Margaret Mead's New Guinea research with Reo Fortune and Gregory Bateson led to the book, *Sex and Temperament in Three Primitive Societies*, in which Mead described three New Guinea societies: The **Arapesh, Mundugamor**, and **Tchambuli**. Mead was exploring the idea that sex roles are the result of culture (nurture), not biology (nature). Compared to American sex role stereotypes, she argued, the Arapesh had a female personality type, the Mundugamor had a male personality type, and the Tchambuli had reversed sex roles. This led her to conclude that culture is more important in determining appropriate behavior for each sex than is biology.

5.2 Gender, Sex, and Coitus

This leads to a discussion of some **misused terms: Gender, Sex**, and **Coitus**.

Gender, literally, refers to **masculine and feminine parts of speech**. There are not too many examples of gender in this context in English, other than personal pronouns such as 'her' or 'him'. Some other languages make heavy use of gender with regard to parts of speech. For example, in French many words are considered to be masculine and feminine, whether they refer to men or women, or not. *Le chapeau*, with the masculine word *le* for 'the' and the masculine *eau* ending means 'the hat'. It can be a woman's hat, but the word has the masculine gender. *La chapelle*, with the feminine word *la* for 'the' and the feminine *elle* ending does not refer to a woman's hat, even though the word has the feminine gender. Rather, it means 'the chapel'. However, since the late twentieth century many people have come to use the word 'gender' to refer to the sex role that a person most feels like, regardless of what his or her personal plumbing may indicate.

Sharyn Graham Davies reports that the **Bugis** in Indonesia have five gender identities: *makkunrai* (feminine woman), *oroané* (masculine man), *calalai* (masculine female), *calabai* (feminine male), and *bissu* (transgender shaman) (2007). **Gilbert Herdt** reports that among the **Sambia** of New Guinea, sexual behavior not only does not define masculinity or femininity, but that ritualized homosexuality is part of warrior training that is abandoned upon adulthood (1987). Herdt cites similar practices in other cultures, from the Ancient Greeks to the Japanese samurai.

5.3 What is Sex?

5.3.1 Sex and Coitus

Sex is not the act of reproduction. The act of reproduction is called **coitus**. You may hear someone say 'We had sex last night'. You always have sex: sex is having the biological equipment that indicates that one is male or female (this is not the same thing as masculine or feminine –see above). What determines sex? It is not as simple as it might appear at first.

5.3.2 Chromosomes

5.3.2.1 XX or XY

At its most basic, sex is the result of what we have at the **twenty-third pair of chromosomes**, the sex chromosomes. Usually humans have 46 chromosomes arranged in 23 pair, and you get one member of each pair from each of your parents. The twenty-third pair consists of 'X's or 'Y's. If you get an X from your mother and an X from your father, you are considered a genetically normal female; if you get an X from your mother and a Y from your father, you are considered a genetically normal male: Females have **XX** at the twenty third pair of chromosomes and males have **XY** at the twenty third pair of chromosomes.

5.3.2.2 XO, XXY, and XYY

Sometimes there is a mistake, and people are born with **XO** (technically, the 'O' is a zero, indicating an absent chromosome, not an 'O' chromosome) (**Turner's Syndrome**), who appear to be sexually immature females, **XXY** (**Klinefelter's Syndrome**), who appear to be 'feminized males', or **XYY** ('**Supermales**') who may be taller than average. Apparently there is something on the X chromosome that is missing on the Y chromosome, but which is necessary for life, because there are no known individuals who are YY or YO.

Someone's **apparent sex** is determined by more than the 23rd pair of chromosomes (the sex chromosomes, X and Y). Someone's apparent sex can be altered *in utero* about nine weeks after conception by a wash of hormones during gestation. Prior to this point, male and female embryos cannot be distinguished from one another: the gonads are inside the body, both male and female tubing is present, and the external gentalia consists only of a 'sex bud' that can develop as male or female. XX embryos get a wash of female hormones; XY embryos get a wash of male hormones. Following the hormone wash, the embryo begins to develop as the sex coded for by the hormones. Sometimes there is a mistake, and an XX embryo will get a wash of male hormones and begin to develop male characteristics, or an XY embryo will get a wash of female hormones and begin to develop female characteristics. This may help to explain why some people say that they feel like one sex, but they are trapped in the body of the other sex – maybe they are.

5.3.3   Apparent Sex

5.3.3.1 Suys

Someone's **apparent sex** also can be altered by clothing, as can be seen from the **suys**. *Suys* are women who live as men in Albanian peasant villages, where only sons can inherit a farm. If a couple has no sons, a daughter is selected to be the heir, and she must live the rest of her life as a man.

5.3.4   Berdache, and Contraries

Another example of clothing altering apparent sex can be found among the nineteenth century **Cheyenne** of the North American Plains; these were the **berdache**. The *berdache* were men who lived their lives as women, sometimes in response to images seen in their adolescent sacred vision quests, in which boys found their spirit companions and saw what their lives' roles were to be. Among the Cheyenne, **contraries** were men who did many things backward, said 'no' when they meant 'yes' and 'yes' when they meant 'no,' washed with dirt, and were esteemed as warriors. Sometimes the contraries and the berdache married each other.

5.3.5   The 'masculine protest'

This has led some Freudian psychologists to see the contraries as examples of what **Sigmund Freud** called the 'masculine protest': males who go overboard to prove their masculinity because they doubt it themselves.

5.3.6   Paraphilias

Because there is so much variation in what is considered 'normal' from culture to culture, alternate forms of sexual expression, once termed perversion, now may be called **paraphilias** (alternate forms of expressing love) by some sex researchers.

5.3.7   Does Everyone Know?

Not all societies are aware of the direct role of coitus in reproduction. In *Baloma: The Spirits of the Dead in the Trobriand Islands*, **Bronislaw Malinowski** described sexual openness on the islands and the influence on it of the belief that pregnancy was caused, not by sexual intercourse, but by ancestral spirits called *baloma*. It was believed that coitus just loosened the path that the baloma, returned to embryo form, had to travel to reenter a woman's body. For this reason descent and inheritance was **matrilineal** (traced only through the mother's family line), and fatherhood was considered a social role, not a biological one. A man inherited his mother's brother's yam garden, not his father's (whose heirs were his sister's children). For this reason the newly married couple moved near the husband's uncle's garden and worked on *it*, not his father's. This is called '**avunculocal residence.**' If a father wanted to leave his wealth or magic to his child, a marriage could be arranged between the child and one of his heirs—his sister's children. In this arrangement, the father acts more like a favorite uncle and the mother's brother is the disciplinarian.

5.4 The Universal Incest Taboo

There is a universal taboo (meaning all cultures prohibit it) on **incest**. What constitutes incest varies from culture to culture; in some places just talking to an in-law is considered incestuous, in others, such as **Gopalpur** in south India, described by **Alan Beals**, a man is expected to marry his own sister's daughter. Nonetheless, all cultures forbid marriage or mating between mothers and sons, fathers and daughters, and sisters and brothers. A few very rare exceptions are the royal houses of **Ancient Egypt**, the **Inca**, and **Hawaii**. This is because the royal families ruled by divine right, and if they had children by people who were not also gods, those children would not have the right to rule. In older couples who have been married for many years, lack of sexual interest in each other is known as 'the Coolidge Effect' after an apocryphal story about President and Mrs Calvin Coolidge.

5.4.1 Edward Westermark

5.4.1.1 Childhood Familiarity

5.4.1.2 The Westermarck Hypothesis

It has been noticed by anthropologists that children who have been raised together under the same roof tend not to be sexually attracted to each other. The '**childhood-familiarity**' theory of the universality of the incest taboo is called the **Westermarck Hypothesis**.

5.4.2 Living Laboratories

Anthropologists try to test hypotheses in living laboratories. Living laboratories are cultural systems in which the hypothesis that we wish to test already exists, and does not have to be artificially created. The Westermarck Hypothesis has been tested in living laboratories around the world, and two of the better-known examples are provided here.

5.4.3 Arthur Wolf in Taiwan

The Westermarck Hypothesis was tested in **Taiwan** by **Arthur Wolf**, who compared divorce rates and **fertility** (actually having children; the ability to have children is called **fecundity**) between the **great marriage**, in which people meet and marry as adults, and the **little marriage**, in which parents arrange a marriage between their children when the children still are small. The girl moves into the boy's family's house, and they grow up together as siblings. When they are adults, the marriage is formalized, and they begin to live together as a married couple. Wolf found that couples in the big marriage had more children than couples in the little marriage, but they also had more divorces. Wolf said that this supported the Westermarck Hypothesis.

5.4.4 Melford Spiro in Israel

The Westermarck Hypothesis also was tested in an **Israeli kibbutz** (commune) by **Melford Spiro**. In this study, unrelated children are raised together in a commune dormitory. Spiro found that most of these children marry out of the kibbutz, supporting the Westermarck Hypothesis.

5.4.5 Sigmund Freud

5.4.5.1 Oedipus Complex

In *Totem and Taboo*, Sigmund Freud insisted upon the universality of the Oedipus complex. The Oedipus complex is a term used to describe a particular developmental stage in which Freud believed boys want to kill their fathers and marry their mothers. He described its origin in the 'primal parricide' (the killing of the father) of the primal horde (the first group of humans). Although Freud's ethnography in *Totem and Taboo* is considered state-of-the-art for when it was written, his theoretical section on the origin of the incest taboo, the origin of the Oedipus complex, and primal parricide led it to be scorned by anthropologists.

    Bronislaw Malinowski contested Freud's argument by citing the **Trobriand Matrilineal Complex** in his book, ***Sex and Repression in Savage Society***, in which boys treat their fathers like uncles, but want to kill their mothers' brothers. Malinowski reasoned that this is because the uncle disciplines the children in the Trobriand Islands, just as the father did in Vienna, where Freud was writing, and it had nothing to do with subconscious incestuous desires—it was just that no child likes to be disciplined and desires to be rid of the discipliner. Malinowski had studied psychology under Wilhelm Wundt, as did Emil Durkheim and Franz Boas, and he was versed in the psychological theory of his day.

5.5 Marriage and Post-Marital Residence

5.5.1 Marriage

Marriage can be defined as a formalized, essentially universal, culturally accepted relationship between two or more people, usually of opposite sexes, who have mutual rights and obligations. How many does one marry? There are several sets of rules for this. In the following list males are represented by triangles (Δ), females by circles (O), and marriages by equal signs (=). **Monogamy** is marriage between one man and one woman.

Monogamy   Δ = O   one man and one woman at a time

    Polygamy is any form of multiple partner marriage, but usually consists of **polygyny**, and **polyandry**.

Polygyny $\Delta = O + O...$ one man and two or more women at a time

Polyandry $...\Delta + \Delta = O$ two or more men and one woman at a time

Consensual unions are non-marital sexual and/or economic unions which may be permanent

Consensual union $\Delta - O$ usually one man and one woman at a time

Monogamy is practiced by about one fourth of the world's societies. The most common *ideal* (culturally revered, as opposed to *real*) marriage form in the world is **polygyny**, which is practiced by nearly half of the world's societies. The reason that 'ideal' is stressed here is that, in reality, one may find many monogamous marriages in polygynous societies because of various stages in the life cycle: a marriage may start out with one man and one woman; then, as finances permit, another woman may join the marriage. Likewise, as people age, some members of a polygynous marriage may die off. Sometimes a couple may just be happy with only the two of themselves and not want to bring in another spouse. Normally, if a man wishes to add another wife to his marriage, he must obtain the approval of his other wives before he can do so. Sometimes it is the wives who wish to add to their numbers because they need farm help, and in horticultural societies it is women who do much of the farm work. In this case, they tell their husband that he is getting married, and sometimes to whom.

A variation on polygyny, called **ghost marriage**, can be found among the **Nuer** of the southeastern Sudan. The Nuer believe that it is a terrible thing for a man to die without having had children, so the dead man's living brother may stand in as proxy for him. Thus a woman may be married to a ghost, and she has children with the ghost's living brother, who stands in as proxy, but the children are the ghost's children, not the living brother's.

Polyandry is rare, but may be best known from the Himalayas. Tibetan people living in **Limi**, Nepal practice fraternal polyandry, in which a woman is married to a group of brothers. This functions to keep the unpaid farmhands (the brothers) together in one place and keeps familial land holdings from being subdivided. Unmarried women may live in town and have their children with the less favored of the rural husbands.

Consensual Unions are common in some parts of the world, including the modern United States. **Judith Gussler** found it to be the preferred reproductive pattern on the island of **St. Kitt's** in the Caribbean. According to Gussler, some Kittitian women prefer not to marry the men with whom they have their children because this limits their **economic potential**. Gussler argues that by having their children with several men, Kittitian women have a larger pool of economic child support from which they can draw; one man on economic migration from the island can only afford to send home a certain amount of money to the mother, no matter how many children they have together, but several men may be able to send back considerably more to the mother to support their offspring.

5.5.2 Same Sex Unions

This was described earlier with regard to the berdache and contraries. The Nuer also have a form of same sex marriage called **woman marriage**, as do the **Anang** of Nigeria. In woman marriage two women who desire the economic benefits of marriage may marry one another, although, according to John Messenger, who conducted field research among them in the early 1950s, it is not a sexual union.

5.6   The Economics of Marriage

Marriage is an economic union, as well as a social and sexual union. Even in the modern world people tend to be more attracted to people who appear to have the potential for being good providers. Our acknowledgement of the fact may be on a subconscious level: we tend to be more attracted to people who wear expensive clothing or drive more expensive cars than we are to people who wear ragged clothing or drive beat-up old 'rust buckets'. In many other cultures the connection between economics and marriage is clearer cut.

5.6.1   Bride Price

Nearly two thirds of cultures practice what is known as **bride price**. Bride price is so called because early western observers saw grooms or their families giving cattle, sheep, horses, or goods to the brides' families prior to marriage. They believed that the groom was buying the bride from her family, but this is not so. The husband is not buying the bride; he is compensating her family for the loss of her economic services to them after marriage (like buying out a player's contract on a sports team). By the time someone has reached her late teens or early twenties in horticultural or pastoralist societies, she has become a valuable employee of the family business—farming or herding. Thus it may be an economic hardship to her family to lose such a trained and skilled employee, who then is going to work for another family's business—the groom's. Because of this, the groom must compensate her family for the loss of her economic services. Among the pastoralist **Zulu** of Natal, South Africa this compensation is known as *lobola*, and it consists of a negotiated number of cows; the higher the bride's rank in Zulu society, the more cows must be included in the *lobola*.

© InnaFelker/Shutterstock.com

5.6.2   Bride Service

When a man compensates his in-laws with labor (instead of animals or goods) prior to marriage, it is called **bride service**, and it is practiced by nearly twenty percent of human societies. Readers may be familiar with the Biblical story of **Jacob and Rachel**. In the story, Jacob desired to marry Rachel, but her father required him to labor for him for seven years prior to marriage (and then switched brides). This is an example of bride service. Another example may be found among the **Ju/'hoansi** of the Kalahari. Among the Ju/'hoansi the groom must live with and hunt for the bride's family until they have children, who must be raised with their father's family. Then the married couple moves to where the husband's family lives, and he hunts for them.

5.6.3   Exchange of Females

Exchange of females is similar to bride service, except that it is not the groom who labors for the bride's family to compensate them for the loss of her economic services to them at marriage, but his sister (or closest available female relative). It is found in about five percent of human societies. The loss of such a valuable farm worker as a bride (who, by the time she was old enough to marry, would have been a skilled and experienced worker) would leave a hole in the employment roster at the bride's farm. This has to be filled by someone from the farm to which she is moving at marriage. This is described by Elanore Smith Bowen's (the pen name of the anthropologist **Laura Bohannan**) in her ethnographic novel, *Return to Laughter*, about field research among the **Tiv** of north central Nigeria in the mid twentieth century. In the book one of Bowen's Tiv friends told her that she would have to be leaving soon because her cousin was getting married, and she had to take the bride's place on the bride's family farm until her own wedding. This is what is meant by 'exchange of females', and it fascinated Laura and **Paul Bohannan** in their writing about the Tiv.

5.6.4   Dowry

Many Americans have a mistaken idea about the nature of **dowry**. Dowry is not what it is called when one man pays another man to marry his daughter, because no one else will marry her; that is Hollywood, it is not dowry. Dowry is mother to daughter inheritance at matrimony, and it is found in nearly ten percent of human societies. **Ernestine Friedl** describes it as being like a **trust fund** that passes from mother to daughter, and the groom just becomes the trust officer. He is expected to maintain or increase the trust until his own daughter marries and inherits the dowry from her mother (his wife).

5.6.5   Gift Exchange

The **Andaman Islanders** in the Bay of Bengal practice exchange of gifts between both families. This is not gift giving to the bride and groom, but between the two families, who communicate through third parties until the marriage takes place. Gift exchange is found in a little over ten percent of human societies.

5.7 Whom may we Marry?

In North America most people probably believe that they marry for love, but whom we fall in love with depends upon whom we meet and who among them is available. Universities are not only places to which one went in order to get an education. Rather, they also were selective breeding farms, in which people of both sexes and of similar social and economic background were removed from the general population at the ages during which they most likely were to find their future mates. That way they were less likely to pick someone from a different social or economic class than the one from which they came; it was acceptable to marry up (**hypergamy**), but not to marry down (**hypogamy**) in class. For this reason some of the more class elite universities not only were more expensive than many others, but some of them also were located in hard to get to rural settings. Williams' argument was that this helps to prevent hypogamy. In many societies marriages are arranged. **Arranged marriages** remove the choice from the marrying couple and put it in the hands of others, usually their parents. This does not mean that the marrying couples may not reject their families' choice in some societies. Certainly they can.

Very often, though, the marrying couple does not have a choice, as Arthur Wolf found to be the case in Taiwan's 'little marriage', or as **C.W.M. Hart** found among the **Tiwi** on Australia's Melville and Bathurst Islands in the 1920s, where girls were born married, usually to adult men, with whom they took up marital residence during, or shortly after, adolescence. Usually arranged marriages are not as extreme as in these two cases, and it is more likely that people are matched by a **go-between**, or **matchmaker**, in their late teens or twenties with an eye to compatibility (economically, as well as socially). **Chung-min Chen** reported that in a village that he studied in Taiwan, it was the future mother-in-law's job to ensure that the patrilineage would be maintained, so she had the final say on the choice of a bride based upon her perception of the bride's potential fertility.

Another marriage rule found in some societies is the **levirate**. In the levirate a woman who has been widowed marries her deceased husband's closest available male relative, usually his brother, although not always, as in the Biblical story of **Ruth and Boas**. When Ruth's husband died, she was forced to marry his kinsman, Boas. This is not a one-sided arrangement, as he was forced to marry her as well. The levirate acts as a form of social welfare in societies with a strict division of labor by sex. Widowed people are provided with a spouse to perform tasks that they may not be allowed or are unable to perform, and single people also are provided with a spouse to perform tasks that they may not be allowed or are unable to perform. The **sororate** is the complementary system in which a widowed man marries his deceased wife's closest available female relative, usually her sister.

Exogamy is a rule that is found in most societies. Exogamy means the spouse is chosen from outside of one's own group ('exo' means 'out of' and 'gamy' means 'marriage'). The most obvious form of exogamy is **lineage exogamy**—you have to marry outside of your family. By contrast, **endogamy** means that the spouse is chosen from within one's own group ('endo' means 'within'). A person can be exogamous for some things (like village of residence) while endogamous for other things (like caste) at the same time.

5.8 Post-Marital Residence Rules

Most human societies have rules about where a married couple may live. These are called **Post marital residence rules**, and they vary from society to society, in ways that may be related to economic practices.

5.8.1 Patrilocal

The most common ideal residence rule in the world is called **patrilocal residence**, practiced by about two thirds of human societies. Patrilocal residence means that a newly married couple will reside with or near the husband's family. A reason for this is that it keeps the unpaid farmhands (adult sons) close together and close to the job. Technically, living with or near the husband's family is called **virilocal residence**. When children are born, they grow up surrounded by their father's family. Then virilocal residence converts to patrilocal residence. Some examples of cultures with patrilocal residence include Arabs, Chinese, Omaha, Shawnee, and Yanomamo.

5.8.2 Matrilocal

Matrilocal residence means that a newly married couple will reside with or near the wife's family, and it is practiced by almost fifteen percent of human societies. Once again, a reason for this is that it keeps the unpaid farmhands (adult daughters) close together and close to the job. Technically, living with or near the wife's family is called **uxorilocal residence**. When children are born, they grow up surrounded by their mother's family. Then uxorilocal residence converts to matrilocal residence. Some examples of cultures with matrilocal residence include Cherokee, Crow, Hopi, Navajo, and Yoruba.

5.8.3 Avunculocal

Avunculocal residence means that a married couple will reside with or near one of the spouses' uncle. It is practiced by less than five percent of human societies. The Trobriand islanders sometimes practice avunculocal residence because the husband will inherit his mother's brother's yam garden, not his father's.

5.8.4 Neolocal

Neolocal residence also is practiced by less than five percent of human societies. In neolocal residence a newly married couple will reside with or near neither spouse's family. This is more likely to be found in modern industrial societies like the United States, England, or France.

5.8.5 Bilocal

Bilocal residence means that a married couple may reside with or near the husband's family at some point in the marriage and with or near the wife's family at another point, like the Ju/'hoansi, who are not considered completely married until they have children, so they live with the wife's family after marriage, and the husband practices bride service. Once children are born, the couple is considered completely married and lives with the husband's family, because they are members of his lineage.

5.9 Kinship

Anthropologists talk about **kinship** (to whom one is related, and how they are related) a lot. This is not done just to confuse students and keep class averages low (it sometimes helps, but, believe it or not, that is not why we do it). We do this because in most societies many, if not all, societal relations are based on kinship. Kinship determines whom we may marry, whom we may not marry, from whom we will inherit, with whom we may or may not work or socialize; even to whom we may or may not speak (this is one form of what is called **avoidance**). An important part of knowing to whom you are related involves knowing who your ancestors and descendents are, so we try to determine types of descent found in the societies that we study.

5.9.1 Types of Descent

Different societies have different sets of rules to determine to whom you are related and to whom you are not related; these are called the **rules of descent**. Why is this necessary? This is necessary because you cannot keep track of all your relatives – you have almost eight billion of them. Based upon **mitochondrial DNA** analysis, there is less genetic variation in the entire human race than there is in one band of wild chimpanzees. All humans alive today are descended from one woman who lived in east Africa about 200,000 years ago; she is known as '**Mitochondrial Eve**' (not to be confused with the Biblical Eve).[1] We all are closely related; therefore it would be impossible for us to keep track of all of our six billion family members. For this reason our societies pick and choose which of our biological relatives are going to be included in our sociological families for purposes of marriage, descent, and inheritance. The following are the different sets of rules used by different societies.

5.9.2 Matrilineal Descent

Matrilineal descent is descent reckoned through the female line only (if it helps, think of it like this: **MAtriLINEal**, your 'ma's line'). This would seem to be the most logical form of descent reckoning, because there probably were witnesses at your birth. Both sons and daughters are members of their mother's matrilineage, but only the daughters' children are members, not the sons' children. The sons' children would be members of their mother's matrilineage. However, only about fifteen percent of human societies trace their ancestry this way (some examples would be the Cherokee, Crow, Hopi, and Navajo). Matrilineal descent can be diagrammed like this: the world (some examples would be Arabs, Chinese, much of India, the Shawnee and the Omaha). Patrilineal descent can be diagrammed like this:

---

[1] This known as the 'Out of Africa' theory. Recent research suggested that this theory may need to be reworked to stay inline with more current DNA data.

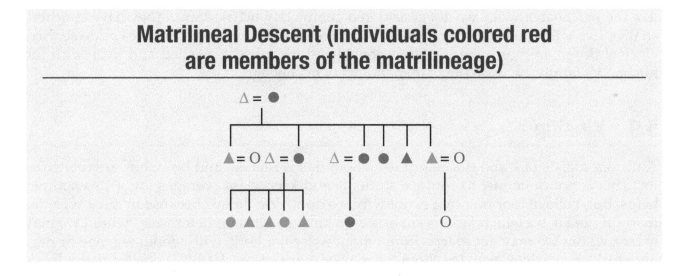

Matrilineal Descent (individuals colored red are members of the matrilineage)

5.9.3 Patrilineal Descent

Patrilineal descent is descent reckoned through the male line only (your 'pa's line'). Interestingly, about forty-five percent of human societies trace their ancestry this way, making it the most common rule of descent in the world (some examples would be Arabs, Chinese, much of India, the Shawnee and the Omaha). Patrilineal descent can be diagrammed like this:

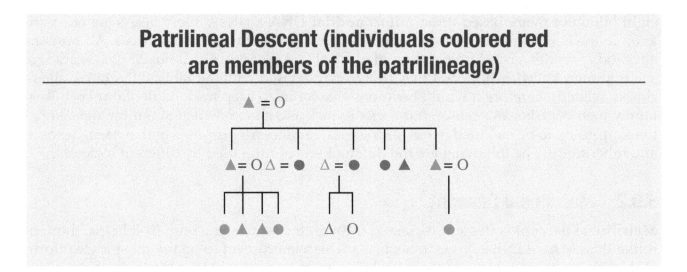

Patrilineal Descent (individuals colored red are members of the patrilineage)

Matrilineal and Patrilineal descent are known as **Unilineal descent groups**, because ancestry is traced through one line only.

5.9.4 Bilateral Descent

Bilateral descent is descent reckoned through both family lines equally. This type of descent is used by about thirty-five percent of human societies, including modern United States citizens, the French, the Ju/'hoansi, and the Inuit.

5.9.5 Ambilineal Descent

Ambilineal descent is reckoned through either parent's line by choice, that is, you can pick and choose to which parent's relatives you are related. Some examples of societies that practice ambilineal descent include Hawaii, Tahiti, and the old Highland Scots.

5.9.6 Double Descent

Double descent is practiced by about five percent of human societies. Double descent is *not* the same as bilateral descent, in which descent is descent reckoned through both family lines equally. It is descent reckoned through both parents' lines, but in *different ways*, like the Ashanti (also spelled Assente), who often are described as matrilineal, but who inherit their bodies from their mothers, but who inherit their souls from their fathers.

5.9.7 Unilineal Descent Groups

Unilineal descent groups, like matrilineal and patrilineal, sometimes are divided into several subsets. One of these is the **lineage**, or **sept**. A lineage is a group of relatives who can trace their descent back to a common ancestor through known links in the chain of descent. As an example, both you and your cousin can trace your descent back to a common ancestor, your grandparent, through known links in the chain of descent: your parents who are siblings and children of your grandparent. Technically a sept is not the same thing as a lineage, and refers to one seventh of a clan, in the Scottish terminology, but beyond that the difference is difficult to distinguish.

A **clan** (sometimes called **sib**) comes from the Scots Gaelic and/or the Irish Gaeilge word *clann*, which can mean 'children' or 'family'. A clan is a group of relatives who believe that they are descended from a common ancestor, but they cannot trace links in the chain of descent all the way back to that ancestor. One of the reasons for this is that it may be a **totemic ancestor**.

A **totem** is the belief that a plant, animal, or force of nature at some point took human form, and while in human form gave birth to the first member of the clan, thus the members of that clan, although they look human, actually are that plant, animal, or force of nature. A good example of this can be found in the cinematic film *The Secret of Roan Inish*, about an Irish family who were descended from a silkie, or seal woman, who took off her sealskin to reveal a woman who married the fisherman who found her. A group of related clans is called a **phratry**.

A **moiety** is half of a unilineal society that is divided into two descent groups. The word moiety comes from the French word *moitié*, which means 'half'. Let's say that you live in a society with just two families, the Smiths and the Joneses. If you are not a Smith, then you are a Jones; if you are not a Jones, then you are a Smith. Smiths, if they marry, must marry a Jones. Jones, if they marry, must marry a Smith. In this society the Smiths and the Jones each are a moiety, or half, of the society. An example of this from the ethnographic literature can be found among the northern **Arunta** (as also spelled Aranda) of central Australia. The northern Arunta have two intermarrying patrilineages, making each of the patrilineages a moiety. In some usages, a clan is localized and/or matrilineal, while a sib may be dispersed and/or patrilineal (see grey box at the end of this chapter).

LINEAGE

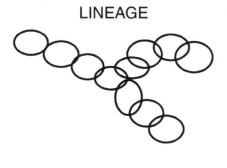

In a lineage, people believe that they are related to a common ancestor, and they can trace the links back to that ancestor in the chain of descent.

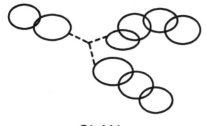

In a clan, people believe that they are related to a common ancestor, but they no longer can trace the links back to that ancestor in the chain of descent.

CLAN

5.10   Family Types

5.10.1   Nuclear Family

Family types vary around the world, just as do descent systems. The basic template of a family is called the **nuclear family**. A nuclear family consists of a married couple and their children:

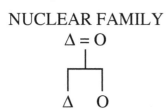

NUCLEAR FAMILY

Of course there are many variations of this basic model: sometimes couples have no children; sometimes children have no parents (an increasingly frequent tragedy in areas where HIV (Human Immunodeficiency Virus) is widespread); sometimes there is only one parent in a household; or sometimes the couple may be same sex, as we saw with woman marriage among the Nuer and the Anang.

5.10.2   Extended Family

The **extended family** consists of several related nuclear families of different generations all living together in the same house, or very close together. Extended families are especially common in patrilocal agricultural societies, in which the primary farmers are men, like the **Jats** of Haryana State in India, as shown in the ethnographic documentary *Dadi's Family*, about a middle aged mother-in-law in an extended family household. In the case of the Jats, the household consists of the P generation (the grandparents); the F1 generation (the sons, their wives, and any unmarried daughters of the P generation - married daughters move into their husbands' extended family households); and the F2 generation (the patrilineal grandchildren of the P generation). Matrilocal extended family households also are found, especially in horticultural societies, in which the primary farmers are women, for example, the **Hopi** of the American Southwest, but they are less common than are patrilocal extended family households. Part of the reason for this is that patrilocal residence is more common than is matrilocal residence.

Patrilocal Extended Family

(Patrilineage members living in the household in red, patrilineage members not living in the household in blue, resident in-laws in green, nonresident in-laws and grandchildren in purple)

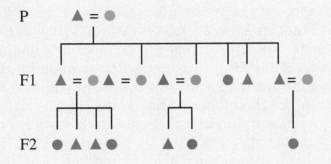

Matrilocal Extended Family

(Matrilineage members living in the household in red, matrilineage members not living in the household in blue, resident in-laws in green, nonresident in-laws and grandchildren in purple)

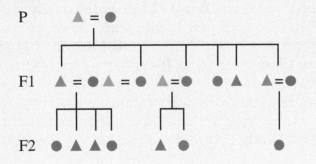

5.10.3 Stem Family

The **stem family** household is in between the nuclear family and the extended family households. It was described by **Conrad M. Arensberg** and **Solon T. Kimball** in their book, *Family and Community in Ireland*, about County Clare, Ireland, in the 1930s, as part of Harvard University's Anthropology department's major, decade long, three subfield study of Ireland. The stem family household consists of the grandparents (P), one son, his wife, and any unmarried siblings of the married son (F1), and any children of the married son and his wife (F2). Although the people of County Clare reckoned descent bilaterally, residence was patrilocal. Farms were too small to subdivide among the F1 generation, so only one member of a family (usually a son) could inherit them. Usually there was only enough for one dowry, so only one daughter could marry. The surplus members of the F1 generation may have been able to enter the seminary or the convent, been apprenticed to a shop in a town, emigrated, or stayed on the farm as unmarried, unpaid farmhands and housemaids, and still referred to as 'boy' or 'girl' into their 60s and 70s—they were stems off the family tree that never bore fruit.

5.10.4 Terms for Family Members of Different Relationships

Your **consanguineal kin** are your biological relatives; con means 'with', and 'sang' means blood, so your consanguineal kin are your 'blood relatives'.

Your **affinal kin** are your relatives to whom you are related by marriage. In other words, they are your 'in-laws', until divorce — or as a friend once referred her ex-husband's family, her 'outlaws'.

Your **cross-cousins** (sometimes written X cousins) are the children of your parent's sibling of opposite sex: mother's brother's son (MoBroSo); mother's brother's daughter (MoBroDau); father's sister's son (FaSiSo); or father's sister's daughter (FaSiDau). Cross-cousins often are considered the ideal marriage partners in unilineal societies (matrilineal or patrilineal), because technically they are not related to you, and by marrying them you may inherit from a parent to whom you are not related (we do not mean that you are not biologically related to the parent) through that parent's heir—your cross-cousin.

Your **parallel-cousins** (sometimes written II cousins) are the children of your parent's sibling of same sex: mother's sister's son (MoSiSo); mother's sister's daughter (MoSiDau); father' brother's son (FaBroSo); and father' brother's daughter (FaBroDau). They are parallel because their parent and your parent have a parallel relationship to your mutual grandparents: they are both sons, or they are both daughters, making their children parallel cousins. Your cross cousins are called cross because their parents do not have a parallel relationship to your mutual grandparents: they are neither both sons, nor are they both daughters, making their children not parallel (that is, not II, parallel, but X, or cross) cousins.

The **family of procreation** is what anthropologists call the family that we create when we marry in order to procreate. The **family of orientation**, by contrast, is the family that we are born into; it orients us on our path through life the way a compass orients a hiker on his or her path through the woods. Kinship specialist **Robin Fox** has shown that some **Tory Islanders** off the coast of County Donegal, Ireland, may return to live with their families of orientation following their weddings. This also appears to be the case in India in the **Nayar** caste's marriage system. In these cases one would live with one's mother, siblings, female sibling's children, and one's own children if one is female, but not if one is male (they are living with their mother's family of orientation).

Stem Family

(Family members living in the household in red, family members not living in the household in blue, resident inlaws in green, nonresident in-laws and grandchildren in purple, priests and nuns in black [note the grandmother has become a family member after her mother-in-law's death)

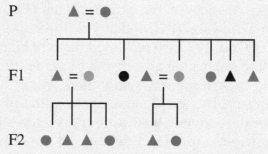

5.11 Kinship Systems

Anthropologists have found six basic kinship systems in the world: the **Crow, Omaha, Iroquois, Hawaiian, Eskimo (Inuit)**, and **Sudanese**. We draw them as **egocentric** kinship charts. They are called egocentric because **ego** means 'I' in Latin, and you ask someone, 'What do you call this relative?' This person responds, 'I call him/her …' In most kinship diagrams ego is pictured as a square, rather than as a triangle or a circle, because ego may be male or female. Most of them are **classificatory** systems, in which people with very different biological relationships are classified under a common term, like 'aunt' in the United States, which describes your father's sister, but also you mother's brother's wife – two very different relationships to ego (you). One is a paternal blood relative, but the other is a maternal in-law (affine). Similarly, in the Omaha system you might call you mother's brother's daughter (MoBroDau) 'mother'. However, the Sudanese system is **descriptive**, in which the term by which someone is called describes his or her relationship to ego. For example, you do not call your father's sister's daughter 'cousin,' instead you would call her 'father's sister's daughter.'

5.11.1 Eskimo (Inuit)

The Eskimo (Inuit) system probably is the simplest kinship system for North American students to understand, because it is practiced in both the United States, Mexico, and Canada as well as in about fifteen percent of other human societies. Generally it is found in bilateral societies in which the nuclear family may practice neolocal residence. Some examples of societies that practice the Eskimo (Inuit) system are the Inuit, the Ju/'hoansi, modern North Americans, and the French. It can be diagrammed like this:

In this diagram, red is father, blue is mother, black is brother, orange is sister, purple is aunt, green is uncle, and brown is cousin. Notice that the parents sisters are called by the same term in both families, the parents' brothers are called by the same term in both families, and the cousins are called by the same term in both families (some societies distinguish between male and female cousins, as in the French *cousin/cousine*).

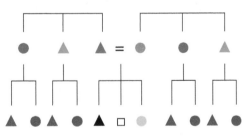

5.11.2 Hawaiian

The Hawaiian system is the absolute simplest kinship system; all the parents' sisters are called mother, all the parents' brothers are called father, and all the cousins are called brother or sister, depending on sex. The Hawaiian system is found in about a third of human societies, especially in ambilineal societies. Some examples would be the Hawaiians, Tahitians, Nuer, and Yoruba. In this diagram, red is father, blue is mother, black is brother, orange is sister.

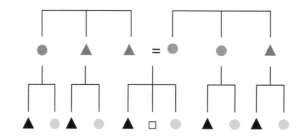

5.11.3 Sudanese

The Sudanese system is found in less than ten percent of human societies, usually in societies with social stratification. This may be an easy one to remember because, ironically, the Sudanese system is the most complex. Because the Sudanese kinship system is descriptive, what you call a relative describes your relationship to him or her. For example, you would call you mother's brother's son 'mother's brother's son', or you father's sister's daughter 'father's sister's daughter'. For this reason, every individual on the following kinship chart will be indicated by a separate color: no terms repeat, so no colors will repeat. Some examples of cultures that practice the Sudanese kinship system include the southern Sudanese, Turkish, Chinese, and the ancient Romans.

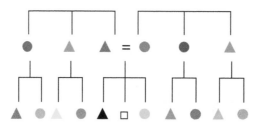

5.11.4 Iroquois

5.11.4.1 Bifurcate Merging

The Iroquois system is found in unilineal societies with bifurcate merging. Bifurcate merging means that the two families are terminologically split (bifurcated) in ego's parents' generation, but then terminologically merged back together again in ego's own generation. It is found in twenty-five percent of human societies, such as the Iroquois, Lakota, Navajo, and Yanomamo.

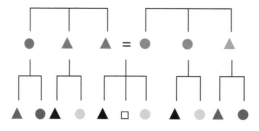

5.11.5 Omaha

The Omaha system is found in ten percent of human societies—usually in patrilineal societies, such as the Omaha, Shawnee, and Dani. In the Omaha system you would call the female members of your mother's patrilineage by the same term (usually we just say to call them 'mother'), you would call the male members of your mother's patrilineage by the same term (usually we just say to call them 'uncle'), you would call the male members of your father's patrilineage of your father's generation by the same term (usually we just say to call them 'father'), and you would call the female members of your father's patrilineage by the same term (usually we just say to call them 'aunt'). You would call your parallel cousins 'sister' and 'brother' because you call their parents 'mother' and 'father'. This may seem simpler if you label the blue figures 'Ms. Jones' and the green figures 'Mr. Jones'. Likewise, label the red figures 'Mr. Smith' and label the purple figure 'Ms. Smith'. Ms. Smith's children are not colored red or purple because they are not members of your father's patrilineage. Rather, they are members of *their* father's patrilineage (apparently their father is 'Mr. Brown').

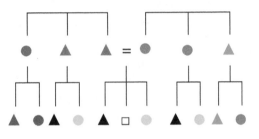

5.11.6 Crow

The Crow system sometimes is called the mirror image of the Omaha system, but is not really. Rather, it generally is found in matrilineal societies, so the cross cousin terminology is reversed from the Omaha system. The Crow kinship system is found in less than ten percent of human societies, for example, the Crow, Cherokee, Hopi, and Ashanti. As with the Omaha system, it may make more sense if you label the blue figures 'Ms. Jones' and the green figures 'Mr. Jones'. Likewise, label the red figures 'Mr. Smith' and label the purple figure 'Ms. Smith'. Mr. Jones' children are not colored blue or green because they are not members of your mother's matrilineage. Rather, they are members of *their* mother's matrilineage (apparently their mother is 'Ms. Brown').

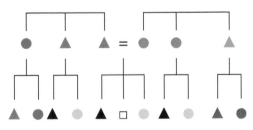

The main difference in the *charts* of the Iroquois, Crow, and Omaha kinship systems appears to be at the cross-cousins' figures.

Residence Patterns

Residence describes where a couple lives after marriage and where their children grow up.

Patrilocal/Virilocal: residence where children grow up in father's family; after marriage the new husband and wife live with husband's family—68.5% of human societies; often associated with patrilineal descent.

Examples: **From Australia & Oceania**: Australian Arunta, Australian Tiwi, Trobrianders, Dani, Ulithi Islanders, Tahitians; **From the Americas**: Maya, Inca, Yanomamo, Shawnee, Omaha, Kickapoo, Yurok; **From Africa**: Nuer, Igbo, Yoruba, Wodaabe, Konso, Ituri; **From the Middle East**: Arab, Turkish, ancient Hebrews, **From Asia**: Chinese

Matrilocal/Uxorilocal: residence where children grow up in mother's family; after marriage the new husband and wife live with wife's family—13.1% of human societies; often associated with matrilineal descent.

Examples: **From the Americas**: Cherokee, Creek, Seminole, Crow, Cheyenne, Iroquois, Navajo, Hopi, Zuni, Inga lik, Zapotec, Siriono; **From Asia**: Khmer.

Neolocal: residence where children grow up in their nuclear family; after marriage the new husband and wife live in a new residence apart from both the husband's and wife's families—4.7% of human societies; often associated with bilateral descent.

Examples: **From the Americas**: contemporary American; **From Europe**: contemporary English, contemporary French, Saami (Laplanders)

Ambilocal: living with either the husband's or wife's family—8.5% of human societies; often associated with ambilineal/cognatic descent.

Examples: **From Australia & Oceania**: Maori; **From the Americas**: Tlingit.

Duolocal/Natalocal: husband and wife each remain in own natal home—0.9% of human societies.

Example: **From Asia**: Nayar; **From Europe**: Tory Islanders

Avunculocal: from husband's view: living with the husband's mother's brother's family (often after cross-cousin marriage to mother's brother's daughter); from wife's view: often living with wife's family (matrilocal/ uxorilocal)—4.3% of human societies.

Examples: **From Australia & Oceania**: high-ranking Trobrianders; **From Africa**: WaMakonde, Ashanti

Amitalocal: DOES NOT EXIST IN REALITY (*Or does it?*): from wife's view: living with the wife's father's sister's family (often after cross-cousin marriage to father's sister's son); from husband's view: often living with husband's family (patrilocal/virilocal)—0% of human societies?

The data in this boxed section were compiled by Sharlotte Neely and Barbara Thiel, November 1, 2005, and generously provided for use in this book.

Kinship Terminologies

Kinship terminologies are systems for determining what kin terms are applied to which relatives.

Be sure, too, to examine the kinship charts for each of the following:

Eskimo: 16% of human societies; most often associated with bilateral descent; most common in bands & states.

Examples: **From the Americas**: many Inuit (Eskimo), Western Shoshone, contemporary American; **From Africa**: Ju/'hoansi (Bushmen); **From Europe**: contemporary English, contemporary French, contemporary Greek

Hawaiian: 32% of human societies; most often associated with ambilineal descent.

Examples: **From Australia & Oceania**: Hawaiians, Tahitians, Trobrianders; **From the Americas**: Nootka, Cheyenne, Kootenai, Netsilik; **From Africa**: Nuer, Yoruba; **From Asia**: Andaman Islanders

Sudanese: 8% of human societies; most often associated with some sort of unilineal descent.

Examples: **From Africa**: Peoples of Southern Sudan; **From the Middle East**: Turkish; **From Asia**: Chinese; **From Europe**: old English (before Norman invasion), ancient Romans

Iroquois: 25% of human societies; most often associated with some sort of unilineal descent; often associated with cross-cousin marriage.

Examples: **From Australia & Oceania**: Australian Arunta, Australian Tiwi; **From the Americas**: Iroquois, Lakota Sioux, Navajo, Western Apache, Chipewyan, Kuskowagamiut, Yanomamo; **From Asia**: Tungus, Peoples of South India

Omaha: 10% of human societies; associated with patrilineal descent.

Examples: **From Australia & Oceania**: Dani; **From the Americas**: Omaha, Shawnee, Mesquakie, Illinois, Kickapoo; **From Africa**: Bunyoro, Igbo

Crow: 8% of human societies; associated with matrilineal descent.

Examples: **From Australia & Oceania**: Ulithi Islanders; **From the Americas**: Crow, Cherokee, Choctaw, Chickasaw, Creek, Hopi, Tlingit; **From Africa**: Ashanti

The data in this boxed section were compiled by Sharlotte Neely and Barbara Thiel, November 1, 2005, and

generously provided for use in this book.

Marriage

Definitions of marriage vary greatly from society to society. The most common function of marriage is to expand the number of one's kin.

Marriage is *unique* to and *universal* among humans.

TYPES OF MARRIAGE:

Monogamy: one man legally married to one woman at one point in time (the most common form of marriage)

Polygamy: a general term for having more than one spouse; either polygyny or polyandry

Polygyny: one man legally married to two or more women at one point in time (a very common form of marriage); in **sororal polygyny** a man is married to two or more women who are sisters

Polyandry: one woman legally married to two or more men at one point in time (a rather rare form of marriage); in **fraternal polyandry** (the most common form of polyandry) a woman is married to two or more men who are brothers

Other forms of marriage include cousin marriage, ghost marriage, and various forms of same-sex marriage, to name but a few. The data in this boxed section were compiled by Sharlotte Neely and Barbara Thiel, November 1, 2005, and generously provided for use in this book.

FUNCTIONS OF MARRIAGE:
- to expand one's number of kin
- to limit and define sexual relationships
- to legitimize children and define who has responsibilities for them
- to establish an economic unit

Many other functions exist and vary from culture to culture. Romantic love is a rather rare purpose for marriage outside Western culture.

Other Important Terms

Family of Orientation: the family in which one is the child

Family of Procreation: the family in which one is the parent

Nuclear Family: a married couple and their minor children living together at home

Extended Family: a nuclear family plus other relatives; the most common versions are either an elderly couple, their unmarried sons and daughters, and their married sons with their wives and children or an elderly couple, their unmarried sons and daughters, and their married daughters with their husbands and children

Lineage: a descent group composed of consanguineal kin where all the generations back to a common ancestor are known; a publicly recognized corporate descent group; usually a segment of a clan or sib

Clan: a descent group who claim a common ancestor; often a *localized* group who claim a common ancestor; often composed of two or more related lineages that form a segment of the clan; in some usage a matrilineal descent group who claim a common ancestor; when a people have only two clans they are termed moieties

Sib: a *dispersed* descent group who claim a common ancestor; in some usage a patrilineal descent group who claim a common ancestor

Moiety: a unilineal descent group that represents half a population; a society can have only two moieties

Ramage: a group of people who have a common ancestor using ambilineal descent

Kindred: a group of people who all have a common living relative; a group of people closely related to one person through that person's mother or father; all the people related to one through one's mother and all the people related to one through one's father; usually associated with bilateral descent

Primogeniture: a system of inheritance in which a person's property and/or rank passes exclusively to the eldest child or eldest son *Exogamy*: marrying outside a defined group

Endogamy: marrying inside a defined group

Bifurcate Collateral Terminology: a system which differentiates the uncles and aunts both from parents and from each other

Bifurcate Merging Terminology: a system which groups the Fa and FaBr as Fa and the Mo and MoSi as Mo; how ever, the MoBr and FaSi are denoted by distinct aunt and uncle terms

Cross Cousin: the child of either one's FaSi or one's MoBr; children of opposite sexed siblings; a situation where one's parent and one's cousin's parent are the opposite sex

Parallel Cousin: the child of either one's FaBr or one's MoSi; children of same sexed siblings; a situation where one's parent and one's cousin's parent are the same sex

Sororate: a man marries his dead wife's sister; common in matrilineal descent

Levirate: a woman marries her dead husband's brother; common in patrilineal descent

Consanguineal Kin: relatives "by blood;" those with a common ancestor

Affinal Kin: relatives by marriage

Fictive Kin: relatives by adoption; unrelated adults who treat each other as kin

Further Reading

Books:

Burton Pasternak's *Introduction to Kinship and Social Organization* Ernest L. Schusky's *Manual for Kinship Analysis* Linda Stone's *Kinship and Gender*

Web Sites:

http://www.as.ua.edu/ant/Faculty/murphy/436/kinship.htm

http://homepages.wmich.edu/~bstraigh/AN120/AN120visuals/kinship.htm

http://www.umanitoba.ca/faculties/arts/anthropology/kintitle.html

The data in this boxed section were compiled by Sharlotte Neely and Barbara Thiel, November 1, 2005, and generously provided for use in this book.

Key Words and Concepts from Chapter 5

Bias	Cheyenne	Virilocal residence
Sex roles	Masculine protest	Matrilocal residence
Sex and Temperament in Three Primitive Societies	Paraphilias	Uxorilocal residence
	Baloma	Avunculocal residence
Arapesh	Nuer	Neolocal residence
Mundugamor	Limi	Bilocal residence
Tchambuli	St. Kitt's	Kinship
Gender	Economic potential	Avoidance
Sex	Same sex unions	Rules of descent
Coitus	Woman marriage	Mitochondrial DNA
Parts of speech	Anang	Mitochondrial Eve
Bugis	Bride Price	Matrilineal descent
Sambia	Zulu	Patrilineal descent
XX	*Lobola*	Unilineal descent groups
XY	Bride service	Bilateral descent
Twenty third pair of chromosomes	Jacob and Rachel	Ambilineal descent
	Ju/'hoansi	Double descent
XO	Exchange of females	Lineage
Turner's Syndrome	*Return to Laughter*	Sept
XXY	Tiv	Clan
Klinefelter's Syndrome	Dowry	Sib
XYY	Trust fund	Totemic Ancestor
Apparent sex	Gift exchange	Gift exchange
Suys	Andaman Islanders	Matrilineal
Berdache	Post marital residence rules	Avunculocal residence
Contraries	Patrilocal residence	Universal incest taboo

Incest
Gopalpur
Ancient Egypt
Inca
Hawaii
Childhood familiarity
Westermarck Hypothesis
Living laboratories
Taiwan
Fertility
Fecundity
Great marriage
Little marriage
Israeli kibbutz
Oedipus complex
Trobriand Matrilineal
  Complex
Sex and Repression in Savage
  Society
Post-marital residence
Marriage
Monogamy
Polygamy
Polygyny
Polyandry

Consensual unions
Ghost marriage
Totem
Phratry
Moiety
Arunta
Family types
Nuclear family
Extended family
Jats
Dadi's Family
Hopi
Stem family
Family and Community in
  Ireland
Consanguineal Kin
Affi nal Kin
Cross-Cousins
Parallel-Cousins
Family of Procreation
Family of Orientation
Tory Islanders
Nayar
Hypergamy
Hypogamy

Arranged marriages
Tiwi
Go-Between
Matchmaker
Levirate
Ruth and Boas
Sororate
Exogamy
Lineage exogamy
Endogamy
Kinship systems
Crow
Omaha
Iroquois
Bifurcate merging
Hawaiian
Eskimo (Inuit)
Sudanese
Egocentric
Ego
Classifi catory
Descriptive
Totem

Key Names from Chapter 5

Sally Slocum
Eleanor Leacock
Margaret Mead
Sharyn Graham Davies
Gilbert Herdt
Sigmund Freud
Bronislaw Malinowski

Alan Beals
Edward Westermark
Arthur Wolf
Melford Spiro
Judith Gussler
Laura Bohannan
Paul Bohannan

Ernestine Friedl
Conrad M. Arensberg
Solon T. Kimball
Robin Fox
Thomas Rhys Williams
C.W.M. Hart
Chung-min Chen

References and Suggested Readings Chapter 5. Male and Female: Sex, Marriage, Family, and Kinship

Arensberg, Conrad M. (1968) (1937) *The Irish Countryman*. Prospect Heights, Ill.: Waveland Press, Inc.

____and Solon Kimball (1974). *Family and Community in Ireland*. Cambridge: Harvard University Press.

Beals, Alan R. (1962). *Gopalpur: A South Indian Village*. New York: Holt, Rinehart and Winston.

Bowen, Elenore Smith (1964) (1954) *Return to Laughter*. New York: Anchor Books.

Davies, Sharyn Graham (2007). Challenging Gender Norms: Five Genders among the Bugis in Indonesia. Belmont, CA.: Thompson Wadsworth.

E. E. Evans-Pritchard (1940). *The Nuer: A Description of the Modes of Livelihood and Political Institutions of a Nilotic People*. Oxford: Oxford University Press.

Fox, Robin (1978) The Tory Islanders: A People of the Celtic Fringe. Cambridge: Cambridge University Press.

Friedl, Ernestine 1967 Dowry and Inheritance in Modern Greece, In Peasant Society: A Reader, Jack M. Potter, May N. Diaz, and George Foster, eds. Boston: Little, Brown and Company. pp. 57 – 62.

Freud, Sigmund 1918 Totem and Taboo. New York: Moffat, Yard.

Goldstein, Melvyn C. 1987 When Brothers Share a Wife: Among Tibetans, the Good Life Relegates Many Women to Spinsterhood. Natural History, March 1987, pp. 39–48

Gussler, Judith D. 1980 Adaptive Strategies and Social Networks of Women in St. Kitts. *In A World of Women*, Erika Bourguignon, ed. pp. 185 – 209. Brooklyn, NY: J. F. Bergin Publishers, Inc.

Hart, C.W.M., A. R. Pilling, and J. C. Goodale 1988 The Tiwi of North Australia. New York: Holt, Rinehart and Winston.

Herdt, Gilbert 1987 The Sambia: Ritual and Gender in New Guinea. Fort Worth: Harcourt Brace Jovanovich College Publishers.

Hoebbel, E. Adamson 1960 *The Cheyenne: Indians of the Great Plains*. New York: Harcourt, Brace, Johanovich College Publishers.

Leacock, Eleanor (2000). (1983) Interpreting the Origins of Gender Inequality: Conceptual and Historical Problems. In Jon McGee and Richard L. Warms (eds.) *Anthropological Theory: An Introductory History*, 2nd ed. Mount View, CA.: Mayfield Publishing Company. pp. 429–444.

Lee, Richard B. (1984). The Dobe !Kung. New York: Holt, Rinehart and Winston.

Malinowski, Bronislaw (1992). (1916) Baloma; The Spirits of the Dead. In *Magic, Science and Religion*:

And Other Essays. Prospect Heights, Illinois: Waveland Press.

_____ (1927*). Sex and Repression in Savage Society*. London: Routledge and Kegan Paul.

Mead, Margaret (1935). *Sex and Temperament in Three Primitive Societies*. New York: William Morrow.

Service, Elman R. (1978). *Profiles in Ethnology*. New York: Harper Collins Publishers.

Slocum, Sally (1975). Woman the Gatherer: Male Bias in Anthropology. In *Toward an Anthropology of Women*, Rayna Reiter, ed. New York: Monthly Review Press.

Spiro, Melford E. (1965) *Children of the Kibbutz*. New York: Schocken Books

Stein, Philip L. and Bruce M. Row (2010) *Physical Anthropology*. New York: McGraw-Hill

Wolf, Arthur (1968) Adopt a Daughter-in-Law, Marry a Sister: A Chinese Solution to the Problem of the Incest Taboo. *American Anthropologist*, 70: 864–874.

Chapter 6

Expressive Culture: Symbols and Language

Arnaud F. Lambert

"Human behavior is symbolic behavior; symbolic behavior is human behavior."

(Leslie White 1988 [1949])

Language is one of the primary means through which human beings share culture and learn cultural beliefs and values. Language is also one of the most complex, intriguing, and important facets of human life. There are thousands of distinct or mutually unintelligible languages on earth, as different from each other as Mandarin Chinese and German, Samoan and Swahili. According to the *Ethnologue* database, there are 6909 languages around the world (Rowe and Levine 2009:349). The Summer Institute of Linguistics has counted 6784 languages (Crystal 2005:336). To truly understand human culture, it is necessary to have a good handle on how human languages work and change over time and across different societies. This chapter delves into **anthropological linguistics**, the study of human language and communication systems, and examines some of the ways in which language and culture intersect, beginning with the fundamental basis of all human communication, the symbol.

6.1   Does Culture have a Symbolic Basis?

According to Leslie White (1988 [1949]), human culture emerged when our hominid ancestors first began to use **symbols**. Regardless of their form as tools, clothing, ornaments, body decorations, customs, rituals, art, or spoken language, symbols allowed human beings to give meaning to their world.

Symbols are one of the many ways that humans relate signs (i.e., things that represent other things) to objects. According to the C.S. Peirce (1933, 1934), the relationship between signs and the objects they represent can be experienced in three different ways.

Signs can have an **iconic** relationship to objects. In this case, the sign mimics or is similar to the object that it represents. Examples of this sign-object relationship include drawings of cigarettes on "No Smoking" placards or the depiction of a knife and fork when referring to places to eat on a map.

Some signs have an **indexical** relationship with their referents. These signs employ a natural relationship between the sign and the object they represent to refer to the existence of the object. A classic example is smoke. Smoke is often used to indicate the presence of a fire because fire causes smoke. Cultural relationships can also be indexical, such as when a crown is said to signify royalty. This is because kings and other members of royal families are historically known to have worn crowns in Europe.

The symbol, by contrast, is a very different kind of sign. Unlike an index, a symbol is essentially arbitrary. There is often no natural or culture-historical connection between the sign and its object. The only way symbols can represent other things is if we, as members of a society, agree that it works in this manner. As strange as it sounds, most of words people speak are symbolic. Take, for example, the English word "lobster." It is not iconic because the crustacean it represents does not make sounds which resemble the word. Likewise, it is not an indexical sign because capturing, cooking, and eating a lobster does not elicit any activity or sounds relatable to the word. The only reason we know that the word "lobster" refers to a large marine crustacean with a long tail and one pair of oversized claws is that we agree that it does. We learned the word from previous generations and have accepted its meaning.

Notice also that the conventional nature of symbols suggests that they are culture-specific. For example, a different social group such as French-speakers may not agree that the word "lobster" represents this crustacean. They can choose another word, like "l'homard"; while Hawai'ians have agreed to use the term "ula." Since symbols are arbitrary, different social groups are free to invent any word they wish to represent something else (Figure 6.1).

© 2014 Makhanch_S. Used under license of Shutterstock, Inc.

Figure 6.1. A skull and crossbones: In what ways is this image iconic, indexical, and symbolic? How might its symbolic meaning change from one culture to another?

6.2 How does Culture Shape the Way We Communicate?

Symbols, and to a lesser degree icons and indexes, are crucial to the way humans communicate with one another. Although we often take language to be a primarily verbal manifestation, human beings can communicate information to each using all five of our senses—sound, vision, taste, smell, and touch (Crystal 2005: 3–10).

Taste and smell are the least developed modes of human communication but if the importance of food and various fragrances and perfumes is any indication, we certainly know how to manipulate these senses to share information and send messages.

Next to language, the visual and tactile modes of symbolic communication are very important in most cultures. Often referred to as "body language" or non-verbal communication (Ottenheimer 2009), these forms of communication rely on various visual cues to relay information. These cues may involve:

1. **Body movements (kinesics)**: On the basis of the motion of limbs and other major body parts, these visual symbols include the folding or extension of the arms, turning the head, bowing, kneeling, and sitting in various positions (Hall 1959).

2. **Body posture**: Utilizing the orientation of the body, these symbols can take the form of various forms of standing upright, bending slightly forward, or leaning on one side or another.

3. **Hand gestures**: This form of "body language" relies on different configurations of the fingers, selectively extending some and/or bending others.

4. **The use of space (proxemics):** Although it does not involve the movement of the human body, the use of space and relative proximity can also be culturally meaningful in different contexts of interaction (Hall 1982 [1966]).

5. **Facial expressions:** The minute movement, flexing, manipulation, and orientation of different aspects of the human face—the eyes, eye brows, ears, nose, and mouth—can also be meaningful, especially when paired with other body movements and hand gestures.

6. **Haptics:** Encompassing the tactile dimension of "body language," haptics includes forms of communication involving contact between people. Some examples include hugging, shaking hands, and giving someone a high "five."

Since all of these different types of visual and tactile cues are symbolic, they vary markedly from culture to culture.

Although based on hand gestures, sign language is quite different from "body language". Sign language is more akin to writing in the sense that both these systems of communication were invented to represent the sounds of spoken language in other formats. Writing achieves this end through relatively permanent graphic marks on a medium such as paper, stone, or other material (DeFrancis 1989: 5). Writing can also take many forms from pictographic writing that uses pictures to express ideas to logographic writing systems that use graphic signs to represent words and word parts (Robinson 2007). Still other forms of writing use signs to represent syllables or individual sounds, like the Roman alphabet. Sign language, by contrast, uses hand gestures and facial expressions (Ottenheimer 2009). Like writing systems, sign language can also vary from culture to culture because both use symbols that do not inherently correspond to the vocalizations they represent. In this sense, it might be best to think of sign language and writing as systems of symbols that represent other symbols!

Learning Activity: The Meaning of Hand Gestures

Because they are symbolic, hand gestures are essentially arbitrary and their meaning can vary from culture to culture. Many of the gestures that North Americans typically use in everyday social interactions can therefore have completely different meanings in other cultures. Take the following four gestures for example.

© 2014 Christos Georghiou. Used under license of Shutterstock, Inc.

© 2014 okili77. Used under license of Shutterstock, Inc.

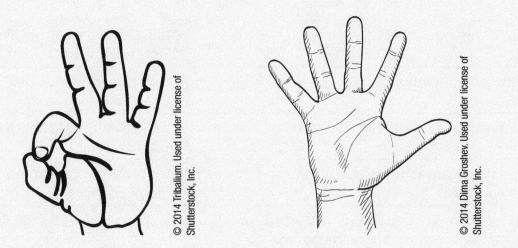

© 2014 Tribalium. Used under license of Shutterstock, Inc.

© 2014 Dima Groshev. Used under license of Shutterstock, Inc.

A. *The "thumbs up" sign for example is used in North America to show approval or to hitchhike. However, in Turkey and Greece, it means "Up yours!" and in Japan, it can signify the number five.*

B. *The V-sign, made by extending the first two fingers, is typically used to denote the number two or to signify the concept of peace in North America. By contrast, in Greece, it means "Go to Hell!"*

C. *The "okay" sign is created by making a circle with your thumb and forefinger. In North America, it means "okay." In France and Belgium, it symbolizes the number zero and in Brazil, it is a sexual insult.*

D. *The "open hand" sign is made by extending all of the fingers and showing the palm of the hand. In North America, when both hands are used in this manner, this gesture is used to communicate surrender or that the person is telling the truth. In Greece, the same gesture means "Up Yours x 2!"*

Now, think of some other common hand gestures that you use to communicate. What is the meaning of these gestures in your culture? Use this online article – https://www.huffingtonpost.com/2014/03/17/theglobal-guide-to-hand-_n_4956860.html — to uncover their meaning in other cultures. Are they similar or different?

6.3 What is Language and How does it Differ from Other Forms of Animal Communication?

In contrast to "body language" that uses tactile and visual modes of communication, language is primarily a verbal system of communication although it too can rely on graphic and gestural forms. Language is perhaps best defined as a system of symbols used to communicate relatively complex ideas because of the way in which arbitrary clusters of verbal, written or gestured signs are systematically put together according to a unified set of rules to create culturally meaningful phrases, sentences, utterances, and speeches (Rowe and Levine 2012).

Non-human animals also have verbal systems of communication but they differ greatly from human languages (Table 6.1). Human language is almost completely symbolic. The

Table 6.1. Comparison of human and non-human (animal) verbal forms of communication.

Human Language	Non-Human (Animal) Verbal Communication
Predominantly symbolic	Predominantly indexical (stimulus dependent)
Can communicate about the past, present, future	Can communicate about the present only
Can communicate about both concrete and abstract objects and ideas	Can communicate about concrete objects only
Vocabulary changes by adding new words or Changing the meaning of existing words	Vocabulary does not change
Endless variety of utterances (productivity)	Repetitive utterances (call and response pattern)

words used in a language are essentially arbitrary. One exception is **onomatopoeia** or the vocal imitation of sounds occurring in nature such as the "moo" of a cow, the "buzz" of a fly, or the "meow" of a cat. However, such words form a minor part of any language and often cannot be used to form complete sentences. By contrast, animal verbal communication is predominantly indexical in the sense that the sounds animals make are intimately connected to a stimulus present in their environment such as food, an intruder, or an internal feeling or drive.

As a result, the symbolic nature of language allows human beings to communicate about the past, present, and the future; while the indexical nature of animal communication is grounded in the present due to its reliance on various stimuli. Likewise, it is possible for human beings to share information about both concrete objects and abstract concepts using language. However, since ideas do not necessarily form enough of a stimulus, non-human animals most often communicate about concrete objects or empirical beings.

Because of its reliance on arbitrary symbols, human language is also capable of rapid change. We can change our vocabulary and grammatical norms many times within a generation. We can create new words by blending existing words, such as creating the word "chillax" from the older words "relax" and "chill." We can invent entirely new words to help us make sense of changing technologies. For instance, how many of us have used the new English verb "to google" lately? We can also opt to change the meaning of words without inventing new ones. In American English, for example, it was once the case that men were described as "pretty" and women were considered "handsome." Today, using these terms in this way could be insulting! In comparison, the vocabulary of non-human animals does not seem to change although it can be quite extensive.

Finally, the flexibility and arbitrariness of human languages permits us to develop a seemingly endless array of utterances. In fact, it is very hard for humans to say the same exact sentence in exactly the same way to refer to the same thing. There are always subtle variations that can change the meaning of our speech. By contrast, numerous studies have demonstrated that animal communication is predicated on the use of repetitive utterances. Sometimes known as the **"call and response pattern,"** these repetitive sequences are common among primates (Figure 6.2).

Figure 6.2.   Two chimpanzees interacting with food.

Language, then, allows human beings to communicate very complex ideas through the use of symbols. Take for example, one of the longest known words in any language, the German term *"rindfleischetikettierungsueberwachungsaufgabenuebertragungsgesetz."* It means nothing less than "the law delegating beef label monitoring." By contrast, the Turkish word *"şehirliles̜ tiremediklerimizdensiniz"* is used to signify that "you are one of those whom we cannot turn into a town-dweller." But how does language transform essentially mean-ingless and arbitrary sounds into deeply meaningful words and phrases? To uncover the power of human language, it is necessary to examine the way in which it is structured.

6.4   What is the Structure of Language?

When linguists try to describe a language and its structure, they run into two related prob-lems. First, the average human can make about a hundred distinct sounds, including con-sonants and vowels. Linguistics refers to these sounds as **phones** (or human-made sounds). Although they form the building blocks of language, not all languages employ exactly the same number or type of sounds. The second major problem is that linguists must have a way to write down or symbolize the sounds used in all languages. This can be problem-atic because the alphabetic and/ or syllabic symbols used in various writing systems only account for the sounds used in their respective languages. For example, the English alpha-bet does not have a symbol for the "énye" sound found in Spanish. Likewise, some of the symbols used in a particular writing system can encompass more than one sound in the language represented by the written symbols.

To overcome these obstacles, linguists have adopted the international phonetic alphabet or IPA (Figure 6.3). It uses a distinct set of symbols to account for every sound is used in any language, such as consonants, vowels, click sounds, trills, whistling sounds, as well as

THE INTERNATIONAL PHONETIC ALPHABET (revised to 2015)

CONSONANTS (PULMONIC) © 2015 IPA

	Bilabial	Labiodental	Dental	Alveolar	Postalveolar	Retroflex	Palatal	Velar	Uvular	Pharyngeal	Glottal
Plosive	p b			t d		ʈ ɖ	c ɟ	k ɡ	q ɢ		ʔ
Nasal	m	ɱ		n		ɳ	ɲ	ŋ	N		
Trill	ʙ			r					R		
Tap or Flap		ⱱ		ɾ		ɽ					
Fricative	ɸ β	f v	θ ð	s z	ʃ ʒ	ʂ ʐ	ç ʝ	x ɣ	χ ʁ	ħ ʕ	h ɦ
Lateral fricative				ɬ ɮ							
Approximant		ʋ		ɹ		ɻ	j	ɰ			
Lateral approximant				l		ɭ	ʎ	L			

Symbols to the right in a cell are voiced, to the left are voiceless. Shaded areas denote articulations judged impossible.

CONSONANTS (NON-PULMONIC)

Clicks	Voiced implosives	Ejectives
ʘ Bilabial	ɓ Bilabial	ʼ Examples:
ǀ Dental	ɗ Dental/alveolar	pʼ Bilabial
ǃ (Post)alveolar	ʄ Palatal	tʼ Dental/alveolar
ǂ Palatoalveolar	ɠ Velar	kʼ Velar
ǁ Alveolar lateral	ʛ Uvular	sʼ Alveolar fricative

VOWELS

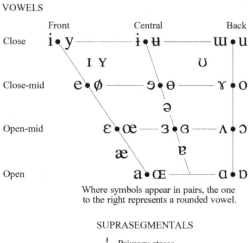

Where symbols appear in pairs, the one to the right represents a rounded vowel.

OTHER SYMBOLS

ʍ Voiceless labial-velar fricative
w Voiced labial-velar approximant
ɥ Voiced labial-palatal approximant
ʜ Voiceless epiglottal fricative
ʢ Voiced epiglottal fricative
ʡ Epiglottal plosive

ɕ ʑ Alveolo-palatal fricatives
ɺ Voiced alveolar lateral flap
ɧ Simultaneous ʃ and x

Affricates and double articulations can be represented by two symbols joined by a tie bar if necessary. t͡s k͡p

SUPRASEGMENTALS

ˈ	Primary stress	ˌfoʊnəˈtɪʃən
ˌ	Secondary stress	
ː	Long	eː
ˑ	Half-long	eˑ
̆	Extra-short	ĕ
ǀ	Minor (foot) group	
ǁ	Major (intonation) group	
.	Syllable break	ɹi.ækt
‿	Linking (absence of a break)	

DIACRITICS Some diacritics may be placed above a symbol with a descender, e.g. ŋ̊

̥	Voiceless	n̥ d̥	̤	Breathy voiced	b̤ a̤	̪	Dental	t̪ d̪
̬	Voiced	s̬ t̬	̰	Creaky voiced	b̰ a̰	̺	Apical	t̺ d̺
ʰ	Aspirated	tʰ dʰ	̼	Linguolabial	t̼ d̼	̻	Laminal	t̻ d̻
̹	More rounded	ɔ̹	ʷ	Labialized	tʷ dʷ	̃	Nasalized	ẽ
̜	Less rounded	ɔ̜	ʲ	Palatalized	tʲ dʲ	ⁿ	Nasal release	dⁿ
̟	Advanced	u̟	ˠ	Velarized	tˠ dˠ	ˡ	Lateral release	dˡ
̠	Retracted	e̠	ˤ	Pharyngealized	tˤ dˤ	̚	No audible release	d̚
̈	Centralized	ë	̴	Velarized or pharyngealized	ɫ			
̽	Mid-centralized	e̽	̝	Raised	e̝ (ɹ̝ = voiced alveolar fricative)			
̩	Syllabic	n̩	̞	Lowered	e̞ (β̞ = voiced bilabial approximant)			
̯	Non-syllabic	e̯	̘	Advanced Tongue Root	e̘			
˞	Rhoticity	ɚ a˞	̙	Retracted Tongue Root	e̙			

TONES AND WORD ACCENTS

LEVEL		CONTOUR	
e̋ or ˥ Extra high		ě or ˩˥ Rising	
é ˦ High		ê ˥˩ Falling	
ē ˧ Mid		e᷄ ˧˥ High rising	
è ˨ Low		e᷅ ˩˧ Low rising	
ȅ ˩ Extra low		e᷈ ˧˩˧ Rising-falling	
↓ Downstep		↗ Global rise	
↑ Upstep		↘ Global fall	

Figure 6.3. The International Phonetic Alphabet

various tones and pitches. The IPA is organized in such a way that anyone can reproduce a sound's **manner of articulation** (the way in which a sound is produced in the mouth and nose) and **place of articulation** (or the parts of the mouth used to produce the sound) even if the sound is not known in their spoken language (Ottenheimer 2009: 50–56). Despite this, many of the symbols used in the IPA chart are intended to match letters in the Roman alphabet. As a result, many correspond to letters with which English speakers are familiar. This can be helpful when trying to understand how to pronounce some of the symbols on the IPA chart. Some consonantal sounds, such as plosives, are relatively straightforward in terms of their manner of articulation. They require a puff of air to push through various parts of the mouth. Examples include bilabial plosives such as the [p] sound in "pen" or the [b] sound in "big". Alveolar plosives require that the air be pushed through the mouth as your tongue flicks the gum tissue behind your upper front teeth. Examples of alveolar plosives include the [t] sound in "tin" and the [d] in "dog." Other plosives require that your tongue flick the back of your palate (known as the "velum"). These velar plosives include the [k] sound in "kite" or "cat" and the [g] sound in "goat." Another class of consonants is equally well represented in English. These are known as fricatives and are formed as air passes continuously through various parts of the mouth. Some are labiodental, like the [f] sound in "fit" and the [v] in "van," and require passing air through the junction of your upper teeth and lower lip. Sounds like the [s] in "sit" and [z] in "zipper" are alveolar fricatives. Some fricatives are represented by less well-known symbols such as [θ] or the soft "th" sound in "thing" and [ð} or the hard (voiced) "th" sound in "other." Another set of fricatives require moving the tongue a little behind the alveolar ridge behind the upper teeth. These sounds are [ʃ] or the "sh" sound in "ship" and [ʒ] or the "s" sound in "measure." Affricates tend to combine the features of plosives and fricatives. They start with a puff of air and terminate with a flow of air. Examples include [tʃ] or the "ch" sound in "chocolate" and [dʒ] or the "j" sound in "judge." Nasal sounds are also fairly common. Such consonants include the bilabial [m] sound in "mild" and the alveolar [n] sound in "nice." These sounds are produce by passing some air through the nose and some through the mouth.

Of course, as noted above, there are a lot of phones but not all of them are used in every language. Languages typically use between 40 and 50 sounds to create words, although some languages such as Hawai'ian use only 12 sounds. Some languages such as the Khoisan languages of southern Africa rely on click sounds not found in any other language. Linguists classify these sounds as **phonemes**, the smallest sound unit (phone) that is used in a language.

Although it is sometimes difficult to recognize all of the sounds used in other languages, linguists have devised a relatively easy test to identify which sounds are meaningful in a language and which sounds have no meaning. The test involves looking for minimal pairs, two words that sound alike except for one sound. If the words signify different things, then these two sounds are considered phonemes. For instance, the English words "cat" and "rat" differ only in their initial sounds. The word "cat" begins with a [k] sound and the word "rat" begins with an [r] sound. Since phonemes are meaningful, changing the [k] sound to an [r] sound should change the overall meaning of the word as it does in the English terms "cat" and "rat." Thus, the [k] sound and the [r] sound are phonemes in the English language. Here is another example. In the Nunavut dialect of the Inuktitut (Inuit) language in northern central Canada, the term "aglu" refers to a seal's breathing hole; while the word "iglu" denotes a house. Both of these are minimal pairs that also differ in their initial sounds [a] and [i]. Therefore, the sounds [a] and [i] are phonemes in this dialect of Inuktitut.

Learning Activity: Khosian Phonemes

The Khoisan languages are found primarily in southern Africa (Botswana and Namibia) and are best known for their use of "click" consonants (Figure 6.4). Some of the neighboring Bantu languages such as Xhosa also have "click" sounds. Below are some examples of typical Khoisan click consonants. They include the IPA (International Phonetic Alphabet) symbol and some clues on how to make the sounds.

| = *dental click (sounds like the English 'tsk'), sometimes shown as a "/"*
‖ = *lateral click (made by sucking on the molars on both sides of the mouth)*
⊙ = *bilabial click (a lip-smacking sound made without pursing your lips)*
! = *alveolar click (tip of tongue is brought forcefully down from the roof of the mouth)*
ǂ = *palatal click (same as above but further back in the mouth)*

Now try to pronounce these Khoisan words from the Dobe Ju/'hoansi language (Lee 1993:189):

1. ‖gangwa - God
2. chulo - a camp
3. ‖gangwasi - ghosts of the deceased
4. !kia - a trance state
5. ǂtum - father-in-law or son-in-law
6. n!ore - an area of land with a Ju/'hoansi camp
7. nlum - "medicine" or energy used for healing
8. !kun!a - an old name

Figure 6.4. A young Khoisan speaker from Namibia.

Of course, phonemes are not the only components of a language (Figure 6.5). It is not possible to effectively communicate by randomly placing phonemes together. Every language has rules regarding how to create morphemes, or words and word parts. Morphemes are the smallest linguistic units that have a meaning in a language. Morphemes can be classified as free morphemes if they can occur by themselves or as bound morphemes if they only occur in the presence of other morphemes. Bound morphemes are usually prefixes or suffixes like the English "un-" or "-able." They cannot exist without another morpheme but they carry a meaning (Ottenheimer 2009: 81–90).

Although words (or **morphemes**) can denote a concept or entity, words are not usually placed in random order when humans communicate verbally or in writing. There are cultural rules for putting morphemes together to create longer sentences and utterances. These rules are known as grammar or syntax (Ottenheimer 2009: 92–100). Syntax helps us put morphemes together to communicate more complicated concepts! These rules differ from one culture to another and from one language to another. One of the simplest ways to order morphemes is known as **word order** or the organization of a sentence/utterance in terms of its subject (S), verb (V), and object (O). There are six ways to organize a sentence with regard to the order of words, although subject-first sentences are the most common form (Eastman 1990: 96; Ottenheimer 2009: 99–101):

SVO—English, French, Russian, Swahili, Thai

SOV—Farsi (Persian), Inuit, Japanese, Quechua, Turkish

VSO—Classical Arabic, Irish, Tagalog

VOS—Fijian, Malagasy, Ch'orti' Maya

OSV—Apuriña, Xavante

OVS—Apalai, Panare

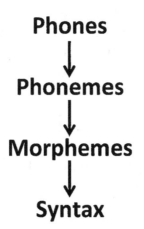

Phones

↓

Phonemes

↓

Morphemes

↓

Syntax

Figure 6.5. The structure of language.

6.5 How do Languages Vary?

We all know that we each communicate somewhat differently using language. We may differ in terms of our fluency or pitch. We may nasalize our pronunciation of specific words or speak with a lisp (Chambers 2003: 3). Anthropologists have also recognized that the features of language (i.e., its phonemes, vocabulary, and syntax) can vary with the social, political, and economic attributes of its speakers, including their social status, ethnic identity, and gender (Rowe and Levine 2012: 194–216). Our use of language also changes as we interact with people in different social settings and communities (Chambers 2003: 5). Some of the best-known examples of the influence of human cultures on the use of language include regional and ethnic dialects (discussed in a separate section of this chapter).

Another well-known example is the manner in which American men and women differ in the manner in which they use language (Chambers 2003: 139–156). In the 1970s, Lakoff (1975) first identified the elements of a distinctive linguistic register used by women. This register featured the use of weak directives in speech, a questioning intonation, and the use of hedges or tag questions such as ending a statement with the phrase, "Is that right?" Researchers have differed greatly on how to interpret these differences. Some suggest that this register reflects deficiencies in women's use of language; others have suggested that they reflect the different social ranking and power of women in American society (Coates 1986). More recently, linguists such as Tannen (1986, 1996) have argued that this register represents cultural differences in the way men and women communicate effectively.

Beyond the issue of gender differences, language use can be used to mark and even legitimize the unequal status of different social groups. For example, Labov (1972) found how speech could be used to identify a person's socioeconomic standing. In New York City, the use of the sound [r] identified white-collar workers, whereas blue-collar workers generally omitted that sound in their speech. Because blue-collar registers tend to have less prestige, Labov also found that a person's class aspirations could influence their speech patterns in order to reflect the social group or class with which they wanted to be identified (Chambers 2003: 45–46). On the other hand, there are also cases in which it may not be practical to change one's speech to reflect the language norms of a higher class. For example, in social situations in which a person wants to highlight their membership in a particular class, they will tend to avoid changing their speech patterns to reflect a different class.

6.6 How do Languages Change Over Time?

Just like any other part of culture, languages and their elements can change over time. Historical linguistics is the study of how languages change over time and diverge from each other (Campbell 2000). By comparing the elements of different languages (e.g., phonemes, morphemes, and syntax), historical linguists try to determine how languages are related. This is known as the **comparative method**. Most commonly, this is done by comparing **cognates**, or words, in different languages with similar meanings. By examining sound correspondences in such cognates, it is possible to determine how closely languages are related and therefore belong to the same language family. In Table 6.2 for instance, cognates from five different languages are compared. Do you notice any differences? How are they similar?

Table 6.2. A Select List of Cognates between Five Languages Belonging to the Indo-European Language Family (Campbell 2000: 139–141; Rowe and Levine 2009: 552).

Sanskrit (India)	Greek	Latin	Gothic (German)	Modern English
Janu	Gonu	Genu	Kniu	Knee
Pitar	Pater	Pater	Fadar	Father
Bhratar	Phrater	Frater	Brother	Brother
Janas	Genos	Genus	Kun-i	Kin
Padam	Poda	Pedem	Fotu	Foot
Trayas	Tris	Tres	Thri	Three
Sapta	Hepta	Septem	Sißun	Seven
Dasha	Deka	Decem	Taihun	Ten
Saitam	(He)-katan	Centum	Hund	Hundred
Nakt-	Nukt-	Noct-	Nahts	Night

Based on the correspondences shown between the cognates in Table 6.2 (among many others), linguists have long recognized that these five languages belong to the Indo-European language family along with Hittite, Persian, Albanian, Russian, Czech, French, Spanish, and Swedish. In addition to Indo-European, several hundred language families can be found around the world. These include Semitic (e.g., Arabic and Hebrew), Algonquian (e.g., Blackfoot, Micmac, Cree, Ojibwa, and Wampanoag), Athabaskan (e.g., Navajo, Apache, Chipewyan), and Austronesian (e.g., Hawaiian, Tahitian, Trukese). In Africa, there are Bantu languages (e.g., Kongo, Tswana, and Zulu), Nilotic languages (e.g., Maasai and Dinka), as well as Khoisan or "click" languages (Campbell 2000: 164–165). Asia, by contrast, is home to the Sino-Tibetan language family (e.g., Chinese, Tibetan, and Burmese), the Austro-Asiatic languages (e.g., Khmer and Vietnamese), and the now disputed Altaic language family (e.g., Mongolian, Korean, Japanese, Turkic, and Tungusic) (Campbell and Mixco 2007).

You may have also noticed some differences in the way these cognates are pronounced. For instance, the voiceless plosives [p], [t], and [k] in the Sanskrit, Greek, and Latin words for "father," "foot," "three," and "hundred" are equivalent voiceless plosives [f], [θ] (a soft "th" sound), and [h] in Gothic and English. Because Sanskrit, Latin, and Greek are more ancient languages than Gothic or English, these differences represent a historical change. In linguistics, this change in pronunciation is known as *Grimm's law* (Campbell 2000: 46; Rowe and Levine 2012: 357). The reasons for it are not altogether clear, but we know that languages can change over time for a variety of reasons. Sometimes, new words are added to a language to represent new ideas or to refer to new technologies. Many languages borrow words from one another because they have no cognates for the term (Campbell 2000: 79–83). For example, the English words "iguana," "canoe," and "barbecue" were borrowed from the Arawak and Taino peoples of the Caribbean. Words such as "coyote," "chocolate," and "tomato" came from the Aztec language. The word "robot" came from Czech and "moped" and "slalom" came from Swedish. In other cases, the meaning of words can change. A good example of this is the English word "wicked" (Ayto 2011: 573). Originating from the Old English word "wicca" meaning "wizard," it eventually came to mean "bad" or "evil." In more recent times, the term's meaning has become much more positive, referring to something "good."

And although part of the process of language change has always entailed the disappearance of some languages, the extinction of languages around the world has steadily increased. Roughly 90% of the world's six thousand plus languages are spoken by less than 100,000 people. Of these, approximately 360 are spoken by only 50 people. When compared to the world's largest languages – e.g., Mandarin Chinese (1.3 billion speakers), Spanish (700 million speakers), English (600 million speakers), Hindi (490 million speakers) and Arabic (280 million speakers) – many of these smaller languages can be considered in danger of becoming extinct (Crystal 2005: 336; Rowe and Levine 2009: 366–367). Some of this situation occurred as a result of deliberate programs of ethnocide and genocide linked to colonialism and imperialism. In other cases, languages may become endangered as new generations of speakers decide to learn one of the major world languages in order to expand their social and economic opportunities. At the same time, there are a number of communities that are actively trying to preserve their indigenous languages by recording current speakers and reconstructing the language so that it can be taught to new generations (Crystal 2005: 339).

6.7 What is the Relationship Between Language, Culture and Human Cognition?

The relationship between language and culture can also be very complex. It might be best to think of language and culture as having a circular relationship (Figure 6.6). According to this view, language is a reflection or expression of culture, such as cultural beliefs and values. But language can also play a role in shaping culture.

Cultural influences on language are much more noticeable so we will tackle this relationship first. One of the simplest ways to observe how cultural beliefs and values impact language is through **focal vocabularies**. A focal vocabulary is an extended list of terms in a language that are used to denote a specific item or behavior that is deemed important to the society. Although the list is often embellished to a ridiculous degree (see Pullum 1991:159–167), the dozen or so words in Inuktitut (Inuit) that refer to snow provide a good example. Due to their arctic environment it would make sense that snow would be the object of vocabulary expansion. Note though that there is a similarly sized focal vocabulary for snow in North American English. Given the popularity of skiing and other winter activities, it is not surprising that this dialect of English differentiates between "snow," "sleet," "slush," "blizzard," "powder," "dust," and several other words for different types of snow. North American English supplies us with an even more concrete example with the concept of "money." Think about how many English words there are for money? Such words include "dollars," "bucks," "mullah," "stacks," "coin," "cheddar," "dough," "cake," "bread," "dinero," "loot," "chop," and many, many others!

Another example of the way in which language influences culture is supplied by the phenomenon of the **dialect**, or a variety of language associated with geographic regions

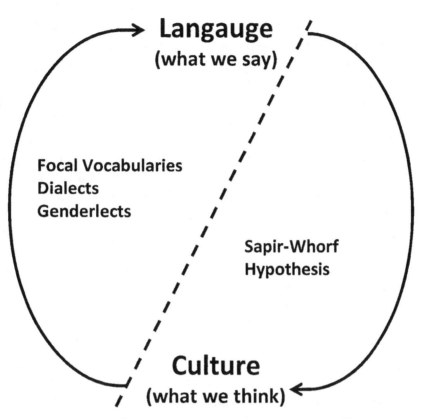

Figure 6.6. The relationship between language and culture.

within a nation, national identities, ethnic groups within a nation, socioeconomic groups (i.e., social classes), and genders. Indeed, there are so many dialects of specific languages that language itself can be thought of as a collection of dialects that are historically related and similar in vocabulary and structure. For example, the English language varies on a national level between England, Scotland, Ireland, Australia, Canada, and the United States. English and American English spellings and pronunciations can differ ("colour" vs. "color," "theatre" vs. "theater") as can vocabulary ("boot" vs. "trunk of a car," "lift" vs. "elevator"). The similarities are due to the historical relationship between countries that speak English; the differences reflect direct and indirect influences from other cultures, changes in technology, and other culture-specific mechanisms of change.

By contrast, the influence of language on culture particularly on cultural beliefs or "what we think" is more difficult to observe. One example of this form of **linguistic determinism** or linguistic relativity is known as the **Sapir-Whorf hypothesis** (Ottenheimer 2009:28–29, 36–39). Originally advanced by the linguists Edward Sapir and Benjamin Lee Whorf in the early part of the twentieth century, this hypothesis claimed that human thought was ultimately shaped by language. If there was no word for it, then you could not think it. In other words, the words and syntax of a language determine how a speaker of that language thinks about and experiences the world.

Classic examples of the Sapir-Whorf hypothesis were at first anecdotal. Whorf, for example, claimed that speakers of Hopi did not have a past or future tense for verbs, suggesting that they did not have a linear sense of time (Whorf 1956 [1941]). It turns out, however, that the Hopi language contains plenty of modifying terms that can be used to chronologically place the object of a sentence (Trask 1995).

Over the last forty years, there have been numerous tests of this idea. Some of the most interesting have come from experiments on monosyllabic color terms (i.e., the basic color terms). Languages vary significantly in regard to number of color terms they use. Some have only two basic color terms; others contain seven or more. This diversity offered a wonderful opportunity for linguists to observe whether cultures with smaller color vocabularies were "colorblind" due to their language (Berlin and Kay 1996). One example comes from the Raramurí or Tarahumara people of central Mexico. Their basic color terms consisted of "red," "orange," "yellow," "grue" or blue and green, and "purple." In one experiment, linguists asked some Raramurí volunteers to label colored cards into categories. As the Sapir-Whorf hypothesis predicted, they lumped blue and green cards under the same category. In another experiment, however, a different group of Raramurí volunteers were asked to categorize the same set of cards into groups based on similarity of color. Interestingly, the volunteers were able to differentiate between 'blue" and "green". What does this experiment and others like it tell us about the idea of linguistic determinism? They show us that language does shape the way you can talk about and represent the world but it does not appear to alter the way you perceive and experience it (Agar 1994).

Chapter Summary

Language, a system of symbols with standard meanings, is a crucial and vital aspect of all human cultures. Through language, members of a society are able to communicate with one another. Some anthropologists study body motions and gestures used in nonverbal communication, or body language. Even non-human animals have basic verbal and visual communication skills. Chimpanzees and gorillas for instance, have been taught non-verbal forms of communication such as American Sign Language. Linguistic anthropologists have also researched the use of language in different human social contexts, a field known as sociolinguistics. These different social contexts can explain dialectal differences in spoken language, or differences in pronunciation, vocabulary, and syntax; honorifics in language, and conversational norms.

Key Terms

anthropological linguistics	icons (iconic signs)	onomatopoeia
bound morphemes	indices (indexical signs)	phones
call and response	kinesics	phonemes
cognates	language	place of articulation
comparative method	linguists	proxemics
dialects	linguistic determinism	sapir-whorf hypothesis
focal vocabularies	manner of articulation	symbols
free morphemes	minimal pairs	syntax
haptics	morphemes	word order

Chapter 7
Ethnographic Studies

Liam Kilmurray

Outline

7.1   Introduction

> The task of the ethnographer is to contextualize insight of local values and practices within wider local significations, and to render them probable; to show how theirs is a meaningful alternative as a way of life. That is the be-all and end-all of anthropology and, as such, central to disciplinary identity. (Howell 2018, 2)

Ethnography, also known as participant-observation or fieldwork, is an essential part of anthropological research. It is based on the simple idea that in order to really understand the cultural practices of a community, it is best to observe its people and interact with them over a long period of time. To do this, anthropologists undertake fieldwork. This involves the anthropologist becoming what is known as an ethnographer—an anthropologist practicing participant-observation. There are other types of participant-observation that do not exactly coincide with the anthropological version—which we will generally call ethnography in this chapter. Participant-observation is also undertaken by sociologists, healthcare or aid workers, writers, historians, and marketers, among many others. These research projects sometimes focus on one individual or one set of workers or prisoners; they do not examine in any great detail the cultural or structural aspects of these communities and so are not really anthropological ethnographic projects. In anthropology, ethnography is defined as the systematic scientific study of the customs and practices of a cultural field by means of total immersion for a period usually lasting a year. The period of one year is important, as it allows the ethnographer to witness the changing seasons and, for example, the full cycle of crops, planting, sowing, and reaping. Within one year or more, the ethnographer witnesses the annual ceremonies and the important dates in the life of the community. Bearing witness to this, the ethnographer will then write up her monograph, or what has been called the "textual rendering of social worlds" (Lila Abu-Lughod 2000, 261). This daily observation of, and engagement with, social life is crucial. Ethnographers seek to uncover and understand local ways of doing things, local values, what is done and not just what is said. In cultural anthropology doing fieldwork was for the longest time (and to some degree remains) a rite of passage. Anthropology teaches us many things about other cultures, specifically when fieldwork is undertaken. It teaches us to examine our own culture with a comparative and more analytical eye. In fact, it is ethnography that helps set anthropology apart from other social sciences. It played a foundational role in anthropology, as from the very early days ethnographers were the first anthropologists who travelled afar to live with and study what were then called the "exotic other." Ethnographers were the first to bring information regarding distant cultures back to their host nations, both fascinating and disturbing European societies.

Ethnography is open-ended and inductive. "Open-ended" means that the questions that are asked and the approach that is taken by the ethnographer do not necessarily have a planned ending and therefore may develop in different ways. An "inductive" approach means building explanations from this field experience. Like all forms of anthropology ethnography seeks to unravel the complexities of social life and to understand these from the local point of view. Indeed, since the very beginnings of ethnography, fieldwork has been the laboratory of anthropology, where theories can be tested against empirical data collected during the ethnographer's residency. Like other fields of anthropology, ethnography straddles both the hard (scientific) and the soft (social) sciences. How scientific or social ethnography is remains dependent upon the approach taken by the individual ethnographer. For some, anthropology and ethnography should remain solidly scientific, rooted in empirical research. Howell notes that ethnography, like much of anthropology, "constructs its intellectual imaginings upon empirical-based knowledge about human worlds" (Howell 2018, 1). This empiricism is essential so that any claims or interpretations may be backed up with hard data. For others, the empiricism and hard data of science should be wedded to a more humanistic interpretation and writing of the culture at hand. They consider empiricism important but would allow also for some creative interpretation.

Unlike hard scientific approaches, where laboratory tests must be conducted under near-identical conditions, ethnographic research is, by definition, never the same (Guest 2018). No two ethnographers would ever write the same report or come up with identical findings regarding any aspect of culture. The eminent French anthropologist Claude Lévi-Strauss examined the psychology of various South American groups, whereas the English anthropologist Radcliffe-Brown chose to focus on the kinship systems of African groups. Other ethnographers, although they have studied the very same populations, chose to examine widely different aspects of society. This is a strength, however, not a failing of ethnography. Polyvocality, the inclusion of more than one voice, and polysemy, the capacity for a sign or symbol to have multiple meanings, are essential to an understanding of the multitude of cultural practices that anthropologists encounter and attempt to interpret. The primary methodology of ethnography is participant-observation. Yet the paradox at the heart of this practice is that the ethnographer is simultaneously participating in *and* observing from a "distance." He or she must straddle this juncture and ensure that an objective—insider/outsider report—results from their fieldwork. This fieldwork is not undertaken in isolation from the broader field of anthropology itself, and it must be intellectually relevant to anthropology as a whole, as will be explained below.

The purposes behind the intensive research efforts of ethnography are many, and they have changed over the years. In the eighteenth and nineteenth centuries it was discovery that was the prime motivation for organizing field research projects. Who lived beyond those mountains, what type of people were to be found deep in this forest, were there "civilized" peoples across this mighty river? As more and more ethnographers spread throughout the world, such as Frank Cushing working among the Zuni in the late nineteenth century United States, or the many British and German expeditions to Africa and Asia, ethnography began to ask more systematic questions of the peoples encountered. In so doing, these early anthropologists laid the foundations for what was to become the hallmark of anthropology—the empirical study of culture. They were the first to work out the logistical and methodological approaches to gathering anthropological data. They constructed genealogical charts for conceptually mapping kinship systems, and they designed questionnaires and interview techniques in order to systematize the data they were gathering. Early scholars such as Malinowski and Boas strived to construct theoretical models in order to interpret and understand the peoples they studied, and to express this understanding in their published monographs. These pioneers of ethnography were therefore responsible for much of the theoretical framework that has been employed in anthropology for the past two hundred years. Those early days of ethnography were also characterized by the "lone" ethnographer striding forth into the jungle or sitting alone among curious "natives." This sort of "anthropologist as hero" trope is now long past and discredited, and today ethnography is usually undertaken by a team of specialists. These teams will not always be comprised solely of anthropologists, and may contain geologists, linguists, archaeologists, and others with skills deemed necessary for particular fieldwork projects. As we will see in the following, the history of ethnography is dominated by fieldwork projects undertaken far from the (usually Western) anthropologists' home base. Given that the goal of anthropology is to understand difference and to seek out other ways of living, most of the early research was undertaken in distant places. This has changed over the past few decades and more and more ethnographic projects are undertaken closer to "home." This is an emergent trend, but it is not exactly new, as occasionally earlier ethnographies tackled issues within their own nation states. Such was the case with W. F. Whyte who produced an ethnography of Italian Immigrants in the Boston (Whyte 1943), or others who examined factory workers and so forth. Still, the general practice was to go afar to study other cultures.

Photo, Elliott & Fry.

SIR EDWARD BURNETT TYLOR.

Source: © Folklore Society

7.2   Development of Ethnography

The word ethnography stems from the Greek words θνoςethnos "folk, people, nation" and γράφω *grapho* "I write." It therefore translates generally as "the writing about people." When and where did it begin? Many different starting points in the distant and dispersed past have been proposed. Some early recorded cases in which we may dimly perceive the genesis of ethnography are found in the works of the Greeks and Romans. Writing in the fifth century B.C. the Greek scholar Herodotus, known as the Father of History, described the various peoples outside of the Hellenic world. He reported on some of their practices, their gods, and their systems of governance. Two thousand years ago, Tacitus and Julius Caesar, both Romans, wrote about the cultural practices of early non-Latin peoples. In his Commentaries, Julius Caesar wrote not just about the conquest of the Gauls but he also examined some of their social practices. These are early examples of ethnographic research, but of course they are not proper anthropology as in many cases the goal was to understand the practices of a society in order to conquer and subdue it, dramatically at odds with modern ethnography.

A more modern form of ethnography began with Edward Tylor in the 1860s, whose field research in Mexico and his comparative accounts of different cultures set the stage for the development of ethnographic studies. Tylor's definition of culture has long been cited in anthropology. However, it was in the context of ethnographic research that he first coined this definition: "Culture or civilization, taken in its wide ethnographic sense, is that complex whole which includes knowledge, belief, art, morals, law, custom, and any other capabilities and habits acquired by man as a member of society" (1871). Among those whom Tylor influenced was Sir James Frazer, whose most famous work, *The Golden Bough* (1890), documented the similarities among magical and religious beliefs around the world. In these early days, much of the ethnography undertaken was actually what is termed "armchair ethnography," so called because anthropologists rarely went into the actual field to conduct in-depth research. Rather, they would rely on reports from people who had been there, such as traders, missionaries, soldiers, and explorers. In the United States of America, Lewis Henry Morgan did actually conduct ethnographic research among the Iroquois in the Finger Lakes region of upstate New York. Morgan wanted to comprehend tribal kinship patterns, so to that end he undertook further ethnographic inquiry on the Great Plains and the Missouri river among the Winnebago, Crow, Yankton, Blackfeet, and others (Morgan 1871). Morgan was therefore no armchair theorist, and in his research into the Iroquois he sought to construct a terminology for classifying different systems of kin-reckoning. His major work, *Systems of Consanguinity and Affinity of the Human Family*, would be put to use by generations of future ethnographers.

Sir James Frazer, Author of the Golden Bough.

Such nineteenth century ethnographers interpreted their data in light of what was then the dominant theory in emergent anthropology—evolutionary theory. This theory was based inappropriately on Darwinian evolution, since Darwin was concerned solely with biological evolution. Nonetheless, culture-evolutionary theorists argued that human societies went through a series of developmental stages, from savagery to barbarism to civilization. The criteria for judging what level of social evolution groups had reached was based mostly on their technology, kinship systems, and other social institutions (Tylor [1881]; Morgan 1871). The goal of these early ethnographic works was therefore to shed light on other cultures, usually remote from Europe, and classify them according to this evolutionary scheme, a scheme long since discarded in anthropology. However, these early scholars set the wheels in motion for establishing ethnography as a relevant approach to anthropological research. By the early twentieth century, "armchair" ethnography can be said to have had its day and a new phase called "verandah" ethnography emerged. In this phase, anthropologists left the armchair but did not exactly go into the field to conduct their research. They did not always make their way through jungles or climb steep mountain tops and cross difficult landscapes. Neither did they sleep or eat in the same place as their research subjects. Instead, they went close to the field, as close as they could, often staying with the local religious mission, or bureaucratic or military representative of the various colonial powers. The "informants" they wished to gather information from came to them instead, to the verandah, where the anthropologist would then conduct interviews. This phase ended by the 1920s and true ethnography—participant-observation—emerged. Eventually researchers such as Bronislaw Malinowski, Edward Evan Evans-Pritchard, A. A. Radcliffe-Brown, and Franz Boas transformed what was once an ad hoc pastime into a rigorous practice now known as participant-observation. These anthropologists were practicing ethnographic research at a time when the theoretical means to do so were still very much in flux, and this remains the case today. They helped pave the way for newer theories and methodologies.

European ethnography was undertaken in the colonies of European nations. In the United States, things were done differently. The absence of overseas colonies and the presence of living indigenous nations resulted in American ethnography focusing on these cultures. Much of the early work in the United States can be described as salvage ethnography. The bulk of ethnographic writings in this period were concerned with recording and interpreting the lifeways of cultures seen to be on the brink of destruction or becoming so modernized or dejected that the old lifestyles, stories, and ways of knowing, were disappearing. The collection of ethnographies from this period demonstrates the attempts of anthropologists to document what were thought to be dying cultures. Beyond any postmodern critique of the obvious imperialism of this approach, many argue that some valuable work was done (we will address this further in the following section on postmodernity).

7.3 Preparation for Fieldwork

The practical aspects of organizing an ethnographic expedition are many and complex. In preparing for fieldwork, the ethnographic team must be highly organized. To begin with, a site must be chosen. The field, as it is known, may be one that is a long way from the home of the investigator. For a European, this would include places such as the Amazon basin or the highlands of Papua New Guinea. Alternatively, more recent fieldwork projects tend to be located closer to the ethnographer's home. For instance, the project might entail the ethnography and observation of the eating habits of students at Carleton University in Ottawa, or the analysis of the lives of homeless people in New York City. Once a site has been selected a project plan must be created, one which will lay out the objectives of the research, the timing, equipment needed, resupply of equipment, and the details of living quarters that must be carefully planned. Depending on where the research will be conducted, visas and permissions must be sought. This is an important point, as frequently in the history of ethnographic research local conditions caused plans to be altered or cancelled. This has occurred with expeditions into countries or regions that have experienced natural disasters, outbreaks of disease, or civil unrest.

Before setting out into the field, financial grants from sponsoring institutions must be secured. Once a location and a plan are decided upon, the anthropological team must submit a proposal for research in order to obtain this funding. This will normally entail the specific questions the ethnographic research hopes to have answered. Usually the application and plan will outline the methodology of the research, such as how information will be gathered; will the methodology include one-on-one interviews with certain segments of the population such as men, women, elders, or will the entire population be included? Ethnographers may also outline a theoretical approach that will be applied to the analysis of the data that they will gather. The ethnographer may state that he or she will undertake emic or etic research, or an admixture of both. Briefly, emic research is undertaken from within the group under study (from the perspective of the subject), while etic research is from the outside (from the perspective of the observer). Emic research will therefore be more likely to use extensive first person quotations than etic research.

There is also the important need for inoculation against disease and germs that the researcher may be exposed to and have no natural protection from. Finally, equipment must be obtained, such as maps/GPS, recording devices, notebooks, archives, genealogical charts, and whatever else the researcher deems necessary for the completion of a successful fieldwork expedition. To aid in their ethnographic enterprises many anthropologists also undertake archival research before and/or during their research. This is known as ethnohistory and along with ethnoarchaeology, it produces a fuller understanding of the people under study.

7.4 Ethnohistory and Ethnography

Actual field research is just one aspect of ethnographic inquiry, albeit perhaps the most important. Ethnohistory is also used. This is the study of social customs through the examination of historical records. Archival research was important to anthropologists such as Boas, whose pioneering work argued that since many cultural practices arise from the past and are modified within contemporary practices, a fuller understanding of any given cultural practice, such as the Potlatch of the West coast of Canada, must incorporate the history of the group and its practices. Before setting out into the field, ethnographers pour over any archival records that may exist which throw light on the culture they will be studying. James Axtel, author of *The Invasion Within* (1986), describes ethnohistory as "the use of historical and ethnological methods to gain knowledge of the nature and causes of change ... "

(1986, 3–4). Ethnohistory has been widely used in the United States in connection with land claims from Indigenous tribes. In ethnographic contexts, it is invaluable as a tool to supplement the knowledge and understanding of a group of people under study.

7.5   Ethnoarchaeology and Ethnography

Ethnoarchaeology is the use of anthropological data derived from living groups as an analogy for understanding people of the past. Archaeologists can then infer that ancient societies likely used the same techniques as their modern counterparts given a similar set of environmental circumstances. Inference in anthropology is a crucial issue; one that Allison Wiley (formerly UWO) called a "necessary evil." Much ethnoarchaeological research has been undertaken into, for example, the Wendat Indians in Canada by Elizabeth Tooker, Conrad Heidenreich, and Bruce Trigger. Such archival research has been invaluable to archaeological and ethnographic research into the Huron confederacy. In particular, the Jesuit documents of the seventeenth century have helped in the reconstructions and interpretations of this time period (Thwaites 1896). Researchers can thus familiarize themselves with the historical background of any culture or people that is being studied. Once fieldwork plans and maps, books, and other relevant data are collected, the researcher is ready to begin the ethnographic enterprise. The challenges of visas, financing, plans and what to study are just the beginning, as once in the field there will be other challenges to overcome. One such example is the difficult of maintaining objectivity, and of not "going native."

7.6   Maintaining Objectivity

One of the major challenges of working in the field is for an ethnographer to remain objective. He or she must not allow personal and cultural biases to get in the way of understanding and interpreting cultures and groups under study. In this regard, the older and offensive phrase – "going native"—is relevant. Going native and thus losing all sense of objectivity, crosses a red line in anthropology and has long had negative connotations within the ethnographic world. If an ethnographer remains aloof and set in their own cultural paths—what is known as being "culture-bound"—they may not be receptive to the nuances of the culture under study. On the other hand, if the anthropologist experiences what is now called "over-rapport," it is likewise seen as abandoning objectivity and thereby undermining the validity of their research. Awareness of the dangers of over-rapport has had an important impact on ethnography. Kenneth Good, an anthropologist who studied the Yanomami (also spelled Yąnomamö or Yanomama) in Venezuela during the 1970s, came close to this accusation of losing objectivity. Good was then a researcher from the University of Pennsylvania and a graduate student of Napoleon Chagnon (another famous ethnographer of the Yanomami). During the course of his fieldwork he was presented with a 9-year-old bride by the Yanomami and he accepted her in accordance with local customs. Apparently, they consummated the marriage when the girl was 14, as is the norm in Yanomami culture. The two lived together with the tribe, and had two sons and a daughter, all of whom grew up in the United States. This incident, while not alone among the annals of ethnographic research, was at the time seen as an ethnographer losing objectivity and it was heavily disapproved of by the academy. At what distance should the ethnographer remain from the people they are sharing daily life with? Understanding at what point the ethnographer has crossed the objectivity red line is not always easy. It remains a challenge to the successful completion of the ethnographic project. A further challenge to conducting research in the field is known as culture shock.

7.7 Culture Shock

Described as a characteristic of fieldwork, culture shock occurs when the ethnographer suffers a loss of familiar symbols and signs that he normally uses to negotiate his social reality. One's normal symbols—those social anchors—disappear, and one's cultural links are challenged. The result can be devastating, as a listless forlorn mood may descend upon the ethnographer and they can become literally culture-shocked. This shock manifests itself in forms of anxiety, and dependent upon the age, experience, and mental fortitude of the ethnographer, it can be fatal to the process of doing fieldwork. While anyone can suffer mild culture shock, an ethnographer is prone to a severe form of culture shock due to long-term immersion in the field. Culture shock can occur almost immediately or can take time. Often the longer one remains in the field, the more culture shock can accumulate. At a certain point the ethnographer will adapt and get over it or give up and return to the familiar surroundings of his or her own cultural setting. An example of an immediate sense of culture shock can be seen from the example of Napoleon Chagnon, who worked on and off for decades among the Yanomami, deep in the Amazon jungle. It is worth quoting at length from Chagnon's experience in 1964

> We had arrived at the village while the men were blowing a greenish powder, a hallucinogenic drug called ebene, up each other's noses [...] with such force that gobs of it spurt out of the opposite nostril of the person inhaling. One of the side effects of the hallucinogen is a profoundly runny nose, hacking and choking, and sometimes vomiting. The nasal mucus is always saturated with the green powder, and the men usually let it run freely from the nostrils. My next discovery was that there were a dozen or so vicious, underfed growling dogs snapping at my legs, circling me as if I were to be their next meal. I stood there holding my notebook, helpless and pathetic. Then the stench of the decaying vegetation, dog faeces, and garbage hit me and I almost got sick. I was shocked and horrified. What kind of welcome was this for the person who came here to live with you and learn your way of life, to become friends with you, to be adopted by you? (Chagnon 2013, 19–20)

Of course, as later recognized by Chagnon himself, the Yanomami were conducting a ceremony that was important to their spiritual and physical healing. Chagnon went on to produce his work *Yanomamö: The Fierce People* (1968), a book, much like its author, that was the subject of much controversy. The monograph itself, with its depiction of Yanomamö (once again offensively) as "noble savages," who could be very warlike (unlike Chagnon's culture?!), was to become a standard ethnographic text for students through the 1960s and beyond. During his time working in the Venezuelan–Brazilian forests Chagnon was attacked by warriors, anaconda snakes, and a jaguar. While not all fieldwork is as dangerous as this, many such events lead to culture shock setting in among ethnographers. The more mundane causes such as loneliness, anxiety, and feelings of isolation, are just as damaging to the practice of ethnography.

What is the impact of culture shock on ethnography? Some have suggested that over time culture shock may indeed have been necessary for the eventual production of ethnographic texts. It has been said that culture shock prepares one for the imaginative leap required to produce insights into a culture. Others disagree, stating that as culture shock sets in, and should it last, then the "production of ethnographic knowledge at this point is hazardous" (Irwin 2009).

Yanomamo snorting embele, a hallucinogenic drug used in ceremonies for spiritual healing.

7.8 Classic Ethnographies

7.8.1 Malinowski

One can gain a flavor of the diversity of the subject matter and the many different approaches undertaken by anthropologists by examining some of the classic yet sometimes controversial works in ethnography. Malinowski's work, *Argonauts of the Western Pacific* (1922) looms large in the canon of ethnographic literature. His work among the Trobriand Islanders laid the groundwork for how ethnography should be undertaken—by lengthy, immersive, participant-observation. The Trobriand Islands are an archipelago of coral atolls off the east coast of New Guinea. The Trobriands' society was matrilineal, the people ate their food alone individually, and they had what has been called "non-lineal codifications of reality" (Lee 1950, 89). This means that like some other groups—the Navajo for example—their construction of time, of cause and effect, differed remarkably from Western notions of the same. In the early twentieth century, this culture was living on dispersed islands thousands of miles from Europe, and therefore they were an attractive source of information for young Western ethnographers. Malinowski was forced to remain in Australia and its islands because he was considered an enemy citizen in World War I and forbidden to return to Europe. He therefore began his ethnographic career among these people. He originated the process of constructing a rigid, structured, and lengthy stay within a culture in order to produce more accurate ethnographic reports. He diligently recorded many of the Trobrianders' customs for the first time, and in fact, as Howell rightly notes (2018, 6), Malinowski's chapter on methodology became an essential work in British ethnography. He insisted upon the importance of long-term immersion in fieldwork and he also argued for the need for methodological clarity. This involves stating clearly for the reader how many and what type of communication his findings were based upon. According to him, the ethnographer should make clear how many women, elders, children, and so on, were interviewed and observed in their daily routines. He was thus among the first to include demographic and statistical information in his ethnography. Malinowski, who went on to become one of the dominant figures in Western anthropology during the first half of the twentieth century, demonstrated that by immersing oneself in a culture over the long term and following a rigid methodology of note-taking and interviews, a more thorough analysis of cultural practices might be obtained. Carefully observing the rituals of daily life among the Trobriand Islanders, he asked

> What is then this ethnographer's magic? By which he is able to invoke the real spirit of the natives, the true picture of tribal life? As usual, success can only be obtained by a patient and systematic application of a number of rules of common sense and well-known scientific principles, and not by the discovery of any marvellous short-cut leading to the desired results without effort or trouble (1922, 5).

Malinowski understood also that in order to produce a good ethnography one must amass sufficient data to base any findings or interpretations upon. Recognizing this, he stated: "I knew well that the best remedy for this was to collect concrete data, and accordingly I took a village census, wrote down genealogies, drew up plans and collected the terms of kinship" (1922, 5).

© Silent O/Shutterstock.com

Malinowski conducted his research on the Trobriand Islands. Shown here is one of the boats used for trading voyages.

Malinowski published his research in *Argonauts of the Western Pacific* (1922), which reveals his careful recording of the details of the Trobriand Islanders' daily life in his notebooks. He applied the theoretical framework of functionalism, wherein he argued that all aspects of culture served some key function in society. He also argued that the ethnographer should conduct research in a holistic fashion. This holistic approach meant that all facets of society—kinship, religion–spirituality, economics, gender, power, and so on be examined together. An organic analogy is often used to describe his functionalist approach: in the same way that lungs, heart, and blood vessels combine to stabilize the human body, so too did the various institutions of society such as kinship, spirituality, and economics function to maintain order and ensure continuity and stability in society. Malinowski changed the face of ethnographic research and is now usually recognized as the founding father of modern participant-observation. This reputation was gained due to his authoritative writing, his lengthy immersion within the culture studied, and his insistence that research methodology be included in the published monograph.

However, Malinowski was also a controversial figure. He attained almost cult-like status among an emergent cohort of young anthropologists, many of them his own students. Others in academia were not so impressed by him, objecting to his aloof style and rather imperious tone. Clyde Kluckhohn, an American anthropologist, once wrote that to some British and many American anthropologists he appeared as "a pretentious Messiah of the credulous" (1943). Nonetheless, there is broad agreement that Malinowski's approach to ethnography had a profound and positive impact on the emergence of ethnographic fieldwork, making it an essential tool of cultural anthropologists. His legacy was the intensive, lengthy immersion in the field, his data gathering tools, and his meticulous note-taking. Furthermore, his application of theory to the interpretation and publication of his data established a more rigorous approach, both in methodology and theory in ethnography, encouraging other early twentieth century Western ethnographers to remain in the field for longer periods and to apply a theoretical framework to their research.

As we will see in more detail in the following, some ethnographers attempted structural functionalist analysis, examining whole kinship systems, such as Radcliffe-Brown's research on African and Australian kinship systems. Elsewhere Evans-Pritchard grappled with the relevancy and interpretive problems associated with the "poison chicken oracle" of the Azande (Evans-Pritchard 1937). Others attempted a more humanistic approach, stressing the emotional and historical elements of given cultural practices, such as Boas undertook among the Kwakiutl in British Columbia. Whatever the particular theoretical approach of the anthropologist as ethnographer, all sought to add to the knowledge of humanity in its diversity. They all also sought regularities, sometimes generalizations that could be applied to understanding humanity as a whole. The accumulation of ethnographic knowledge became the aim of anthropology, whose researchers had spread far and wide to gather firsthand knowledge of the world's cultures. The data they collected was then poured over, interpreted and reinterpreted, critiqued, and finessed until some form of authoritative view emerged. Within anthropology this gives rise to much cross-cultural comparison, that is, the comparative study of ethnographic data, of society, and of culture. As ever, the analysis of different cultures around the word threw up problems and issues that ethnographers had to grapple with. Such is the case with the use of magic and witchcraft among the Azande peoples of Africa.

7.9   Estyn Evans-Pritchard and the Chicken Oracle

> In writing about the beliefs of primitive peoples does it matter one way or the other whether one accords them validity or regards them as fallacious? Take witchcraft again. Does it make any difference whether one believes in it or not? Or can one just describe how a people who believe in it, think and act about it, and how the belief affects relations between persons? (Evans-Pritchard 1976, 244)

The list of classic ethnographic works would not be complete without mentioning Evans-Pritchard, the English social anthropologist who researched the Azande in the late 1920s. Evans-Pritchard also wrote three books on the Nuer people, a pastoralist group in eastern Africa. It was his initial work among the Azande that resulted in his doctorate and which became a classic reading in ethnography through the subsequent decades. In this work, *Witchcraft Oracles and Magic Among the Azande* (1937), he undertook a form of relativism in approaching the beliefs and practices surrounding witchcraft among the Azande. One of the more provocative of his writings was on the poison chicken oracle, a matter of importance that went beyond this particular issue. What is vital regarding this work is that it directly confronts an issue that has been a key challenge of many an ethnographic undertaking—to what degree can one accept the beliefs of a different social system? To what degree can one remain objective in the face of practices that are directly rejected and critiqued by one's own culture? The matter of interpreting witchcraft, magic, sorcery, and a host of other practices that are foreign to the ethnographer has a great bearing on ethnography, for if the ethnographer is to understand the culture and its practices as much as possible, then some sort of empathy or a willingness to entertain these new and alternative beliefs is needed. For Evans-Pritchard, trained in the Western cannons of the social sciences, coming face-to-face with the chicken oracle was a test of his ability to remain objective and nonjudgmental. Most of his contemporaries and even most modern ethnographers argue that he was very successful in this challenge. His ethnography is a masterful work and one of the most thorough attempts of his generation at coming to grips with such practices and translating them for a mostly Western audience of anthropologists.

The Azande are an agricultural group living primarily in the northeastern part of the Democratic Republic of the Congo, in south central and southwestern part of South Sudan, and in southeastern Central African Republic. By way of brief description, the poison chicken oracle as practiced by them is undertaken in order to divine the presence of witchcraft. To do this, the Azande witchdoctor uses termite sticks, rubbing boards, but most of all the poison oracle. Benge, as the Azande call this poison oracle, sought to determine the causes of various misfortunes. In the belief that evil enchantments had been placed upon someone (making them ill, for example) or upon something (diseased crops for example), tribe members would bring a case to the witchdoctor. The sort of challenges that the benge is called upon to investigate are numerous. To the Azande, ordinary ailments or events could be explained by an enchantment or an act of witchcraft being directed by someone. These enchantments were gender specific: women could only bewitch other women and men bewitch other men. The stages of the poison oracle are that the witchdoctor and interested parties go out into the bush, away from others and away from enchantments. The chickens, usually neither too young nor too old, are fed an amount of poison at the discretion of the witchdoctor. Some chickens may die instantly, many after a while, and some not at all. Once the poison is administered to the chicken, the accusation and the name of the accused are called out. If the chicken dies, guilt is established, and witchcraft has been present. Importantly, however, the Azande believed that people might be witches without knowing it. Witchcraft was seen as a substance residing in the stomach and inherited from parents, mother to daughter and father to son. The substance could remain dormant, meaning a Zande might not know that he or she was a witch at the time. When the oracle was pronounced, and once they learned they were a witch, they would stop their "bad thoughts" and cease unknowingly placing others under an enchantment.

What is essential to know is that the benge and other divination methods were part of the Azande legal system, therefore what the oracle revealed is the guilt or innocence of the accused. Thus, the oracle played an important role in regulating Azande society. Evans-Pritchard went so far as to say that "there is no niche or corner of Zande culture into which it does not twist itself." Much of what Evans-Pritchard learned of the use of witchcraft had to be observed, even coaxed from the people he lived among. In fact, although the use of the oracle and witchcraft in general were profuse, he noted that much of this was just taken for granted, and that the Azande spoke of it a lot less that any other matter. It was just there, a part of their background reality. Debunking the notion of some form of separate Azande logic, he concluded that the Azande belief system, rooted in witchcraft, oracles, and magic, was quite rational in the sense of well adapted to their physical and social contexts, despite prevailing Western opinion at the time.

Only through the daily observation of Azande behavior could Evans-Pritchard understand the importance and intricacies of Azande belief in witchcraft. He understood that when it came to causation the Azande fully accepted that people were killed or hurt, for example, because a granary collapsed on them. Termites ate the support beams and the structure collapsed, killing or injuring those resting in the shade below. Despite this recognition of causation, these particular people were killed because of witchcraft. They happened to be at that particular spot at that particular time due to the presence of witchcraft. Likewise, if a woman was bitten by a snake on the way through the bush the physical cause of her death was the venom of the snakebite. Yet witchcraft was ultimately to blame because she chose—under an enchantment—that particular pathway at that particular time of day when that particular snake was passing. That we know in quite significant detail this fascinating aspect of Azande life broadens our understanding of human lifeways. Our knowledge of these people, the Azande, adds to the storehouse of human cultural creativity and the fascinating ways in which people deal with and create a social reality.

7.10   Franz Boas

The German American scholar Franz Boas studied the Kwakiutl (Kwakwaka'wakw) people of Western Canada for more than 40 years. His teaching career spanned five decades, and the longevity of this long tenure at Columbia University meant that he would be highly influential on generations of anthropologists to come. His theories of historical particularism and cultural relativism had a profound impact on many fields of anthropology. Historical particularism argues that each society has its own unique historical development and must be understood based on its own specific cultural context (Boas 1967). Closely linked is the concept of cultural relativism, which states that anthropologists should have the ability to view the beliefs and customs of other peoples within the context of that culture rather than their own. Conceptions of truth and moral values are not absolute but are relative to the persons or groups holding them. This encouraged many young ethnographers to throw off the shackles of tradition and interpret Indigenous practices on their own terms, not with reference to some overarching theoretical scheme or evolutionary system, and not based against their own culture. Native people's practices were understood for how they operated within their own communities and within their own logic.

Maps and mapping have been central to ethnographic research for centuries.

Franz Boas, the German American anthropologists worked in Canada for decades among West Coast Indigenous peoples.

Franz Boas worked among the Kwakiutl (Kwakwaka'wakw) First Nation for decades. He held an abiding interest in their art. Shown here are Kwakwaka'wakw Feast Dishes and Bentwood Chests. Photo: L. Kilmurray (2010).

Boas was a pioneer in visual anthropology. He was fascinated by Native artwork, particularly costumes used in ceremonies, and also had an abiding interest in totem poles. He took some of the earliest and finest photographs of Kwakiutl regalia and architecture, and in fact he pioneered the filming of these and other West Coast peoples. Boas is attributed with the solidity of the "four-field" approach, and with it being adopted in the United States. He argued that all fields of anthropology (biological, archaeological, linguistic, and cultural) should be taught and practiced. His work still resonates today, not least within the field of ethnography (Stocking 1992; Boas 1967).

7.11   Clifford Geertz and Thick Description

An intriguing approach to an ethnographic study was undertaken by Clifford Geertz among the people of a Balinese village in Indonesia (1973). Professor of social science at the Institute for Advanced Study in Princeton from 1970 to 2000, Geertz was instrumental in the development of what became known as interpretive anthropology or symbolic, anthropology. This was a reaction to the long-established stance of objectivity in ethnography. The epistemology of interpretive anthropology saw culture as a series of texts to be read and these could be described employing the writing methodology of "thick description" (Neni Panourgiá 2016). An ethnographic thick description is also reflexive—it includes subjective explanations and meanings provided by the people who are themselves being studied. Geertz took the term thick description from Gilbert Ryle (2009[1968]).

> Geertz holds that anthropology's task is that of explaining cultures through thick description which specifies many details, conceptual structures and meanings, and which is opposed to "thin description" which is a factual account without any interpretation. Thin description for Geertz is not only an insufficient account of an aspect of a culture; it is also a misleading one. According to Geertz an ethnographer must present a thick description which is composed not only of facts but also of commentary, interpretation and interpretations of those comments and interpretations. His task is to extract meaning structures that make up a culture, and for this Geertz believes that a factual account will not suffice for these meaning structures are complexly layered one on top and into each other so that each fact might be subjected to intercrossing interpretations which ethnography should study (Cultural Reader 2012).

Geertz undertook his fieldwork in Morocco, Africa, and in Bali on the Indonesian island of Java. At that time there was much debate within anthropology regarding the most productive methodology for conducting field research. Theoretical approaches were under scrutiny, ethnographers vied for both attention and anthropological relevance as they sought to describe the special realities of different cultures and interpret them in often unique ways. Geertz argued that "[m]an is an animal suspended in webs of significance that he himself has spun" (Geertz 1973, 5) signaling his concern with meaning over structure. To untangle or get inside the "webs of significance," Geertz used thick description. In anthropology thick description starts with scientific observation of human behavior, yet it interprets not just the behavior, but also its context. One particular example from Geertz's work may shed light on what he meant by this thick description—the Balinese cock fight. In front of the male spectators two roosters are set upon each other inside a pen or courtyard. A six-inch spur called a *tadji* is attached to one leg of each rooster. The fight ends when this spur cuts deep into the loser, and he becomes the main course for dinner—usually eaten by the winning cock's owner. The Balinese cockfight was interpreted by Geertz as a symbolic microcosm of Balinese society, wherein social status, prestige, and hierarchy were all on display as men "fight with their cocks" (Geertz 1972). What Geertz discerned in the cockfight was the symbolic representation of something very real in Balinese social life. The fight channeled aggression and rivalry into a symbolic sphere of engagement (Cultural Reader 2012). The fight both represented and took part in forming the social and cultural structures of the Balinese people, which were dramatized through the cockfight. Geertz opined that rituals such as the Balinese cockfight are a type of text which can be read. It is a society's manner of speaking to itself about itself—and is therefore of prime interest to the anthropologist. Geertz's ethnography sought to translate the social importance of this ritual—whose performative force was fundamental to power relations in the community. His thick description sought to convey the importance of the cockfight. Its attendant symbolic aspects such as seating order, body language, stances, and other elements had to be performed to have public force (Erikson and Murphy 2017, 132). In another analysis Geertz chose a singular act—that of winking, in order to elaborate on his thick description approach.

7.12 Winking

Geertz attempted to elaborate on the nuances and intricacies of human behavior that an ethnographer practicing thick description might analyze. He also discussed actions that were not as public as a ritual or ceremony, but smaller events such as a wink (Geertz 1973). Geertz took his cue from the work of the English philosopher Gilbert Ryle, whose article *The Thinking of Thoughts: What is "Le Penseur" Doing?* (1968) analyzed the myriad meanings associated with systematically misleading expressions. When is a wink not a wink, but a twitch, or a conspiratorial action, asks Ryle? Observing, for example, the closing of eyelids from a thin descriptive view would see this action as a twitch, or a mere wink. But as Geertz stresses, from the ethnographic point of view, the context and inner cultural meanings associated with the "wink" must be understood. The wink could be a false wink, disguised as a twitch, or a twitch signaling a wink, and so on. The point was that the winker is communicating according to a "socially established code." In the same way that one can observe the social power strategies at play in the cockfights, this code must be understood to perform thick description.

> If ethnography is thick description and ethnographers those who are doing the describing, then the determining question for any given example of it, whether a field journal squib or a Malinowski-sized monograph, is whether it sorts winks from twitches and real winks from mimicked ones. It is not against a body of uninterpreted data, radically thinned descriptions, that we must measure the cogency of our explications, but against the power of the scientific imagination to bring us into touch with the lives of strangers (Geertz 1973, 317).

Thick description as an ethnographic method had a mixed reception within anthropological studies as a whole. Some lauded the novel insights that this approach offered, while others worried that it was so subjective as to be hard to replicate and opened up ethnography to the myriad ways in which a person perceived a wink, that is if the wink was noticed at all. Abbot (2004) pointed out that much of the approach of thick description was in fact already in use in literary criticism. Carneiro (1995) thought that Geertz's thick description as well as his methods of interpretive anthropology lacked the scientific structure that is requisite for quality ethnography. Others pointed to the fact that thick description and the textual analogy do not produce any overarching theory. Whether one agreed or disagreed with his approach, it remains a watershed in ethnography.

To use Geertz's own words, what we observe in small actions such as winking are a "speck of behavior, a fleck of culture." But Geertz did expand to some degree the awareness within ethnographic studies of the different approaches that one might take and the minutiae of cultural actions that are of social importance.

7.13 Problems with Ethnography

Once the touchstone of cultural anthropology, ethnography has fallen on somewhat harder times in the past few decades. What one might call classic ethnography, that is, fieldwork among distant cultural settings conducted by people from the First World, has been heavily criticized and "deconstructed" from a number of sources (Austin-Broos 1998). Much of the criticism is indeed merited; it is not hard to find the old colonial and imperial, often racist and sexist, attitudes held by many anthropological practitioners in many of the classic works. However, the same can be said of many other social sciences. Perhaps the most important critique of ethnographic studies stems from the postcolonial and postmodern perspectives. Here, we will address some of the major problems that have been found in ethnographic inquiry, ranging from bias, misrepresentation, racism, and, even the *raison d'être* for undertaking ethnographic research.

7.14 The Postmodern Critique

Beginning in the 1980s anthropology underwent a period of profound reexamination, and ethnography was not immune from this. Many classic works were reevaluated and criticized for a variety of perceived faults. Certain ethnographic works were seen as colonialist apologies. Some ethnographies of the 1970s and 1980s were critiqued for their *lack* of a postmodern approach, when in fact no real genre of postmodernism existed at the time of the fieldwork in question. Other ethnographic publications were attacked for not portraying the peoples they studied accurately or indeed fairly. Many anthropologists did recognize that they could not ever really describe with any degree of accuracy what it means to be an Ilongot, or an Azande. However, they understood this and accepted that the vision and version of the peoples under study presented within ethnographic publications were just that, a vision and a version, an outsider's view. Perhaps that is what is sought by some: an understanding not *from* the Azande but an understanding of an outsider's views *of* the Azande. What happens in much of the postmodern critique is that we learn much about the errors of the individual original anthropologists, and about the theoretical bent of the anthropologists making the critique. Yet, we tend to lose sight of the peoples under study. This happens in other fields, such as in archaeology, where conferences, books, and debates pour over the symbolic attributes that *may* be discernible or not from a given archaeological site. But eventually, amidst all the clamor and reevaluations and accusations, we tend to lose focus on the material culture and the original archaeological site. Much of the postmodern critique was indeed productive, and accepted within the field as long overdue. Yet, in describing a cultural field from the insider–outsider perspective, there will always be areas of hazy understanding, partially viewed realities and even errors. Ethnography does not claim to be a perfect translation of a cultural field; rather it is a representation of what the ethnographer or team understand of this cultural field. Of course, the ethnographer must seek to be in tune with social realities, to treat the point of view of the peoples studied with respect and be aware of biases and assumptions they bring to their work. However, some postmodern critiques claim that ethnography itself is politically incorrect and that having moved on from the imperialist days of anthropology we have substituted the exotic colonized "other" with the "suffering other" (Robbins 2012). These are the downtrodden, migrant, starving, or to use Fallon's phrase the "wretched of the earth." This is an area worthy of future consideration, but it should not stymie ethnographic research entirely. As Robbins suggests, anthropologists are "capable of recovering some of the critical force of an earlier anthropology without taking on its weaknesses" (2013, 447, cf. Howell 2018).

7.15   Colonialism

When we speak of a culture-historical period, or a "turn" toward reflexivity or a "feminist era" in ethnography, we should note that there always existed earlier works taking these approaches. These defined periods in theoretical schools are so defined because they are repeated, echoed, and expressed as a *genre*. Yet there always existed early risers, anthropologists who sounded the alarm on colonialism or sexism much earlier that the recognized era of postcolonialism or feminism in ethnographic studies. However, the 1980s and the 1990s witnessed a sustained critique of some of the prior practices of ethnographers.

Criticism in recent years (argues that ethnography grew out of a "master discourse of colonization" (Robin 2003). This is a critique echoed by Marcus and Fisher in their excellent analysis of ethnographic writing (1986). In it they rightly point out that many earlier ethnographic accounts were replete with imperialist and racist undertones or took an analytical approach that paid little if any attention to differences in gender, for example, within the communities being studied. Malinowski has been criticized for negating the role of women in his work on the Trobriand Islanders. Whereas he urged ethnographers to grasp the Trobriand point of view, this view was often just the male view. Our task, he claimed, was to "to grasp the native's point of view, *his* relations to life, to realize *his* vision of *his* world" (Malinowski 1922, 25, cf. Howell 2018, 6). Annette Weiner attempted to "unmask the myth" of male dominance in the Trobriand Islanders that shines through Malinowski's work. In her reethnography of the Trobriand Islanders from a feminist perspective, she highlighted many areas where women held power, arguing that previous ethnographic accounts were gender-bound and missed the important roles women play in the Trobriand Islands (Weiner 1976).

Certainly, as in other fields of anthropology, ethnography contains many past failings. Reevaluations were needed, recalculating what was missed is important, and correction of any fallacious analysis or data certainly needed. However, one might be as revisionist as possible and still appreciate the early work that was done. This is not in any way an excuse for those ethnographies that misrepresented peoples or that contained dismissive or derisive accounts of other groups. It is a recognition of the times, the period in which some of these works were undertaken. It is quite easy now to point out that Evans-Pritchard, for example, was very cozy with colonial authorities in his studying of the Azande people. It is easy to judge with hindsight that Malinowski did not appreciate the diversity of gender roles and women's work among the Trobriand Islanders, or that Geertz made sweeping structural statements based on one ritual. Many ethnographic works are just victims of their own times. That the origin of many ethnographies undertaken in Africa, for example, were located squarely in the colonial world is an unfortunate aspect of the past. As Harrison states, anthropologists are "well aware of these origins and, as a foundation of contemporary disciplinary training, debate the extent to which past ethnographers were willingly and/or unwillingly complicit in furthering these efforts" (Harrison 2018, 30). The postcolonial critique is one that anthropology, and specifically ethnography simply had to go through. It has resulted in a reappraisal of some of the classic works, and some of the former tenets of ethnographic research. Ethnography can emerge stronger and more relevant from this critique. Newer approaches to fieldwork incorporate the voices of the other collaborative projects are becoming the norm, as ethnographers work *with* the communities more than they had in the past. There are other issues that have troubled ethnography, and in fact are still pertinent today. One such issue is what ethnographers term "contamination".

7.16 Contamination

Contamination was a potent challenge to ethnographers at a time when there still existed many cultures that had not had much if any contact with the outside word, particularly the world that anthropologists came from. An example of contamination is seen in the case of the Yir-Yoront, an Aboriginal people inhabiting the Cape York Peninsula in Far North Queensland, Australia. The Yir-Yoront subsisted by hunting, fishing, and gathering shellfish and plant foods. Their technology was what anthropologists termed Stone Age, meaning they did not use metals and employed stone or wooden tools for most tasks. First visited by Europeans in the early nineteenth century, the Yir-Yoront were given steel axes as gifts from the initial European missionaries. As the missionaries returned, many more steel axes were handed out. These axes were preferred over stone axes due to their technological advantages in cutting down trees and performing other tasks. However, the stone axes, which had been used from time immemorial, were in fact woven into the cultural structures of Yir-Yoront society. Certain lineages quarried the stone, others performed ritual rites associated with making the stone axes, others transported it, and women were forbidden to use stone axes. This all changed with the introduction of numerous steel axes through missionaries and traders. The result was a classic example of cultural contamination of some aspects of Yir-Yoront society. As Sharp puts it

> The most disturbing effects of the steel axe, operating in conjunction with other elements also being introduced [...] developed in the realm of traditional ideas, sentiments, and values. These were undermined at a rapidly mounting rate, with no new conceptions defined to replace them. The result was the erection of a mental and moral void which foreshadowed the collapse and destruction of all Yir Yoront culture, if not, indeed, the extinction of the biological group itself. (Sharp 1952, 71).

There are other examples from the ethnographic record of outsiders introducing items that "contaminated" in the anthropological sense, various communities. Contamination can result from the introduction of firearms, diseases, alcohol, and other deleterious aspects of outsiders' societies. This happens much more rarely today, as modern teams of ethnographers are more aware of these issues, or communities have already adapted to the introduction of newer technologies in this much more connected world. As modern ethnography redresses some of the failings of the past, it should not lose confidence in its importance to understanding ourselves and others. There is still much to be understood about the world and the peoples who reside in it. There is still much more to be learned, and with the advent of the internet revolution and the shrinking of the world, there is more and more data to be analyzed by the ethnographer.

7.17   The Internet and Ethnographic Research

The World Wide Web has spawned much research in anthropology, some confusion, some despair, and an explosion of unfinished and fragmented works. Anthropological theory was slow to engage with the Internet as a whole, perhaps because much of the "virtual" research was ongoing, prone to change due to rapid, daily updates, and came from a bewildering variety of sources and places. Despite the challenges that the digital revolution has posed for anthropologists, it is, as Hallett and Barber argue, "no longer imaginable to conduct ethnography without considering online spaces" (Hallett & Barber 2013, 307). They suggest that the online world should be seen as another "level" or "site" where participants live. This is challenging for the old school, face-to-face ethnographers, who are urged to become cyber-ethnographers, and to design studies that examine blogs, chat rooms, and a host of other online interactions (Hallett & Barber 2013, 308). However, this emerging digital culture is a "tension that anthropologists have little choice but to navigate" (Erikson and Murphy 2016, 192). More and more applications to undertake ethnographic research into "virtual worlds" are made in anthropology each year. But, as Michael Fisch notes: "resistance within anthropology to the idea of virtual worlds as legitimate objects of ethnographic inquiry has made it difficult to support such projects without some reservation" (Fisch 2013, 599). Perhaps it is too early to tell whether ethnography can successfully navigate the online world. It has opened up a vast new horizon for ethnographic research, but one that will have to be firmly structured to ethnographic needs and skills for it to be productive (Boellstorff et al. 2012). It does bring ethnography to a wider audience, one that can promise an exciting future for ethnography.

7.18   Conclusion: The Future of Ethnography

What is in store for the future of ethnography? Newer approaches include the emergence of multisite fieldwork, where more than one location, village or cultural field are visited by either the same ethnographer or members of a team. This form of ethnographic research can be valuable in that it allows for more than one setting to be analyzed. It can enable research into diasporas, or it can allow the tracing and analysis of a certain cultural practice over wider areas. Multitemporal ethnography is also an increasing practice witnessed in anthropology. In this form of ethnography, participant-observation is practiced on a site over the long term (Howell and Talle 2012). The researchers will return over what may amount to years to follow-up on prior research, to analyze changes that may have occurred, and to review and compare differences witnessed in different practices. This is a form of diachronic research that can indeed be very productive (Marcus 1995).

> Although multi-sited ethnography may not necessarily forsake the perspective of the subaltern, it is bound to shift the focus of attention to other domains of cultural production and ultimately to challenge this frequently privileged positioning of ethnographic perspective (Marcus 1995, 101).

"The world has changed, Bilbo Baggins". The elvish queen certainly states it correctly: the world as we knew it has indeed changed. Since the 1990s and with the gathering speed of globalization the world is now much more connected. Most villages and communities are no longer as isolated. As distant from large population or commercial centers or difficult to physically access through modern travel as they may be, they have their own Facebook pages, Wikipedia entries, and real-time skyping capabilities. What does this all mean for ethnographic research? In 1995, the renowned sociologist Anthony Giddens spoke of the "evaporating subject matter" of anthropology (Fardon et al. 2012, xxix). Was this prescient, pessimistic, or mistaken? Marcus (1995, 101) spoke of the "loss of the subaltern," referring to the fact that modern ethnography must tackle newer, less isolated, and less "primitive" peoples. This coincides with the advent of multisited ethnography, which, combined with the opening up of "virtual worlds," promises to shake ethnography from its historical lethargy and enter modernity poised to study not just the other, those subalterns, or the "suffering other," or the isolated "tribe," but to engage in the modern world and the demands it places on this new ethnography. However, while globalization and instant communication adds immeasurably to the data available, increasing the opportunities for collaboration and for the democratizing of anthropology, the sheer amount and speed of information now available does not produce deep cultural understandings. For this ethnography is still required, perhaps even more so given the scale of new data and the speed of interactions. There is a need for contextualization, comparison, analysis, and categorization. Ethnography helped create anthropology as a coherent social science. Despite the oft-repeated claim that ethnography has had its day, it remains an essential aspect of cultural anthropology, still a "rite of passage" for many budding anthropologists. In fact, many have come to regard ethnography as a fifth, separate field of the anthropological program. Allied with archaeology, linguistics, biological anthropology, and cultural anthropology, ethnography completes the holistic approach that is the signature of anthropology. It continues to thrive, having reexamined its own past failings and having undergone sometimes torturous self-examination and theoretical debate, it has persisted. While ethnography may never again encounter undiscovered cultures or isolated communities, it is still very relevant in today's world. Ethnography remains anthropology's unique portal into diverse societies and changing cultures. It will adapt, just like culture. It will endeavor to still get inside the point of view of the "other" and contribute to human knowledge, helping us to understand ourselves and each other.

Further Reading

Abbot, A. 2004. *Methods of Discovery*. New York: Norton.

Abu-Lughod, Lila. 2000. "Locating Ethnography." *Ethnography* 1, no. 2: 261–67.

Austin-Broos, Diane J. December 1, 1998. "Falling Through the 'Savage Slot': Postcolonial Critique and the Ethnographic Task." *The Australian Journal of Anthropology* 9, no. 3: 295–309.

Boas, Franz. 1967. *Kwakiutl Ethnography*. Chicago: University of Chicago Press.

Boellstorff, Tom, Bonnie Nardi, Celia Pearce, and T. L. Taylor, eds.). 2012. *Ethnography and Virtual Worlds: A Handbook of Methods*. Princeton: University Press.

Carneiro, Robert. 1995. *Godzilla Meets New Age Anthropology: Facing the Post-Modernist Challenge to a Science of Culture*. Cagliari: Edizioni M & T.

Cultural Reader. 2012. *Article Summaries and Reviews in Cultural Studies*. Accessed June 12, 2019., http://culturalstudiesnow.blogspot.com/2012/05/clifford-geertzs-thick-description.html

E.E. Evans-Pritchard 1976. *Witchcraft Oracles, and Magic Among the Azande*. Oxford: Oxford University Press.

Erikson, Paul A., and Liam D. Murphy. 2017. *A History of Anthropological Theory*. Toronto: University of Toronto Press.

Evans-Pritchard, E. E. 1937. *Witchcraft Oracles, and Magic Among the Azande*. Oxford: Clarendon Press.

Fardon, Richard, Oliva Harris, Trevor Marchand, Cris Shore, Veronica Strang, Richard Wilson, and Mark Nuttall, eds. 2012. *The SAGE Handbook of Social Anthropology*. Los Angeles: Sage.

Fisch, Michael. 2013. "Review of *Ethnography and Virtual Worlds: A Handbook of Method*". Boellstorff, Tom, Nardi, Bonnie, Pearce, Celia, and Taylor, T. L. (eds.). Princeton: Princeton University Press, 2012. *American Ethnologist* 40, no. 3: 599–600.

Geertz, Clifford. Winter, 1972. "Deep Play: Notes on the Balinese Cockfight." Daedalus 101, no. 1. "Myth, Symbol, and Culture": 1–37. Published by: The MIT Press on behalf of American Academy of Arts & Sciences.

Geertz, 1973. "Thick Description: Toward an Interpretive Theory of Culture." In *The Interpretation of Cultures: Selected Essays*. New York: Basic Books.

Guest, Kenneth J. 2018. *Essentials of Cultural* Anthropology. New York: W. W. Norton & Company.

Hallett, Ronald E., and Kristen Barber. 2013. "Ethnographic Research in a Cyber Era." *Journal of Contemporary Ethnography* 43, no. 3: 306–330.

Harrison, Anthony Kwame. 2018. *Ethnography*. Oxford: Oxford University Press.

Howell, Signe. 2018. *The Cambridge Encyclopedia of Anthropology*. Accessed June 1, 2019. https://www.anthroencyclopedia.com/entry/ethnography#h2ref-6

Howell, Signe and A. Talle, eds. 2012. *Returns to the Field: Multitemporal Research and Contemporary Anthropology*. Bloomington: Indiana University Press.

Irwin, Rachel. 2009. "Culture Shock: Negotiating Feelings in the Field." *Anthropology Matters* 7, no. 1: 13–26.

Lee, Dorothy. March–April 1950. "Lineal and Nonlineal Codifications of Reality." *Psychosomatic Medicine*.

Malinowski, Bronislaw. 1922. *Argonauts of the Western Pacific*. London: G. Routledge & Sons.

Marcus, George E. 1995. "Ethnography in/of the World System: The Emergence of Multi-Sited Ethnography." *Annual Review of Anthropology* 24: 95–117.

Marcus, George E., and Michael M. J. Fisher. 1986. *Anthropology as Cultural Critique: An Experimental Moment in the Human Sciences*. Chicago: University of Chicago Press.

Morgan, Lewis Henry. 1871. *Systems of Consanguinity and Affinity of the Human Family*. Washington: Smithsonian Institution.

Napolean A. Chagnon 2013. *Noble Savages. Toronto: Simon and Schuster.*

Panourgiá, Neni. 2016. *Interpretive Anthropology*. Oxford Bibliographies. Accessed May 15, 2019. http://www.oxford bibliographies.com/view/document/obo-9780199766567/obo-9780199766567-0048.xml.

Robbins, Joel. 2012. "Beyond the Suffering Subject: Toward an Anthropology of the Good." *Journal of the Royal Anthropological Institute (N.S.)* 19: 447–62.

Robin, Patric Clair. 2003. *Expressions of Ethnography: Novel Approaches to Qualitative Methods*. Albany: State university of New York Press.

Ryle, Gilbert. 2009 [1968]. "The Thinking of Thoughts: What is 'Le Penseur' Doing?" In *Collected Essays 1929–1968: Collected Papers, Volume 2*, 494–510. London: Routledge.

Sharp, Lauriston. Summer, 1952. "Steel Axes for Stone-Age Australians." *Human Organization* 11, no. 2: 17–22.

Stocking George, W., Jr. 1992. *The Ethnographer's Magic and Other Essays in the History of Anthropology*. Wisconsin: Wisconsin University Press.

Thwaites, Reuben Gold. 1896. *The Jesuit Relations and Allied Documents: Travels and Explorations of the Jesuit Missionaries in New France, 1610–1791*. Cleveland: The Burrows Brothers Company M DCCCXCVIII.

Weiner, Annette B. 1976. *Women of Value, Men of Renown: New Perspectives in Trobriand Exchange*. Austin: University of Texas Press.

Whyte, William F. 1943. *Street Corner Society: The Social Structure of an Italian Slum*. Chicago: University of Chicago Press.

Chapter 8
Subsistence Systems and Material Culture

Paul V. McDowell

Outline

8.1   Making a Living Cross-Culturally: An Introduction

In this chapter we examine subsistence, or food-getting systems, and the role they play in forming and structuring cultures.

Because our cells do not contain chlorophyll, we, as members of the animal kingdom, cannot produce food with photosynthesis; plants with this capacity do this. Like other species, we ultimately rely on plant foods, even though we also depend on other animals for subsistence. The pork bellies futures are safe on Wall Street.

Why are many anthropologists so oriented toward subsistence techniques of various sorts? The tradition of **cultural materialism** takes the view that cultures are what its members eat—or at least work for. This is the notion that focuses primarily on technoenvironmental and economic factors that constrain culture, and the primary sector involves the transfer of energy by technological means from the environment to members of a culture. This orientation reflects an academic Marxist tradition, and indeed might represent what C. Wright Mills called vulgar Marxism (1962).

The basic model entails a technoenvironmental base, combining an environmental base—grasslands, northern forest, desert, tropical rain forest—with the tools that a human population has at its disposal. In grasslands, for example, a society with a gasoline-driven tractor and plow has an advantage over one with a horse and plow—so long as the oil doesn't run out. In turn, the society with a horse and plow enjoys an advantage over one with nothing but a hoe or digging stick in the same grassland environment; in fact, the hoe-bearing farmer cannot penetrate the sod at all. Then there are the herders, with another adaptive advantage; with cattle or sheep, who needs plows or tractors?

Then who does the work? Who assigns the tasks? Who owns the property on which the cattle graze or the crops are grown? Who owns the cattle and the crops? How are the workers compensated for their labor? In short, how is the **economy** organized?

Like other species, our forebears were **foragers**, or **hunters and gatherers**, or, to use a term used by some, **food collectors**. Whatever term is used, they relied strictly on what nature could yield; a few populations in the world may still be foraging, and others, such as !Kung or Eskimo (Inuit) did so until recently.

© franco lucato/Shutterstock.com

Groups such as the San people of Botswana still practice hunting and gathering.

The constraints of foraging were evident: Laws of nature governed human populations as it governed nonhuman populations; population had to be within carrying capacity of environment, for example, or some members would die out.

Some human measure of control over the food supply came with the domestication of animals and plants, probably about 9,000 to 11,000 years ago. Even then, domestication did not free our forebears from ecological forces, nor (even with industrial agriculture providing almost all our food) is this the case today. Indeed, we may be running out of oil needed to do the job.

This is where cultural materialism makes its strongest case: the genre of anthropological thought that links cultures to their respective subsistence systems. To survive, every culture must adapt to its physical environment through the use of whatever food-getting or food-producing technology is at its disposal.

Therefore, this chapter first examines five main types of subsistence systems:

1. **foraging** (hunting and gathering, food collection, and in some instances fishing);

2. **horticulture**, or hoe cultivation, some of which involves **slash-and-burn**, or swidden cultivation;

3. **pastoralism**, or herding of animals of various sizes from goats and sheep to cattle and horses;

4. **equestrian hunting**, which, although it involves hunting, involves the use of a domesticated animal (horse or reindeer) to hunt other animals; and

5. **intensive agriculture**, which involves the use of the plow or other means of making high agricultural yields, some using fossil fuels.

8.2   Foraging or Hunting and Gathering

Often known as **hunting and gathering**, the term **foraging** refers to the hunting of animals (including fish) and the gathering of vegetation (including nuts, fruits, edible leaves, roots, tubers, and everything else borne by plants). As omnivores, we rely on both animals and plants. We make and use tools—spears and arrows to hunt animals, baskets and digging sticks to gather plant foods—to forage. With minor exceptions, tool manufacturing and use separates us from other animal species.

Once upon a time, our ancestors were all foragers. Until the Mesolithic period, they practiced **simple foraging**, which involved all the attributes that will take up most of this section; low yield technology, nomadism, reliance on sharing. Then, in a few areas of the world, some of our ancestors took on **complex foraging**. Here, the people could rely on large animals to feast on, or could rely on several sources of food at one place; at that point, they abandoned nomadism and could develop fairly complex societies. The only contemporary example we have of this are the Indians of the Northwest Coast, who relied on rich salmon runs and abundant game in the forests, and other cultures, such as the simple chiefdoms of the Chumash along the Santa Barbara Channel (Feder 2004; Fagen 2004).

8.2.1   Simple Foraging

The foragers of today—or more accurately, of the recent past—have several common attributes. First, they are found in **marginal environments**, those unsuited for most forms of intensive cultivation (cattle ranching may be a relatively recent exception). The environments include deserts like the Kalahari of southern Africa and most of the interior in Australia; tropical rain forests in inaccessible places, such as central Congo, the outliers of the Thai and Malay Peninsulas, and parts of Amazonia in South America; and the arctic regions of Canada, Alaska, Greenland, and northern Russia. The deserts are too dry for intensive cultivation, the tropical rain forests too moist, and the arctic too cold (Scupin 2003).

Foraging strategies are clearly environment-specific. Desert and rainforest peoples have a relatively simple hunting technology: bows and arrows tipped with a weak poison among the !Kung (also known as the Ju'/hoansi, San, and the politically correct or incorrect Bushmen); spears, bows and arrows, and nets among the Mbuti "pygmies" of the Ituri Forest in Central Congo; blowguns and harpoons among the Semang of Malaysia. The notable exception are the Inuit of Arctic Canada and Alaska; they rely on harpoons, spears, kayaks and uniaks (boats of animal skin), and a sophisticated assemblage of other tools and weaponry. Gathering is even simpler; women use digging sticks to harvest and baskets, karosses (a leather cape among the !Kung), and skin pouches. Except for the Inuit, whose climates preclude vegetation except for short seasons, plant foods form a greater portion of the forager diet than meat; percentages range between 60 percent and 80 percent. Game, especially large animals, are hard to track and harder to kill. Each !Kung is lucky to bag 10 large animals per year; the Semang stopped hunting water buffalo years ago (Lee 2003; Turnbull 1963, 1983; Balikci 1970).

Among all regions, the primary attribute for simple foragers is the overreliance on natural sources of food. Nature rules. Resources fluctuate by time and place. In the Kalahari Desert, the mongongo nut tree that is abundant one year may be stingy the next—perhaps because the rainy season was too wet. Waterholes filled to the top one year may be empty the following year. Some places may vary in the same season. Some waterholes are empty, others full, all in the same year. The same rule applies to plant foods, animals, and fish (Lee 2003).

© Oleg Znamenskiy/Shutterstock.com

The Kalahari Desert in South Central Africa has been home to the San people have lived here for 20,000 years as hunter-gatherers.

Second, because of fluctuation in resources, the people have to move around a lot. When the tubers are exhausted, the nuts overpicked, or the game not showing up, the band must migrate to a more promising site. Nomadism means minimal possessions— all that can be carried—so it is unsurprising that the material culture is thin at best. An exception are the Inuit, who can carry a lot of material on their dog sleds and rely on kayaks and uniaks to move around when the ice is thin (Lee 2003; Balikci 1970).

Third, the environment imposes upper limits on population: the **carrying capacity**, or the upper limit of population that a specific environment— desert, rainforest, ice field—can support. Carrying capacity affects all cultures—even our own if we paid attention—but the effects are direct among foragers. Therefore, **Liebig's Law of the Minimum** is most evident. Formulated by Justus von Liebig, a German fertilizer manufacturer in the 19th century, the law states that lack of growth is limited not by the total of resources available, but by the scarcest resource. In crop science, the limit was imposed by the scarcest nutrient. In human populations, the limit is imposed by the scarcest resource: food supply in all three environments, and water supply in desert environments. The leanest year imposes the upper limit under this law, regardless of the abundance in other years (Wynne-Edwards 1986; Scupin 2003:152; Bodley 2001:71).

Fourth, again with the exception of the Inuit, foragers lack means of storage, particularly of meat.

This provides an incentive to consume meat, soft fruits, tender leaves, and other perishable foods as quickly as possible. Less perishable foods can be stored and consumed at leisure. One example is the mongongo nut among the !Kung; it can be stored for up to 18 months. Root crops also take longer to decay (Lee 2003; Balikci 1970).

Fifth, partly because of the relative absence of storage means, foragers are known for their propensity to share; in other words, their primary mode of transaction is **generalized reciprocity**. Among the !Kung, for example, if a party of hunters bags a wildebeest (an ungulate resembling an ox) or a giraffe, they own the meat—but it is theirs only to distribute. Whoever owned the arrow that first entered the beast—the owner may be a child, a woman, an old man who is not at the kill site—is also part owner of the meat, but again only to give away. This mode of exchange provides security for the less successful hunter, or one who may be down on his luck. Making gifts of meat also strengthens kinship ties, and there are rules as to who receives priority (Lee 2004).

Sixth, the foregoing description suggests that foragers are ever on the edge of starvation, but studies show that they may be nowhere near that level. Lee, for example, finds that although preferred foods may be exhausted before the next harvest season, not all food is. The !Kung of Dobe simply had to settle for the food they least desired, once the preferred mongongo nuts were exhausted (Lee 2003). Sahlins (1972) argues for a "Zen road to influence," or **affluence hypothesis**. Foragers, not knowing about all the amenities of civilization—television, cars, or cell phones to update the examples—do not miss them; in the meantime, they are gathering enough to live comfortably. Forager needs are few, the hypothesis runs, and they do not need to spend time pursuing the means of satisfaction.

There is documentation, however, that foraging peoples are at the brink of starvation. Some are: the Inuit may have fit this description, if Balikci's portrayal on film is to be believed. Among San (Bushmen), the Nyae Nyae !Kung San are described as being in a less productive environment than the Dobe !Kung San (Marshall 1965). In any case, it is true that foragers' diets are much more varied than that of many food producers, particularly intensive agriculturalists. Whether there is more then enough to eat appears to depend on the location (Scupin 2003).

Seventh, a corollary to the affluence hypothesis suggests that foragers do not spend much time working for a living. Lee (2003) calculates that the Dobe !Kung spend fewer than 20 hours of week in nonintensive labor hunting game or gathering vegetation, and Sahlins reports the same results on a comparative sample of other cultures (Sahlins 1972).

Eighth, there are suggestions that foragers are relatively egalitarian in both property and power. Among the !Kung, property notions are minimal. Game is owned only to be given away. Plant foods are owned by women who harvest them, and their family. Waterholes are freely available to all and to visitors, who need only request permission from the headman, who freely gives it (Marshall 1965). Indeed, Lee denies that there is any such thing as a headman among the Dobe !Kung (2003).

Finally, there is the longstanding debate as to whether foragers are our "contemporary ancestors." In other words, are foragers of today or the recent past similar to foragers of the Paleolithic? Although at first an appealing notion, there are several shortcomings of this view. First, the undisturbed foragers (if there are any) have existed in the same past 10,000 years as the nonforagers (including ourselves). Much can happen in the meantime, including culture change among the foragers themselves. Second, most foragers live in marginal areas; they cannot necessarily resemble the foragers who hunted game in the richer plains of East Africa, the moderate climates of Italy or Spain, or the rich floodplains of the Indus or Yangtze rivers. Third, their very presence in marginal areas suggests they were forced to the margins by the stronger, more technologically sophisticated populations who took the best lands and other resources (Carneiro 1967, 1970; Scupin 2003). A possible exception are the Australian Aborigines—some 500 bands—who had lived in isolation since they migrated to the continent 40,000 years ago. Even then, there is reason to believe that inhabitants of the richer coastal regions forced weaker populations into the vast, arid lands of the Outback. Archaeological evidence suggests exactly this pattern; the coasts were populated first, then the inland (Feder 2004).

8.2.2 Complex Foraging

By definition, **complex foraging** refers to the hunting and gathering of food whose energy yield approaches that of the food-producing systems that involve domestication. Complex foraging was more commonplace in the Upper Paleolithic and Mesolithic than it is in the recent past. For example, the Japanese site of Nittano, known for the Jomon tradition in pottery, showed signs of a permanent village. Fish was caught in the summer, game, in the winter, and a wide variety of wild vegetation was available in all seasons but winter. Other sites, such as Monte Verde in Chile and Dolni Vestonice in the Czech Republic, relied on megafauna—big game—such as mammoths, mastodon, giant bison, and wild cattle (Sanders and Price 2004).

© Dotted Yeti/Shutterstock.com

Megafauna such as the woolly mammoth were hunted during the Upper Paleolithic period.

The best known contemporary examples are the villages strung along the Northwest Coast of the United States and the west coast of Canada. (Ozette, Washington, contains archaeological characteristics that fit in with the Northwest Coast complex.). The Northwest Coast consists of moderate climate rainforest, mostly comprising cedar and several varieties of pine: ponderosa, fir, and balsam. The communities relied heavily on salmon, which were harvested every salmon run in the hundreds. Salmon was preserved by smoking, rendering it edible for several months. Game was also plentiful, from small game such as rabbits up to deer and elk. Flora was in abundance as well, with several varieties of berries and other wild plants. They did not cultivate crops, nor did they domesticate animals, which in any case were not amenable to domestication (Drucker 1955; Sanders and Price 2004).

Given a plentiful supply of wood, the Northwest Coast natives were known for their longhouses, seagoing canoes, totem poles, boxes, and other objects, beautifully carved and painted. The high-yield subsistence base rendered a nomadic existence unnecessary. Although war often occurred, the villages maintained a complex ranked society headed by a chief, whose validation was secured by a major feast known by the Chinook name potlatch. Unlike most simple foraging societies, the Northwest Coast native people recognized property ownership of not only salmon streams but also houses, canoes, and even intangible rights such as particular dances (Drucker 1955).

Thus, complex foraging societies are highly different from simple ones. The energy yield is much greater, whether because of megafauna or because of a rich and diverse food source. Sources do stand the risk of yearly fluctuation but, at least in the case of salmon, were unlikely to vary much from one year to the next. The environmental carrying capacity is much higher than that of simple foragers, as is the limit specified in Liebig's Law of the Minimum. Thus, settled communities are more likely to develop from complex foraging, although humans do not exercise control over their crops that domestication would bring. The institutions associated with simple foraging—communal control over resources, minimal power of headmen where they exist, sharing and generalized reciprocity—are nonexistent. Societies may be characterized by extended families, perhaps lineages and clans; ranking is likely to occur, and property is important, though more clan-based than individual-based (Sanders and Price 2004).

8.3 Food Production

We now take up the four major **food-producing** subsistence systems, which may be defined as all forms of subsistence technology whereby a population obtains its food through domestication of plants, animals, or both. These modes of technology consist of **horticulture**, **pastoralism**, **equestrian hunting**, and **intensive agriculture**. We discuss these modes in technology in turn.

All four systems share common characteristics. First, compared with food collection, food production is steady from year to year, with the exception of drought, soil exhaustion, plant disease, and plant decimation by insects or other pests. Second, storage facilities are made or constructed. Often, the food itself is nonperishable, such as maize, wheat, barley, or other seeds. Preservation techniques have been devised for other foods, such as a freeze-drying technique the Inca developed for preserving potatoes and duck, then storing them in ceramic containers. Third, permanent or semipermanent settlements accompany domestication. They may be villages, such as the communal *shabono* or corral among the Yanomamö; cities that are familiar to us all; or semipermanent camps, such as the herding peoples who, unlike simple foragers, move seasonally rather than opportunistically. Fourth, part-time or full-time artisans arise to pursue their craft. As energy production rises, more and more specialists outside the primary sector (hunters, gatherers, fishers, or cultivators) come into existence.

Finally, one should bear in mind that each of the food-collection systems does not necessarily exist in isolation. Some do; the cattle-herding Masai do not hunt, nor do they plant and harvest crops. Others combine two or more food-production systems. Yanomamö combine hunting with garden cultivation. Some central Asian herders plant gardens before moving their herds to their summer quarters, and harvest any crops that survive weeds, insects, and weather.

8.4 Horticulture

Horticulture entails the growing of crops of all kinds with relatively simple tools: digging stick and hoes for turning the soil, and axes or machetes to clear the brush and to weed. Two types of horticulture predominate: cultivation of long-growing tree crops, such as coconuts and breadfruit in Samoa and other Pacific islands; and **slash-and-burn** (also known as *swidden*, *extensive*, and *shifting*) cultivation. Secondary characteristics include higher productivity compared with simple foragers, small permanent (sometimes semipermanent) settlements; incipient part-time craft specialization; and, in some instances, status differences among kin groups.

Horticulture is still practiced today, for example in Coa bang, Vietnam as shown in this picture.

8.4.1 Tree Cultivation

A classic example of tree cultivation is represented by Samoa, a chain of islands formed by volcanic action, whose porous soils prevent overwatering from the frequent heavy showers that range up to 200 inches per year. The combination of heavy rain and warm, sunny weather fosters a lush plant cover. The main sources of crops are three fruit-bearing trees: breadfruit, coconut, and banana, none of which requires much maintenance. Taro is also another source of starch, and these are planted on sloping land; when the soil is exhausted, Samoans clear other sites for cultivation. Weeding is nonexistent; the leaves and combined shallow-root and deep-root structures of taro plants and weeds prevent the erosion of a loose volcanic soil from the torrential rains. Samoans obtain their protein primarily from fishing, though they also keep chickens and pigs.

As this brief discussion indicates, tree cultivation may be interspersed with slash-and-burn cultivation, as we see for taro in Samoa. The Yanomamö, while relying primarily on slash-and-burn cultivation, also harvest the fruit, a highly prized delicacy, of peach palms, hearts of palm, Brazil nuts, and cashews (Ember and Ember 2002:73–74).

8.4.2 Slash-and-Burn Cultivation

Of all systems of horticulture, **slash-and-burn cultivation** is the best known and most widely practiced. The commonalities are evidence enough. The process begins with cutting brush and trees at the beginning of the dry season in tropical regions. Once dried toward the end of this season, the slash (brush and felled trees) is burned, and around the start of the rainy season, seeds, cuttings, or both are planted. Once the garden is planted, it is usually typical for harvests to take place on an as-needed basis, and often the actual planting may be staggered so that the crops mature at different times of the year. When the soil is exhausted, anywhere between two to three years, the plot is abandoned, a new site is cleared, and a garden is planted. Inasmuch as 12 to 24 years are needed for the soil to regenerate, extensive territory is required and so this type is also called extensive cultivation.

8.4.3 Tropical Cultivation in Amazonia

Rain forest cultivation in Brazil's riverine basin known as Amazonia has been extensively studied, so it is perhaps worth one's while to bring it to closer scrutiny. A systematic comparison of five Amazonian tribes has been made in Betty Meggers' appropriately titled book *Amazonia: Man and Culture in a Counterfeit Paradise* (1996). Meggers describes the general features of the Amazonian rain forest, its adaptive features to an extremely hot and wet climate, and how the slash-and-burn cultivation of tropical rain forest Indians is an unconscious imitation of the real tropical rain forest. We'll go through this here.

Amazonia is divided into two ecological zones: the Várzea, or the riverside silt that accumulates every spring when the banks of the Amazon and its tributaries are flooded; and the Terre Firme, or the Amazonian basin away from the rivers. Lands in the Várzea are replenished by silt deposited by the floods, and so are extremely rich and capable of cultivation. The description that follows refers

Slash and burn horticulture is still practiced today. Shown here is a cleared area in the Peruvian Amazon region.

to the Terra Firme, which is a plain, lush with trees but with thin and poor soil; "counterfeit paradise" is an appropriate part of the book's subtitle.

Ecology of Tropical Rainforests. The combination of intense heat and torrential rains is destructive to any exposed soil in the tropics. For Amazonia, Meggers describes three absolutes that affect the soil. The first is high atmospheric temperature, which affects several biological and chemical processes crucial to soil maintenance. For example, humus, the topsoil essential to all agriculture, cannot form if the soil temperature is above 77 degrees Fahrenheit. Below that temperature, humic materials, formed from the decay of animal droppings combined with plant and animal remains, can build up. Above 77 degrees, the rate of decomposition of humus exceeds its rate of formation, because much of the carbon and nitrogen in the compounds escape as gasses into the air.

A second constant is rainfall, which acts on the surface of the ground in two ways: erosion and leaching. As the water scours the surface of the soil, particles are carried off. The erosion rate increases exponentially, meaning that if the rate of flow is doubled, the scouring capacity quadruples, the carrying capacity of water increases 32 times, and the size of the particles transported increases 64 times. Leaching acts on the composition of the soil, so that soluble nutrients such as nitrogen are removed to levels below the reach of plant and tree roots. The higher the temperature of the moisture, the more the soluble nutrients that are lost.

The first two constants—high solar temperature and torrential rainfall—combine to induce a chemical reaction in the terrain. All tropical soils contain trace amounts of iron and other minerals. The intense heat and extensive moisture serve as catalysts in the oxidation of these minerals in a process that converts the minerals, and the soil itself, into **laterite**. Called **laterization**, the process also removes phosphorus, another nutrient essential to plant growth. The soil also loses its perme-ability and so is unable to retain other essential nutrients, such as ammonia, lime, potash, and magnesia. Once initiated, laterization is irreversible. It is worth noting that most mining in the tropics involves separating the ore from its oxides with a process that involves intense heat, which requires high fossil-fuel intake. The process becomes unprofitable if the price of petroleum increases.

The age of soil is the third constant. The terrain in Amazonia is one of the oldest geological formations in the world. The processes already described have been going on for millions of years, so that the soil is so devoid of nutrients that they would be barren in a temperate climate. Soils are acidic, some moderately and others extremely so. Soils consist primarily of sand and clay. The soil is perennially short of calcium, an essential nutrient for plants with high protein content.

Features of Tropical Rainforests. The main features of tropical rainforest serve as an adaptive means to minimize the effects of sunlight and tropical rains. These consist of a protective canopy, diversity of species, and high rates of growth. We discuss these in turn.

First, the forest canopy is so thick that the forest floor is dark; it lacks foliage for that reason, and, indeed, requires an explorer to carry a flashlight to make his or her way through the forest base. The canopy contains not only the leaves of the trees, but also several species of **epiphytic plants**, which anchor themselves on the treetops and derive their nutrients from the atmosphere-borne moisture and minerals. Their vines are trailed like streamers from the treetops.

This canopy has several functions that protect the soil. First, it provides a shade keeping the soil temperature below the 77 degrees necessary to ensure topsoil formation and minimize loss through gasification of nitrogen and carbon compounds. Second, it breaks the heavy rainfall. Some—25 percent—of the rainfall is absorbed by the leaves and epiphytic plants; the remainder falls to the ground in a fine spray. Thus, reduction of water flow minimizes erosion, and the reduced water volume also minimizes leaching.

Also preserving the soil is the juxtaposition of species with differing nutrient requirements in the same space. As Meggers puts it, such vegetation is "consequently characterized by a great proliferation of species but low concentration of individuals of the same species" (1996:17). Estimates are that the number of species of trees is more than 20 times the number in European forests; nevertheless, they look the same to the untrained eye. The interplanting ensures that all nutrients will be used; what one tree does not use, another tree does. An added bonus are the different root characteristics and penetration, so that the resultant root mat improves the structure of the soil during the life of the plants, whose death contributes to the organic matter to be processed into humus (Meggers 1996:18). Their dispersal also lessens the spread of disease and pests.

Even the spectacular growth rate observed for tropical forests have a function. Because of their volatility, nutrients have to be processed at a high rate. The intense heat and high rainfall make for this acceleration. Not surprising, then, is that the rate of litter fall (animal remains and waste, combined with dead vegetation) is four times the rate of New York woodlands; the nutrients range in proportion from double in phosphorus to tenfold in nitrogen. Adding to the rapid processing are the nutrients captured from the atmosphere through rainwater, which contributes 75 percent of the potassium, 40 percent of the magnesium, and 25 percent of the phosphorus absorbed by the topsoil (Meggers 1996:17).

Meggers summarizes two major conservation functions of the primary tropical rainforest: (1) It sets up and maintains a closed cycle of nutrients, so that the same ingredients are kept in continuous circulation and loss is reduced to a minimum, and (2) it mitigates the detrimental effects of the climate to the extent that soil impoverishment by erosion or leaching is either arrested or reduced to a very slow rate (1996:18).

Slash-and-Burn Cultivation Primary Forest in Microcosm? In lesser respects, tropical horticulture performs adaptive functions not unlike the mature tropical rain forest. To some extent, tropical gardens maintain a continuous circulation of the same nutrients and reduce the rate of soil impoverishment.

The Mundurucú provide a representative illustration of slash-and-burn cultivation as practiced throughout Amazonia. At the beginning of the dry season, they first clear brush and small trees. Then they fell the larger trees systematically, by partially cutting all trees in the path of a "keystone" tree, which knocks the others down. Trees left standing are felled individually. After two months, the slash is burned on a day a slight breeze serves to fan the flames, but not strong enough to leave behind unburned slash. The burning must be completed by the end of the dry season.

Planting begins at the onset of the rainy season, with cuttings interplanted. A hole is made with a digging stick, cuttings or seeds are inserted, and the soil is moved over them with a foot. Usually, twelve or so food plants are raised, with sweet potato and manioc (a root cultigen highly prized throughout Amazonia and known in Spanish as *yuca*) interplanted at the center and other crops planted at the edges. Planting is staggered, so that when one crop (especially manioc) is harvested, a cutting is immediately planted. Weeding is done usually twice annually. Decline in productivity leads to abandonment of the field, usually by the third year (Meggers 1996).

Yanomamös' cultivation is similar, but varies in certain details. First, once a site is planted, the Yanomamö clear and plant a new plot every year. This makes it unnecessary to do all the work of clearing a new plot, and the site shifts as new plots are cleared and the old ones abandoned. Their crops include a nonnative plantain tree, which produces a high energy yield for a tropical plant, and the tree may be harvested years after its site has gone back to brush and forest (Chagnon 1997).

The two sites share common characteristics. First, the larger plants provide shade for the smaller ones and the soil itself. Ground cover is additionally maintained by harvesting a few plants at a time and staggering the planting, so that the soil is rarely exposed to the sun and rain. Interplanting ensures maximal utilization of nutrients by plants whose requirements differ, and discourages the spread of pests and diseases that attack specific plants. Weeding is of mixed value; although gardeners remove weeds competing with crops for space and nutrients, they also hasten soil deterioration by removing shade and protection from erosion. Finally, burning the slash returns some nutrients to the soil, as do decomposing trunks and large branches; they also divert certain pests and diseases from crop plants (Meggers 1996).

Finally, the genuine poverty of the Amazonian environment is evident when one considers the scarcity and dispersal of wild foods, coupled with their low nutritional value. Amazonia contains the most varied plants in the world, yet they are not concentrated. Furthermore, protein sources are scarce. With the exception of the Brazil nut and other nuts, seed-bearing plants are scarce. A great deal of protein is required for seed reproduction. Therefore, most plants reproduce by vegetative means, whereby new plants grow from the shoots of their parent. Most animals are thin, isolated, and often nocturnal. Monkeys and peccaries (wild pigs), which are large and move in groups, are the exceptions. The primary factor of this poverty of protein in the environment is the age of the soil, dated back to the Tertiary, whereas most soils of Europe and North America date back only to the Pleistocene of the Quaternary. Thus, most Terra Firme soils consist of clay and sand, and are highly acidic which, to Meggers, would render them barren in moderate climates. Low calcium content in tropical soils is one primary factor in this poverty of protein (1996:35–37).

It is not surprising, therefore, that most peoples of Amazonia supplement a diet, consisting mostly of starch and of plant foods that reproduced by vegetative means rather than by seed, and seek their protein by hunting and fishing. "Over the millennia," Meggers contends, "each aboriginal group succeeded in developing a seasonal cycle that combines hunting, fishing, gathering, and agricultural of various intensities, but which in every case assures the availability of nutrients indefinitely without endangering the equilibrium of the ecosystem" (1996:37).

We cannot conclude without recalling the so-called "Protein Debate" between Marvin Harris, who never set foot in Yanomamö territory, and Napoleon Chagnon, who spent at least 66 months over several years with them. In his *Cows, Pigs, Wars, and Witches*, Harris explains Yanomamö war-fare in terms of protein scarcity; when two tribes converge at the same hunting ground, they start fighting over game animals. Chagnon counters with the argument that the abduction of women, not game, sparks off the war. The argument went on for decades until Harris's death in 2001, and involved Kenneth Good, a student of Chagnon's who nonetheless supported Harris's protein scarcity theory. Harris sees the evolutionary significance of the Protein Debate in light of competition for resources; Chagnon sees the significance of the Abduction-of-Women theory in light of reproductive success. For a review of the arguments—and the infighting—see Harris (1974, 1979), Chagnon (1997:91–97) and Good (1997). The student should be cautioned against the kind of futile—or feudlike—arguments such as this one.

Native Brazilian man from Tupi Guarani Tribe.

© Filipe Frazao/Shutterstock.com

8.5 Pastoralism

Some cultures domesticate animals, but not plants. In other words, they practice **pastoralism**, or the primary dependence on the products of domesticated herd animals. They range in size from goats and sheep to cattle, horses, and camels. They occur primarily in grassland regions, whose soil is too impenetrable for horticulture or preindustrial agriculture. The climate may also be too hilly, too arid, or too cold to support intensive cultivation. So long as there is grass or like vegetation, pastoralism is a feasible strategy of subsistence (Sahlins 1968).

Pastoralists move their animals as the seasons change. They may be transhumant or nomadic. **Transhumant pastoralism** occurs when men and boys move their herds from one region or elevation to the next and back again, while their families stay in one place. East African herdsmen are transhumant pastoralists. **Nomadic pastoralism** occurs when entire families move with the herds throughout the year and there are no permanent villages. Central Asian peoples, who live in transportable yurts, are examples.

Animals vary with the climate, region, and purpose. The Bedouins of Arabia, for example, use camels primarily for transportation, and rarely consume the meat; other Middle Eastern peoples, such as the Basseri of southern Iran, raise sheep, goats, horses, and donkeys. East Africans are particularly famous for their cattle, which they value in the way we value money.

Because they can produce only animal consumer products—milk, hides, meat, and in East Africa blood—some anthropologists refer to pastoralists as **incomplete food producers**, because they do not also grow crops. Therefore, they often depend on settled communities for plant food products—nuts, fruits, root crops—and for crafted goods. Sahlins argues that there develops a hostile symbiosis between herders and community folk— symbiotic because each depends on the other, but hostile because herders may find it more profitable to raid the communities than to trade with them. Indeed, warfare is often associated with pastoralists. An entire age grade is devoted to defending the tribes' own herds or raiding their neighbors' (Sahlins 1968; Sangree 1965).

Because of the need to move, valuables are small and portable; they include coins, jewelry, ornaments of gold or other precious metal, and so on. Generally speaking, property is limited in amount and size by the need to be carried in carts or on the backs of animals.

Because males often (though not always) raise animals and defend their herds, male cooperation is usually important among pastoralists. Therefore, residence tends to be patrilocal (where the wife moves in with her husband and husband's kin), households tend to center around a core of related males, and descent tends to be patrilineal.

Because pastoralism is an incomplete food-producing system—animals but not plants are domesticated—it was early thought that animal husbandry was a transitional phase between hunting and gathering and agriculture. However, most archaeological evidence suggests that pastoralism arose during, or even after, the domestication of plants and animals both; this suggests that some populations may have left settled communities, by choice or by force, to develop this complex (Sahlins 1968).

Many contemporary Maasai people continue to practice pastoralism.

In recent years, governments have encouraged or forced nomadic pastoralists to move into settled communities, in the interest of maintaining control over them. Called *villageization* in Kenya and by other names elsewhere, the effect has been a marked reduction of nomadic peoples as they take up agriculture or wage work.

8.6   Equestrian Hunting

As you may know, the classical stereotype of "The Indian" is one who hunts buffalo while riding on a horse, wearing a war bonnet, brandishing bow and arrows or lance, and who lives in a tipi—in short, everything you see in this or that cowboys and Indians movie or the over-romanticized *Dances with Wolves*. **Equestrian hunting** refers using draft animals—horses—to hunt other animals (Sahlins 1968).

In anthropological fact, this practice is rare. In North America, this kind of hunting was not an aboriginal trait in North America, even in the Great Plains. Before the horse was introduced in the Great Plains in the 17th century, plainsmen either hunted on foot—the Comanches for one—or practiced horticulture along the major rivers, as did the Cheyenne. Horses indigenous to North America died out in pre-Columbian times; the horse population domesticated by the Plains Indians were probably introduced by Spaniard colonists who settled northern Mexico and what is now New Mexico between the 16th and 19th century. The greatest known period of diffusion of horses was from 1740 to 1800.

The use of the horse in hunting spread quickly as horses became more plentiful. It may be that settled peoples took to the horse because of its economic superiority to river-bottom agriculture, but a more likely explanation was the importance of the horse in warfare—higher mobility and speed of mounted warriors as compared to foot warriors—so that village-dwelling peoples had no choice but to defend themselves.

Trade with whites may have also contributed to the spread of equestrian hunting, as individual tribes hunted even more buffalo—or stole horses for trade—and fought each other to gain trading advantages. Guns, which gave even greater military advantages to their owners, were also prized.

In many respects, equestrian hunting was similar to pastoralism. Buffalo moved wherever there was good pasture, and this changed with the seasons; Native Americans moved with the buffalo. Buffalo moved in huge herds during late spring and early summer (when the grass was tallest—and it was also rutting season), then dispersed in late summer through winter, when grass was sparser and in winter under snow. Accordingly, the Cheyenne and other Plains Indians massed during the spring and summer, and dispersed in smaller bands in the fall (Sahlins 1968).

Communal hunting was the most common and the most productive. Unlike the environmentalist image that *Dances with Wolves* projects, the real Cheyennes' aim was to kill off the entire herd if they could. Mounted men stampeded the herd into an ever tighter circle, picked off any buffalo they could, and repeated the process. Then the skinning and butchering began, with women doing the greatest amount of work in preparing the meat and dressing the skins. Meat was dried into jerky (derived from the Spanish word *charqui*), then pounded with berries to make pemmican, which was stored in rawhide sacks. In this case, large amounts of meat could be made to keep the winter, and it was no advantage to consume it immediately, as it would be among the !Kung.

8.6.1 Intensive Cultivation

Known also in the anthropological literature as intensive agriculture, **intensive cultivation** refers to food production that is characterized by the permanent cultivation of fields, high levels of productivity, and sometimes sophisticated technology such as irrigation canals or terraces, plows drawn by draft animals, and varieties of farm machinery. However accomplished, all forms of intensive cultivation share the following attributes.

Intensive Cultivation: Common Attributes. Intensive cultivation provides a high yield per unit of land as compared with horticulture, but it can vary. For the peasants in the Chinese village of Kaihsienkung, who rely on terraced irrigated fields, 186 work-hours are required to produce 1 million calories (yearly requirement for one person); in the United States back in 1947, 2.2 work-hours were required to produce the same amount.

Generally, most land is devoted to a single crop. In the case of Kaihsienkung, 90 percent of land was devoted to rice, with wheat, beans, cotton, and soybeans accounting for the remainder. Elsewhere, the staple crop(s) consisted of maize in Mesoamerica; potatoes in Andean America; grain, predominately wheat, in the Near East and, later, Europe; millet in northern China; and rice in southern China and southeast Asia (Service 1978).

Intensive cultivation involves risk of famine. Drought, insect pests, or disease could wipe out a single crop, the major disadvantage that is not found in horticulture. In many high civilizations, grain was stored against this contingency. The intercropping practices found in many horticultural systems minimize this risk (Sahlins 1968).

Most staples can be stored. Grain, unless moist, is slow to decay, and can be stored for several years. Means have been found to store such perishable root crops as potatoes; for example, the Inca of Andean America froze their potatoes (among other foods, such as duck) at night and dried them during the day—an originator of the freeze-dry technique of food preservation (Steward and Faron 1959).

Formation of Intensive Cultivation: Some Explanations. Did our ancestors take up agriculture because it was obviously superior to foraging when it comes to yield? Most anthropologists, including especially archaeologists, reject this explanation. This is because farming is an arduous task. One has to plan each season—for that matter, each day—carefully. Seeds must be planted; then there is watering to be done, frequent weeding, protection against predators, harvesting, storage, and selection of seeds for next year's crop. Add animals to the equation, and there is more work to be done, from helping cows or mares birth their young through maintenance while the animals are in their nonproductive periods to milking, slaughtering, butchering, and meat preservation. Foraging is a much simpler life, and not much less productive per capita per year.

Why take up farming then? Perhaps a partial answer to this question may lie in the fact that, whereas foraging, horticulture, and pastoralism all are *extensive* strategies—they take up a great deal of territory—intensive cultivation, by definition, takes up relatively small areas of land and makes efficient use of it. Perhaps the reason lies in population increases relative to usable land.

Most of the explanations for the **Neolithic Revolution**, defined by plant and animal domestication, center around the theme of population density relative to land and water availability, although occurrence of plants and animals that can be domesticated play a part. The **oasis hypothesis**, formulated by Vere Gordon Childe (1951), posits that agriculture emerged where there was water in an increasingly water-scarce environment;

communities developed along the Tigris, Euphrates, Nile, Indus, Huang Ho, and other rivers, all in regions where land was fertile but water was otherwise scarce. Lewis Binford's **edge hypothesis** (1983) suggests that land use became intensified at the edge of natural hunting and gathering habitats by populations that otherwise might have been forced out. Arguing from a similar premise, Cohen (1979) suggests that intensification occurred everywhere because population densities increased everywhere, beyond the region's carrying capacity. Each explanation has its problems. Some point out, for example, that agriculture developed in places where water was not particularly scarce, nor the population dense.

Other explanations are more complex. For example, Braidwood offers a **natural habitat hypothesis** (1960), which proposes that agriculture emerged where domesticated plants developed at the site of their natural ancestors. Jarmo, for example, developed at the edge of the Fertile Crescent, which extended from the eastern shores of the Mediterranean, eastward through southern Turkey, Syria, and northern Iraq, and thence into Iran. Most archaeologists would argue for a multivariate theory, one that posits several contributing factors—population, habitat ideal for cultivation, domesticable plants, and so on. The relative importance of these variables also varies by location and by cultivation techniques employed.

Intensive Cultivation Technologies. Although preindustrial civilizations are often identified with irrigation canal systems (Mesopotamia) or flood plain irrigation (Egypt), the term covers a large variety of techniques. This can be accomplished by a combination of the following factors:

One of the most common forms of intensive cultivation is **irrigation**. The simplest known technique involves **flood plain irrigation**, in which fields are abandoned to flooding during the rainy season and planted when the flood recedes. This form was best known in Egypt during the Old and Middle Kingdoms, but was supplemented with the **shaduf**, a lever with a bucket that was dipped into the Nile and the water transferred to a sluice and thence to the field (Price and Sanders 2004). Other irrigation systems involved the construction of canals from the river (as was the case for the Tigris and Euphrates Rivers in Mesopotamia), and the construction of **terraces** in Meso-America, China, and southeast Asia. One unique system was the construction of **chinampas**, or raised fields constructed from alternate layers of earth and decayed vegetation to form a rich—and relatively dry— platform for the crops. This was characteristic of the swamps around the Aztec capital of Tenochtitlán, but Mayan city states may also have been sustained by these platforms (Schele and Miller 1986; Berdan 1982).

Many agricultural systems rely on draft animals, such as the horse or ox, and plow. Plows with wooden shares (some tipped with metal) were common throughout the Near East, where the soil is mostly silt, which is light and pliable. In Europe, where much of the soil is heavy, a metal share was a necessity.

Chinampas horticulture is still practiced in many parts of the world, including Central America as shown here.

Much of the civilizational world, however, relied on what Scupin (2004) calls **intensive horticulture**, whereby most of the cultivation, including canal construction, is or was done by hand. Except for the llama in the Andes, the New World lacked draft animals of any kind, and practically all work was done by human power.

At the opposite end of the scale, modern agriculture has replaced draft animals with the tractor, but the plow has been refined rather than replaced; it has many rather than one share, so a wide swath of soil can be turned on one trip; harrows, with spikes to smooth and pulverize the soil; and other devices. More important is the question of energy consumption. In a comparative study of energy consumption, Earl Cook (1971:136) finds that the daily per capita consumption in kilocalories (kc) was 5,000 kc among hunters and gatherers (foragers), 12,000 kc among horticulturalists, and 26,000 among agrarian (preindustrial intensive cultivators); in contrast, modern industrial societies shot up to 230,000 kc (Scupin 2003:272).

Although industrial agriculture is highly productive in comparison with preindustrial agriculture and other subsistence systems, there is substantial evidence to indicate that when calculated as a ratio-to-energy input, food energy output is much lower in comparison with nonindustrial subsistence systems. Nor is the input confined to the cost in gas and oil for running farm equipment. First, there are the energy costs to manufacture this equipment in the first place. Second, as Heinberg points out,

> nitrogen fertilizers are produced from natural gas; pesticides and herbicides are synthesized from oil; seeds, chemicals, and crops are transported long distances by truck; and foods are often cooked with natural gas and packaged in oil-derived plastics before reaching the consumer. [Therefore] from farm to plate, depending on the degree to which it is processed, a typical food item may embody input energy between four and several time its food energy. This energy deficit can only be maintained because of the availability of cheap fossil fuels, a temporary gift from the earth's geologic past (2003:175).

There are secondary effects. With the advent of intensive cultivation, a large number of workers are freed to pursue other, nonagricultural crafts. Thus, a high degree of craft specialization is likely to emerge, and trade develops not only among specialty craftspersons within but also between communities or cities. Settled communities not only accompany the intensification of agriculture (indeed, the complex foragers of the Upper Paleolithic and the Mesolithic were able to found settled communities) but sooner or later develop into cities.

8.7 Conclusion

We have presented five basic subsistence strategies as ideal types—as if each culture employed only one of these strategies. In fact, most cultures employ two or more strategies. The complexities were hinted at for Amazonia, where most cultivators also hunt animals and gather wild fruits and other plant foods. A reason was also suggested: Amazonia is a protein-poor environment. Nor are they all of one type: pastoralists may herd cattle, horses, sheep, goats, or some combination thereof. Cultivation techniques vary as well. Some involve flood plains, others canals from rivers, still others in terraces, and yet others in raised fields in swamps.

Chapter 9
Religion and Culture

Richley H. Crapo

Learning Objectives

After reading this chapter, you should be able to:

1. Critique the various definitions of religion.

2. Analyze the ways in which people conceive of the supernatural and their relationship to it.

3. Discuss the relationship between religion and practical aspects of human survival and cultural adaptation.

4. Define the structure and diversity of religious ideology.

5. Define the relationship between religious ideologies and social organization.

6. Analyze the nature and functions of ritual.

7. Explain the different forms of religious social organization.

8. Illustrate the role of borrowing in religious change.

9. Explain the role of religion in the United States.

10. Describe the revitalization movement.

11. Discuss the social and psychological functions of religion.

12. Analyze the cognitive characteristics of religious thought.

Cultural Anthropology by Richley H. Crapo, along with © 2014 Bridgepoint Education. Reprinted by permission.

Outline

Religion is a cultural universal—that is, even though not all individuals are religious, anthropologists have found no society in which religion is absent. Religion is a socially shared supernatural ideology and a system of rituals by which human beings strive for greater control over themselves and their social and natural environments. Psychologically, the beliefs and rituals of a particular religion symbolically express the kinds of stresses and anxieties common among members of the society or societies in which it is found. In this chapter we will examine both the psychological and the social aspects of religion.

9.1 Why Are People Religious?

Creationists, generally speaking, believe that the earth is no older than 6 or 10 thousand years and that many of the findings of anthropology are therefore incorrect. In the southern state of Georgia, in 2002, a warning label appeared on books dealing with evolution and Darwin. Like others elsewhere in the USA, it said: "This textbook contains material on evolution. Evolution is a theory, not a fact, regarding the origin of living things. This material should be approached with an open mind, studied carefully, and critically considered" (Cobb County Board of Education 2002). To some, this warning sounded quite reasonable, but to many, including most anthropologists, it was seen as an infringement of free speech and an attempt to undermine scientific inquiry into the human past. In placing warning labels on textbooks, the actions of this school-board testify to the sometimes-fraught relationship between the anthropological community and certain religious views regarding how where, and when our species came to be. Elsewhere, the creationist museum that was opened in Kentucky in 2007, presents a recreated Noah's arc. The display cases, literature, and publications all refute the teachings of Wallace, Darwin, and any field of anthropology that addresses the ancient past or physical evolution. These strongly anti-evolution institutions see the idea of evolution as a falsehood, and they also offer to teach visitors how to fake fossils in 15 minutes.

Feelings run high when anthropologists claim that we are descended from apes, and, that this was a process that occurred over millions of years. This is as true today as it was true over 150 years ago when Darwin claimed that all life had a common ancestor and that we evolved by means of natural selection. Darwin delayed the publication of one of the greatest theories that mankind has ever produced for 20 years due to his fears that religious and social ostracization would follow. Vehement denials and denunciations have been the lot of many an anthropologist studying prehistory or the evolution of mankind. There is no easy fix to many of the disagreements, faith versus science is a face-off never won cleanly. However, from the anthropological perspective the goal is never to pass judgement on the beliefs of others. We are interested in the way that religion manifests itself in the social world, how it transforms and impacts people. We approach the study of religion, spirituality, and ritual with an endeavor not to make value statements or to make any truth claims. Anthropology focuses on the tangible elements such as written texts, rituals, patterns of behavior or opinions, that can be studied using standard anthropological research tools. The aim is to examine the social practices associated with religion and spirituality and to analyze their effects on people and groups. The study of religion is approached in much the same manner as one would analyze the institutions of kinship, economics, or gender.

Although cultures differ considerably in their religious beliefs, practices, and organizations, there is no known human culture from which religion is absent. The question of whether people are interacting with a true supernatural realm cannot be answered through anthropological study because the supernatural realm itself cannot natural and what they do when they are engaging in religious thought or practices. And these observable characteristics explain the various benefits religion has to societies and to individuals have served to perpetuate it in all human cultures.

9.1.1 The Reduction of Anxiety

There are psychological benefits for the individual in the practice of religion. People do not always have as much control over their lives or circumstances as they need in order to feel secure. In his research among the Trobriand Islanders of Melanesia, Malinowski (1922) found that people used their skills and practical knowledge in contexts in which they had control but resorted to magic and other ritual means to influence situations over which they had none. When gardening they relied on their knowledge of plants, soils, and cultivation techniques to ensure good yields, but when preparing for long distance voyages they turned to magic to ensure the stability of their canoes in the rough seas, favorable winds, and good weather. In cases such as this, the performance of rituals to gain added control through supernatural means can alleviate potentially debilitating anxiety. This is especially true when the anxiety stems from problems for which no secular remedies are known. More than one anthropologist has noted parallels between religious curing rituals and Western psychotherapeutic practices.

In frightening situations, religion can be a source of strength by enabling one to stand up to one's fears and overcome them. The prayer uttered privately or the blessing given by another before a dangerous undertaking may provide just enough confidence to ensure success. Plains Indian warriors like Plenty Coups, the famous Crow leader, often went on vision quests to acquire Guardian Spirits that they could turn to from then on for advice and help in times of need (Linderman, 1930). This gave them added confidence as they face the many challenges in their lives. Religion also provides means of dealing with guilt and shame. In some religions, guilt can be overcome by acts of penance and sacrifice, and shame can be counteracted by demonstrations of piety that restore one's reputation.

People who are unable to remove unjust obstacles in their lives sometimes release their anger by acting it out with rituals that direct the supernatural power against the source of their frustrations. At times of loss, religion may also console the grieving In these and other ways, religion helps people cope with troubling emotions.

Religion can also produce anxieties by teaching its followers to avoid things that are believed to be spiritually dangerous (see the discussion of taboos in *Section 2: The Building Blocks of Religion*). These induced anxieties provide the motivation to avoid things that may, in fact, be dangerous in the mundane world—things such as caves, precipices, or waterfalls that are physically dangerous may be regarded as spiritually powerful and to be avoided. Such beliefs may reinforce respect for the larger society of which people are a part, as when secular leaders are believed to be spiritually powerful (see the discussion of mana in *Section 2: The Building Blocks of Religion*).

9.1.2   The Maintenance of Social and Moral Order

Socially, religion teaches people that they have a place in the universe and a relationship to it. Through the ideology of a religion and through its rituals, people gain a sense of identity and a feeling that life is meaningful. The practice of a religion creates greater solidarity among its participants, enabling them to work more effectively together and accomplish more.

Religion provides guidelines about how human life should be properly conducted and what values should be held. In so doing, it motivates people to follow the customs of their society even in the absence of practical insights about how their actions may benefit it. For instance, farmers suffering the effects of a prolonged drought may, after several failures, be too discouraged to dig yet another well until a "water witch" assures them of the presence of water at some location. Without such religious sources of motivation, the short-term costs of trying one more time in the face of the previous failures might seem to outweigh the potential long-term benefits. Social rules necessary for the maintenance of order may be supported by the threat of supernatural punishments for their violation or supernatural rewards for their acceptance. This can be especially beneficial in a society that lacks secular means of ensuring obedience to the rules. Viking men were promised the reward of Valhalla for valor in warfare, and Aztec warriors were assured that death in battle led to an eternity in the most glorious of the Aztec heavens, that of their war god, Huitzilopochtli. Among the Rwala Bedouin of northern Saudi Arabia, the pains of Hell awaited those who lied, and for the ancient Egyptians a similar fate was reserved for the stingy.

In situations in which disagreement might be divisive, religion may provide the means to achieve consensus without hard feelings. For instance, divination can be used to find the answer to a question about which the group is hopelessly divided. That solution then can be accepted by all without loss of face. Barry S. Hewlett (2012) and his colleagues discovered that the Aka and Ngandu of Central African Republic administer poison to a healer in order to divine answers to questions of such a sensitive nature that their resolution is best left to the supernatural. Such questions might include, for example, which wife is responsible for the illness of a man's youngest wife or who caused the death of a well-liked neighbor. Oftentimes, those deemed guilty by such methods were turned over to the police for punishment.

Finally, the rituals of religion provide emotional release from stresses that might otherwise lead to socially disruptive behavior. When Zuñi farmers blame their crop failures or illness on the malevolent use of religious rituals against them by people in another town and take action to protect themselves through rituals, they may be sparing themselves the strife that might otherwise disrupt their own village if they took out their frustrations on neighbors or relatives.

9.2 The Building Blocks of Religion

Despite their tremendous diversity in beliefs and rituals, all religions have certain things in common. Any religion can be described by examining four basic building blocks: the way it is organized socially; its ideology (that is, the system of religious beliefs and values that are shared by its adherents); its ritual practices; and the psychological states involved in the personal spiritual lives of its followers. Each of these will be considered in turn in this chapter.

9.2.1 Ideology in Religion

Religious ideology, which comprises the super natural beliefs and sentiments of society, is more diverse than most kinds of nonreligious ideology. Some religions emphasize impersonal supernatural forces such as fate, destiny, karma, luck, mana (defined later in this section), or kismet. Others emphasize personified supernatural entities as diverse as gods, demi-gods, demons, ghosts, goblins, or elves. Some religions include a belief in witches, or human beings who have an innate power to harm others. Others do not. A few believe in one supreme deity, while others believe in many more or less co-equal deities who possess different kinds of power. Some religions have rigid restrictions on when and where sexual behavior is permissible while others do not, and a few even treat sexual relations as a religious sacrament. The great diversity within religious ideology exists because religious beliefs and feelings are typically less restricted by practical consequences of immediate concern in daily life than beliefs and feelings about nonreligious matters. For instance, our ideas about how to make and use the tools upon which our society depends for survival must conform to the facts of physics relevant to their effective functioning. Thus, it will not be difficult to recognize a bow and arrow no matter what part of the world it comes from, and ideas about how to make and use this weapon will have much in common in all societies. beliefs and feelings are typically less restricted by practical consequences of immediate concern in daily life than beliefs and feelings about nonreligious matters. For instance, our ideas about how to make and use the tools upon which our society depends for survival must conform to the facts of physics relevant to their effective functioning. Thus, it will not be difficult to recognize a bow and arrow no matter what part of the world it comes from, and ideas about how to make and use this weapon will have much in common in all societies.

9.2.1.1 Belief in Supernatural Beings

Sir Edward Burnett Tylor (1871), a 19th-century Victorian scholar, provided one of the first anthropological definitions of religion. As did most anthropologists of his era, Tylor used an evolutionary framework for studying culture, including religion. In his view the defining feature of religion is **animism**, a belief in souls. According to Tylor, religion functions to provide human beings with explanations for such perplexing phenomena as unconsciousness, sleep, dreams, and hallucinations. He argued that religion originated when early humans postulated the existence of a human soul to account for such phenomena. Unconsciousness, fainting, sleep, and even death could be explained as the soul' departure from the body; dreams could be memories of the soul's experiences as it traveled outside the body during sleep; and visions or hallucinations could simply be apparitions of souls and other spirit beings. The idea of the soul also implied the possibility of other spiritual entities such as ghosts and ancestral spirits. The idea of more powerful supernatural beings such as gods and goddesses, Tylor suggested, eventually evolved from ancestral spirits whose original human identities were forgotten over the generations.

9.2.1.2 Belief in Supernatural Power

One limitation of Tylor's definition was its narrowness in excluding from the realm of religion the belief in formless supernatural powers. Robert Marett (1909) first raised this criticism of Tylor and introduced the Melanesian word **mana** to refer to the concept of impersonal spiritual power. He labeled such beliefs **animatism**. Marett reasoned that because the idea of an impersonal spiritual force was simpler than that of supernatural beings, it must have preceded the rise of animism. Mana, which might be thought of as a kind of supernatural electricity, can reside in objects such as a rabbit's foot or a four-leaf clover, in powerful natural phenomena such as thunderstorms, or in anything strange, rare, or dangerous. In doses too large, it can cause harm, illness, or even death, but properly channeled it can be used by human beings to accomplish ends that are unattainable by other means. Mana can increase one's luck, skill, and ability to gain knowledge of hidden things. It is the force behind magic; it is the holiness in the ground around the burning bush; it is the sacredness of the Host in the Eucharist; it is Luke Skywalker's Force. As the embodiment of spiritual power in its rawest form, mana inspires the sense of awe and reverence that people of every religion experience when they perceive themselves to be in the presence of the holy. Although mana makes things more powerful than they normally would be, it does not come and go of its own accord. Like its secular equivalent, electricity, humans must manipulate it to benefit from its power. However, unlike electricity, the manipulation of mana is accomplished through rituals.

Where mana plays a prominent role in religion, the concept of taboo is also likely to be important. A **taboo** is a supernatural rule that forbids contact with certain things or people, oftentimes those filled with so much mana that careless contact with them may harm the unwary. People who violate such prohibitions are thought to face some sort of supernatural punishment. The term "taboo" was derived from a Polynesian word, *tapu* or *tabu*, which means both "forbidden" and "sacred." Polynesian chiefs were sacred and their bodies contained so much mana that it was taboo for commoners to touch them, as to do so might kill an ordinary person. Because Tylor's definition failed to encompass mana, an important aspect of religious practice and ideology, Marett broadened it by defining religion as the belief in supernatural things in general.

India's Sacred Cow

Religious beliefs often serve practical purposes, even though these purposes may not be obvious. Such is the case with the sacred cows of India.

Since the British colonial occupation of India, the English phrase "sacred cow" has stood for any custom that is maintained in spite of all rational reasons for its change. The zebu cow, held sacred by Hindus of India, symbolizes gentleness, life, and India itself. The cow is so greatly revered that its protection was written into the constitution. The cow may be neither killed nor molested as it wanders the streets. To the British, for whom cattle were an important food resource, it seemed the height of folly for a society in which hunger and even starvation were significant social problems to support cow reverence instead of cow eating. In spite of the thinly veiled ethnocentrism in this opinion, there is some intuitive merit to the idea that protection of the cow is irrational when its use as food might alleviate a major social problem.

Marvin Harris (1974), who believed that the material conditions of life have a greater impact on an ideology than an ideology does on those conditions, argued that the custom of cow reverence is integrated with other facets of Indian life in such a way that using cows for food would create more problems than it would solve. Those whose only contact with cattle is the meat section of their local supermarket may be unaware of the great expenditure of resources that goes into the raising of cattle as food. In the United States, for instance, beef cattle are fed from farm-grown foods. Three fourths of the agricultural land in the United States is devoted to growing food for cattle. Since U.S. farmers are still able to produce sufficient food for domestic consumption and export, this cost is well within their means. In India, though, the establishment of this kind of beef industry would remove acreage from the production of

(Continued)

(*Continued*)

food for human beings. The result would be the displacing of millions of farmers and an increase in food costs and hunger.

Indian farmers pen their cows at night but allow them to wander during the day, scavenging their own food. Eating the weeds and plants that they find away from the farm, the cows consume things that are not edible to humans for about four fifths of their diet. The custom of permitting cows to range freely greatly reduces the amount of labor and feed that farmers must devote to the upkeep of their animals. Allowing cows to wander and fostering cow love benefits the poorest farmers who otherwise could not afford to own a cow or keep it during times of hardship.

Although the cow is not food for its owner, it is an important part of that farmer's means of food production. Teams of oxen are harnessed to pull plows. Cows provide a small amount of milk for their owners and a few milk peddlers. Cattle also produce dung, which is valuable as fertilizer and fuel in India, a country with little oil, coal, or wood. Cattle dung takes the place of expensive petrochemical fertilizers. It is also burned within the home as a cooking fuel. Finally, when cattle die from natural causes, the meat is not wasted, for most of it is eaten by members of the lowest castes, who have little access to other sources of quality protein. The custom of cow worship ensures that the meat reaches the tables of those who could least afford to buy it if it were a market item sought by all.

Perhaps someday beef will be routinely eaten in India, but under current circumstances beef eating would not be cost effective, whereas cow reverence is. Far from being a case of the irrationality of religious symbols, the sacredness of the zebu cow in India reflects the real importance of the cow as a resource and means of livelihood under the current economic conditions.

9.2.1.3 What Is a "Supernatural" Belief?

Throughout the 20th century, definitions of religion usually incorporated the word "supernatural" to contrast ordinary things in the mundane world with the realm of powers and beings, which are believed to be fundamentally different. The **supernatural** has generally been understood to be a realm that transcends the natural senses. Again, whether such a realm actually exists is beyond the scope of science to determine, but we can ask whether the world's diverse beliefs about such a realm have anything in common that will enable us to identify what it is about religious beliefs that give them an air of being otherworldly or supernatural. One commonality appears to be that supernatural beliefs involve anthropomorphic thinking.

Anthropologist Stewart Guthrie (1993), who undertook a major survey of the studies of religion, discovered that the common denominator in all religious thinking is **anthropomorphism**, or the attribution of humanlike agency to things that are not human, in this case spiritual beings. Guthrie argues that the concept of anthropomorphism can replace the notion of the supernatural in the definition of religion. In this case, religion can be described as a system of (1) beliefs in which the nonhuman realm is portrayed as having humanlike qualities, including the ability to respond to symbolic communication; (2) feelings related to those beliefs; and (3) ritual practices that elicit and control those feelings and are carried out either to portray the beliefs or to influence the universe by symbolic communication.

According to Guthrie, such anthropomorphic explanations are plausible for three reasons: (1) Humans are complex and multifaceted, so similarities can be found between many phenomena and some parts of the human condition; (2) human beings are likely to be found wherever the human observer may be; and (3) humans are the most important factor in the human environment. Therefore, anthropomorphic models are readily used by human beings to interpret their experiences, and it is these models and interpretations of the universe as created and governed by unseen humanlike beings that we call religion.

In Guthrie's view, our understanding of our experiences is initially ambiguous, but by interpreting experiences in human terms, we reduce this ambiguity. Whether we do so religiously or scientifically does not matter. We understand new things by finding similarities between them and things we already understand. Thus, by thinking of nonhuman phenomena in human terms, Guthrie's hallmark of religious thinking, we create plausible explanations for the unknown.

9.2.1.4 The Sources of Religious Symbolism and Beliefs

Religious beliefs and feelings must at least be compatible with the ways of thinking and the values that are held by their adherents as they go about their daily lives. No religion is likely to flourish if it demands beliefs or attitudes that are incompatible with those that are necessary for survival, whether in the economic, political, or reproductive lives of its members. Thus, many differences in religious ideologies may be accounted for as adaptations of culture to differing environmental, technological, and social circumstances.

Religious symbolism draws heavily on features of the natural environment that are important to the survival of the group. Thus, in aboriginal Australian religions, one important concept was that every human was born with a special spiritual relationship with a particular food animal. For Pygmies of the Ituri Forest, the forest, as the source of all necessary resources, was religiously personified as the spiritual parent of humans, and religious rituals emphasized the tie between humans and the forest. Such beliefs inspire an attitude of being in a symbiotic rather than exploitive relationship with the environment, which can have very positive outcomes for society.

The social organization of the society in which a religion is found also affects religious ideology. Guy Swanson (1960) tested the idea that religious beliefs are symbolic representations of what he calls the "sovereign groups" of society and, consequently, have the power to inspire respect and compliance in their members. Sovereign groups, he noted, have "original and independent jurisdiction over some sphere of life" (p. 20). Using a sample of 50 societies from around the world, he found that strong statistical relationships existed between several common religious doctrines and social traits that could logically be expected to be symbolized by those doctrines. The social correlates of various kinds of religious beliefs that he found are summarized below.

Monotheism, the belief in a high god or supreme being who either created and ordered the universe or at least maintains order within it now, is most likely to be found in societies in which the sovereign, decision-making groups are organized hierarchically so that one is superior in rank to at least two levels of groups below it. In such societies, the supreme sovereign group, like the supreme god, can create and maintain order among subordinates. Thus, in contemporary nation-states worldwide, monotheistic religions with their single supreme being have come to have the greatest number of adherents. Even the followers of Hinduism, which has many specific deities, tend to view all those deities as different manifestations of an ultimate Supreme Being.

In contrast to monotheism, the belief in multiple (but not supreme) gods who have different characteristics, powers, and functions, and who may exert control over different domains, is called **polytheism**. Polytheism reflects specialized purposes in human affairs. A society with many unranked occupational specialties is more likely to have a polytheistic religion than is a society with few such specialties. Similarly, societies with distinct social classes are more likely than egalitarian societies to have polytheistic religions. For example, traditional Indian society with its hereditary social castes and numerous jati occupations had comparably diverse, specialized polytheistic deities, which are now coming to be seen as simply different aspects of a single monotheistic deity (as described earlier).

Many traditional societies emphasized the role of **ancestral spirits** who were believed to remain active in human affairs long after the ancestor's death. This was most common in societies in which the economic and political life of the people was primarily controlled by kinship organizations such as lineages and clans. The idea that ancestral members of the clan or lineage continue to be interested in the ongoing economic and political lives of its members would have been seen by Durkheim (discussed in *Section 3: The Psychology of Religion*) as an example of the current social values of the kin group being projected into the group's religious symbolism. A symbolically similar belief is the idea of **reincarnation**, in which the human soul does not simply continue to interact with its descendants but is reborn within the human community. Reincarnation beliefs are most common in societies in which continuity from one generation to the next is maintained by small, isolated groups whose members are economically interdependent and occupy a common settlement smaller in scale than a village.

Belief in some form of **human soul**, which embodies an individual's personality and personal memories, is almost universal. But Swanson distinguishes between societies in which the soul is believed to be lodged in the individual's body and those in which the soul transcends the body. The belief in souls intimately tied to the individual's body is more common in societies in which each individual's unique, personal social identity is highly important, whereas in societies where personal success is more a matter of fitting in and functioning within the larger social group as a team player, the soul is more likely to be conceived as an impersonal vitalizing essence, part of a transcendent spirit that animates everyone.

Although all societies have moral and ethical rules that govern the conduct of individuals toward each other, not all societies use the threat of supernatural punishments for the violation of their moral rules to maintain compliance. **Supernatural sanctions for violations of moral rules** are most often seen in societies where interpersonal differences in wealth are prominent—that is, where different groups within society benefit unequally from those rules.

9.2.2 The Social Organization of Religion

A hallmark of religion is ritual involvement with others. By participating in the religious rituals of their society, people express a sense of togetherness, unity, and belonging. This group aspect of religious practice fosters deeper loyalty to one's society. To be sure, all religions include rituals that individuals may perform for their own benefit: private prayer to petition the spirits and gods for aid; magic to achieve the same ends more coercively; taboos that are followed to avoid misfortune; and positive acts that foster luck, skill, and safety. However, no religious system is built solely from these individualistic ritual activities. Many other rituals have reference to and are part of belonging to a broader religious community and ideology. For instance, all religions have, in addition to the personal rituals practiced by individuals, at least part-time religious specialists who perform rituals for others, and some are organized into more complex communal or ecclesiastical religious groups (Wallace, 1966).

9.2.2.1 Shamanism

Ritual may be performed by any adherent of a religion, but all religions also have some individuals who specialize in the use of spiritual power to mediate between supernatural beings and mortals. The most common kind of ritual specialist in human societies is the inspired and often charismatic medical-religious curer called a **shaman**. Shamans are believed by adherents of the religions in which they are found to be quite capable of using their rituals to harm as well as help others. The shaman's power may be used with the intent of causing illness or even death, or to inflict a myriad of other harms upon people. This is not necessarily done for antisocial purposes but in order to bring wrongdoers to justice by using religious power against them. That is, just as a police officer may use force against those who harm others, a shaman may act as a spiritual enforcer of a society's values. These are aspects of shamanism not fully understood or appreciated by practitioners of what has been labeled "neo-shamanism." Michael Forbes Brown (1989) has used a description of shamanism as practiced by the Aguaruna of Peru, among whom he conducted extensive research, to challenge the romantic naiveté of adherents to the Neo-shamanism Movement in the United States. Among the Aguaruna, the shaman plays an important and beneficial role but one fraught with danger. Unlike American adherents to neo-shamanism, the Aguaruna understand that the shaman's tremendous power can be used for good or evil. Shamans, in turn, know that if they get it wrong or attract suspicion, they can easily be labeled sorcerers and killed.

Of all forms of religious organization, **shamanic religions**, those in which the only ritual specialist is the shaman, are the socially simplest and perhaps the oldest. Shamans may perform rituals to divine the future or to gain answers to their clients' questions. As spirit mediums, they may be called on to increase the success of a hunt, the fertility of the game, or the growth of crops. The charms that they make protect their clients from harm or increase their luck and skill. However, shamans are best known for their skill at manipulating the supernatural to cure illness. Their spiritual powers do not differ in nature from those that nonspecialists may use on their own behalf, but their special status grows out of their reputation for greater skill at manipulating these powers. In addition to their spiritual powers, shamans often possess an impressive body of knowledge about the natural medical effects of a broad range of native plants and other curative materials and techniques. Shamans also draw upon their patients' awe and reverence for religious power, thereby increasing the patients' confidence in the likelihood of recovery.

Mircea Eliade (1964) has shown that the central feature of shamanistic practice is the ecstatic experience achieved in trance. In the trance state, shamans may send their spirits on errands in service to their clients, or they may invite powerful spirits to enter their bodies and give them power. In spirit travel and possession trances, shamans experience the ecstasy of visions of a world not seen by ordinary eyes. In some societies, seizures are perceived as evidence of soul flight and, hence, shamanic abilities. The Hmong, for example, perceive seizures, or as they describe it, "The spirit catches you and you fall down," as a sign that a person has been called to be a shaman. This had disastrous consequences for one little Hmong girl, whose parents were among the 12,000 people who moved from Laos to Merced, California, in the final decades of the 20th century (Fadiman, 1997). Due a lack of Hmong translators at the local hospital, the child's seizure disorder, which her parents suspected to a spiritual calling, was misdiagnosed by the doctors who attended her until it had done irreversible damage to her brain.

Willie Blackeye: A Nevada Shoshone Shaman

On the reservation in Nevada where I did my fieldwork, a Shoshone *puhakanten*, literally a "possessor of power," named Willie Blackeye, cured the sick when he was called upon by persons in need of his services. The shaman's spiritual power was brought to him by a spirit partner, a *newe puha-pea*, the Eagle, who first appeared to him in a vision and gave him the power to cure.

When a prospective patient approached this shaman, the first task was to determine whether he would be able to perform the cure. At the direction of his spirit partner, certain cases—such as those that he diagnosed as cancer—had to be referred to a medical doctor. To facilitate the diagnosis, the individual who consulted him would be given an "eagle wing," a fan made of eagle feathers to place above his or her bed that night. That evening, the shaman would consult his spirit partner for a diagnosis. On the next day, he would either accept or reject the petitioner as a patient, depending on the diagnosis.

A cure usually began at sunset in the shaman's home. It was sometimes attended by other interested members of the community. Attendance at a curing ceremony is believed to foster good health in general among those who participate. The patient, who had bathed that morning at sunrise in a local hot spring, provided tobacco that was smoked by the shaman as part of the ceremony. After smoking, the shaman began a chant that he was taught by his spirit partner in his first vision. This chant was a call to the Eagle to come down from his mountain abode and enter the shaman to give him power to cure his patient's illness. Willie Blackeye alternately smoked, chanted, and massaged the patient's body to remove the illness. Following the ceremony, the patient might be given some tasks to perform to complete the cure. For instance, a patient who was suffering from nosebleeds may be required to collect the blood and dispose of it on a red anthill. Patients were required to abstain from alcohol to ensure the efficacy of the cure.

Willie Blackeye's basic fee was just $8. Over the decades since his fist vision, he never increased that charge, as it was set by his spirit partner, and to do so would cause his power to cure to be withdrawn. However, as an expression of thanks for his work, a patient might bring him a voluntary gift such as a blanket.

Korean religious tradition also includes an important role for shamanic rituals, which are performed by a class of female shamans called *mansin*. They obtain their power by becoming possessed by spirits and deities, during which time they carry out rituals that benefit both individuals and groups. Brian Wilson (1980) reports that *mansin* divine the causes of both psychological and physical illnesses, undertake their cures, communicate with the spirits of the dead, placate angry gods, and purify villages plagued by evil spirits.

Lewis (1971) and Wilson (1980) have both pointed out that spirit possession is a religious practice in which socially powerless members of society are able to assert themselves in ways that society ordinarily forbids and thereby "press their claim for attention and respect" (p. 32). This view of the psychological role of spirit possession seems valid when applied to the Korean *kut* ceremony performed by female shamans. In Korea, the social roles of women provide few opportunities for achieving high public status. In her shamanic role, a Korean shaman can be dominant over the males who are present, even ordering her own husband around during a *kut*. Her authority is based on the belief that she is possessed of a powerful spirit, often a male deity. Playing such a dominant role provides an emotional safety valve for women whose predisposition is toward dominant behavior (for instance, women who as children are seen as "tomboys") and who would otherwise be required to conform to a submissive female set of roles.

The blurring of gender lines seen in the case of the Korean shaman is not characteristic of shamanism in all its forms, but the sacred status of shamans does give them a symbolic "betwixt and between" (see discussion of liminality later in this section) spiritual quality. While mixed-gender characteristics were not part of the shamanistic role in most shamanistic religions, neither is it infrequent. For instance, in Chukchee shamanism, male shamans were expected to adopt the dress of women as a symbol of their sacred status. On the other hand, where supernumerary genders have been found, those genders have been typically viewed as having unusual spiritual abilities necessary for such shamanistic practices as the ability to cure (or cause) infertility (Crapo, 1995), as well as other gender-related spiritual roles such as religious performances at weddings.

9.2.2.2 Communal Religions

A more complex form of religious organization tends to be found in societies that have slightly larger local social groups than those in which shamanic religions predominate. In these societies with larger social groups, **communal religions** serve to celebrate the cohesiveness of the group or ease the transition of individuals from one status to another by publicly proclaiming that change in a rite of passage

The group rituals of communal religions permit broader social participation in the shared concerns of the community or of groups of specialists than do individual or shamanic rituals. The rituals that are most often celebrated in communal religions include rituals to increase the fertility of game or ensure success in hunting; annual rituals to influence the weather, the fertility of crops, and the harvest; social rituals to celebrate changes in status or reinforce the importance of social divisions by sex or age; and ceremonies to reenact the mythology of the group or commemorate cultural heroes, ancestral spirits, or particular deities.

The foraging people of central Australia provide a good example of the importance of communal religious rituals in perpetuating bonds of unity within the social groups of which they are a part. These people lived in local groups, each of which belonged to one of a number of different clans. Each clan, which united local groups that were dispersed over large areas, was named for a species of animal or plant that was sacred to its members and symbolized the unity of the dispersed clan members. As the clan **totem**, this species was believed to be spiritually related to clan members; their souls were believed to be the same kind of spirit as that of their totem species. On certain occasions clan members came together from diverse areas to perform rituals that were intended to increase the numbers of the clan's totem species. By participating with one another in this religious ritual, the members of the clan reinforced their common social bond. Thus, communal religious rituals intended to influence the clan's sacred totem simultaneously perpetuated the solidarity of the clan itself. Anthropologists often refer to such rituals as rites of intensification in recognition of the role they play in fostering group cohesion.

9.2.2.3 Ecclesiastical Religions

Ecclesiastical religions tend to be found in agriculturally based societies, particularly in those with large enough populations to support a variety of full-time specialists. The **ecclesiastical religions** make use of individual, shamanic, and communal rituals, but they add to them a series of rituals performed by **priests**, religious practitioners who have been trained to perform rituals for entire congregations. In ecclesiastical religions, priests may perform some shamanistic roles, such as confessor, counselor, and faith healer. However, the priestly hierarchy may not be tolerant of some shamanistic activities, such as séances, faith healing, prophecy, and psychic readings by separate specialists. The hierarchy of priests often frowns on similar behavior in the lay congregation as well and may forbid such practices as spirit possession trances and ecstatic speaking in tongues by members of the congregation.

Priests may be organized into a professional priesthood, a bureaucracy that both coordinates the activities of its members and regulates the ritual calendar of the congregation. Unlike shamans, who often are highly charismatic individuals who follow the inspiration of the moment in modifying their ritual performance to fit the needs of their clients, priests maintain the traditional ritual forms that they have learned. Priests often learn those rituals during an extended period of rigorous training, as Gerardo Reichel-Dolmatoff (1976) found was the case for the *mámas*, the ritual priests of the Kogi of Columbia. Young male Kogi train for 18 years to become *mámas*, during which time they live apart from the community, remain separated from their families and all females, stay indoors during the daylight hours, and eat special foods.

Roman Catholic Baptism

The ecclesiastical religious rite of baptism is normally practiced shortly after the birth of a child as the first religious rite of passage for Roman Catholics. As is common throughout the world for rites of passage for infants, the baptismal rite includes naming the child and introducing it to others present as a new member of the community.

The rite of baptism ideally takes place on Sunday in the presence of other church members, relatives, and friends, under the direction of a priest. It begins with the godfather and godmother presenting the child for baptism. The priest meets them at the door of the church. The priest asks them, "What name do you give your child?" to which they respond with the name of the child. Then, using the name to identify the child, the priest asks the godparents what they are requesting on behalf of the child, to which they respond, "Baptism." Thereupon the priest charges the godparents with their responsibility for the spiritual training of the child. After they agree to accept this duty, the priest welcomes them on behalf of the Church and traces the sign of the cross on the forehead of the child.

The welcoming of the child to the Church is followed by scriptural readings regarding the rite of baptism and a short sermon on the significance of baptism. This may be followed by a brief period during which all present are invited to pray silently. The congregation is then led in a vocal prayer regarding the death and resurrection of Jesus, who is asked to receive the child into the Church and to grant that the godparents will be examples of faith to the child. The priest then prays for God to free the child from sin and to send the Holy Spirit to the child, after which the child is anointed with consecrated oil.

After being anointed, the child is taken to the baptismal font, where the priest reads a blessing reminding all those present that water is a rich symbol of the grace of God and of religious cleansing. The priest baptizes the child by immersing it in the water or by pouring water on it three times while saying, "I baptize you in the name of the Father, and of the Son, and of the Holy Spirit."

Following the baptism, the congregation sings a short hymn, the child is anointed again, and it is clothed with a white garment provided by the family. The priest lights a candle, a symbol of the light of Christ, and reminds the godparents of their duty to help the child walk in the light and to keep the flame of faith alive in the child's heart.

9.2.3   Ritual in Religion

In the mid-20th century, American anthropologist Anthony F. C. Wallace (1966) shifted research attention to ritual as a fundamental building block of religion. He contended that ritual is performed to bring about or to prevent changes in human beings or in nature. Religious beliefs give meaning to rituals by explaining and interpreting them and by directing the energy of the ritual performance.

Ritual differs from other sorts of behavior in three important ways: It is symbolically meaningful; it is often performed in a repetitive, stereotyped, and predictable way; and it has the intent of manipulating nature through the power of symbols rather than by mechanical means.

Ritual plays three central roles in religion: (1) It unites a community emotionally; (2) it portrays or acts out important aspects of a religion's myths and cosmology; and (3) it influences the spiritual world and thereby the natural world for human beings, or conversely, it helps human beings adjust to the conditions of the natural and spiritual realms. These roles of ritual as symbolic communication may be present simultaneously in a single ritual and are not always clearly distinguished in the minds of the participants themselves.

9.2.3.1 Ritual as Communitas, Liminality, and Social Order

Victor Turner (1969) has emphasized the role of ritual in helping people achieve feelings of unity with each other, a kind of social relationship that he calls **communitas**. During the state of communitas, the normal structure and hierarchy of society is forgotten, and members of the group experience themselves as a community of equals whose individuality may even be submerged into a general sense of fellowship. According to Turner, the experience of communitas is a source of deeply felt bonding and allegiance between a group's members—a kind of "mystery of intimacy"—that every society needs (p. 139). However, communitas is also potentially dangerous and disruptive to society, as it challenges the basic system of social hierarchy, rank, and power differences as they are usually experienced in day-to-day interaction. The dangers that communitas might otherwise pose to society's power structure are restrained by the fact that this state is typically achieved only during the ritual process.

Rituals, Turner noted, are often described as having three phases. In the first phase, sometimes described as a period of "separation," the participants in the ritual may be literally removed from their normal place of work to a place set apart for the purpose of disentangling themselves from the web of symbols that define the ordinary reality of their culture. The middle phase of a ritual is often described as a period of pilgrimage within a spiritual landscape. Turner calls this transition stage between the beginning and end of a ritual the **liminal period**. This is a "betwixt-and-between" period in which the normal social hierarchy is dissolved and replaced by an emphasis on the commonality of the group itself. It is during the liminal phase of a ritual that communitas is characteristic of the participants' feelings toward each other. Finally, participants in rituals are returned to an awareness of the mundane world of normal social life during the phase of reintegration. This tripartite pattern of ritual is particularly common in the rites of transition that societies commonly use to mark the status changes that occur during the lifecycle. However, liminality, the state of being "betwixt and between," is also found in social settings where people experience themselves as outside the normal social order—either as marginal or inferior in the eyes of others or as somehow distinct from the normal categories of life. Thus, people with low-ranked or marginal social statuses—such as slaves, prostitutes, or street people—may experience a strong sense of camaraderie such as is experienced by mainstream members of society only during the communitas of the ritual process. For more on communitas and rites of passage see Figure 9.1.

9.2.3.2 Ritual as Portrayal

Rituals often involve symbolic portrayals of myths. The Christian ritual that is sometimes called the Sacrament of the Lord's Supper, in which wine and broken bread are shared by members of a congregation, may remind people of the final meal that Jesus and the disciples had together before Jesus's arrest and crucifixion. At the same time, the broken bread and the wine may symbolize or become the body and the blood of Jesus, who Christians believe died as a vicarious sacrifice on behalf of humankind. In addition, the ritual may represent purification and renewal of the spiritual bonds that unite members of the congregation with their religion as they receive and eat the sacramental meal. Similarly, the baptism by immersion that is practiced in some Christian churches may represent simultaneously a washing away of sin; a portrayal of the death, burial, and resurrection from the dead that most Christians believe Jesus experienced; the spiritual death and renewal by which the individual enters the Christian religion; or the individual's own future death, burial, and hoped-for reawakening to a life beyond the grave. Part of the beauty of a ritual

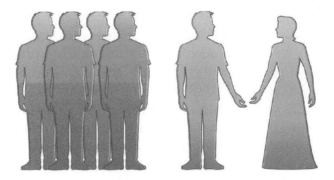

Separation

Communitas

Reintegration

Figure 9.1: Rites of passage: American bachelor party

The traditional North American bachelor party is an example of communitas.

for its participants lies in the multiplicity of meanings it may have for them, a characteristic that may give them the feeling that the ritual embodies meanings transcending those of ordinary symbols.

9.2.3.3 Ritual as Influence

Rituals are also performed to influence the supernatural for the sake of human beings. The purposes of such rituals—for instance, regaining health or avoiding illness, protecting oneself in times of danger, discovering a lost watch, bringing rain in times of drought, winning at gambling, or winning someone's love—are as diverse as are human needs. The role of rituals may be perceived as only mildly influential or as powerfully effective. The former type, called **petitionary rituals** by anthropologists, are often most prominent in religions that emphasize the worship of powerful deities who may choose to decline the request. In such religions, petitionary rituals may combine expressions of praise and thanksgiving with requests for desired benefits, as a good relationship with the supernatural being may increase the chances of the petition being positively received.

On the other hand, rituals that are considered powerful and effective, even compulsive of the supernatural, and therefore more likely than mere petition to achieve the desired results, are called **magic**. This should not be confused with nonreligious stage "magic," which even the audience may recognize as nothing more than skilled illusion. Magic of the religious variety is ritual that its audience truly believes will work by virtue of its ability to coerce supernatural beings or influence powers such as mana. Unlike petitionary rituals, which include general guidelines to be followed but often involve much personal latitude in how they are performed, magical rituals are presumed effective only if they are performed correctly. Therefore, magic is typically executed with mechanical precision, and with great care and attention given to its details.

In earlier times, anthropologists treated magic as a system based on supernatural beliefs that was somehow different from religion, or they ethnocentrically contrasted the magic that they described in non-Western societies with the religions of Europe, which emphasized petitionary rituals. Today, we consider such contrasts too sweeping and instead describe magic as one variety of religious ritual. In other words, we think of rituals as falling along a continuum whose endpoints are petition and compulsion, with magic falling nearest the compulsive end of the scale. Usually, rituals are more coercive when people feel an urgent need to have more control over events than they have by nonreligious means. Magic, in other words, is more typical of religious behavior when the successful outcome of the magical act is crucial to the performers. George Gmelch's (2011) analysis of baseball magic clearly illustrates this relationship between magic and uncertainty. Hitters and pitchers, who have little control over the outcome of their efforts, are renown for respecting taboos, relying on fetishes or "good luck charms," and mechanically following particular routines—all forms of magic—to enhance their chances of a winning performance. Fielders, who know they have a better than 97% chance of catching a ball hit in their direction, face little uncertainty in their performance and don't bother with magical interventions.

Sir James Frazer (1922) noted long ago that magic the world over seems invariably to make use of the same two principles: imitation and contagion. **Imitative magic** acts out or portrays what it is intended to accomplish. It uses a principle that Frazer called the **Law of Similarity**. This principle seems to be based on the idea that performed activities similar to the desired outcome increase the probability of its occurrence. Thus, magical rituals that follow this principle imitate the thing that they are designed to bring about. Christians who immerse a convert in water to "wash away sin" and Pueblo Indians who whip yucca juice into frothy suds to "bring rain" are both making use of the Law of Similarity. So is the child in the United States who takes care to step over the cracks in the sidewalk, following the admonition in the childhood rhyme, "Step on a crack, and you break your mother's back." Note in this last case, the crucial similarities in the sound of the words *back* and *crack* and in the appearance of the line of sidewalk blocks and the line of vertebrae in the spinal column.

The idea that once two things have been in contact with each other they will remain in contact on a spiritual level so that the magical manipulation of one will also affect the other is called the **Law of Contagion**. **Contagious magic** follows this law. It may be performed on anything that has had contact with the person to be influenced: a lock of the person's hair or a piece of his or her clothing are ideal; fingernail or toenail clippings, dirt from under the nails, or excrement will do just fine; even dirt from the bottom of a footprint will help. In magic designed to harm, the magical poison can simply be poured into the victim's footprint. The Law of Contagion is one reason why many people all over the world have two names, one for public use by others and a true, private name known only to themselves and perhaps a few close relatives. Because the name is an extension of the self, so the logic goes, to know someone's true name is to be able to use it as a form of contact in speaking a magical spell. In some parts of the world, when illness is thought to have been magically induced, the victim will customarily change his or her name as a part of the cure. This denies the **sorcerer**—a person who uses magic to harm others—the chance for continued mischief by magical use of the victim's name.

Often, magic employs elements of both the Law of Similarity and the Law of Contagion at the same time. My grandmother in Arkansas, for example, practiced the custom of protecting her children from tetanus by carefully washing the farmyard nail that had been stepped on, covering it with lard, and placing it on the kitchen windowsill. This magical ritual made use of the object that had inflicted the wound—the Law of Contagion—and treated it in a way that she believed would prevent germs from reaching it—the Law of Similarity.

An important use of rituals to obtain supernatural aid or knowledge is **divination**. Methods of divination can be very creative. They may include examining the entrails of animals for unusual signs, considering the flight direction of birds or the shapes formed by molten lead poured into water, or checking the lines on people's hands or the date of their birth. These methods have been used to answer such questions as, where is my lost watch? Who committed a particular crime? What kind of person should I marry? Methods of divination fall into two main categories: those in which the results can be easily influenced by the diviner and those in which they cannot. The former include practices such as reading tealeaves or interpreting an astrological sign, casting the *I Ching*, spreading *Tarot* cards, or randomly selecting a Bible verse. Each of these techniques gives the diviner a good deal of latitude for subjective interpretation. These methods permit the diviner's knowledge of the client's circumstances to play a role in providing answers that are psychologically satisfying to the customer.

Methods that give responses that the diviner is unable to control include such techniques as casting lots or checking whether an object floats on water. Like flipping a coin, these tend to randomize the answers. This approach to divination is especially useful when conflicting secular information causes confusion or when divergent opinions must be resolved. Frank Speck (1935), for example, once described how during lean times, Naskapi hunters of Labrador resorted to scapulimancy to improve their chances of finding game. Scapulimancy entails heating an animal shoulder blade—a caribou shoulder blade in the case of the Naskapi—and then reading the cracks that form much as one would read a map. This map, then, tells hunters where to go next in their search for game, leaving the success or failure of their quest in the hands of the supernatural rather than opening band members to the risk of blame in the event of continued failure.

Magic also may be used with the intent of causing ill health. Illness is a problem with which people must cope in all parts of the world. Although health-related magic is most common in societies that lack complex secular medical technologies, one finds religious rituals for the curing and causing of illness in all the world's societies.

According to Forest Clements (1932), there are six major theories of disease in the world's societies: natural causes, magic, the intrusion of disease objects into the victim's body, soul loss, spirit possession, and taboo violations. Each of these is associated with an appropriate approach to curing the illness.

Those diseases or infirmities that are thought to be the result of natural causes are treated by pragmatic techniques such as setting broken bones and using herbs. Even societies that treat most illnesses with magic and rituals will have practical methods for dealing with minor injuries and herbal and other remedies for common maladies. They may, nonetheless, attribute those injuries and illnesses to supernatural causes.

When magic is used to bring about illness or death in a victim, the sorcerer's favored materials may include things that have been in intimate contact with the victim, as they invoke the Law of Contagion and direct the magic more surely to its intended victim than the Law of Similarity alone might. Magic-caused illnesses must be cured by corresponding countermagic.

Sending a foreign object, called a **disease object**, into the body of a victim by magic is another favored technique of sorcerers and witches for bringing about illness or death. When a foreign object such as a barbed stick or a stone is believed to have been supernaturally projected into the victim's body, thereby causing pain and illness, the object is removed by massage and sucking.

The fourth cause of illness is **soul loss**, a malady commonly found where independence and self-reliance are important social values. When a soul has left a person's body—whether dislodged from the body by a sudden fright, simply lost during its nightly wanderings, or stolen by another's magic—the body is left without the vitality that it needs to survive. If this is believed to be the cause of the victim's ill health, a healer must coax the wayward soul back into the patient's body or recapture it and bring it back.

Spirit possession, the control of a person's behavior by a spirit that has entered his or her body, is common in societies where people are expected to be dutiful and compliant rather than independent and assertive. It requires a ritual of exorcism to remove the offending spirit.

In many cultures, especially those in which people are expected to learn a lot of rules, it is believed that illness may come not as punishment but simply as a natural consequence of breaking a supernatural rule. Thus **taboo violation** may include not only willful rule breaking but also rule breaking that is accidental or even done without the actor's awareness. As a result, the rule breaker is not necessarily held morally responsible for the act, as in the Western concept of sin, but he or she may still suffer the consequences. For instance, Apache Indians of the southwestern United States believe that illness may result from using firewood that has been urinated on by a deer, even though one is unlikely to know whether or not this is the case. Furthermore, in some societies the illness that follows a taboo violation may strike someone other than the rule breaker—a relative or a neighbor, for instance. When taboo violation is thought to be the cause of illness, confession will play a role in the cure.

The use of rituals to harm another person supernaturally is called **sorcery**. This practice is most common in societies in which individuals must interact with each other but in which socially approved means for one individual to control another do not exist. In an earlier study of sorcery, Beatrice Whiting (1950) showed that it was most likely to be practiced in societies that lack "individuals or groups of individuals with delegated authority to settle disputes" (p. 90), leaving retaliation by peers as the main tool of social control. In addition, beliefs in sorcery and **witchcraft**—a related phenomenon in which the evildoer has an innate ability to harm others without using rituals—are most common in societies that engender severe anxiety about the expression of aggression or sexuality in children during their socialization (Whiting & Child, 1953).

What determines whether people will attribute the cause of an illness to the malicious acts of others (sorcerers or witches, for example), or to another cause? As has been noted, Beatrice Whiting (1950) and Guy Swanson (1960) have linked the presence of societal conflicts and the absence of effective social means of resolving them to the belief that sorcery can work harm. Specific conflicts surrounding sexual jealousy also have been suggested as a basis for witchcraft and sorcery. On the other hand, the belief that illness may be caused by nonhuman spiritual beings (spirit possession) seems to symbolize anxiety about the kind of social role one is expected to play. Bourguignon and Greenberg (1973) found that spirit possession is most common in societies in which people are expected to be submissive and compliant, and that spirit loss is most common in societies in which people are socialized to be independent and self-assertive. Illness as a result of taboo violation is found in societies in which conformity to rules is important. For instance, taboo violation is an important cause of illness among the arctic Inuit, whose environment can be deadly if one is lax or careless in following the established rules of life.

The belief in evil supernatural powers as a source of harm to human beings is far from absent in the contemporary world. Adam Ashforth (2005) discusses the ongoing difficulty faced by the South African government over how best to respond to the widespread belief in what is called "witchcraft" there, a local term that encompasses what in this text is termed "sorcery." The dilemma for the government is whether witchcraft should be accepted as a legal concept because not doing so alienates the legal system from the people and their sense of justice by not responding to deaths and other harms they attribute to "witchcraft."

In some cases, victims of sorcery actually die. Anthropologists have tried for decades to understand the phenomenon of death by magic. Cannon (1942) analyzed cases of so-called **voodoo death** and suggested that the actual cause of death in such cases may be prolonged shock induced by extreme fear. Cannon quotes Herbert Basedow (1925), who graphically described the terrifying effect of sorcery by **bone-pointing** in Australia:

A man who discovers that he is being boned by an enemy is, indeed, a pitiable sight. He stands aghast, with his eyes staring at the treacherous pointer, and with his hands lifted as though to ward off the lethal medium, which he imagines is pouring into his body. . . . His cheeks blanch and his eyes become glossy, and the expression of his face becomes horribly distorted, like that of one stricken with palsy. He attempts to shriek but usually the sound chokes in his throat, and all that one might see is froth at his mouth. His body begins to tremble and the muscles twist involuntarily. He sways backwards and falls to the ground, and after a short time appears to be in a swoon but soon after he begins to writhe as if in mortal agony, and, covering his face with his hands, begins to moan. After a while he becomes more composed and crawls to his wurley [hut]. From this time onwards he sickens and frets, refusing to eat, and keeping aloof from the daily affairs of the tribe. Unless help is forthcoming in the shape of a counter charm administered by the hands of the *"Nangarri"* or medicine-man, his death is only a matter of a comparatively short time. If the coming of the medicine-man is opportune, he might be saved. (Basedow qtd. in Cannon, 1942, p. 181)

Normally, both fear and anger stimulate the sympathetic nervous system, which regulates the inner organs and the circulatory system. This stimulation prepares the body for prolonged muscular exertion and aids in such things as escaping from danger. However, adaptation to unusual levels of stress cannot go on indefinitely; the stress of remaining in this state of preparedness will eventually cause exhaustion and damage to the bodily organs, which may result in death.

Reo Fortune (1932a) gave a graphic account of the use of sorcery to kill among the Dobuans, inhabitants of the Melanesian Islands near New Guinea. The sorcerer and one or more assistants approached the area of the victim's garden in the forest. They rubbed their bodies with magically powerful herbs to make themselves invisible and then crept to the edge of the clearing where the victim was working in the garden. Suddenly, with a characteristic scream, the sorcerer jumped into the clearing. The victim, taken by surprise, would realize what was happening from the cry and actions of the sorcerer. He or she would be overcome by fear and fall immediately into a faint. The sorcerer was then free to prance about and dramatically act out, in symbolic form, the surgical opening of the victim's abdomen and the magical removal of the entrails and vital organs. After closing the magical wound, the sorcerer would ask the victim, "What is my name?" The victim could not respond, ensuring that the sorcerer would not be identified.

After the sorcerer departed, the victim gradually recovered enough to stagger home and crawl up the ladder to his or her house. Relatives, recognizing the expression of shock and fear on the victim's face, knew what had transpired and began to make arrangements for the funeral. The victim lost all appetite and could die from shock within the next few days.

Just as ritual is believed to play a prominent role in the causing of illness or even death, religious power is called on in many societies to cure illness. Curing illness is the primary concern of shamans, or inspired religious healers. In societies in which shamans are able to congregate in sufficient numbers, they may form organizations in which they discuss their practices, cooperate with one another in curing patients, and initiate apprentices into the shared secrets of the trade. For instance, among the Iroquois, a Native American people who live in northern New York and whose earlier culture was described extensively by Morgan (1851a), various illnesses were treated by the members of specialized medicine societies. Among these were the False Face Society, the Bear Society, the Pygmy Society, the Otter Society, the Chanters for the Dead, and the Eagle Society. Each specialized in the treatment or prevention of particular ills and had its own songs and rituals. Those who asked a particular society for a cure became members of that society if the cure was successful, as did persons who dreamed that they must join a society, as such a dream was believed to have been a message from the supernatural. Thus, following a cure, individuals acquired a new social status and were expected to play a role in the curing of others who became afflicted by the same disease.

9.3　The Psychology of Religion

In this section we will explore the personal and subjective characteristics of religion.

9.3.1　Spirituality

While the word *religion* is commonly used to refer to the social organization that followers may participate in and the ideology they share, the word **spirituality** is typically used to refer to the religious psychology of those who are adherents of a religion. Americans sometimes say "I'm spiritual but not religious," meaning that although they do not actively participate in a religious body such as a church, synagogue, or mosque, they nevertheless personally experience life in spiritual terms. Spirituality is this personal or psychological side of religion, whether it is experienced in an organized group setting or privately.

9.3.2　Trance States

Religious rituals are often accompanied by **trances** (also called **altered states of consciousness**). These are subjective states of mind characterized by the individual's disassociation from a normal state of consciousness. Although not everyone is susceptible to such altered states of consciousness, the trance experience tends to be culturally specific: In other words, susceptible individuals learn how, when, and why to go into trance and what form the experience should take. The trance experience of one late-19th-century Lakota Ghost Dance participant was much the same as that of another: Everyone danced the same round dance steps to the same drum beat, sang the same songs, and acted in pretty much the same way when they went into trance. That is because the Ghost dancers shared an understanding of what they were doing and why: They were dancing a prescribed dance to bring back the ancestors and restore their life to the way it had been before it was so badly disrupted by Euro-American influences and domination (Andersson, 2008; Mooney, 1896).

　　Trances may be rather mild and undramatic experiences, such as the state of daydreaming or fantasy that we all engage in occasionally when we are tired or bored with our current environment. They also may be rather vivid and dramatic occurrences, such as visionary experiences. It is this later type of trance that is of most interest to anthropologists.

9.3.2.1　Socialization and Trance States

Bourguignon and Greenbaum (1973) have noted that different cultural patterns lie behind two different forms of trance: spirit travel trance and spirit possession trance. The first is characterized by passivity or even unconsciousness during the altered mental state, which is interpreted as a "trip" in which the spirit leaves the body and communes with supernatural entities. Possession trances, on the other hand, involve a great deal of bodily activity, thought to be under the control of a spirit visitor. These trances are often entered with the aid of repetitive chants and dancing. Unlike participants in spirit travel trances, people who engage in possession trances often experience amnesia about what they said and did while possessed. In spirit travel trances, hallucinations may be vividly recalled, and drugs are more likely to be used as an aid to entering the trance.

The spirit travel trances are most likely to be found in societies that place the heaviest stress on independence and assertion. Spirit possession trances, on the other hand, are most common in societies where compliance is expected. In each case, the common form of trance is that which most effectively reduces the kind of stress typically found in that culture.

9.3.2.2 Biological Explanations of Trances

Trances are the result of the effects of various forms of stress on the human brain. The cerebral cortex of the human brain is divided into two major halves or hemispheres. The left hemisphere has specialized centers that make possible the symbolic skills embodied in language. Stress, however, interferes with the symbolic capacity of the human organism. The right hemisphere, which takes the lead in nonsymbolic behavior, plays the dominant role during the expressive acts common in rituals because it communicates by direct representation with signs.

9.3.2.3 Producing Trance States

Ludwig (1972) reports five main ways of producing altered states of consciousness: (1) a prolonged reduction of sensory input and/or motor activity; or (2) the opposite condition, namely, sensory and/or motor overload; (3) prolonged increased alertness or mental involvement; or (4) the opposite condition, a prolonged decrease in mental alertness or involvement; and (5) changes in body chemistry. The first of these may be exemplified by trances induced through meditation. Much like the Lakota Ghost dancers, whirling dervishes achieve their transcendent mental state by means of the second method—hyperkinetic movement. Examples of the third method include the spiritual state achieved by the practice of maintaining hyper-awareness found in Eastern religions that treat every action as a sacred act and by practices such as fervent but quiet solitary prayer. Restricted Environment Stimulation Therapy (REST), which relies on such techniques as deprivation chambers and flotation tanks, would be an example of Ludwig's fourth type. Finally, many of the religions studied by anthropologists have made use of psychoactive plants to achieve trances through changes in body chemistry. All of these conditions interfere with the normal functioning of the central nervous system and produce stress, the source of the signalized ritual behavior that accompanies altered states of consciousness.

9.3.2.4 Near Death Experiences

Recent research on the neurochemistry of the brain suggests that many of the characteristics of spiritual experiences such as the feeling of being in the presence of a great transcendent being, like a deity, are physiologically induced. One category of such experiences, called **near death experiences (NDEs)** can occur when the parietal lobes of the brain (areas just above and in front of the ears) are oxygen deprived. This may account for what has happened to people who report near death experiences in which they have feelings of tremendous well-being, detachment from their bodies, and sometimes even what seems to be out-of-the-body experiences that may include visitation by spiritual beings or even entering the presence of a divine being (see van Lommell et al., 2001).

Although trance states may be spontaneously induced by stressful experiences, their occurrence is not necessarily random and unpredictable. This is, in part, because many life stresses are not random events but are culturally patterned, being more or less likely in specific circumstances, and thus varying from one culture to another. In addition, individuals in any culture may learn how to enter a state of trance when it is socially appropriate and expected—for instance, while participating as audiences in religious rituals or artistic performances. Thus, although in some instances trance is an unwelcome consequence of prolonged anxiety, there are also numerous instances where trance is sought after and fully congruent with accepted social roles. This is particularly well illustrated by the religious specialists known as shamans who, in many societies, are expected to enter trance states as a normal part of the performance of religious rituals. To the extent that altered states of consciousness are responses to stress, they may be culturally shaped along two dimensions. One dimension is the cultural nature of the stress itself; the other is the way in which altered states of consciousness are culturally defined. For instance, Tanya Luhrmann (2004) described the importance of trance states in the process in some Christian denominations of becoming "born again" and in rearticulating a relationship to God in a way that expresses alienation from contemporary technological and secularized society.

9.3.2.5 Dream Control of the Supernatural

One example of how cultural definitions of trance influence its role in society is the use of dreams to control the supernatural. D'Andrade (1961) compared societies in which people attempt to contact and control the supernatural through dreams with those societies in which dreams play no such role. He found that societies in which young men move far from their parents when they marry are more likely to make such use of dreams. He suggests that this may be a response to the loss of a parent as a source to turn to in times of need. Societies that have the capacity to store food are less likely to use dreams for supernatural purposes than those that do not preserve food. Because the latter is also likely to emphasize independence and self-reliance as a natural consequence of its small accumulation of foodstuffs, Bourguignon (1974) regards the use of dreams to control supernatural power as a response to stresses generated by the lack of human support that the expectation of self-reliance implies.

9.3.3   Feelings in Religion

Supernatural things are believed to be a source of great power that can be influenced for human ends. Whether perceived as gods, spirits, or mana, they have the quality of being both nonhuman and humanlike in their response to symbols. Because they are both powerful and mysterious, they are capable of inspiring strong feelings in humans who approach them. Rudolf Otto (1923) described these intense feelings as the uncanny or eerie sense of awe and dread that people sometimes experience when they are confronted by mysterious things. Such feelings are easily interpreted as a perception of a transcendent, supernatural presence that can fascinate even while it may be feared.

French anthropologist Émile Durkheim (1912/1915) focused on the feelings that religion creates in a community of people. To him religion was a system of beliefs and practices pertaining to **sacred** things, by which he meant things that inspire feelings of awe, respect, or reverence because they are set apart and forbidden.

Durkheim was concerned with the question of what lies at the root of religious ideas and what maintains them through the generations. He suggested that sacred things and religious ideas about them are symbolic representations, or metaphors, for those aspects of society and culture that inspire feelings of respect, fear, and awe among its members. Durkheim believed that by maintaining and manipulating these feelings in symbolic form, religion perpetuated the sentiments that people must have toward their society if it is to survive. In other words, religion transforms social norms into sacred obligations. Durkheim illustrated his belief in the intimate connection between a religion's sacred symbols and society's fundamental institutions by examining the native people of central Australia, whose communal rituals were described above. In Durkheim's view, each religion is best understood as a society's symbolic worship of itself. In a Durkheimian sense, religious symbolism arises through the same kind of psychology that may also sanctify other symbols of a society, as when Americans express outrage at the desecration of the country's flag or occasionally entertain efforts even to amend the country's constitution to outlaw shows of disrespect for this "sacred" symbol.

Another influential view of religion that also focuses on the importance of feelings has been that of Clifford Geertz. His approach emphasizes religion's role in creating or expressing feelings that lend stability to society. He expressed this when he described religion as a symbolic system that functions to "establish powerful, pervasive, and long-lasting moods and motivations" in people by "formulating conceptions of a general order of existence and . . . clothing these conceptions with such an aura of factuality that . . . the moods and motivations seem uniquely realistic" (Geertz, 1966, p. 4). Geertz's approach, like that of Durkheim, focuses on the role of religion in validating people's allegiance to their society and culture. Religion, in this view, consists of important symbols that affirm a culturally valued worldview by providing people with ritual settings in which they will feel that those valued beliefs are true even though they may be challenged by experiences outside the religious setting. Thus, for instance, religion can rescue people's faith in spite of disasters, tragedies, and personal difficulties that might otherwise challenge it. Religious concepts that explain life's evils as "God's will," punishment for sin, the results of witchcraft, or in terms of similar religious ideas help people cope with the difficulties of life that might otherwise undermine their social commitments. According to Geertz, it is especially by participating in religious rituals that people repress any contradictions between the world as it ought to be and the world as it is.

Geertz's approach also invites comparisons between religion and other institutions that traditional definitions have contrasted with religion—for instance, the similarities in the deep commitment and behavior of followers of theologies such as Islam or Christianity and of strong adherents of various political ideologies.

9.3.4 Religious Extremism

For most people, religion and spirituality are important parts of life but not all-consuming. Most followers of a religion spend the bulk of their time participating in the workaday world and participate in religion only on special occasions such as a day of worship, saying grace at meals, or offering personal prayers at certain times of the day. Sometimes, however, religion can reach the point of being an obsession for an individual or the prime motivator of an entire religious group, both in the world of politics and during strictly religious observances. Under what circumstances is this the case?

Hyper-religiosity in individuals is best understood as an artifact of that individual's personality rather than as something caused by his or her religion itself. Psychologically, this form of religious extremism, which is sometimes called religious compulsivity, is behaviorally and mentally identical with the extreme obsessive-compulsive behavior seen in some individuals in nonreligious contexts. In other words, religion is not the cause of the hyper-religiosity found in some religious individuals. Rather, it is simply a form of individual compulsivity that happens to be manifested in a religious context.

The label of "religious extremism" is usually applied to an entire religious movement or group rather than an individual. Religious extremism occurs when a religious body (such as a particular denomination) becomes the predominant vehicle of political expression for its followers. This typically happens when a social or ethnic group experiences discrimination, economic deprivation, or societal stigma and also shares a common religious bond. Under such circumstances, responses that otherwise might be made in purely political terms may begin to be made using the shared religious system to express political dissatisfaction and motivate group members to engage in political acts, up to and including terrorism, in the name of religion.

At the milder end of such religious extremism are the various forms of Christian, Jewish, Islamic, Hindu, and Buddhist fundamentalism. **Fundamentalist religions**, wherever they are found, are espoused by members of society that feel economically and/or politically disenfranchised and socially stigmatized. Such was the case with the serpent-handling Christian fundamentalists Mary Lee Daugherty (1976) studied in rural Appalachia. At the time of her research, their life was a struggle: They were all poor, and many were unemployed. Those who did have jobs worked in the coal mines in very dangerous conditions. Their religion, and the feeling of closeness to God created by their willingness to handle poisonous snakes as a sacrament, gave them the strength to carry on. Daugherty's serpent handlers shared two commonalities with fundamentalists around the world. All such groups espouse a literalist understanding (one that requires no special theological training) of scriptures that they regard as infallible sources of truth, and all believe that their religious truths should be implemented in their political lives within their larger society. That political activism, however, may simply involve voting for candidates they believe will support laws that are in harmony with their values. Sometimes, however, on the fringe of such fundamentalist groups are subgroups that believe that their cause is based on absolute truths, which they are entitled to use coercive means to achieve. It is on this fringe that one finds religious movements emerging that engage in terrorist acts to support their political agendas.

Mainstream religions are those that teach and reinforce social values that are in harmony with the larger society of which they are a part. New religious movements tend to arise, in part, as protest movements in regard to social issues and values that are important enough to potential converts to recruit new members from the larger society. Such movements are sometimes referred to as "cults" in the mass media, a term most anthropologists reject as value-laden. The concept of "religious extremism" as used here is not a value judgment but simply a reference to religious ideologies that, in contrast with the mainstream religions, are notably at odds with the larger society of which they are a part.

Economists Iannaccone and Berman (2006) have suggested that a religious group is correspondingly more likely to espouse an extremist ideology the more forms of sacrifice its members are expected to make. Such sacrifices might include demonstrations of devotion such as monetary donations to the religious body and requirements that isolate members from the societal mainstream (e.g., rules against dancing, alcohol, and other widespread social practices). Such prohibitions reduce the ability of group members to participate in activities within the larger society. This, in turn, makes the religious meetings and social fellowship provided by the group even more important to its members. The social isolation of such groups may lead to their becoming quite skilled at providing their members with a variety of services, including schooling, social services, and other benefits that further enhance group loyalty and isolate members from the broader society. None of these things necessarily mean that the group will not remain benign, but the self-sufficiency that such internal services provide does seem to be a necessity if the group's extremism is to shift from a mere ideological gap between themselves and others to a more militant form. The most militant of extremist religious groups tend to offer many such services to their members.

9.3.4.1 Religious Extremism and Violence

Although religion typically reinforces prosocial values as a means of uniting followers, religious groups are not always benign. Religious extremism tends to develop when a religious group perceives itself as politically or economically threatened by other, more powerful groups. Under such circumstances a group can become highly politicized as a means of what it perceives as necessary self-defense. In short, religious extremism is most likely to be found in religious groups that are in tension with their current social environment, and mere separatism seems to them to be an insufficient means of maintaining their own welfare. Under such circumstances, religious groups can become highly politicized in their opposition to those they view as adversaries. It should be noted that most of the world's terrorist acts are purely political with no religious underpinning. For instance, the Tamil Tigers have engaged in more suicide bombings for their political cause than have terrorist movements that claim a religious motivation. What both kinds of extremism have in common is their economic and political motivations.

It is economics and political circumstances that lead a religiously extremist organization to become politicized in its willingness to engage in violence. This can happen, for instance, if an isolationist religious group perceives itself as threatened by the surrounding society or its government, as in the case of Jim Jones's People's Temple, in which 920 members died by ingesting poison in response to a perceived threat by government. A similar thing happened with the Branch Davidians, a Christian extremist group that literally went down in a blaze of glory when besieged by federal agents at Waco, Texas (Barkun, 1993). It can also occur if a religious organization with an extremist ideology has little or no competition from other, less extremist religious groups—for instance, if it has become the state-sanctioned religion. This latter case is exemplified by those parts of the Inquisition that occurred under Catholic Church control in the Middle Ages. Religious support for and organizational control of the Inquisition during some periods of its history have been analyzed by Cullen Murphy (2012). While most of the centuries of that era involved Inquisitions (such as the Spanish Inquisition), in which the violent acts were carried out under the authority of the political sovereigns, there were cases where the Church organization combined its religious desire to purify the faith with its political power and conducted similar acts of torture and persecution of heretics and nonbelievers. Murphy demonstrates that it is not simply a certitude of exclusive control of religious truth, but also the addition of the organizational machinery to carry out political action, that is necessary for religious extremism to turn violent, as has recently occurred in the religiously motivated killing of abortion doctors in the United States and in terrorism carried out in the name of religion in various parts of the world.

The Crusades

Eleventh-century Western Europe was dealing with the effects of repeated invasions from the north, south, and east. Internal order was collapsing, and local authorities were often brutal in their oppression of the poor. For several centuries, Western Europe had been feeling the effects of repeated Viking raids all along its north and west coasts. From the East, Magyar tribes were moving into the middle regions around northern Italy and Bavaria. And Islamic military action had resulted in Moorish rule in Sicily and Spain. Through this century, the Church had been trying unsuccessfully to instill a greater allegiance to "Christian morality" in the treatment of peasants by brutal overlords, but the fractured nature of Western European politics and the constant external threats made it profitable for local leaders to continue their rule by brutality.

In the middle of the 11th century, there arose a new political threat—the rise of the Seljuk Turks who pushed back the borders of the Byzantine Empire and took control of the Holy Land. Prior to this, the "Saracens," who controlled Jerusalem and the Holy Land, had allowed free passage to Christian pilgrims. One of the first effects of the shift of political control from the Saracens to the Seljuks was the massacre of 3,000 Christian pilgrims. This changed the political situation for Europeans dramatically.

Western Europe was highly Balkanized with no dominant political power at the time. Consequently, political leaders called on Pope Urban II to support a unification of Western European military efforts by granting his religious support to a war against the East that would reopen trade and pilgrimage routes (the two being synonymous) through Byzantium into the Holy Land, a region rich in spices and other important resources. Urban II also saw this as beneficial to something the Church had been unsuccessfully attempting to accomplish within the politically fractured western half of European Christianity: a shift of the military power base of the local power elites from Europe to its borders in common cause against an external political threat, a shift that would weaken the ability of local lords to brutalize the peasantry by removing their enforcers to the East. This appeared to Urban II to support the Church's goal of establishing a more humane "Christian" system of life within the western Christian nations, so in 1095 he began to preach his support for what came to be known as the First Crusade. Interestingly, Urban II spoke of the crusade he called for in terms of protection of Western Europe's Rome-oriented Latin Christianity against the "infidels," but he did not actually single out "Muslims" by name. In the popular culture of the day, it was not just pagans and Muslims who were thought of as "infidels" but also

(Continued)

(*Continued*)

Jews and even the Orthodox Christianity of Byzantium. Jews felt the wrath of the soldiery of all of the crusades, not just in the Holy Land but also in Europe as the military passed through. And Christian Byzantium itself became a victim as well in the Fourth Crusade that began in 1204, when Constantinople was conquered and pillaged by the Crusaders, who for 3 days killed, raped, and looted the city and desecrated Hagia Sophia, perhaps the greatest of all Christian churches of its day. The political element of the crusades is also illustrated by the fact that during the time of the Second Crusade there was also a crusade organized against the pagan Slavic peoples of the Baltic region, a crusade that had nothing to do with the Holy Land but furthered the political goals of European leaders to expand their authority to new lands.

The important question is not whether the rallying cry was versed in religious terms, but why so many people of high and low status supported the call for military action so far away. Urban II envisioned a crusade of militarily trained aristocratic knights, but those who flocked to participate in the First Crusade were primarily peasants— the poor, the dispossessed, the indebted, and those sought by the law. Secondarily, it received support from lawless brigands and their followers, who had been preying on the peasantry and were lured by the belief in greater opportunities to loot the wealth of both Byzantium and the Middle East. Some aristocrats (and a greater number in later crusades) looked forward to the possibility of establishing their own kingdoms in the east. The merchants of Venice and Genoa were particularly enthusiastic because wars need logistic support and they saw the crusades as promising great profits.

An important idea that we should take from this is that the First Crusade had secular political and economic roots rather than religious ones. Urban II's support aided perhaps sped up a political process that was likely to have happened anyway.

9.4 Religious Change

Religion tends to be a conservative institution that functions as a stabilizing influence within society by emphasizing the importance of tradition and perpetuating beliefs and rituals that have been handed down from the past. Yet religion does change. Usually, religious beliefs and practices lag behind social change and then make small adjustments when the discrepancies grow too large.

9.4.1 Syncretism

Religion is not immune to the influences of diffusion. One way religions change is by borrowing beliefs, practices, and organizational characteristics from other religions, a process called **syncretism**. These borrowed elements, however, are often given new meanings or functions. For example, the Native American Church, which now has an estimated membership of 250,000 people drawn from 50 Native American tribal groups, has blended elements of Christian and indigenous peyote (a hallucinogenic cactus) rituals into a distinct religion that is highly meaningful to its adherents (LaBarre, 1938; Stewart, 1993). In doing so, it has changed the functions and meanings of elements from both traditions to meet its needs. The idea of one religion's being receptive to ideas and rituals that have their origins in a different religious tradition is likely to surprise people raised in Western cultures, where most religions portray themselves as deriving solely from a specific body of exclusive ancient scriptures. However, most of the world's many religions have been open to the idea of borrowing practices and beliefs from other religions on the assumption that "if it works for them, maybe we should try it too." And despite the common formal attitudes, religious borrowing does occur within Western religions as well.

The Haitian religion of vodou (voodoo) is an excellent example of one that has combined many elements of religious traditions from West Africa, especially the Yoruba religion, and Europe into a synthesis of beliefs and practices that meet the needs of its contemporary adherents, including people in Brooklyn, New York, as so carefully documented by Karen McCarthy Brown (2001) in her study of a vodou priestess named Mama Lola. For instance, the Christian deity, called by its African name, Bondye, is accepted as the only god, while many other traditional West African deities are viewed as his intermediaries with humans. Many of these, while identified with traditional Catholic saints, are nevertheless referred to by their African names. Saint Patrick, associated with the expulsion of snakes from Ireland in European tradition, is called Dambella, the Dahomean rainbow serpent deity. The Yoruba spirit Ogun, who was associated with metal and metalworking, has become the vodou patron of soldiers (Brown, 1997). His day of special ceremonies is the Catholic feast day of Saint James the Elder, the first martyred apostle, who was known as one of the "Sons of Thunder" because of his unruly temper. It is through "serving the spirits" by spirit possession rituals that followers of vodou seek to influence the supernatural realm for human benefit, as Bondye is too important to be directly involved in helping people himself. Because vodou draws heavily on Catholic symbolism and practice, its members also feel comfortable participating in Catholic Church ceremonies as well.

9.4.2 Secularization

Growth in technological complexity tends to accompany growth in population and increasing social complexity and specialization. Both forms of change lead to a decline in the public visibility of religious symbolism and in the reliance on religious values in decision making. These factors make it increasingly likely that people will feel lost in a sea of strangers, and that they lack the power they would like to have in day-to-day social life. When people are alienated from the mainstream secular values of their society in such a way, they are also less likely to believe in the supernatural.

Because religious rituals reaffirm people's commitment to the fundamental goals and values of their society, stresses experienced by the socially alienated tend to be channeled into coping mechanisms other than traditional religion, an adaptation referred to as secularization.

Secularization is the process by which nonreligious beliefs expand within an ideology at the expense of religious ways of thinking. It is a natural outcome of the more complex technologies and the greater level of social specialization that results from increased population densities. The users of these technologies learn to think of the parts of their environment that their tools allow them to manipulate in a pragmatic and matter-of-fact way. Compared to peoples who rely on rainfall for their food supply, those utilizing crop rotation, the plow, fertilization of the soil, and efficient irrigation systems are unlikely to think of the growth of crops as dependent upon mysterious spiritual forces. As the number of specialists grows, people are apt to become increasingly aware that many of their survival needs are fulfilled through the services of other human specialists, a perception that can also breed a secular view of life.

Secularization can also occur within the religious organization itself. Where technologies produce an economic base that supports a variety of religious specialists such as full-time theologians, religious belief tends to place more stress on organized rational doctrine; characteristics such as religious ecstasy and altered states of consciousness are likely to be less valued. Thus, when there are full-time religious practitioners who specialize in the performance of rituals, the congregation moves toward less active participation. The congregation also may be motivated largely by a secular desire to be accepted as a conforming member of society rather than by an immediate spiritual need for the rituals.

9.4.3   Revitalization Movements

Revolutionary change can also occur in religions through a process that Anthony Wallace (1966) called a **revitalization movement**. Wallace described a revitalization movement as a "conscious, organized effort by members of society to construct a more satisfying culture" in response to unusual social and cultural stresses (p. 30). According to Wallace, revitalization movements are frequently the bases of new religions, often millenarian in outlook, that promise a return to a more stable and harmonious society.

Revitalization movements typically involve four stages, which Wallace termed the steady state, the period of increased individual stress, the period of cultural distortion, and the period of revitalization. The steady state is the normal moving equilibrium of any culture during which change is relatively slow and incremental. A culture can be pushed out of its usual steady state by forces such as "climatic and biotic change, epidemic disease, war and conquest, social subordination, or acculturation" (p. 159). Such forces cause a growing number of individuals to experience individual stress because they interfere with society's ability to meet people's needs. During the period of increased individual stress, crime and illness increase, individual deviance increases, and society appears increasingly disorganized.

A period of cultural distortion can arise if some members of society respond to the increasing stresses by organizing special interest groups that no longer support the established social order. Instead, the special interest groups struggle to obtain the old benefits of life for their members through previously unacceptable behavior. The period of cultural distortion is a time of widespread

> alcoholism, venality in public officials, the 'black market,' breaches of sexual and kinship mores, hoarding, gambling for gain, 'scapegoating' by attacking other groups or a central bureaucracy, and similar alienated behaviors which, in the preceding period, were still defined as individual deviances. (p. 159).

At such times, the old religious rituals, beliefs, and values may be less than satisfying to many because they are too rooted in earlier, less stressful times to help people cope with new, current problems.

The period of revitalization begins when an "individual or group of individuals constructs a new, utopian image of sociocultural organization" (Wallace, 1966, p. 160). This often occurs when a man or woman who was personally distressed by the lack of order in society undergoes a hallucinatory experience perceived by the distressed person as a religious revelation from a supernatural source. It seems to account for society's turmoil and provides a series of new religious rituals that are intended to help people cope with the new problems that the old religions appear to have failed to address.

When the prophet of the new religion preaches the message to others, those who have been trying unsuccessfully to cope with the same widespread social ills may accept it as a divinely revealed answer to their problems. In fact, converts may be attracted so quickly that the revitalization prophet cannot personally coordinate the activities of the growing organization. At this point, a group of full-time disciples may be appointed to do that. The rapid growth of the new religion is often perceived as a threat by those members of society who still have a vested interest in the old, established institutions, such as the government and the previous religious organization. Sometimes the conflict that develops out of this perceived threat ends in the destruction of the new movement by its opponents, but sometimes the revitalization movement achieves dominance and establishes a new steady state.

Revitalization movements were common in many parts of the world among indigenous peoples after they were contacted by the technologically and militarily more powerful European societies. They have included the so-called Cargo Cults of Melanesia (Worsley, 1957) and Australia and several nativistic religious movements among American Indians, such as the Handsome Lake religion of the Iroquois (Wallace, 1970), the Ghost Dance religion of the U.S. Great Basin region (Mooney, 1896), and the Native American Church (LaBarre, 1938; Stewart, 1993), which has spread to many parts of the United States. Similar Christian movements also have histories that follow the pattern of revitalization movements. They include Mormonism; Seventh-Day Adventism; the Reverend Sun Myung Moon's Unification Church; Bhagwan Shree Rajneesh's utopian movement in Rajneeshpuram, Oregon; the Reverend Jim Jones's People's Temple settlement at Jonestown in Guyana; and David Koresh's Branch Davidian group in Waco, Texas.

Chapter Summary

1. Religion is found in all cultures but is subject to greater diversity than any other aspect of culture.

2. Universal aspects that define religion in all societies are the belief in supernatural beings, the belief in supernatural power, the symbolic expression of feelings, and ritual behavior.

3. The great diversity in belief systems may be related to variation in people's social, environmental, and technological contexts and may be seen as helping them adapt to those particular circumstances.

4. Ritual behaviors may serve any of three general functions: uniting a community emotionally, portraying human needs or sacred beliefs, or influencing the supernatural. Rituals may be the province of solo practitioners—shamans, sorcerers, or witches—in small-scale societies.

5. In somewhat larger societies, religion is often a communal matter, with group ceremonies.

6. In large, socially stratified societies, religious specialists are commonly full-time practitioners, organized into the hierarchical systems that characterize ecclesiastical religions.

7. The majority of people in the United States belong to some religious group, and it has been argued that most also subscribe to a patriotic "civil religion."

8. New religions often arise during times of social stress as revitalization movements that offer solutions to society's problems.

9. Religion seems to help maintain social order, reduce individual anxiety, and help people make sense of the often puzzling world around them.

Discussion Questions

1. What three things must always be included in any comprehensive description of a religion?

2. Briefly summarize Harris's ideas about how the Hindu veneration of the potentially edible cow actually may be beneficial for Hindu society in spite of a historic problem of hunger in India.

3. What are the defining characteristics of rituals? According to Wallace, why are rituals so important in religion?

4. What is the difference between sorcery and witchcraft?

5. According to Forest Clements, what are the four common religious explanations for illness? What social conditions seem to make each more likely?

6. Why did Robert Marett believe that a belief in mana was more ancient than a belief in gods or spirits?

7. How are taboos related to the concept of mana?

8. What difficulties are avoided by using the concept of anthropomorphic beliefs instead of the concept of supernatural beliefs in a definition of religion?

9. What are the four stages of a religious revitalization movement?

10. In Guthrie's view, what do concepts of gods, spirits, and mana all have in common?

Key Terms

altered states of consciousness   See *trance.*

ancestral spirits   Souls of ancestors who remain interested and involved in affairs of their descendants.

animatism   A belief in supernatural beings such as the soul, ghosts, spirits, and gods and goddesses.

animism   The belief in supernatural power or mana.

anthropomorphism   Using human qualities to explain the nonhuman realm; interpreting or acting toward the nonhuman realm as if it were human, especially as if it were able to respond to symbolic communication.

bone-pointing   A magical ritual for killing in which a sharp bone or stick is pointed at or ritually cast into the body of the intended victim.

communal religions   Religions that include the performance of rituals by groups of lay practitioners, shamans, or individuals.

communitas   Turner's term for a social relationship achieved through ritual in which people feel a sense of unity with each other.

contagious magic   Ritual coercion of the supernatural realm by the use of the Law of Contagion.

disease object   An object such as a barbed stick or stone that is magically cast into the body of a victim to cause illness.

divination   The use of ritual to obtain answers to questions from supernatural sources.

ecclesiastical religions   Religions that include not only individual, shamanic, and communal ritual practices but also a coordinating body of priests who perform rituals on behalf of congregations.

fundamentalist religions   religions that (1) espouse a literalist understanding of scriptures that are regarded as infallible sources of truth and (2) the belief that their religious truths should be implemented in their political lives within their larger society.

human soul   The supernatural part of the human being that is believed to animate the human body during life or perpetuate the individual's memories or life goals after death.

imitative magic   Attempted ritual coercion of the supernatural realm by use of the Law of Similarity.

Law of Contagion   The principle that things that have been in contact remain supernaturally in contact or that contact between things can be used to transfer mana from one to the other.

Law of Similarity   The principle that things that are similar to one another are spiritually identical and can be used in rituals to influence a desired outcome.

liminal period   Transition stage between the beginning and end of a ritual.

magic   The use of rituals that, when performed correctly, are believed to compel— as opposed to simply making requests of— the supernatural to bring about desired results.

mana   Supernatural power or force.

monotheism   The belief in a high god, a supreme being who either created the physical universe and other spiritual beings and rules over them or who at least maintains the order of the universe today.

near death experiences   a sense of wellbeing and detachment from the body that may occur when the parietal lobes of the brain are oxygen deprived and that are sometimes accompanied with out-ofthe-body experiences that may include a experiences understood as the presence of spiritual beings.

petitionary rituals Ritual requests for supernatural aid that are believed to increase the likelihood of the requested result but not guarantee it.

polytheism The belief in superior (but not supreme) gods, each of whom controls or rules over some major aspect of the universe.

priests Religious practitioners who perform rituals for the benefit of a group and who often are full-time specialists whose emphasis is on preserving the established ritual forms, rather than on inspiration and innovation in the application of their rituals.

reincarnation the belief that the soul of a human being may be repeatedly reborn into the human group to which it previously belonged or as an animal that may be symbolically associated with that group.

revitalization movement A change in religion that represents a conscious effort to construct a more satisfying culture.

ritual A behavior, often performed in repetitive and stereotyped ways, that expresses people's anxieties by acting them out and that may be performed with the desire to influence supernatural beings or supernatural power to achieve greater control over the natural world.

sacred The quality of inspiring feelings of respect, awe, and reverence that is possessed by things set apart and forbidden.

secularization The process by which nonreligious beliefs expand within an ideology at the expense of religious thought.

shaman Part-time religious practitioner who is believed to have access to supernatural power that may be used for the benefit of specific clients, as in healing or divining.

shamanic religions Religions in which the only ritual specialist is the shaman, and which contain only shamanic and individual ritual practices.

sorcerer Practitioner of magical rituals done to harm others.

sorcery The learned use of rituals to magically control the supernatural realm to achieve human goals.

soul loss The belief that the departure of the soul from the body, usually caused by a sudden fright, causes the body to weaken and die.

spirit possession A trance in which individuals feel as if their behavior is under the control of one or more spirits that have entered their bodies.

spirituality religious psychology of those who are adherents of a religion.

supernatural That which is believed to transcend the natural.

supernatural sanctions for violations of moral rules Punishments for immoral acts by spiritual agencies as opposed to human agencies. In most societies, the enforcement of morality is a strictly human responsibility, rather than a religious preoccupation.

syncretism   The borrowing of beliefs, practices, or organizational traits by one religion from another.

taboo   A rule forbidding contact with sacred things, those containing mana.

taboo violation   The breaking of a supernatural rule, whether intentional or not; often believed to be a cause of illness.

totem   A plant, animal, or, less commonly, nonliving thing that is a sacred symbol of the unity of a social group.

trance   Subjective state of mind where experiences are not interpreted in terms of normal symbolic categories of one's culture.

voodoo death   Death that occurs following a magical ritual performed to kill.

witchcraft   The belief in the innate ability to influence supernatural forces, usually to operate in ways that are harmful to others, without the necessity of using rituals.

witches   Persons believed to be supernatural beings and believed to have an innate power to harm people.

Chapter 10
Archaeology and Prehistory: Fragments from Antiquity

Liam Kilmurray

Outline

The excavation of early hominid remains is a central part of archaeology.

10.1   Introduction

Archaeology is a field of anthropology that garners much public attention. Whether it is in films, documentaries, or new discoveries, archaeology captures the public imagination like no other area in anthropological studies. In many anthropology departments, however, courses in archaeology are quite hard to come by. Since the late 1990s, "stones and bones" were out and cultural anthropology became even more dominant. In this chapter, we attempt to demonstrate some of the history of archaeology and provide a glimpse into the development of theory in this field. We also examine some key excavations, and we address select subfields of archaeology in order to provide a small window onto the diversity of practices within the archaeological world.

10.2   When did archaeology begin?

The word archaeology stems from the Greek word for *archaios* meaning ancient or old, and *logia*, which means learning or study. Archaeology therefore translates as the study of the past. Archaeologists are those anthropologists who study the past through an examination of material remains. This means that they focus mainly on durable items, nonorganic things that survive the vagaries of time. Unless there are circumstances where remains from the past do not perish, such as a deoxidized environment—ice, bog, alkaline cave sediments, and so on—archaeological remains consist mostly of stone, bone, and pottery.

There are many places and times that we could point to as the beginning of archaeology. For instance, in the sixth century BC Thusmose IV partially excavated the Sphinx. Nabondius—the last king of the Neo-Babylonian Empire—undertook many excavations in Babylon. Such examples demonstrate that the ancients were also curious about *their* past, whether to further their reign by associating themselves with the potency of the past or to preserve former temples. During the Renaissance, various popes in Rome and the rulers of Florence

(Cosimo de' Medici and Lorenzo de' Medici) sponsored individuals such as Poggio Bracciolini (1380–1459) to collect ancient manuscripts and examine ancient buildings. This inspired budding artists, among them Leonardo de Vinci and Michelangelo, to rediscover the architectural, literary, and archaeological secrets of Ancient Rome. In Britain and United States during the eighteenth-century archaeology, began to take on a more distinct and organized form, with gentlemen scholars taking to the fields and towns to unearth the secrets of the past. This period is generally known as the Antiquarian period, roughly the seventeenth and eighteenth centuries. Many excavations were undertaken, particularly in Britain, where the antiquarians, among them John Aubrey and Sir Richard Colt Hoare, began excavations at such spectacular Neolithic monumental sites such as Avebury, Stonehenge, and Silbury Hill. In the United States, Thomas Jefferson excavated ("dug into" might be a better term for this period) Indian burial mounds in Virginia (Trigger 1989, 69). Others, such as Squier and Davis (1848), also excavated the so-called effigy mounds of the upper Mississippi Valley. The construction of these mounds was originally attributed to Europeans, or lost tribes of Israel, since the prevalent belief was

Silbury Hill, the Neolithic mound in Southern England constructed around 2500 BC, is 131 ft. high.

that they were too complex for the Native peoples to have built. This idea is known as the moundbuilder hypothesis, and it denied local agency or creativity to the indigenous peoples of the Mississippi and Ohio valleys where many such monuments were built. It is now known that they were in fact built by indigenous peoples, some around 1000 AD. This was a sign of the inherent racism, or at least paternalism, of early American archaeology.

Many of the excavations of the nineteenth century were undertaken with rudimentary

Native peoples built hundreds of mounds along the Mississippi and Ohio rivers. Shown here is an Etowah Indian Mound dating to between 1000 and 1200 AD.

technologies, some doing damage to various sites. However, despite this, and the occasional air of treasure hunting that surrounded antiquarian archaeology, the systematic excavation of the past had really begun. As Sir Richard Colt Hoare himself once said, "We speak from facts, not theory." These early archaeological excavations were of varying quality, but they did establish archaeology as an emergent field and paved the way for the recognition of a time before history, as the title of John Lubbocks' book proclaims: "Prehistoric Times."

10.3   Where did the past go?

In many cases, in institutions and entire national anthropology programs, the past has, well, just disappeared from anthropology. One of the reasons for the decline of the past is the often-dominant position that sociology and cultural anthropology hold in many institutions that teach the social sciences. Many North American faculties have a joint sociology–anthropology department with sociology usually more favored in terms of financing, course offerings, number of faculty members, and so on. In a majority of institutions in North America, the dominant type of anthropology that students are likely to be exposed to is cultural anthropology, rather than linguistic, biological, or archaeological anthropology. Other reasons include the sheer volume of anthropological attention and literature devoted to globalism. It is not that sociology, nor indeed globalism, are not areas worthy of intense study, but these areas of study present only a limited view of humanity. They usually pay scant attention to the past, a situation that saddens many an archaeologist. As the great historian David Lowenthal once wrote, "[a] past beyond recovery seems to many unbearable" (Lowenthal 1985, 14).

What separates four-field anthropology from the dominant cultural anthropology is what the eminent French prehistorian François Bordes called *la longue durée* (the long term). For anthropology to be holistic the past must also remain alive and not be covered over with quick references to "long ago," or "founding fathers." Rather, discovering what once was, and how we came to be, is what initially guided anthropology. Knowing the past does not mean that we fossilize anthropological studies. On the contrary, understanding the long term enables us to grasp the structural and cultural relevancies of modern globalism.

To comprehend the challenges of modernity and the complexities of multiculturalism, for example, anthropologists need to understand the trajectories of cultures and economies and how they came to be. Knowledge of primitive communism of egalitarian societies or the collapse of great civilizations is needed to properly assess and understand today's world. This chapter aims to present to the student an introductory level discourse on some of the main developments in Western archaeology.

© krugloff/Shutterstock.com

Archaeological find-pieces of ancient pottery.

10.4 Prehistory

Prehistory, generally considered the time before the advent of writing systems, was not always considered real, valid, or possible. Reasons for this are to be found in many religious beliefs and readings of scripture. For example, in the 1650s, James Ussher, the Archbishop of Dublin, proposed that the earth was created at nightfall on October 22, 4004 BC. Ussher's logic for using this date was based on the counting of the generations mentioned in the Book of Genesis. He was not alone in portraying the world as young, as created according to religious belief, by the gods. For the Classical Greeks, the universe as created by the gods was characterized by what they termed the "Great Chain of Being." In this scheme there existed a "Fixity of Species," with humans on top and lesser animals below. No evolution occurred, no change was possible, and the world existed in a state of stasis. Just like the Ussherite Doctrine, there could be no prehistory that predated such a godly chronology. Slowly, through the periods of the Renaissance, the Scientific Revolution and the Enlightenment, things began to change. The great works of Charles Darwin and Alfred Wallace demonstrated *how* species may change over time. Geologists such as James Hutton and Charles Lyell argued convincingly that the geological record could not have formed within only 6000 years. Around the same time, amateur archaeologists were making discoveries of ancient fossils and associated tools that raised the possibility of a time before creation, so to speak. It took centuries, and many remain unconvinced, but the weight of scholarship and the very foundations of anthropology and allied sciences such as geology rested upon the belief that there existed a deeper past than previously accepted, and that there was in fact such a thing as prehistory. It would be up to archaeologists, palaeontologists, and others to populate and understand these prehistoric times.

10.5 Ground-breaking archaeological excavations and the thrill of discovery

> Discovery asserts our autonomy; it means the past in some sense belongs to us because we found it. [...]. Discovery is also about immediacy. To find something is to have immediate contact of a sort with its original owner; and this is as close as we can get (Shanks 1992, 58).

"As close as we can get" to the past is an apt phrase. For while we may hold the skull of Homo erectus in our hands, we will never know what dreams it once held. We may quite accurately detail the construction sequences of Newgrange or Stonehenge, but when it comes to fully understanding the motives and emotions that drove the building of these monuments, we will likely come up short. When archaeologists try to write about and interpret the past, it would be well to recall the title of a wonderful book on archaeology by John Barrett: we, and our audience, must remember that we are forever dealing with "fragments from prehistory" (1994). During the course of an archaeological excavation, whether large-scale or small, every single shovel full, every shake of the framed mesh, *could* contain a priceless fragment from antiquity. This could be a Celtic golden torque or a hoard of Roman gold coins. Each square dug into the ground might reveal the outlines of an Iroquois longhouse, or a burial from the historic period. More likely than not it may be a broken piece of pottery, a sherd, or frequently a piece of a projectile point used in some ancient hunt. The thrill of discovery drives many archaeologists on; the thoughts that some small piece of a prehistoric lifeway might be illuminated by a tiny fragment is part of the reason for the perseverance in digging holes in often unwelcoming soil and traipsing through hot sandy landscapes or rainy forests. While the archaeological world consists of thousands of small-scale, perhaps less glamorous excavations annually, there have been in the course of the years many spectacular excavations that have changed our understanding of the past and brought archaeology out of the dusty archives and into the spotlight of international public attention.

Also, these high-profile excavations have been exceptionally important to our understanding of the past. Current and past excavations have helped archaeologists understand the dynamics of power and change in the past, contributing to a revaluation of ancient societies. For example, the excavation of the terra cotta army in Lishan, China in 1974 that revealed the power and intricacy of the rule of Qin Shi Huang, the first Emperor of China. Recently, aerial drone "archaeology" has revealed new Nasca lines in Peru, and in the summer of 2017 archaeologists from Tübingen's Institute for Ancient Near Eastern Studies excavated an archive of ninety-two clay tablets that revealed (or confirmed) the location of the ancient royal city of Mardaman in Northern Iraq. Elsewhere, mummification workshops were uncovered in Egypt in 2018 that promise to dramatically increase our understanding of the process and importance of mummification. Other major excavations have contributed to our understanding of the past in a profound manner, such as the complex excavations at Çatalhöyük or the discovery of the first European settlement in North America, at the site of L'Anse aux Meadows, a Viking site in Nova Scotia, Canada, occupied some five hundred years before Christopher Columbus.

10.5.1 Çatalhöyük

Between 7500 BC and 5700 BC the archaeological site known as Çatalhöyük flourished on the Konya Plain in what is now south-central Turkey. This site was one of the earliest complex settlements that practiced agriculture, that is, the domestication of plants and animals. As such it sits astride a very important juncture for our understanding of the processes behind domestication and the associated social changes that occurred in the Middle-East at this time period. The site itself is still under annual excavation and consists of a remarkable eighteen successive layers of buildings that reveal the multiple stages of the settlement's history. First excavated by James Mellaart in 1958, the site contains the well-preserved remains of dozens of buildings sitting on 32 acres and was home to approximately 3000 to 8000 people. Remarkable at this site is the layout of the houses, which are back-to-back with no doors and only roof access. It is assumed this was for defensive purposes as well as to keep out the growing

The excavation of Çatalhöyük revealed one of most fascinating sites of the Neolithic Period in Turkey.

populations of rodents that accompanied the storage of food surpluses and the garbage that this large settlement would have accumulated.

Çatalhöyük is also renowned for the preservation of so many shrines that were discovered within the houses. That these shrines are predominantly found within individual houses is also revealing. This has led archaeologists to consider the role of the family, or individual, within the broader community. There are no obvious public buildings so far discovered at Çatalhöyük, but rather each individual household seems to have maintained its own shrines and buried its dead beneath the floors, often separating the skull. Thus, it might be inferred that this early community maintained some sense of individuality in terms of households. However, Hodder has recently suggested that analysis of discovered teeth indicates that closely related kin were not buried in the same household, leading us to marvel further at the nature of households and relationships at this enigmatic site. Equally interesting are the many auroch heads (a wild ancestor of the cow) found mounted on the walls in many houses. The symbolism of these auroch heads and horns, and their prevalence within the site, have led some such as Hodder to speculate that the people at Çatalhöyük were domesticating the wild, both physically by domesticating crops, and symbolically by bringing the aurochs into their settlement and houses. The significance of the aurochs is attested to by Twiss and Russel (2009), who state

> Within the general body of cattle symbolism, a particular emphasis on heads and horns is apparent. [...] [C]attle horns figure prominently in the site's iconography, its ritual activity, and even its architecture. Sometimes the 'horns' are mere artistic representations of cattle horns, but actual *Bos* crania remains are frequently used. They are embedded in walls and benches, installed in the architecture, ceremoniously deposited in caches and abandoned buildings, and even included (rarely) in burials (2009, 21).

The excavations at, and interpretations of, Çatalhöyük are far from complete; the site raises many more questions than it has so far answered. Some see a focus on women due to some of the figurines being of females; others argue that symbolic anthropology may indeed be reading too much into the "ritual" artifacts. However, Çatalhöyük is an exceptionally important archaeological site, one provides glimpses into prehistoric life, and, at the very least, its structure and artifacts are highly suggestive of a complex ritual and ceremonial life. Çatalhöyük is revealing of the time period when human groups began the process of settling down, of living together in large numbers for long periods of time. How this process played out, and what the social implications were, is tremendously important for our understanding of prehistoric life.

10.5.2　Newgrange

The excavation of Newgrange in Ireland, beginning in the late 1960s, was an important event in Irish archaeology and indeed in the reconstruction of European prehistory. Newgrange (*An uamh Grainne*/the Cave of the Sun) is perhaps the finest example of a type of monument known as a passage grave. These are monuments built in the Neolithic Age (the New Stone Age) which were constructed without metal tools of any kind. A passage grave consists usually of a stone corridor leading to a central corballed arched tomb with recesses, the

Decorated kerbstone at Newgrange.

whole of which is covered by a gigantic mound of soil, shale and sod. The passage grave tradition in Western Europe was long-lived and quite widespread. From around 5000 BC to 2000 BC these monuments were built from Malta in the Mediterranean to the West coast of Ireland. Many are found in southern Scandinavia, western Spain and Portugal, the British Isles, and Ireland. Built around 3300 BC, Newgrange is one of the largest and most exquisitely constructed of the surviving passage graves. It was, and remains, the centerpiece of the *Bru Na Boinne* complex, where in a bend on the River Boyne in Ireland there can be found at least three major passage graves and an assortment of other types of Neolithic monuments (such as a standing stone circle, cursus, and many smaller tombs and monuments). Newgrange is renowned for its famous corbelled arch, its profusely ornamented kerbstones and the fact that it is one of the few monuments with an accepted astronomical alignment.

Statistically, Newgrange is one of the largest of the passage graves. The cairn, comprised of water-rolled pebbles and turfs, reaches some 78.6 to 85.3 m in diameter. Turfs from the mound give a radiocarbon date of 3300 BC. It has been convincingly argued that the vast amount of material for the cairn, some 200,000 tons, came from what is now the "figure eight" pond to the south of Newgrange, toward the river Boyne (O'Kelly 1982).

Around the cairn there are ninety-seven revetment slabs. Many of these are richly engraved, including the K1, K52, and K67 stones. These revetment slabs measure from 1.7 to 4.5 m wide, averaging 1.2 m high. For the retaining wall, on the front of the revetment only, white quartz and black grandolite were built into the face of the mound (O'Kelly 1982; Jones and Bradley 1999, 113). Elsewhere ordinary stones were used. This is a significant factor, and the quartz may have been intended to reflect moonlight and sunlight, drawing specific attention to the front entrance of the monument. The passage is almost 19 m in length, containing twenty-one orthostats on the west and twenty-one on the east, averaging 1.5 m in height. Of special interest is the "roof-box" at Newgrange, which is the slot in the wall directly above the entrance. It is this construction—90 cm high, 1 m wide, and 1.2 m "deep"—through which the winter solstice sun shines, and which is one the most arresting displays in the entire complex of passage graves in the Boyne territory.

10.5.3 The roof-box at Newgrange

It has been claimed of many Neolithic monuments that they were astronomically designed, meaning they were oriented upon specific times of the year such as the Solstice, or the azimuth, or any key calendrical date that is marked by the height and position of the sun, moon, or stars. However, not many monuments can actually be proven to have astronomical significance. This is due to a circular monument intersecting with any number of celestial events; the key is finding the location at the monument where the celestial event is marked. At Stonehenge, the rising sun probably shone between the portal stones to mark the summer solstice. It was thought that the heel stone marked the summer solstice, but this stone has slipped sideways, and it is believed it was not originally in line with the rising solstice sun (Pitts 2001, 149–150). The excavator, O'Kelly, reported a local belief that had persisted into modern memory that the rising sun illuminated the three-spiral stone in the interior of Newgrange. This encouraged O'Kelly to investigate the winter solstice there leading to the "discovery" of the roof-box which funnels the solstice sunlight into the back of the chamber (O'Kelly 1982, 123). The roof-box of Newgrange allows the light from the winter solstice to penetrate the interior of the mound. The Newgrange roof-box is a remarkable feat of engineering, technological, and astronomy. For a few days before and after December 21st, a small band of light creeps into the mound directly over K1, the famous entrance stone, and illuminates the inner recesses. Inside these recesses are some of the finest examples of Neolithic art anywhere in the world. The function, if such can be determined, of this roof-box, may have been to mark the change of seasons, to welcome the suns return and the lengthening of days. Such times were important to farming communities. Those who built the Boyne passage graves and other monuments still inspire us today. Newgrange, after 5300 years of existence, still stands. The sun still penetrates the roof-box, and the ancestors represented within are illuminated, not forgotten. It is one of the most remarkable archaeological sites and one of the greatest engineering feats of prehistory.

10.5.4 Canada

Much of the archaeology undertaken in North America is known as cultural resource management (CRM). In this type of archaeology, private archaeological companies bid on contracts for clearing plots of land, such as for new housing divisions, roads, or any alteration of land that needs to be mitigated, meaning cleared of significant archaeological relevance, in the sense that construction can proceed since no substantial findings were made. In Canada, archaeology is a thriving area of research and industry, albeit confined in terms of excavation seasons, due to the climate of most of the country. However, across the nation in just the past few years there has been a series of remarkable and important excavations. One example is the recent excavation and ongoing investigation of the Mantle site, a Huron village from the late precontact period. In the early sixteenth century this site northeast of Toronto was one of the largest and most complex villages of its time, housing some 1500 people. It lay undiscovered for 500 years and its excavation sheds new light upon the development of the Wendat people in Ontario (Williamson 2012).

In the province of Quebec, the archaeological dig at Pointe-à-Callière in Montreal is equally important to a clearer understanding of nineteenth century politics. The 2017 excavation of the site which housed the Parliament of the United Province of Canada between 1844 and 1849, has revealed thousands of artifacts, including ink wells, parliamentary seals, and old books. The site is open to public tours and has received tens of thousands of visitors curious about early nineteenth century Montreal.

10.5.5 L'Anse aux Meadows—Canada

Archaeologists often refer to their work as filling in the blank spaces of prehistory. The UNESCO site of L'Anse aux Meadows can be said to have done just that for the first non-indigenous occupation of North America. For the longest time, however, it was believed that the famous voyages undertaken by Christopher Columbus, John Cabot, or Ferdinand Magellan had been the first to cross the Atlantic Ocean and "discover" the New World (see Lester 2009 for an interesting discussion of this subject). In fact, it was neither new nor discovered, as Indigenous peoples had of course been in North America for thousands of years, arriving from Siberia roughly 17,000 years ago. Located in the northwest of the Canadian province of Nova Scotia and Labrador, L'Anse aux Meadows (the bay with the meadows) is the oldest discovered European settlement in North America, predating the European voyages of the late fifteenth century by some 500 years. Founded approximately at 1000 AD, this is the only known Viking site in North America. The excavation in 1960 by the husband and wife team of Helge Ingstad and Anne Stine Ingstad attempted to understand the nature of the settlement. The Ingstads' excavation revealed eight wooden framed houses topped with sod roofs which supported perhaps some 30 to 100 people who subsisted largely on hunting (there is no evidence of domestication of either plants or animals). The Viking inhabitants of L'Anse aux Meadows hunted for fox, caribou, wolf, bear, lynx, birds, fish, seal, walrus, and whale. They also ate butternuts which are found far to the south, so they may have travelled beyond their settlements in search of other usable resources. There was evidence of workshops for the repair of boats, an iron smithy with a forge, and a carpentry workshop. The Ingstads speculated that this may have been a place to repair boats, used as a sort of station to enable both trade and discovery. Certainly, the Norse sagas speak of other lands, presumably to the south due to their mention of vines. What we know of relations with the Indigenous people, who at this time were likely Inuit, is that within a fairly short period of time hostilities broke out. This is reported in the Viking Sagas, which relate that the when Norse first encountered the indigenous people they traded peacefully, but there were also violent clashes between them. The outpost was likely abandoned due to these attacks and in part due to climate change and the decline in the Norse Greenland community itself due to conflict and people leaving for either Greenland or back to Scandinavia. L'Anse aux Meadows remains the sole European settlement of the Americas that dates to roughly the first millennium BCE, and it is a provocative archaeological site that still draws the attention and curiosity of scholars and the public.

Aerial image of L'Anse aux Meadows, Newfoundland, Canada.

When archaeologists move from excavating and measuring houses, or classifying the scatters of faunal remains, and then try to interpret what these may mean, they begin to apply theoretical frameworks. Some of these are accepted for many years, others rejected, and others linger for years before new evidence debunks their findings. Theory, whether at L'Anse aux Meadows, Çatalhöyük, Newgrange, or a Wendat village, is an essential component of archaeology if we are to move on from the what, where, and when, and attempt to ask why.

10.6   Theory in archaeology

Many archaeological publications address theory (see e.g., Erikson and Murphy 2017; Johnson 2010; Bentley et al. 2007; Hodder 2001; Trigger 1989). Here, we will cover just the broad outlines of this area. Understanding theoretical developments in archaeology teaches us not just about the great theories themselves but about the contingent and changing nature of archaeological theory itself. New theories in archaeology have frequently led to different and fuller understandings of the past. For example, when archaeologists began to seriously contemplate gender disparities in how prehistory was written, such as in the work of Gero and Conkey (*Engendering Archaeology*, 1991), it led to a rewriting of certain areas of European prehistory to include the often-overlooked role of women in the past. When Shanks and Tilley (1987) shook up the archaeological world with their postmodern critique of archaeological claims to objectivity, the result was an explosion of interpretations of both old and new data. Many understandings of nineteenth century archaeologists, for example, are now viewed as either too general, somewhat speculative, and in some cases clearly wrong or even racist and sexist. Theoretical developments rarely go unchallenged and many theories fade away. Some linger on and become part of the orthodoxy of archaeological interpretation. Yet theory remains important as without some theoretical grounding, archaeologists would be consigned to collecting, classifying, and displaying the remnants of antiquity. Theory is necessary in order to "read the past," to attempt to reconstruct meaning in peoples' actions from their material remains.

In archaeological literature, the general coverage of excavations rarely addresses the broader picture that archaeologists are usually trying to construct. Often, theoretical debates are conducted in journal articles or specialty books. While celebrated discoveries such as King Tutankhamun's burial chamber or the terra cotta army in Lishan are portrayed as enriching our understanding of ancient rulers and their wealth, archaeologists often seek more information. Earlier archaeologists, for the most part, concentrated upon discovering, excavating, and classifying artifacts and archaeological sites. As the twentieth century dawned, archaeology grew more complex technically and more sophisticated theoretically, asking more of the archaeological record. What, for instance, might the presence of ceramics at hunter-gatherer sites (an abnormal discovery) signal about the changing nature of hunting and gathering or the movement of goods and people in prehistory? Why did some societies change from chiefdoms to tribal polities and what were the circumstances that drove such change? Were these archaeologically detectable? What did the presence of elite grave goods in select graves signify? In short, as time progressed archaeologists tried to account for social and historical change and to do so they needed theoretical frameworks. Below, we examine three major archaeological theories.

The astonishing site of the terra cotta army of the Emperor Qin Shi Huang includes some 6000 life-size figures of warriors and was part of an associated necropolis and mausoleum.

10.6.1 Culture historical archaeology

Culture-history, or the cultural-historical approach in archaeology, placed an emphasis on classifying societies based on their material culture signatures. Typologies for world pre-history were drawn up and groups, sometimes referred to as ethnic groups, were identified through their archaeological remains and their geographical and chronological spread. Between approximately 1900 and 1960 the culture-historical approach was fairly dominant in archaeological thinking. The roots of this approach lie in the last few decades of the nineteenth century in Germany. Gustav Kossina, a linguist and professor of archaeology, was influential in the development of culture-history. Kossina, himself influenced by other German historians and ethnographers, believed that archaeological excavations could reveal regionally delimited ethnic groups, which were defined by their material culture. From the beginning culture-history contained a strong element of nationalism. Kossina sought to trace back in time the Germanic tribes, which he called the Arians, and demonstrate their cultural longevity, their long occupation of central European areas, and their great achievements.

The timeframe within which the culture-historical approach was prominent coincides with a period of major expansion of archaeology. The decades from 1900 to 1960 witnessed prolific excavations on a very large scale. Numerous complex and well-funded excavations took place in Egypt, Babylon, and throughout the Middle East, as well as in Europe, the United States, and beyond. The Second World War, despite retarding excavations during its duration, was actually a great stimulus for the *number* of archaeological excavations undertaken in the decades immediately prior to the outbreak of hostilities. The prewar period saw massive state investment, particularly in Germany, Russia, and Italy. Great interest and expenditure were lavished on the search for the first farmers in the Middle East, or the oldest Germanic settlement in Eastern Prussia. Others sought to determine the presence of their own ethnic group on lands that were now contested, and competing archaeological discoveries and interpretations were made.

At the same time, less overtly nationalist archaeology continued apace. Major digs were sponsored by American, French, English governments, and other institutions and departments. The result was a major increase in the number of archaeological sites, dates, artifacts, and knowledge in the first few decades of the twentieth century. More houses, roads, train tracks, and people resulted in the disturbance of lands on a scale not seen since perhaps the early Neolithic period (when early farming first transformed the landscape on a large scale). In order to fully understand and classify all these new data a theoretical framework was required, and culture-history was one such theory. It viewed cultures as bound together by common and distinct sets of norms and believed that the archaeological record could be read as a reflection of these norms and therefore of the cultural group itself. In order to classify ancient cultures, these culture-historians focused on similarities rather than on dissimilarities while attempting to construct typologies. An example of this approach is seen in the works of Gordon Childe, who published *The Dawn of European Civilization* in 1925. It was followed by a series of books with similar sweeping narratives in which large chunks of European prehistory were classified and ordered. The culture historical theorists painted Europe was populated by groups based on their material culture: the Bell Beaker people, the Battle Axe people, or the Linearbandkeramik peoples, and so forth. Culture-historians have been criticized for being too normative; that is, for simplistically labeling sites and groups based on assumed similarities in the archaeological record. Yet these culture historians—who never really saw themselves as such—did contribute to the classifying and typological sorting of many archaeological cultures.

One important component of the culture historical approach was the idea of diffusionism. Diffusionism believed that inventions such as agriculture or metal-working occurred only once and then spread by diffusion to other regions. This diffusion could happen by either the movement of ideas or of peoples themselves with their new practice. Diffusionist reconstructions of European prehistory or American hunters and gatherers, for example, were based on the presence of similar cultural "traits" (see Story and Jones 2011 for a detailed discussion of diffusionism in anthropology). However, these perceived traits were based on excavated material culture whose functions might be known or generally agreed upon. However, it was not known, or agreed upon, how these artifacts might have been interpreted by these societies themselves or how the material culture was deployed in social relations. Thus there were limitations, sometimes gladly accepted by archaeologists who wished not to reconstruct any local meanings from artifacts. The axes cut and the pots held liquid, traits diffused across entire continents were generally assumed to always serve similar functions and represent similar cultural actions. Culture-history archaeologists therefore sought to trace the spread of these actions and date them from an original source. Some of these archaeologists (such as the processualists we will meet shortly), accepted that certain inventions did spread from an original source, such as agriculture from the Middle East where wheat and sheep were to be found. However, they argued that the reliance upon external forces to explain many cultural, technical, and other developments lessened the agency and abilities of local peoples. In addition, the grand schemes of diffusionism were of little help in understanding the immediate archaeological record. This would lead to processualist archaeology, an approach that relied more on hard science and positivist theory. Thus, diffusionism and the approach of culture-history in general, once such a dominant theory in archaeology, have fallen out of favor, thanks in part to the critique of the processual theorists.

10.6.2 Processual archaeology

With its peak in the 1970s, processual archaeology focused on the processes of culture. Culture was viewed as an adaptive mechanism to enable people to cope with the vagaries of life and the environment. Also known as New Archaeology, its most famous proponents were David Clarke, Lewis Binford, Colin Renfrew, and Michael Schiffer. Processualists, and other approaches loosely associated, focused their interpretations of archaeological material on the processes of technology, on adaptations to the environment, on what caloric information faunal remains might reveal and so on.

Processual archaeology was dominant in North America, and to a lesser degree in Western Europe. It spawned numerous exciting excavations and reinterpretations of prior excavation reports by those of the "old" archaeology. With a strict adherence to scientific evaluation of data, and an application of positivist theory. Danny Miller provides a succinct definition of the processualist approach and its reliance on positivist theory as relying on only those facts which can be sensed, tested, and predicted as knowable (1984, cf. Trigger 1989, 344). This New Archaeology resulted in a vast deal of literature and many excavations. Perhaps its greatest achievement, other than the advances made in compiling American Indian chronology, or in excavations of European and Middle-Eastern prehistoric sites, was in the critique of the findings and long-held beliefs of earlier archaeologists. As David Clarke wrote in 1973, archaeology—having come of age during the Culture Historical period—had now, in critiquing and revaluating its past approaches, and in its strict adherence to the raw data and eschewing of general evolutionary schemes, ensured there would be a "loss of innocence" (Clarke 1973). No longer would the broad conjecturing of culture historians or the sweeping statements of diffusionism hold sway in archaeology, it had come of age through this loss of innocence.

In later years, processualists were fully aware of the debate among the emerging postprocessualists regarding whether meaning and context could be retrieved from the archaeological record, rather than just assemblages and raw facts (see the following). A common response from processualists was to argue that in very many cases there is little that remains of a past context, and that seeking deep structures of meaning from archaeological sites was a futile task. The physical distribution of artifacts in the archaeological record rarely mirrors, nor can be used to measure, their social significance (Schiffer 1972). Whatever meanings were attached to material culture in the past were not, as postprocessualist themselves argue, static. The result of this is that an artifact that once symbolized masculinity or leadership could over time be shorn of this meaning and become just another artifact that no longer symbolized its original meanings. In our day, we can use the example of ripped jeans, which were once a symbol of poverty but over time became a designer symbol. So, processualists argue that meanings change, and contexts cannot fully be read, so it is better to stick to hard science and descriptive approaches to presenting the past. The basic tenets of the New Archaeology were therefore that they viewed archaeology as a science; a branch of history, that they were concerned with the gathering of hard data to set chronologies and to excavate site-specific assemblages. The new archaeologists also argued that archaeology should focus on explanation of the past as opposed to explication (Krieger 2017). It is with this latter idea that past context might be pursued from durable fragments of the past, which set processual (New) and postprocessual archaeologies apart in the mid to late 1980s.

10.6.3 Postprocessual archaeology

Pioneered by such scholars as Ian Hodder, Daniel Miller, Christopher Tilley, Michael Shanks, and Peter Ucko, postprocessual archaeology followed on from processual archaeology. It was born at the University of Cambridge, mainly under the direction of Dr. Ian Hodder, who wanted archaeologists to embrace the multiplicity of contexts and meanings that adhere to artifacts. The attempt to interpret archaeological sites as texts which could be read has also given this type of archaeology the name of interpretive archaeology. The differences between processual and postprocessual archaeology are numerous, not so much in the manner or technology of actual excavating, but rather in the postexcavation process: the interpretation. Hodder and others argue that archaeological interpretation was rife with subjectivity, which differs from the processualists as we have seen. Processualist archaeologists want to stick to the known facts. Hodder (2015) would urge archaeologists to go further and to inquire as to the nature of symbolism in the past. The deposition and discard of specific artifacts may be read as potent symbols that were relevant in past contexts. His famous argument regarding pots asks, "when is a pot not a pot?" When is it more than a vessel for holding food but also a potent symbol of masculinity, femininity, and initiation rites? In short, these artifacts might be read as "symbols in action," and ethnographic research, allied with ethnoarchaeology, can make direct comparisons between living examples and past remains. Postprocessualists argue that material culture is active; it is, to cite Hodder again, "meaningfully constituted," and played an active role in the construction of past society.

The debate between processualism and postprocessualism has often been conducted under a "downpour of Latin tags," with each side outdoing the other in high-sounding language and discourse. On the one hand, a valid criticism of the interpretive, postprocessualist approach is that it obfuscates and complicates more than it clarifies. Processualist, positivist approaches, on the other hand, present a past that is somewhat static and limited in terms of what it says about past lives. The objectivity that processualists adhere to and are staunch defenders of simply does not exist according to postprocessualists. There are no totally objective facts, they argue, and the claim of scientific neutrality and facts speaking only as facts is a fallacy. Scholars such as Ian Hodder and Michael Shanks insist on a polyvocality to the past and polysemous interpretations. Students of archaeology may be excused sometimes for being bewildered by the arcane nature of the theoretical debate between the processualist and postprocessualist schools of thought. The most interpretive of the postprocessualist approaches seem to want to write a poetics of archaeology and argue that interpretation begins at the trowel's edge. For the processualists, this moves archaeology away from hard facts and is, they argue, a license to print anything.

Despite the sometimes-polarizing nature of the debates in archaeological theory, archaeology itself eventually benefits from the energy and attention that these creative, intelligent people, with a passion for the past, bring to the table. Whether the pot was just a pot in the end or not, the pot was found, excavated, cleaned, classified, and scrutinized. The pots are known, and their significance is at least debated, enriching our understanding of the past.

10.7 Technological developments in archaeology

The technology of archaeology continues to improve. Noninvasive excavation techniques such as electrical resistance tomography and ground penetrating radar enable archaeologists to locate and identify buried villages, monuments, or kings and queens without the need to bring shovels. Drone and satellite technologies also aid in the spotting and mapping of ancient sites that would otherwise have been financially challenging. The ability to peer under the soil using radar means that remote and inaccessible sites, for example, villages in the Amazon, or Inca shrines high in the Andes mountains, can at least be identified and plotted before costly and time-consuming excavations need take place. Of course, once located and mapped, such sites eventually may need to be fully excavated. However, the costs of seeking and identifying remote sites are now not as prohibitive a challenge to archaeologists. Light Detection and Ranging (LiDAR) technology was used recently to fully map the resting place of Richard III, an English king from the fifteenth century. The value to archaeology of such developments goes beyond monetary savings, as the all-important context of archaeological sites can be preserved *and* plotted. As José Manuel Valderrama Zafra, a visiting academic at the University of Leicester's School of Archaeology and Ancient History puts it, "In an archaeological context, the value of this noninvasive approach is that you can document the grave of King Richard III and generate a highly accurate and detailed virtual representation whilst minimising any disturbance caused. This really is the 21st century approach to the sketchpad" (University of Leicester 2013).

The application of LiDAR technology allows archaeologists to "see" through the dense canopy of the Honduran rainforest and reconstruct the outline and heights of any features revealed.

Source: PLOS ONE

Elsewhere, 200 km north of the Arctic circle, Canadian underwater archaeologists are currently examining HMS Erebus and HMS Terror, the two ships of the doomed Franklin Expedition. Franklin set out in 1845 hoping to discover the Northwest Passage. Trapped in the ice, suffering from lead poisoning (thought to have been the result partially from eating food out of lead-sealed cans), fatal decisions were made to abandon ship and attempt to winter over. The tale is well known now: none survived, some resorted to cannibalism, and the English Admiralty spent years seeking information as to the plight of the 129 sailors on board. For 150 years the location of the ships was unknown, but in 2014 and 2016 both ships were found. They were located using Inuit folklore and social memory as well as high-tech sonar devices and a mighty combination. Parks Canada is currently sending teams of underwater archaeologists down beneath the frigid waters to excavate the ship in what they think will be a 5-year process. Technological developments, better equipment and, in this case, finally listening to the Inuit peoples who had long preserved memories and descriptions of the ships' rough whereabouts, has resulted in an excavation under the frozen waters of the Arctic Circle.

LiDAR was also recently used to "find" and map the mysterious site of La Ciudad Blanca, located deep in the Mosquitia region of eastern Honduras. This so-called lost city was long sought after, and at one time called the City of the Monkey God. LiDAR technology was used to locate the site in a National Geographic project. This mapping revealed much that was previously unknown, leading to excavations that began in 2016 and are ongoing. LiDAR is relatively easy to use compared to hacking through this particularly dense and dangerous jungle. However, as LiDAR was originally a military technology, it and other newer technologies are not always well received in archaeology. The project at La Ciudad Blanca, for example, was criticized by dozens of archaeologists who were opposed to such a quick and publicized discovery by the National Geographic team. The renowned Mayan specialist Rosemary Joyce said that proper excavation was required—what she called "ground truthing"— and that in some cases "good science becomes bad archaeology" (June 7, 2012, see Fisher et al. for a scientific explanation of LiDAR and a report on its use in Honduras).

10.8   Ethnoarchaeology

In 1969, Louis Binford began ethnographic fieldwork among the Nunamiut people in Alaska. His goal was to observe fist-hand the manufacture of stone tools. He was practicing what is known as ethnoarchaeology. Binford wanted to observe the stone tool makers in action in order to aid in the interpretation and understanding of prehistoric stone tool sites. By directly observing these activities he could try to grasp where specific tasks were carried out, how far from other task-specific areas in the archaeological site, and where the debitage from tool manufacture might spread during manufacture. Since Binford's pioneering project, ethnoarchaeology has been an instrumental aspect of the archaeological toolkit, enabling educated guesses and extrapolations to be made from the ethnographic record and applied to the archaeological record. Ethnoarchaeology allows us to ask, "archaeological questions of ethnographic data" (Hodder 1994, 108).

Similar research projects have shed light on certain aspects of what archaeologists call "site formation processes." William Rathje's "garbage project" in 1973 in Tucson, Arizona could be said to fall into this category. In excavating landfill sites, Rathje observed the depositional processes and waste materials of the people in that city. He was able to compare these findings to what people actually *said* concerning their consumption choices. Knowing what people consume, what they discard, and what they consider garbage enabled insights into the formation of the archaeological record. Ethnoarchaeology can be compared to ethnography—the long-term observation of a cultural group in its natural setting. In the case of ethnoarchaeology, what is really sought is a comparand, a template of people's actions that can be linked to the archaeological record. Certain questions have in fact been answered by using ethnoarchaeological data: for instance, how far stone flakes may scatter from a stone core during the process of tool making, and what marks and shapes are produced by left or right-handed people. Ethnoarchaeological observation can also reveal to the archaeologists what they may be missing from the analysis of just the material record of peoples' actions. Ian Hodder, for example, argues that ethnoarchaeology can guide archaeologists in the search for the relevance, importance, and meaning of certain artifacts. without any ethnographic or historical information to guide them archaeologists are left wondering what does it mean for example if only black pottery is found at one particular place in a village and not elsewhere? The question becomes even more interesting when it is noted that red pots are found on other parts of the site. If, say, stone axes are found in one place and projectile points in another, can we say that task-specific groups were in operation in the ancient past? Are these actions reflected in the social relations of people being observed by ethnoarchaeologists? The basic argument, as we saw earlier, between processualist and postprocessualist archaeological interpretations revolves around what information can, or should be, sought from the dispersal and context of material remains, of axes, bones, and stone tools. Ethnoarchaeology has an important role to play in this debate, as it can, if conditions are right, learn much from living people and how materials end up in the archaeological record. So ethnoarchaeology, whether it answers questions directly about past behavior or whether it provides archaeologists with the knowledge that artifacts are not always just leftovers or rubbish, is important to contemporary archaeology.

10.9 Environmental and ecological archaeology

Archaeology contains a large number of subfields and areas of specialization. Notable among these are environmental and ecological archaeology, which for the purposes of this book will be dealt with as one area of study. Environmental archaeology is not new however it has gained a momentum within the past decade as environmental issues have become a subject of great interest and concern to modern society. Environmental archaeology can be defined as the study of cultural adaptations to environments as detected through the archaeological record. Generally, environmental archaeologists study how we adapt to a particular ecological niche and the impact our adaptations have had on it. Excavated material remains are analyzed and ancient environments are reconstructed, known technically as paleoecology. Paleoarchaeologists can determine for example whether a past environment was first desert, and then lush forest, followed by sea level inundation and a reversion to desert. Elsewhere, environmental studies reveal the movements and sequences of the great glacial periods which altered the landscapes and left behind valleys, rivers, and glacial till. These sequences are essential to an archaeological understanding of the past, and of human occupation and movements in prehistory. Environmental archaeology also examines human effects on the environment, whether deforestation, over-farming, over-hunting, or other impacts. Environmental archaeologists also study ongoing formation processes and our contemporary impacts on, and adaptations to, environmental systems.

10.9.1   The collapse of the Classic Maya

Central and South America have long been of interest to archaeologists. The stunning plazas of Teotihuacan built around 0 AD, and the great temples of the Classic Mayan cities such as Copan and Tikal have been repeatedly excavated, interpreted, and argued about. Why did Teotihuacan suddenly cease to be a massive center of activity, or why did Copan become deserted in the ninth century AD. The case of Teotihuacan is instructive. This city was among the first of the so-called ceremonial plaza centers, one that influenced the trajectory of later Toltec, Maya, and Aztec architectural wonders. Sometime in the seventh or eighth century AD the city was systematically burned and abandoned. The cause of this abandonment remains unclear and archaeologists have speculated that the city was invaded, or that changes in the environment, such as a lack of rainfall, may have caused a reduction in the food supply which rendered the area basically uninhabitable for its estimated 100,000 people. The answer remains to be found perhaps a new generation of archaeologists will discover the answer.

Cases such as the abandonment of Teotihuacan can demonstrate the links between culture and environment, encouraging archaeologists to address the issue of climate change and environmental degradation due to cultural practices. The well-known case of the "disappearance" of the Classic Maya has been well documented (Willey and Shimkin 1971, also see Deborah L. Nichols 2012, for recent discussion of this subject). During the ninth century AD classic Mayan cities such as Copán and Tikal were abandoned. Although there was substantial population decline, the Mayan peoples themselves did not disappear, as is so often reported. Rather, their political polities and their cities were depopulated, abandoned and became the home to howler monkeys as the tropical forests reclaimed these once thriving cultural centers. It is thought that the people returned to the forests, took up with other villages, and generally melted into the landscapes around them.

The Temple of the Moon at Teotihuacan, Mexico.

Photo courtesy of Liam Kilmurray

The once flourishing city of Tikal, Guatemala, was abandoned by the end of the tenth century AD.

© Diego Grandi/Shutterstock.com

This sudden collapse of the Maya kingdoms raises many questions. Was it due to disease, starvation, invasion, persistent warfare, or a combination of all these factors? A single explanation may not account for the demise of these Mayan cities. In terms of attributing the collapse to environmental factors, archaeologists must be cautious. For example, it is known that the Maya did in fact practice conservation of forest resources (University of Cincinnati 2009). There are also indications that they linked the fecundity of their soil with religious significance (Fisher, Hill, and Feinman 2011). However, by the late Classic Period this seems to have come undone with the result that many of the great Mayan centers were rapidly emptied. In attempting to reconstruct these last days of the Mayan cities, it does seem likely that the abandonments were linked to a mixture of deforestation and the fact that the climate became drier during this period. Since most land surrounding Mayan cities was under cultivation, the tree cover was significantly reduced with the result that the soil was no longer anchored by the roots of these trees. This led to a loss of top soil and the withering away of the vitality of the landscape that provided the Maya with their food supply. Hansen et al. (2002) have convincingly argued that the monumental architecture of the Maya also contributed to the loss of forest cover. To convert limestone into lime stucco requires intense heat, so many trees were cut down to fuel the fires to produce it for use in monumental architecture. Added to this was population growth in the years before the collapse, which required more building and more deforestation for construction materials and firewood.

Environmental archaeology can contribute to our understanding of the rise, duration, and collapse of ancient societies. Ongoing research into many sites around the world is proving the relevance of an archaeology that attempts not just to unearth and wonder at the achievements of past societies, such as Teotihuacan and Tikal, but also to these societies' relationship to their environments. If there is evidence of maladaptation, a misuse of resources, or mismanaged forestry, then this is a contribution not just to understanding the past but also to addressing current concerns regarding climate change. As Fisher et al. conclude, "We are not alone in our concern that past records of human-induced environmental change be invoked for considerations of modern policy" (2011, 249).

10.10   Conclusion

Archaeology has travelled a very long way from the days when Paleolithic projectile points were identified as elf-shot, the leftover arrowheads of elves shooting in the nighttime forests. Paleoanthropologists—those anthropologists who excavate fossils—have identified more and more members of the genus Homo, such as the new members called the Denisovans, discovered just recently (Reich 2018). The archaeological community has demonstrated clearly that the human evolutionary tree is actually more like a bush, with species coexisting and disappearing through time. Archaeologists have argued convincingly that the world is far, far older than creationist theories would suggest. Ancient kingdoms and entire city–states have been revealed from deserts and jungles and from underneath European cities. Theoretical debate continues regarding different ways to interpret these excavated materials. But archaeology has made tremendous technological and theoretical strides in recent years.

In this chapter, we have touched upon some of the major issues in archaeology today. We have examined some of the history of archaeology's development. We have also discussed, however briefly, some of the theoretical debates and approaches within the field. We have seen that, opinion is rarely unanimous regarding the "correct" method of interpreting the past, the nature of theoretical debate and refinement demonstrates the contingent nature of our understandings and the self-correcting mechanisms of scientific debate. From an almost endless list of fascinating archaeological excavations and sites, we have explored just a few whose impact on archaeology has been profound. Sites such as L'Anse aux Meadows, Çatalhöyük, and Newgrange reveal something of the nature of major archaeological excavations and their interpretations. Certain areas of archaeological specialization were discussed, such as ethnoarchaeology and environmental archaeology. Although far from an exhaustive examination, these examples should serve to demonstrate the very wide variety of approaches, methodologies, and subject matter that archaeologists deal with. Indeed, it is this diversity of approaches, sites and artifacts, and theoretical perspectives, which characterizes the broad field of archaeology today. Anthropology needs archaeology to examine and understand prehistory. Archaeological inquiry is broad, and it remains essential to both anthropology and to today's world and our understanding of our place within it. Hopefully this chapter will inspire students and others to continue to research and take an active role in the archaeological reconstruction of our past. There is much more to be discovered. With glaciers melting, shorelines changing, and as projects like vast highways and pipelines are being constructed—the is being earth disturbed and fragments from antiquity will be found.

Further Reading

Bentley, R. Alexander, Herbert Maschner, and Christopher Chippindale, eds. 2007. Handbook of Archaeological Theories. Lanham: Alta Mira Press.

Childe, Vere Gordon. 1925. *The Dawn of European Civilisation*. London: Routledge and Keegan Paul Ltd.

Clarke, David. 1973. "Archaeology: The Loss of Innocence." *Antiquity* 47: 6–18.

Erikson, Paul A., and Liam D. Murphy. 2017. *Readings for a History of Anthropological Theory*. Toronto: University of Toronto Press.

Fisher, Christopher T., Brett J. Hill, Gary M. Feinman, eds. 2011. *The Archaeology of Environmental Change*. Tucson: The University of Arizona Press.

Gero, Joan M. and Conkey, Margaret W. 1991. *Engendering Archaeology: Women in Prehistory*. Oxford: Wiley-Blackwell Publishers.

Hansen, Richard D., Steven Bozarth, John Jacob, David Wahl, and Thomas Schreiner. 2002. "Climatic and Environmental Variability in the Rise of Maya Civilization." *Ancient Mesoamerica* 13: 273–95.

Hodder, Ian. 1994. *Reading the Past: Current Approaches to Interpretation in Archaeology*. Cambridge: Cambridge University Press.

Hodder, Ian, ed. 2001. *Archaeological Theory Today*. Cambridge: Polity.

Hodder, Ian. May 2015. "Origins of Settled Life; Göbekli and Çatalhöyük." Accessed May 13, 2019. *Talks at Google*, https://www.youtube.com/watch?v=zKwSg7OyvoE

Johnson, Matthew. 2010. *Archaeological Theory: An Introduction*. Etobicoke: John Wiley & Sons.

Jones, Andrew and Bradley, Richard 1999. 'The Significance of Colour in European Archaeology'. Cambridge Archaeological Journal 9:1, pp. 112–114.

Joyce, Rosemary. 2012. "Good Science, Big Hype, Bad Archaeology." *Berkley Blog*, June 7. Accessed April 13, 2019. https://blogs.berkeley.edu/2012/06/07/good-science-big-hype-bad-archaeology/

Krieger, William H. 2017. "Processual Archaeology." *Oxford Bibliographies*. Last Reviewed 22 November 2016. Last Modified 28 February 2017. doi:10.1093/obo/9780199766567-0056 Accessed May 11 2019. https://www.oxfordbibliographies.com/view/document/obo-9780199766567/obo-9780199766567-0056.xml

Lester, Toby. 2009. *The Fourth Part of the* World. Toronto: Free Press.

Lowenthal, David. 1985. *The Past is a Foreign Country*. New York: Cambridge University Press.

Nichols, Deborah L., ed. 2012. *The Oxford Handbook of MesoAmerican Archaeology*. Accessed May 23, 2019. https://www.oxfordhandbooks.com/view/10.1093/oxfordhb/9780195390933.001.0001/oxfordhb-9780195390933

O'Kelly, Michael J. 1982. *Newgrange*. London: Thames and Hudson.

Pitts, Mike 2001. *Hengeworld*. London: Arrow Books.

Reich, David. 2018. Who We Are and How We Got Here: *Ancient DNA and the New Science of the Human Past*. New York: Pantheon Books.

Schiffer, M.B. 1972. "Archaeological Context and Systemic Context." *American Antiquity* 37(2): 156–65.

Shanks, Michael. 1992. Experiencing the Past: On the Character of Archaeology. London: Routledge.

Shanks, Michael, and Christopher Tilley. 1987. *Re-constructing Archaeology: Theory and Practice*. London: Routledge.

Squier, E. G., and E. H. Davis. 1848. Ancient Monuments of the Mississippi Valley: Comprising the Results of Extensive Original Surveys and Explorations. Washington: Smithsonian Institute.

Story, Alice J., and Terry L. Jones. 2011. "Diffusionism in Archaeological Theory: The Good, The Bad, and The Ugly." In *Polynesians in America: Pre-Columbian Contacts with the New World*, edited by Terry L. Jones, Alice J. Story, Elizabeth Matisoo Smith, and Jose Miguel Ramirez-Aliaga, 7–24. Lanham: Altamira Press.

Trigger, Bruce. 1989. *A History of Archaeological Thought*. New York: Cambridge University Press.

Twiss, K. C., and N. Russell. 2009. "Taking the Bull by the Horns: Ideology, Masculinity, and Cattle Horns at Çatalhöyük (Turkey)." Paléorient *Année* 35(2): 19–32.

University of Cincinnati. July 23, 2009. "Ancient Maya Practiced Forest Conservation 3,000 Years Ago." *Science Daily*. Accessed March 17, 2019. www.sciencedaily.com/releases/2009/07/090722150825.htm.

University of Leicester Press Office. July 10, 2013. *Experts Create 3D Map of Richard III's Grave*. Leicester.

Willey, Gordon R., and Demitri B. Shimkin. Spring, 1971. "The Collapse of Classic Maya Civilization in the Southern Lowlands: A Symposium Summary Statement." *Southwestern Journal of Anthropology* 27, no. 1: 1–18. Chicago: The University of Chicago Press.

Williamson, Ronald F. 2012. "What Will Be Has Always Been: The Past and Present of Northern Iroquoians." In *The Oxford Handbook of North American Archaeology*, edited by Timothy R. Pauketat, 273–84. Toronto: Oxford University Press.

Outline

Key Questions

1. What Is Applied Anthropology?

The areas in which the applied anthropologist is "put to work" are wildly diverse. Anthropologists work in human resources departments for corporations; they are employed in marketing, the military, the government, and in health and education.

2. How Did Applied Anthropology Develop?

Applied anthropology developed from a variety of sources in the United Kingdom, Canada, and the United States. Central to this emergence was the need for anthropologists to work outside academe and to apply their skills to private and government issues such as land claims and the needs of the corporate world. The Second World War was a major impetus to the establishment of applied anthropology.

3. What Are Some of the Challenges Facing the Applied Anthropologist?

Many of the challenges facing applied anthropologists relate to the differences between applying research in the academic and the non academic worlds. Applied anthropologists also face the issue of bias. Yet another issue is the peril of having their work co-opted by government agencies or private firms. Other challenges relate to the question of who, ultimately, controls the data they produce, and what use might be made of it.

4. What Does the Future Hold for Applied Anthropology?

The future of applied anthropology is quire bright in terms of employment prospects, with more and more graduates in anthropology finding employment outside the academic realm. However, the use to which anthropological data are put causes some anthropologists to voice concerns, specifically in terms of the growth of applied anthropology in the military arena.

Applied anthropologists work in many different settings, such as among the Mursi people, a Nilotic pastoralist ethnic group in Ethiopia.

11.1   What is Applied Anthropology?

The question "What is applied anthropology?" is a complex one. One approach is to view it as consulting work undertaken by anthropologists relating to practical problems. An applied anthropologist uses a holistic knowledge of culture, behaviour, social relations, and social structures to address practical concerns. An applied anthropologist, then, is someone employed by an agency or company to generate data that are relevant to solving some practical issue. Essentially, an applied anthropologist applies the skills, training, and knowledge of anthropology to venues outside the academic setting. This covers a wide area, such as nongovernmental organizations (NGOs), international bodies, museums, band councils, and a variety of research institutes, some of which we will discuss below.

Many applied anthropologists are also academic anthropologists; that is, they sometimes work as applied anthropologists while remaining academics. Being an applied anthropologist does not therefore rule out an academic career. Indeed, experience in applied anthropology can be quite beneficial to a later academic or research career.

The diverse realms of applied and academic anthropology are always tethered to the anthropological perspective; it could not be otherwise. But as practices, applied and academic anthropology are quite distinct from each other, in terms of both practice and expectations. For example, applied anthropology entails more interdisciplinary work. Also, different expectations arise when it comes to publishing findings: Within academe the anthropologist usually publishes under his or her own name; on the applied side, by contrast, publications typically appear under the company or employer name. Also, most applied anthropology is not aimed at an academic audience and is published in internal reports rather than, say, as journal articles. Another important difference between academic and applied anthropology relates to how the data gleaned from the anthropological perspective are put to use—which can be problematical (see below).

This chapter aims to provide a solid understanding of what applied anthropology is and where it is practised and to highlight some of the challenges and successes associated with it. We will begin with a history of the field. We will then examine some of its various branches, such as health, business, and the military.

11.2 The History of Applied Anthropology

I think that in the very combination of practical and theoretical interests lies the proper task of the Institute. There is a gap between the theoretical concerns of the anthropology of the schools on the one hand, and practical interests on the other. This gap must be bridged over, and in doing this the Institute can make itself very useful.[1]

Not until Bronislaw Malinowski published *Practical Anthropology* in 1929 did a clearly defined applied anthropology begin to emerge. This is not to suggest that he invented it. The term "practical anthropology" had been coined much earlier, in the 1860s, by James Hunt, the founder of the Anthropological Society of London. In fact, anthropological data had been used throughout the 19th century in a variety of contexts. For example, the Canadian and American governments employed physical anthropologists to classify immigrant populations based on their skull and facial characteristics. Also, linguistic anthropologists had a long albeit stormy history of employment during treaty negotiations in both Canada and the United States. For this reason, many Aboriginal peoples continue to look askance at anthropologists, viewing them mainly as ethnographers with forms to fill out, or as linguists with charts and graphs to document their communities. Much of the present-day distrust stems from the roles that early anthropologists played in treaty making, which invariably resulted in the loss of land and culture for many Aboriginal peoples. Anthropologists are still trying to move beyond this legacy; many people, especially indigenous people, remain wary of them.

In the middle of the 19th century, the Ethnological Society was founded in London, England, as were similar organizations. This marked the beginnings of applied anthropology. Initially, applied anthropologists were attached to the foreign offices and the military units of various countries. These early anthropologists set out to study and document the life ways of "exotic" cultures. However, anthropology did not fare well during colonial times, for its practitioners had competing goals. On the one hand, they wanted to apply their skills to gathering information about the peoples and places they were encountering; on the other, the colonial authorities were more interested in statistics pertaining to military and government projects. This created problems that would reverberate down through the years, for anthropologists became associated with foreign domination, despite their lofty goal of helping "emancipate" humanity.

In the early 19th century the U.S. Congress asked Henry Schoolcraft to compile a report on the status of American Indians. The resulting report,[2] which detailed conditions on American Indian reservations, was among the first North American projects of applied anthropology. However, in his capacity as Indian agent, Schoolcraft also negotiated the Treaty of Washington (1836). That treaty deprived the Ottawa and Chippewa peoples of enormous tracts of land—some 55,997 square kilometres—and for that, Schoolcraft was partly responsible. In his defence, he was genuinely concerned (though paternalistic) about the well-being of the Native people who were being affected—indeed, for the welfare of *all* Native American Indians. Even so, he was a product of the times, in that he supported government schools and mission schools, believing that they were necessary in order to educate and "Christianize" Native Americans. He also urged that the Native people be taught agriculture to compensate for the loss of their hunting grounds and he took a firm stand against the distribution of alcohol among American Indians.

Another notable applied anthropologist was Philleo Nash, an American who began his academic career as a prehistoric archaeologist at the University of Toronto. But he is mainly remembered as "an anthropologist in the White House," to which he served as an adviser on race relations as well as on military affairs. For many years he was also commissioner of the U.S. Bureau of Indian Affairs.

Despite these early developments, the promise of an applied anthropology soon faltered. This was partly because administrators and governments wanted immediate data on Aboriginal peoples that included clear judgments on, for example, the suitability of certain Aboriginal populations for farming, conversion, and "civilizing." Simply put, the goals and approaches of anthropologists were at odds with the needs and goals of government agencies.

Then, during the Great Depression of the 1930s. a distinct field of applied anthropology began to emerge. Much of its work involved social analyses of poverty and government aid policies. As a further important development, the Society for Applied Anthropology was founded in 1941. Its first president was Eliot Chapple, and among its founding members were luminaries such as Margaret Mead and Fred Richardson. The SfAA was a professional organization devoted to addressing a host of issues outside of the academic domain, including social and political ones. At that time, anthropology as a discipline was just over a century old, but during that century it had compiled a vast store of ethnographic and other cultural knowledge relating to kinship systems, social structures, and so on. It had forged an impressive and sophisticated set of theories and concepts for describing, explaining, and interpreting human cultures. This knowledge, which coalesced with the founding of the SfAA, would be put to use on the battlefields of Europe and Asia during the Second World War.

The anthropologist Margaret Mead was instrumental in the creation of the Society for Applied Anthropology.

Source: Library of Congress

11.2.1　Second World War

The Second World War was a sad opening for applied anthropology. Just as with many other fields (technology, for example), the needs of the war spurred developments in both practice and theory. In 1942, as the war entered its third year, the *Journal of Applied Anthropology* was launched (renamed *Human Organization* in 1949). Among the early contributors were Margaret Mead, Ruth Benedict, Clyde Kluckhohn, and Gregory Bateson—people who would set the agenda for much of American anthropology over the following decades.

In Britain, too, anthropologists were heavily involved in the war effort, and in much the same way as in North America (see below). Between the 1930s and the 1960s, British anthropologists wrote a great deal about the social problems and challenges facing the various peoples who were under British colonial rule. The North American and European organizations devoted to applied anthropology shared a similar broad goal: to construct a platform for applying anthropological skills to social arenas such as employment, immigration, indigenous peoples, land claims, and so forth. However, the war effort soaked up much of the energy and time of early applied anthropology.

When the Second World War began—in 1939 for Canada and most of Europe, in 1941 for the United States—anthropologists were actively sought by government departments and especially by the military. They were expected to do their civic duty as loyal citizens and their professional duty as anthropologists. Applied anthropologists contributed to the war effort in a number of ways. Many worked as translators of Japanese, German, and a host of other languages. Many others worked as "cultural translators," providing information, insights, and analyses as well as predictions of the enemy's behaviour. They helped familiarize their country's forces with the social and cultural practices of other peoples, whether enemy or allied. It was hoped that by explaining the cultural bases of certain practices, anthropologists might help mitigate misunderstandings and contextualize "exotic" practices and beliefs.

Anthropologists also worked on the home front throughout the war, helping gauge the mood of the population and working to predict shortages and needs that might arise from the massive reorganization of the labour force. Internationally, anthropologists applied their learning to help ease the many issues arising from, for example, the stationing of millions of North American soldiers in European countries. Essentially, anthropologists like Margret Mead and Clyde Kluckhohn were providing an understanding of culturally grounded behavioural patterns. Anthropologists with specific skills were matched to specific military needs. For example, experts on Russia liaised with intelligence personnel dealing with Russia, while anthropologists with knowledge of Japanese customs worked with the U.S. forces when they were sent to the Pacific arena. The book *The Chrysanthemum and the Sword* is an example of the type of literature that anthropologists produced during this period.[3] Ruth Benedict, the author, undertook ethnological research of the Japanese and German cultures in order to provide cultural information to the American government and army, for both military and diplomatic purposes.

After the war, applied anthropologists continued to work for the Allies as they established new modes of governance in the defeated nations. The collapse of Imperial Japan and Nazi Germany, and the large-scale movement of peoples during and after the war, led to the founding of, literally, new nations. In many ways the war was a crucible for applied anthropology, one in which these experts excelled, thereby proving not only that anthropology had a practical side but also that anthropological knowledge of the world and its cultures was essential. The Second World War had provided applied anthropologists with a window of opportunity to demonstrate their particular skills in a large number of areas.

After the war, most anthropologists returned to their academic pursuits. Some had become disillusioned with the use that had been made of their training on the killing fields of Europe and the Pacific. In their view, the "science of humanity" had been recruited to the cause of killing, and the mere presence of anthropologists in a war sat uneasily with them. This unease was exemplified, perhaps, by Project Camelot, a controversial social science project designed to study national conflicts and social breakdowns, using Chile as an example. Concern from both government and anthropologists that this project was too close to military goals and covert operations led to its cancellation by Congress in 1965.[4]

Over the next few decades, applied anthropologists were still engaged with practical issues, such as the conditions on American Indian reservations and Canadian Indian reserves. As Western nations and companies extended their political and economic reach after the war, anthropologists were called on occasionally to provide pertinent information in many areas, such as ethnic relations and social housing. Generally, though, anthropologists returned to their quiet academic pursuits in the 1950s and 1960s. Today, applied anthropology is a vast field, one that draws from both professional applied anthropologists and academic ones. Organizations abound, especially in North America and Europe. In the United Stares there are a multitude of large umbrella organizations, including the Consortium of Practical and Applied Anthropology (COPPA), which links American departments of anthropology with applied components and acts as a repository of journals, news, and information on applied anthropology.

11.2.2 Applied Anthropology in Canada

Applied anthropology was practised in Canada in the late 19th century. The work of George Mercer Dawson of the Geological Survey of Canada serves as an example. While not strictly what we might term applied anthropology today, the ethnographic work of Dawson and others certainly drew from their anthropological training. They were employed as part of the major survey of Canada's West Coast, and they made recommendations to the federal government relating to the conditions and treatment of several First Nation peoples, including the Haida and the Kwakwaka'wakw. In the early 20th century, famed ethnographer Diamond Jenness worked with Inuit peoples in the North and, controversially, was involved in discussions about relocating several Inuit bands. In his later years, Jenness opposed the relocation of Inuit bands, calling the practice a "form of apartheid."[5] Jenness was responsible for some of the earliest ethnographic research among the Inuit. He also provided the earliest known sound recordings of any Inuit group, whose voices, songs, stories, and mythologies were all captured by this intrepid anthropologist.

In Canada, applied anthropology was not as affected by

Members of the Geological Survey of Canada and Canadian Pacific rail road survey parties during their 1871 expedition to British Columbia.

Source: Toronto Public Library

the war as it was other places. Not until after the war was practical anthropology carried out on any great scale. The Hawthorne-Tremblay Report is the best example of anthropology being applied to social issues during the postwar years. This report, commissioned by the **Department of Indian Affairs**, beginning in 1948 employed around 50 researchers, most of whom were anthropologists.[6] The goal of this report was to compile a databank of information on Canada's Aboriginal population, for the purposes of a policy review relating to the Indian Act. The Hawthorne-Tremblay Report made more than 150 recommendations, many of which were never acted on; even so, it had a strong influence, for it showed that large, cooperative teams employed to compile practical anthropological data could succeed. Also, the report, although later governments left it to languish, did raise public awareness of the successes of Aboriginal peoples with regard to their survival in harsh environments and their technological mastery. The same report highlighted some of the awful conditions and intrusive legislation that bedeviled many communities.

Applied anthropologists in Canada, like their counterparts in the United States, put their cultural training to work for various government bodies, for which they addressed issues such as immigration and Aboriginal peoples. But despite large projects such as the Hawthorne-Tremblay Report, applied anthropology in Canada was limited in both scope and employment opportunities until the late 1960s. In fact, anthropology itself was just beginning to gather steam in Canada as an important social science. In 1960 there were only two Canadian departments of anthropology; by 1969 there were more than 20, with 13 augmented departments, most of which were attached to sociology.

Beginning in the 1970s, Canadian applied anthropologists engaged in research involving Aboriginal peoples, and such projects accounted for most applied research.[7] Another main area of employment was immigration studies, given that each year throughout that decade more than 200,000 new immigrants entered Canada. In this regard, anthropologists studied and compiled reports on resettlement, multiculturalism, ethnic relations, and a host of other areas. Alongside work on Aboriginal issues and immigration, applied anthropologists involved themselves more and more in the corporate world—for example, in marketing, advertising, human relations, and various other areas that together are often referred to as the "anthropology of business." A crucial part of business anthropology sets our to provide employers with information on consumer behaviour.

Applied anthropology in Canada is today a prominent field. In 1992 the Society for Applied Anthropology in Canada established the Weaver-Tremblay Award, which is presented to the anthropologist who best reflects the ideal of social and political engagement in anthropology.[8] In the following sections we discuss some of the domains of applied anthropological research.

11.3   Domains of Applied Anthropology

Applied anthropologists today work in a wide variety of settings ranging from the identification of human remains using forensic anthropological skills, to the design of ergonomic chairs for students, to analyses of market trends for large corporations. Applied anthropology has a fascinating history within the broader discipline of anthropology, ranging from the battlefields of the Second World War to the advocacy of human rights in today's conflict zones. By examining the world of applied anthropology, we can learn about the practical aspects of anthropological expertise and how anthropologists have an impact in many different areas.

As we have seen throughout this text, anthropology is an eclectic field of diverse research interests united by the "anthropological perspective." That perspective incorporates a holistic approach to cultural phenomena, one in which all aspects of society, and all components of individual and group life, are examined through the anthropological lens. Because of this diversity and anthropology's staggered origins in fields such as botany, natural history, ethnography, and geology, anthropology lends itself strongly to practical applications. Next we discuss only some of the domains of applied anthropology.

Srebrenica Massacre site.

TABLE 11.1. Applied Anthropology Fields and Associated Anthropological Study Areas

Domain	Possible Anthropology Study Focus
Housing	Architecture, health
Health/disability studies	Medical/physical anthropology
Corporate	Anthropology of business, economic anthropology
Indigenous issues	Cultural anthropology, archaeology, Aboriginal studies
Cultural resource management	Archaeology
Military	Linguistic/medical/cultural anthropology
Ethnography	Cultural anthropology, ethnographic studies
Museum	Cultural anthropology, archaeology
Environmental/ecological	Physical/ecological/palynology, etc.
Environmental impact assessment	Cultural ecology, environmental anthropology
Social impact studies	Environmental/biological/ecological anthropology
The 'mega' project	Variety of anthropology skills

11.3.1 Forensic Anthropology: Grave Evidence

Forensic anthropology applied to human rights cases raises different kinds of questions in relation to how anthropologists might engage social and political worlds and what kind of "products" might emerge from this engagement. The goals of our work, and the methods, techniques, and engagements used to achieve them, are often quite different from the concerns of anthropologists based in academic institutions.[9]

The skulls were slowly uncovered, the dust and soil of recent years brushed off carefully. Other human bones emerged as the forensic anthropologist worked diligently, focused on his craft and on the hard task ahead. As the excavation continued, the members of the forensic team were surrounded by the media, mourning families, and security forces. Forensic anthropologists had done this type of work before, in Rwanda, Kosovo, Guatemala, and even British Columbia.

Their archaeological and forensic expertise takes applied anthropologists to many disaster sites around the world. They use their skills to find, excavate, clean, and classify ancient hominids or—in the applied area—victims mass of murder, plane crashes, genocide, and natural disasters.

Forensic anthropology is the analysis of skeletal remains for legal purposes. Law enforcement authorities call on forensic anthropologists to identify human remains and to determine, if possible, the cause of death. Forensic anthropologists specializing in skeletal remains commonly work closely with **forensic archaeologists**. The relationship between the two is rather like the one between a forensic pathologist, who examines a corpse to establish time and manner of death, and a crime scene investigator, who searches the site for clues. The forensic anthropologist deals with human remains—often only bones and teeth; the forensic archaeologist controls the site, recording the position of all relevant finds and recovering any clues associated with the remains. From skeletal remains, the forensic anthropologist can determine the age, sex, race, and stature of the deceased, as well as physical abnormalities or trauma (e.g., broken bones).Even some details of an individual's health and nutritional history can be determined from the bones. Thus several kinds of anthropologists analyze human remains for a variety of purposes, contributing to the documentation and correction of violence committed by humans past and present.

One of the best-known forensic anthropologists in North America is Clyde C. Snow. He has been practising in this field for more than 40 years—first for the U.S. Federal Aviation Administration and more recently as a freelance consultant. Besides the usual police work, Snow has studied the remains of General George Armstrong Custer and his men from the 1876 battle at Little Big Horn. In 1985 he went to Brazil, where he identified the remains of the notorious Nazi war criminal Josef Mengele.

Dr. Snow was instrumental in establishing the first forensic team devoted to documenting cases of human rights abuses around the world. This began in 1984 when he went to Argentina at the request of a newly elected civilian government to help identify the remains of *desaparecidos*, or "disappeared ones"—the 9,000 or more people who were eliminated by death squads during seven years of military rule. A year later, he returned to give expert testimony at the trial of nine junta members and to teach Argentineans how to recover, clean, repair, preserve, photograph, X-ray, and analyze bones. Besides providing factual accounts of the fate of victims to their surviving kin and refuting the assertions of revisionists that the massacres never happened, Snow and his Argentinean associates provided crucial evidence to convict several military officers of kidnapping, torture, and murder. Since Snow's pioneering work, forensic anthropologists have become increasingly involved in investigations of human rights abuses in all parts of the world, from Chile to Guatemala, Haiti, the Philippines, Rwanda, Iraq, Bosnia, and Kosovo. Meanwhile, they continue to do important work for more typical clients. In the United States these clients include the FBI and city, state, and county medical examiners' offices.

Forensic anthropologist Dr. Owen Beattie teaches biological and forensic anthropology at the University of Alberta in Edmonton and serves as consultant in physical anthropology for the Office of the Chief Medical Examiner in Alberta. Beattie has conducted forensic investigations for coroners, police departments, and medical examiners across Canada and has helped investigate human rights violations around the world. In the mid-1990s, he served as part of a UN team that exhumed and analyzed victims of the 1994 Rwandan massacres.

Beattie has used his considerable forensic expertise to help solve some of the most fascinating mysteries of the Canadian Arctic. He is most famous for his work on the remains of members of the doomed 1845–48

Exhumation of mass grave site in Compalapa, Chimaltenango (2005).

Source: USAID

Frozen in Time: The Fate of The Franklin Expedition by Owen Beattie and John Geiger Bloomsbury Publishers. 2004.

The frozen remains of Franklin crewmember John Torrington, who died shortly after the expedition's ships, the *Erebus* and *Terror*, became trapped in ice.

Original Study 1

Forensic Anthropology and the Pickton Farm Murders

Tracy Rogers

Tracy Rogers is a forensic anthropologist, the director of the Forensic Science Program at the University of Toronto Mississauga, and an associate professor in the Department of Anthropology.

Forensic anthropology is the application of anthropological skills and knowledge to assist the police, coroners, medical examiners, and pathologists in their investigations. In North America, forensic anthropology usually involves applying bioanthropological and archaeological expertise, while in Britain these specialties are divided between forensic anthropologists (in the lab) and forensic archaeologists (on the scene). In practical terms, North American forensic anthropologists attend a crime scene to determine whether the bone is human, to clarify the nature of the remains (archaeological, historic, forensic, etc.), and to help locate clandestine graves, human remains, and related evidence. They help the police with the proper documentation and recovery of the body and exhibits at the scene. This includes mapping the grave and excavating the body and related evidence to help reconstruct the events that took place at the crime scene. Once the body has been taken to the morgue, the forensic anthropologist provides a biological profile (age, sex, ancestry, stature, unique characteristics) of the skeletal remains to help police identify the deceased. Forensic anthropologists also examine the bones for evidence of injury or damage that could be useful to the pathologist in determining the cause of death or anything that happened to the body after death (e.g., dismemberment).

In 2002, the RCMP and the Vancouver Police Department undertook the largest serial killer crime scene investigation in Canadian history. Over approximately 20 years, more than 60 women had disappeared from Vancouver's Downtown East Side. The police investigation progressed sporadically over the years, but it was not until the spring of 2002 that the Pickton property in Port Coquitlam could be concretely linked to the disappearances. The 16-acre crime scene was a small-scale pig farm. It was not clear how many of the missing women might be associated with this scene, nor where their bodies or related evidence might be concealed. Investigators decided to be as thorough as possible. Besides examining the 53 vehicles and 16 buildings on the farm, they ordered a full excavation of the property in an effort to locate buried remains and/or evidence. Civilians with specialized knowledge in operating heavy equipment were hired to excavate materials and take them to the screening and sorting area, where a team of anthropology graduates from across Canada searched the dirt for anything not natural to the soil. The property was divided into 20 by 20 metre squares and systematically excavated and documented. Undergraduate and graduate students with training in forensic anthropology, bioarchaeology, and archaeology worked in shifts to examine the excavated soil by hand as it moved along a conveyor belt. Nonbiological objects were removed for evaluation by an identification police officer, and Tracy Rogers, a forensic anthropologist. was hired to examine bone and biological material recovered from the scene in order to determine whether it was human, provide a biological profile and/or identifying features, and assess trauma/damage. Two additional forensic anthropologists, Richard Lazenby and Owen Beattie, helped in this process over the course of the 18-month investigation.

As a result of the investigation, more than 16,000 exhibits were seized, more than 130,000 scene photos were taken, 542 fingerprints were lifted, thousands of animal bones were examined and eliminated from the case, human remains were discovered both above and below ground, and Robert Pickton was charged with 27 counts of first degree murder. Due to the complexity of the case and associated evidence, six of the counts were severed and the trial proceeded on those six. In December 2009, Robert Pickton was convicted of 6 counts of second degree murder; he was ultimately sentenced to 25 years without parole, the maximum penalty for such a crime in Canada.

Forensic anthropologists are valuable members of the investigative team at outdoor, fire, and unusual crime scenes. Their knowledge of body dumpsite characteristics, search indicators, and animal activity helps investigators narrow potential search sites for clandestine graves and scattered bones/body parts. Their training in scene documentation, mapping, and excavation ensures that the context and relationships of objects and landmarks at a scene are recorded, allowing the investigative team to reconstruct the events that occurred at the scene leading up to and following the death and/or deposition of the body. At the Pickton property, for example, the forensic anthropology search team was responsible for recovering most of the buried exhibits, and the forensic anthropologist, Tracy Rogers, made recommendations about the search protocol that led to the recovery of human remains in their proper context. Forensic anthropologists also analyze human skeletons, provide information to help identify the deceased, and in some cases help the pathologist determine the sequence of events that led to the death. Most American states and Canadian provinces have at least one forensic anthropologist on staff or working on a contract basis, and those with large populations and high crime rates may employ several forensic anthropologists. To become a forensic anthropologist, one must earn a PhD in anthropology, preferably with a specialization in forensic anthropology. During this process, graduate students usually gain practical experience by working on forensic cases with their supervisors.

Sources: Owen Beattie, Young Alberta Book Society, 1998, http://www.culturenet.ucalgary ca/yabs/beatt1eo.html, accessed October 16, 2000, Owen Beattie, 8th Annual Young Scientist Conference, n.d., http://ftp.ea.educ.ab.ca/dept/ins/beattie/html, accessed October 16, 2000.

Franklin Expedition to find the Northwest Passage. This work, published as *Frozen in Time: The Fate of the Franklin Expedition*,[10] was an international bestseller. Beattie's forensic examination suggests that the men died in 1846 of lead poisoning stemming from faulty soldering of the seals of their canned goods.

In 1999, Beattie supervised removal of the frozen remains of a 15th-century hunter discovered in a remote glacier in Tatshenshini-Alsek National Wilderness Park, British Columbia. The ancient hunter and the artifacts associated with his body have generated strong interest among the scientific and First Nations communities. Beattie has also conducted archaeological and forensic investigations into the 1719 disappearance of Captain James Knight's ships, the *Albany* and *Discovery*, on their way to explore Hudson Bay. Beanie's 1989–91 excavations raised doubts about the theory that the explorer and his men died of starvation. These conclusions are found in *Dead Silence: The Greatest Mystery in Arctic Discovery*.[11]

The field of forensic anthropology has grown significantly over the past few decades and has become popularized in many television shows that depict crime-fighting detectives using the skills of forensic and physical anthropologists. Whether forensic anthropologists are excavating the remains of a recent massacre or uncovering enigmatic prehistoric individual human remains, their work is an important subfield of modern applied anthropology. This importance is illustrated by the contribution that anthropologists and graduate students made in the sad case of the Pickton murders in BC.

11.3.2 Ethnography

Ethnography, as we discussed earlier, is the controlled participant observation of a given cultural field. It is one of the subfields of cultural anthropology, but it is also a large part of applied anthropology. A vital component of ethnography—indeed, of all anthropology—has always been ethics.[12] The Society for Applied Anthropology developed its *Code of Ethics* in 1949, based on a diligent set of rules pertaining to the treatment of participants and the information they reveal or that is gathered from studying them. Notwithstanding its problematic links with colonialism in its very early days, the history of ethnographic inquiry has long reflected that the purpose of most ethnography has been purely academic and that ethnographers are held to a very high ethical standard. Most ethnographic research is undertaken from within academe and for purely academic reasons, such as to teach students or advance knowledge. Increasingly, however, anthropologists are being hired by the private sector, and this development has raised specific challenges. The place of ethnographic research in applied anthropology is quite complex and can raise troublesome issues of ethics and questions about the use of the data that are gathered by ethnographers.

© Oscar Espinosa/Shutterstock.com

Ethnography involves living amongst the people the anthropologist is studying. Here a village of the Dassanech Tribe in Ethiopia is shown.

Even when applying their expertise for practical purposes, ethnographers must still adhere to the ethics codes of the various anthropological associations (the American Anthropological Association, the Canadian Anthropological Association, and so on).

In modern applied ethnography, the purpose of the research and the use of the resulting data can raise some very troubling questions. For example, a large mining corporation may employ a team of anthropologists to conduct ethnographic or archaeological research into indigenous peoples who use and/or reside near the land sought by the company. What would be the purpose of such research? It is likely not knowledge for the sake of enlightenment; it is not to fill in the blank spaces of prehistory and to contribute to our understanding of these peoples. The employer—here, the mining company—may be seeking to gain leverage over the indigenous people, to be forewarned of possible complications resulting from their mining ventures, and to be informed enough to present their case to the public or in the courts should a debate arise about the safe or ethical use of lands and resources. This places the traditional standards of ethnography under severe stress. The researcher's data may in the end cause harm to the indigenous people nearby, or harm to their environment. There is no easy answer to these troubling questions for applied anthropology. The simple fact that one is "selling" one's anthropological skills outside the academic setting can result in the loss of control over the resulting data and the purposes to which it is put.

Other examples of applied ethnography can be found in the corporate world. A case in point: A corporation may hire an ethnographer to study how the members of a large, possibly multicultural workforce interact with one another and with management. Corporate anthropology is addressed in this chapter's Original Study 2.

Whether applied ethnographic research is undertaken in Cree towns or in the offices of major corporations, the same anthropological skills are needed. These anthropologists must also practise very similar techniques, such as interviews and the use of assistants from the local community (formerly referred to as "informants," a term now out of favour owing to negative connotations of "informing" on one's community). Similar ethnographic research skills are thus seen in both academic and applied ethnography: Immersion within, and a thorough knowledge of, the community, is required. This is true whether the ethnography takes place among Llongot headhunters or in a major industrial plant.

However, there are differences between academic and applied ethnography. For instance, where once the ethnographer could choose which community to work with, now the actual "community" is chosen by the stake holders, those who "pay the bills." Also, the standard ethnographic time frame of around a year spent living and working with any given community is no longer really feasible in many cases, as the stakeholders usually require data in a hurry. This situation often results in the skills of the applied ethnographer falling under the laws and rules of the "market"—a development that surely would have horrified the founders of ethnographic research.

11.3.3 Corporate Anthropology

Applied anthropology has many facets, and we have examined just a few of these so far. We turn our attention now to the fast-growing field of corporate or business anthropology. This is not the same as the "anthropology of business," which is the anthropological analysis of business, and not an applied field. Applied business/corporate anthropology itself includes marketing, systems analysis, cross-cultural understanding in the business world, advertising, and human resource studies for large corporations. What corporate managers want from anthropologists is detailed information on how their company and workforce actually function, as opposed to their own internally generated organization charts and graphs. The corporate anthropologist is required to explain how the company's operations might be improved, streamlined, and made more effective. What the anthropologist is really doing is an ethnography of the business environment. Indeed, some see ethnography as "an excellent approach to understanding products within a consumer landscape."[16] As the late business anthropologist Brian Burkhalter added, "In brief, in any business or public situation requiring extensive knowledge about how a local community, culture, group, or group of businessmen think, feel, believe, or act, there is an opportunity for applied anthropology to make policy suggestions based on ethnographic research."[14] In the following Original Study, Anishinaabeg applied anthropologist Rodney Nelson discusses not only the corporate world and applied anthropology, but also how these can intersect with indigenous cultures and traditional knowledge.

11.3.4 Applied Anthropology and the Military

We have already seen how applied anthropology played an important role in the military during colonial days and the Second World War. We will therefore confine our discussion of the military to just a few current observations. Some anthropologists today are hired by military organizations in a variety of areas. In the United States, the *New York Times* reported recently on a semi-secret project known as the Human Terrain System, an experimental program run by the Pentagon, which assigns anthropologists (among other social scientists) to U.S. army combat units fighting in Afghanistan and Iraq. In October 2007, U.S. Defense Secretary Robert Gates "authorized a $40 million expansion of the program, which will assign teams of anthropologists and social scientists to each of the 26 American combat brigades in Iraq and Afghanistan."[15] Their mission is to liaise with local people, and to translate and understand the specific characteristics and cultural practices such as local customs and taboos, so as to smooth the path for military—civilian cooperation. "Since early September, five new teams have been deployed in the Baghdad area, bringing the total to six."[16]

Some anthropologists are uncomfortable with the role that anthropology is being called on to play in war zones. Dr. Patricia Omidian, an associate professor and the head of social sciences for the Aga Khan University's Faculty of Arts and Sciences in Karachi, Pakistan, claims that "militarized anthropology subverts our work and puts us on an ethical slippery slope."[17] In response, Col. Martin Schweitzer, commander of the 82nd Airborne Division unit working with the anthropologists in Afghanistan, reports that the unit's combat operations were reduced by 60 percent after the anthropologists and other scientists arrived, and that this allowed the soldiers to concentrate more on improving security, health care, and education for the local population. Whether other sociopolitical factors contributed co such a decline in combat operations is not stated, but it is suggested that the presence of anthropologists in the field reduced the need for combat operations.

Even so, most anthropologists are extremely wary of becoming involved in military projects. In late 2008 the Association of American Anthropologists amended its *Code of Ethics* specifically in response to this militarization, stating that "in accordance with the Association's general position on clandestine and secret research, no reports should be provided to sponsors that are not also available to the general public."[18] This, along with other amendments, is geared toward ensuring that anthropologists do not conduct covert operations and become embroiled in military operations.

Original Study 2

A Tale of Two First Nations: Traditional Knowledge in Today's Business World

Rodney Nelson

I often get asked what I do for a living. I usually respond saying that I am an anthropologist and then wait for the typical responses: "I always liked dinosaurs! It must be fun to dig up all those bones," or, "Wow! I love ancient cultures like Egypt and Greece." I always smile and prepare my typical response: "I am a corporate anthropologist. I work mainly with First Nations helping to set up businesses and promote economic development." I usually get a confused look and some people even admit that they don't think they know what an anthropologist does. In reality, anthropologists

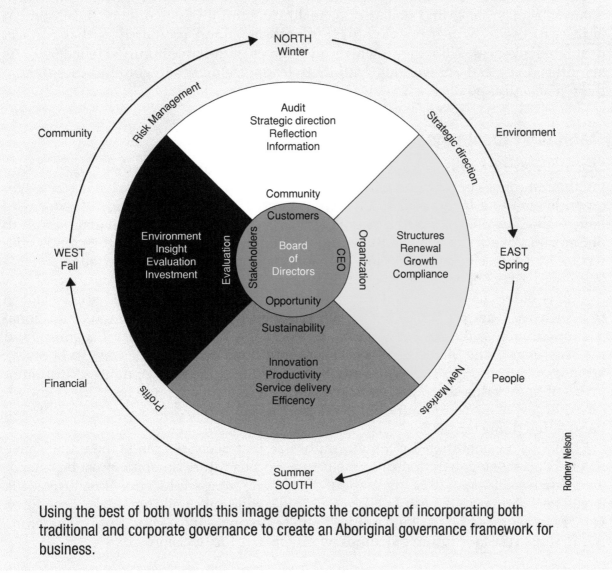

Using the best of both worlds this image depicts the concept of incorporating both traditional and corporate governance to create an Aboriginal governance framework for business.

(Continued)

(Continued)

are working in many fields and disciplines. We are involved in every aspect of human society and culture, including business.

Today there are more than 200 First Nations communities across Canada (Statistics Canada 2006). Many of these communities are facing ongoing social and economic hardships such as low employment, high suicide rates, and increasing diabetes and other health issues. Many communities do not have safe drinking water or access to the medical treatments that others in Canada enjoy. To help alleviate these issues, many First Nations leaders and elders are looking toward economic development as a way to create wealth and prosperity in their communities. As Northwest Coast Tsimshian businessman Calvin Helin says, "First Nations have been doing business for thousands of years so being in business is not new or a colonial process" (CCCR 2010). Several elders and leaders such as Chief Sophie Pierre of the Ktunaxan/Kinbasket Nation, Chief Clarence Louie of the Osoyoos, and Chiefs Sam Bull and George Halfe of Whitefish Lake First Nation see economic development as a way for First Nations to attain self-governance and sustainable, healthy communities. Economic development is the process by which people build organizations and partnerships that connect profitable business with other interests and values of the community (Helin 2009). As an anthropologist. I am working with these leaders, elders, and communities to help them realize this goal.

Traditional Teachings

Discussions of traditional knowledge for First Nations often generate images of saving the rainforests or protecting fishing areas. But traditional knowledge is more than an understanding of the land and the environment. It is the knowledge of those who have walked before us (our ancestors) that has been passed on through generations to define and govern the way we think and act today and in the future. It grounds who we are and forges our identity and decision making. Traditional knowledge extends into every aspect of our lives (Nelson 2010).

Many elders have told me that we all have a responsibility to one another and to the earth we walk on. These beliefs are reflected in many First Nations traditional teachings, such as the Seven Generations Teachings, the Grandfather Teachings, and the Teachings of the Medicine Wheel. These traditional teachings or ways of knowing are passed on through stories, traditions, ceremonies, medicines, dances, and other forms of knowledge sharing (Crawshaw 2005). Elders are often the traditional knowledge holders of the community, but everyone can hold, follow, and share in traditional knowledge (Johnston 2005).

The Seven Generation Teachings emphasize that decisions made today will have an effect on seven generations into the future. So this future outcome must be considered when decisions are being made (Seven Generations Education Institute 2010). Seven generations in the future is our children's children's children. It is a generation we will never meet. but looking out for them is looking out for your family. Therefore, we all must consider future outcomes when making life decisions.

The Seven Grandfather Teachings come from many stories passed on from generation to generation and reflect the concept of *mino bimoadiziwin*, or how to live "the good life". The Ojibway story of the Grandfather Teachings tells of how the Creator gave seven grandfathers the responsibility to watch over the people. To do this they sent a helper to share the teachings of how to live in harmony with the world. The boy helper was visited seven times and was given the teachings to spread to the four directions (Benton-Banai 1979). The teachings of the seven grandfathers are *zaagidwin* (love), *dbaadendiziwin* (humility), *gwekwaadiziwin* (honesty), *aakwade'ewin* (bravery), *nbwaakaawin* (wisdom). *debwewin* (truth), and *mnaadendimowin* (respect) (Albert 2010). This philosophy provides guidance on how we are to govern our actions and behaviours.

The Teachings of the Medicine Wheel are another set of teachings that represent the four directions, east, south, west. and north:

- The east signifies the eagle and represents birth, renewal, vision, the mental, wisdom, and spring.

- The south signifies the wolf and represents youth, community, engagement, enlightenment, the spiritual, and summer.

- The west signifies the buffalo and represents reflection, emotions, objectivity, and fall.

- The north signifies the bear and represents the elders, reflection, insight, the physical, and winter.

Today, the challenge facing First Nations is to keep these traditional teachings alive and to incorporate them into everyday life. These traditional teachings are guides for how we are to act and make decisions. This can also apply to the corporate world when businesses incorporate traditional teachings into their governance structures.

Traditional Knowledge and Business

I have been fortunate to be able to work closely with several Mohawk and Anishinabeg (Odawa, Ojibwa, Nipissing, and Algonquin) leaders and elders, helping them incorporate. traditional teachings into their businesses. Many First Nations businesses are different from non-First Nations businesses because they have the added responsibilities to their communities and the goal of overall betterment of their culture. Success is measured not only in profits but also in social contributions to the community. In some cases, profits are sacrificed for the betterment of community. This philosophy runs counter to the typical business model of making profit for a few shareholders.

Traditional teachings can guide business in making important decisions such as whether to invest in communities, expand the business, or support environmental policies. Traditional knowledge can also provide a foundation for the values of an organization. The Grandfather Teachings provide the foundations of supporting the

(Continued)

(Continued)

nation, community, and family along with notions of honesty, integrity, peace, and wisdom. These values can be incorporated into corporate value systems, thus guiding the organization in how it does business. Traditional teachings such as the Seven Generations Teachings can help a business create a strategic direction. This strategy will sustain the organization for many generations to come, and not just be geared towards immediate profitability.

Traditional Knowledge and the Environment

Traditional teachings can offer insights into understanding First Nations businesses. One of the most common forms of incorporating traditional knowledge into business practices is in the area of environmental protection. Many businesses today have adopted "green practices" that protect the environment while maintaining profits. The Seven Generations Teachings are part of this philosophy. When a business considers how its decisions will affect seven generations from now, their environmental policies will reflect these decisions. Many businesses call this corporate social responsibility (CSR) and are slowly adding environmental policies to their business practices. For First Nations, CSR is more than environmental policies; it is a way of life and is ingrained in traditions and teachings.

Seven Generations Teachings and Goodfish Lake Development Corporation

The Goodfish Lake Development Corporation (GFLDC) is one First Nation business that has embraced traditional knowledge and applied it to its environmental policies (Nelson 2007). It is owned and operated by the Whitefish Lake First Nation, which is home to more than 2,300 Cree, in Alberta 200 kilometres north of Edmonton. In the 1970s, the band faced high unemployment and many people were leaving the community to find work in the nearby oil sands. The band needed a sustainable business that would keep its members in the community and employed. Chief Sam Bull had a vision to create an industrial dry-cleaning and garment-sewing business that could service the nearby oil sands. This led to the creation of the GFLDC. The company is now one of the largest dry-cleaning companies in Canada. GFLDC has taken the Seven Generations Teachings into its own boardroom and, on the advice of its elders and community representatives, has developed strict environmental guidelines to protect the land for generations to come. These traditional teachings have been directly integrated into its business philosophy and policies. The company views protection of the environment for future generations as a corporate priority and has attained the International Organization for Standardization's ISO 14001-2004 standardization for environmental management systems.

Success in Traditions—St. Eugene Mission Resort

Many First Nations have succeeded in business and are seeing their communities begin to prosper. But many more are struggling to find solutions to their problems. Many

First Nations do not have the location or land base to support large-scale-economic development. Some bands look to business development off-reserve in order to find success. Others have become innovative, using their land and history to create economic opportunities. The St. Eugene Mission Resort is one business that has taken a tragic history and turned it into a success story.

The St. Eugene Mission Resort is a five-star resort with a golf course and casino. It provides revenue and jobs to the community and is a source of pride for its members. But it is also part of a drink time in Canadian history. The resort started off as a mission school in 1912 and was one of the first industrial and residential schools in Canada. Many residential survivors tell of the hard-ships and devastating emotional and physical abuse they experienced in the years when St. Eugene was a school. One of its own survivors, Sophie Pierre, became chief of the St. Mary's band and has been instrumental in making the change from the school building being a source of pain and a reminder of darker days to it being a source of pride and success for her community.

Chief Pierre is the past chief of St. Mary's First Nation in Cranbrook, BC, and is the administrator of the Ktunaxa-Kinbasket Tribal Council, which represents more than 1,500 Ktunaxan/Kinbasket people. Chief Pierre is also one of the great First Nations leaders of today and has worked for her community for more than 30 years. She is a strong supporter of economic development that maintains traditional knowledge and world views. When the time came for the community to decide what to do with the old residential school, the debate was heated and ongoing. Chief Pierre describes the time as one of anger, frustration, and pain over what many had experienced at the school (Pierre 2007). At one meeting, an elder stood up and spoke the words that would lead the community to where it is today. The elder said the mission represented too much pain and has been a bad thing for their community for so long. He suggested that there needed to be a way to turn it into an opportunity for the community to begin a healing process. That was the birth of the $40 million St. Eugene Mission Resort, a world-class hotel, golf course and casino.

The resort was a result of the community trying to heal from a tragic situation. The concept of healing is a principal teaching of the Medicine Wheel. It maintain that, while life is forever interrelated by the four directions, we all have freedom of choice in everything we do. The St. Eugene Mission Resort offered a chance of rebirth and hope for the community. This hope represents the eastern direction of the wheel. The south represents the mental healing the survivors need. The west reflects letting go and emotional healing, while the north represents the link to spiritual healing, as well as reflection on the historical past of the mission and the impact it had on the community.

Conclusion

As a corporate anthropologist, I help businesses and communities merge their traditional teachings with their business practices. Many businesses that take this path are accepted and respected by the communities because they are still using traditional values. I often find myself in the middle of a disagreement between the band office that runs the development corporation and the community, which has its own expectations of the organization. My background in anthropology allows me to negotiate

(Continued)

(Continued)

an understanding based on the traditional values of the culture and the expectations of business.

Today many first Nations still do not have the means to create economic development in their communities. Barriers such as lack of funding, ongoing social issues, politics at every level, and the restrictions of the Indian Act make it difficult to promote economic development. Many First Nations are becoming more creative and looking internationally for opportunities that may help their communities. Some still fight to get water they can drink, as well as access to the health care and social services that many take for granted. Economic development may be an answer to these issues by creating opportunities and wealth in communities. Wealth brings infrastructure such as housing, health facilities, roads, hydro and water and sewage mains. It increases social services such as education, suicide prevention, social assistance, and day care. It creates employment and opens opportunities to promote cultural activities and pass on traditions. It helps restore the wellness and wellness and pride of a community and nation. It might even reduce the ongoing issues of substance abuse and reduce the high suicide rate of First Nations youth–a rate that is five times the national average. Until this happens, many first Nations will continue to live in Third World conditions in one of the wealthiest countries in the world. Today, First Nations are taking control of their own density and working towards economic sustainability through economic development. They are doing it on their own terms, and one of their strategies of success has been to incorporate traditional knowledge into business practices.

Sources: B. Johnston, Ojibway Heritage (Toronto: McClelland & Stewart 2005); C. Crowshaw, Scared Ways of Life. Traditional Knowledge (Ottawa: National Aboriginal Health Organization, 2005); C. Helin, Dances with Dependency *(Woodland Hill: Raven Crest Publishing 2009); R. Nelson, "Traditional Knowledge in the Board Room: A Quest for a New Model of Corporate Governance."* Journal of Aboriginal Management *(2010): 28–35; Statics Canada, "Aboriginal Identity Population" (Ottawa: Statistics Canada, 2006); CCCR (Canadian Centre for Community Renewal), "Community Economic Development." 2010, http//www.cedworks.com/CEDdefinition.html; Seven Generations Educations Institute, "Anishinoobe Mino Bimoadizwin: Principles for Anishinoobe Education" 2010, http//www.7generations.org; E. Benton-Banai,* The Mishomis Book: Voices of the Ojibway *(Minneapolis: University of Minnesota Press, 1979); J. Albert, Elder [interview by Rodney Nelson],* in Conversation with an Elder, *2010; R. Nelson,* From Vision to venture *(Ottawa: Conference Board of Canada, 2007); S. Pierre interviewed by Rodney Nelson 2007.*

In Canada, scholars of the military speak of the emergence of an "embedded anthropology," where the contribution is geared more toward understanding the intricacies of military life. For example, anthropologist Anne Irwin of the University of Calgary studied the behavioural patterns of Canadian soldiers on deployment to Afghanistan. Irwin's study is more a social anthropological analysis of military life than research for the purposes of military intelligence. She examined how soldiers bolster their identities by sharing their battlefield experiences through storytelling with their peers.[19] While the Canadian military does not have anthropologists on Human Terrain teams, soldiers are provided with cultural awareness training, and it may be argued that a militarization of applied anthropology is developing. Others might argue that there is an "anthropologicalizing" of the military under way. Anthropologists in the military possess the capacity to aid the soldiers who employ them and to do good work on the ground. However, many in academe are opposed to the use of anthropologists for military purposes. As applied anthropology becomes, once again, linked with military endeavours, and analyses of the military demonstrate the growing role of women, questions surrounding sex, gender, and violence become increasingly germane, and are addressed in the Gender Perspectives feature box below.

11.3.5 Medical Anthropology

One area in applied anthropology that has seen prolific growth in recent years is medical anthropology. **Medical anthropology** is the subfield of cultural anthropology that analyses how cultures and societies are organized around health and related issues. It has been suggested that *all* medical anthropology is applied anthropology, and indeed that is mostly true. Much of the growth in applied medical anthropology has involved a multitude of large projects that have been undertaken over the past few decades. An applied medical anthropologist, much like a forensic anthropologist, may work as part of a UN project in the developing world, or for a private charity such as *Medicins Sans Frontieres*, or for organizations such as Oxfam. Much like a forensic anthropologist, a medical anthropologist must deal with a host of political and social challenges that in many cases impede their research. Applied medical anthropologists—or more accurately of late, medical anthropological teams—must overcome these challenges in order to deliver their services. These include working in war zones or in famine areas and dealing with often hostile environments. Such issues are not normally encountered in academic anthropology, and this makes medical applied anthropological research a very special subfield. Whether in the academic or the applied domain, almost all medical anthropology has practical applications.

© Sk Hasan Ali/Shutterstock.com

Medical anthropologists tend to work in conflict zones and among the displaced, such as this UN camp for Rohingya people fleeing violence in 2017.

11.3.6 Environmental Health and Justice

Our contribution could be most effective, we decided, in broadening the definition of victims of environmental rights abuse and in illustrating the processes and mechanisms which initiate, structure, legitimize, and reproduce victimization. As anthropologists, we could provide the descriptive rationale for human environmental rights.[20]

Much of the work of applied medical anthropologists involves environmental health and justice. Throughout the 19th and 20th centuries, as the industrial system of production grew, so did the production of pollutants. Thousands of new chemical compounds were released into the atmosphere, water, and soil and found their way into the food chain and into our bodies. For decades the industrial world celebrated its triumph over nature and the wealth of new products created. But gradually the unpaid bills for unbridled growth began to come due. Mounting levels of cancer, asthma, and birth defects led to a search for causes. Today, increasingly conclusive evidence links many of these conditions to the expansion and intensification of the industrial system.

One outcome has been the environmental movement, made up of citizen activists who are determined to defend their families and communities. Closely linked to medical anthropology, the **environmental justice** movement has emerged to explore environmental pollution and health. Medical anthropologist Harriet Rosenberg of York University has researched one of the best-known cases of toxic pollution and citizen response—the infamous Love Canal.[21]

Although it is quite an old example, the case of Love Canal demonstrates the need for impact assessments and applied anthropologists. Medical anthropologists, had they been involved from the start, might have galvanized the academic community to act on behalf of the Love Canal residents. As it transpired, they were on their own initially. Love Canal is just upriver from Niagara Falls on the southeastern edge of the city of Niagara Falls, New York. Dug at the turn of the 20th century, the actual canal never carried barge traffic, but from 1920 to 1945 it served as a dumpsite for toxic wastes from the nearby Hooker Chemical plant, a division of Occidental Petroleum. After the dumpsite was filled to capacity, it was closed, buried under a clay cap, and covered with soil.

© Vito DeFilippo/Shutterstock.com

The physical, social, and spiritual health of a northern Cree community in an era of rapid change is the subject of Naomi Adelson's insightful monograph Being Alive Well.

Gender Perspective

Sex Gender, and Human Violence

At the start of the 21st century, war and violence are no longer the strictly male domains that they were in many societies in the past. War has become embedded in civilian life in many parts of the world, and it impacts the daily lives of women and children. Moreover, women now serve in the military forces of several states. although their participation in combat is often limited. Some female soldiers in the United States argue that gender should not limit their participation in combat; they consider themselves as strong, capable, and well trained as their male counterparts. Others believe that biologically based sex differences make war a particularly male domain

Scientists have long argued that males are more suited to combat because natural selection has made them on average larger and stronger than females. This idea, known as sexual selection, was first put forward by Charles Darwin in the 19th century. Darwin contended that the physical specializations of males in animal species—such as horns, vibrant plumage, and, in the case of humans, intelligence and tool use—demonstrate selection acting upon males to aid in the competition for mates. In these scenarios, male reproductive success is thought to be optimized through a strategy of "spreading seed"-in other words, through sexual activity with as many females as possible

Females, on the other hand, ar gatekeepers who optimize their reproductive success through caring for individual offspring. According to this theory of sexual selection, in species where male-male competition is high, males will be considerably larger than females and aggression will serve males well. In monogamous species, males and females will be of similar sizes.

Primatologist Richard Wrangham has taken the idea of sexual selection even further. In his book *Demonic Males*, he explores the idea that both patriarchy and male aggression have an evolutionary basis. He writes that humans, like our close cousins the chimpanzees, are "party gang" species characterized by strong bonds among groups of males who have dominion over an expandable: territory. These features "suffice to account for natural selection's ugly legacy, the tendency to look for killing opportunities when hostile neighbors meet" (Wrangham and Peterson 1996, 168). Violence in turn generates a male-dominated social order· "Patriarchy comes from biology in the sense that it emerges from men's temperaments out of their evolutionarily derived efforts to control women and at the same time have solidarity with fellow males in competition against outsiders" (ibid., 125). Wrangham allows that evolutionary forces have shaped women as well, but he suggests that females, evolutionary interests cannot be met without cooperation with males.

Feminist scholars have pointed out that these scientific models are "gendered" in that they incorporate the norms derived from the scientists' culture. Darwin's original model of sexual selection incorporated the Victorian gender norms of the passive female and active male. The Canadian pnmatologist Linda Fedigan (1986) suggests

(Continued)

that in Darwinian models, women evolved in positive directions only by a "coat tails" process whereby females were "pulled along" toward improved b1olog1cal states by virtue of the progress of the genes they shared with males. Wrangham's more recent *Demonic Males* theory has been similarly shaped by culture; that is, it incorporates the dominant world order (military states) and the gender norms (aggressive males) it values. In both cases, the putatively scientific theory has created a natural basis for a series of social conventions.

This does not mean that biological differences between the sexes cannot be studied in the natural world. Instead, scientists studying sex differences must be especially sensitive to how they may be projecting cultural beliefs onto nature Meanwhile, the attitudes of some women soldiers continue to challenge generalizations regarding "military specialization" by gender.

Sources: L.M. Fedigan, "The: Changing Role of Women in Models of Human Evolution," Annual Review, of Anthropology, 15 /1986) 25–66, R Wrangham and D. Peterson, Demonic Males (Boston Houghton' Mifflin 1996).

The city government then took over the land, and during the post war housing boom built a primary school directly on top of the former dump. By the 1970s, developers had built a subdivision there of more than 700 homes.

The families of Love Canal, in the course of raising their children, began to notice ominous signs. Children jumping in rain puddles in the schoolyard found the soles of their sneakers melting away, and mothers as well as doctors were alarmed by the number of newborns with birth defects and by the appearance of rare cancers in older children. Asthma, allergies, skin disorders, and chronic respiratory ailments also appeared in disturbingly high numbers.

Families were demanding answers, and under the leadership of the Love Canal Homeowners Association (LCHA), they began to lobby municipal and state health authorities to address the multiplying health problems. The government's response followed a pattern that has become familiar to all environmental justice activists. There was nothing unusual about the high level of ailments, officials insisted—this was just the usual variation around statistical norms. When the mothers in the community pressed the officials, they found their concerns dismissed as the fears of "hysterical housewives." Nevertheless, news reports spread word of the health problems, and real estate values plummeted. The largely working-class families had sunk their life savings into their homes and simply couldn't afford to abandon them and live elsewhere.

Their situation seemed hopeless until a few academics at local universities accepted the concerns of the homeowners at face value and began to conduce independent environmental studies. These studies confirmed the LCHA's worst fears: unacceptably high levels of a list of toxins had been found in the schoolyard and the soil of backyards, and was even oozing from the walls in the basements of homes. Most prominent among these was dioxin, the most toxic chemical ever created, dangerous at a few parts per billion.

A young mother named Lois Gibbs took the leadership of the LCHA, and the Love Canal community rose to state wide and then national prominence as a toxic disaster area. Finally, the cumbersome government bureaucracy acknowledged the serious health dangers facing the residents of Love Canal, and in 1979 President Jimmy Carter authorized the relocation of residents as well as compensation for the lost equity in their homes.[22]

The Love Canal story became a prototype for communities all over North America that faced health threats from unacknowledged sources of toxic waste, smokestack industries, and the release of pollutants into the water and air. Lois Gibbs became an internationally prominent environmental crusader and founded what is now the Center for Health, Environment, and Justice in Falls Church, Virginia. For its part, the U.S. government set aside a budgetary allocation, known as the Superfund, for the massive clean-up required to remove toxic wastes and restore sites to human use. Anthropologists, spurred on by concern for the environment and for those suffering from environmental injustice, launched and participated in forums and debates about Love Canal. Anthropological publications on environmental justice increased in number, and applied anthropologists contributed a nonpartisan (or so they argued) voice to the debate, helping at least to air out the issue of environmental health.

Similar examples of communities affected by toxic pollution in Canada include the tar ponds in Sydney, Nova Scotia; the tar sands in Alberta, which affect neighbouring First Nations groups; and the tainted-water tragedy in Walkerton, Ontario, in May 2000, when runoff from a local livestock farm infected the water supply with *E. coli*, which cost seven people their lives and injured many others." While environmental scientists conduct research in such cases to determine the level of toxic risk to humans and animals, medical anthropologists chronicle the social movements that spring up to fight the polluters and, at times, governments that are slow to acknowledge the legitimacy of their concerns. These are just some of the issues facing applied medical anthropology; there are many more, which we have not the space to address. Medical anthropology is one of the largest fields of applied anthropology. As long as there exist issues such as poverty, starvation, and environmental injustice, there will be a need for medical anthropologists to work in these areas.

11.3.6.1 Disability Studies

Other applied anthropologists bring medical and ethnographic expertise to disability studies. In what is sometimes called the "disabled community," anthropologists' training is put to much use. The disabled community is broad and diverse; it is found in hospitals, retirement homes, universities, the workplace—everywhere disabled people are found. It can thus be a subject of ethnographic analysis as much as the Bedouin or the Hazdabe, with the caveat that the community being studied will have different needs than other communities. For those who work with the disabled community, there are of course other challenges besides, which require a wide knowledge of fields such as physiology and psychology, and also compassion. The applied anthropologist in the disabled community may be employed by a hospital to study the delivery of medical services to cultural minorities or any identifiable group with disabilities or health issues.

The student of medical anthropology may end up being employed as a disability specialist working with a major national organization such as the Canadian National Institute for the Blind or War Amps of Canada. Cultural anthropologist Pamela Block is an associate professor in the Occupational Therapy Program of the School of Health Technology and Management at Stony Brook University in New York State. She describes disability studies as "in direct contrast to medical and rehabilitation models of disability, which focus on the physiological aspects of disability, the 'fixing' of atypical. 'broken' physiology."[24] Her anthropological training has brought a different approach to disability studies, where "disability is seen as part of the continuity of the human condition, as part of an identity reliant as much on socio-economical factors as on physiological factors."[25] For an applied anthropologist, the disability community is one that must be studied just like any other cultural grouping. Along with medical treatments, the dynamic of the group and both its collective identity and the identities of its individual members must be understood in order for analysis to succeed.

Elsewhere in the realm of disability studies, others with anthropological training may be hired to conduct research on disabled student communities. Such was the case with the National Educational Association of Disabled Students (NEADS), based in Ottawa. In 2003, NEADS conducted a major national research program that aimed to understand the range and quality of academic materials in alternative formats for students with disabilities in Canada's postsecondary schools. Two detailed surveys were created, one directed at students, the other for service providers such as librarians. This project highlighted the need for improved access to technologies such as Kurzweil 3000, tactile graphics, and other alternative technologies.[26] An anthropologist was hired to construct these surveys and to quantify the responses. The skills of the anthropologist were needed for a variety of reasons. The anthropologist was required to construct pertinent questions for surveys of both the student body and the service providers, to understand the specific pedagogical challenges facing the disabled student body, and to collate the data using SPSS (the Statistical Package for the Social Sciences). The result was a comprehensive analysis of the current conditions of access to academic materials in alternative formats at many of Canada's postsecondary institutions, from both the student and the service provider perspectives. The project identified the strengths and weaknesses of current systems and reported on the needs and expectations of the disabled student population.[27] Applied anthropology therefore can also be directed toward educational institutions—in this case, the large disability community within the broader academic community.

11.4 Salvage Archaeology

The domain of applied anthropology that incorporates archaeological skills is known, generally, as **salvage archaeology**. However, this type of archaeology also falls within the broader field of **cultural resource management (CRM)**. CRM deals with more than archaeology; it includes the management or mitigation of historical landscapes, historical records, old buildings, heritage sites, and so forth. Here we will focus on the archaeological side of CRM in Canada. Some countries, including the United Stares, Britain, and Australia, have laws to protect their

Here, Liam Kilmurray surveys a line of test squares that will be excavated in order to outline proto-Huron longhouses at this 15th-century village site at Jarrett-Lahmer.

Photo courtesy of Heather McLeod-Kilmurray

archaeological heritage. In this regard, Canada "has been a pioneer, with an early, computerized national archaeological survey." CRM exists in Canada because developments on Crown or private property may require that the builder obtain a clearance certificate from the relevant ministry (usually the Ministry of Heritage).

An exquisitely made Ohio Dovetail Indian arrowhead.

© Mark_Kostich/Shutterstock.com

In the United States, developments on federally owned lands, or on private lands using federal funds , require similar clearance from archaeological firms, which are contracted to excavate or mitigate sites.

Dynamic Anthropology 1

The Baby Formula Controversy

Liam Kilmurray

The provocative headlines that reverberated in the media in 1974 included "Baby Killer!", "Third World Action Group Guilty of Libel." and "Anthropologist Takes on a Major International Company Called Nestle." Such headlines highlighted the fact that anthropologists working in developing countries normally can be relied on to stick up for peoples who are sometimes oppressed, while avoiding the condescension sometimes associated with colonial or development projects. The notoriety of what became known as the "baby formula controversy" brought much attention to applied anthropology and to attempts by anthropologists to make a difference. The baby formula controversy really began with the charity organization War on Want, who reproached Nestle for its advertising campaign for the sale of baby formula in developing nations. Many people were incensed by what they perceived to be the overbearing and underhanded approach of Nestle's marketing campaign, and concerned about the damage that might result should its marketing succeed, and a boycott of Nestle was launched. Penny Van Esterik, a Canadian anthropologist, documented and participated in this campaign, which aimed to convince mothers in (mainly) developing countries to abandon the ancient human method of nurturing infants, known as breast-feeding, in favour of bottled formula. Most of the target audience for Nestle's advertising and sales campaign were impoverished, uneducated, and often illiterate.

The Nestle Corporation used its substantial economic might to promote its powdered milk formula. It did so through a major advertising campaign, which

(Continued)

(Continued)

suggested that mothers who continued to breast-feed were endangering the health of their children, and by co-opting local doctors to support the promotion of the bottle formula. The campaign promoted the bottle formula as providing physical and psychological advantages over breast milk. The formula was advertised as safe, modern, progressive, and beneficial to both mother and newborn baby. On the other hand, breast-feeding was cast as backward and associated with disease, danger, and poverty.

In this light, Penny Van Esterik was involved in the campaign, along with UNICEF and the WHO, to bring to light the pressures that Nestle was placing on women in developing nations. The campaign had its highs and lows, and Nestle had some successes, including proving that its product was safe. But Van Esterik was able to demonstrate the associated needs that came with the bottle formula, which were substantial yet had been overlooked by many. For example, the baby bottle formula required regular, daily access to clean-flowing water, and little heed was given to the fact that fresh running water was very often simply not available in these areas.

The flaw in Nestle's plan had not been an oversight, and Van Esterik argued that it simply wanted to start mothers on the bottle (after which there could be little going back) so that they would be obliged to keep purchasing Nestle products. The media campaign and the coalition of major charitable bodies along with the determination and anthropological training of Van Esterik eventually resulted in a victory for natural breast-feeding, in the lifting of the breast-feeding stigma, and in the demise of formula sales in the developing world. All of this illustrates the importance of applied anthropology and the life-or-death scenarios that applied anthropologists are sometimes involved in.

Sources: M. Muller. "The Baby Killer A War on Wont Investigation into the Promotion and Sole of Powdered Baby Milks in the Third World·" (London. War an Wont. 1974).

Dynamic Anthropology 2

Development Anthropology and Dams

Over a 35-year career in scholarly and applied work, Michael M. Horowitz, president and executive director of the Institute for Development Anthropology (IDA) and distinguished professor of anthropology at SUNY-Binghamton, has made pioneering contributions to applied anthropology. His work has focused on equitable economic growth, environmental sustainability, conflict resolution, and participatory government in the former colonial world.

Since co-founding IDA in 1976, Horowitz has been its principal leader. He has played a key role in bringing anthropology forward as an applied science in international development organizations such as the World Bank, the UN Fund for Women, and the U.S. Agency for International Development (USAID). as well as NGOs such as Oxfam and the International Union for the Conservation of Nature. He has mentored several generations of young scholars and professionals-paying particular attention to those from developing countries—encouraging the application of anthropology's comparative and holistic methodologies and theories to empower low-income majorities in the so-called underdeveloped world.

Horowitz's work with pastoralists and floodplain dwellers has had substantial positive impact on the well-being of small producers and landholders in developing countries. A clear example of this is the impact of his work on the lives and livelihoods of people living downstream of a hydroelectric dam in West Africa. Beginning in the 1980s, he and his IDA team carried out rigorous anthropological research along the Senegal River, which flows through Mali, Senegal, and Mauritania. Their study showed that traditional, pre-dam, flood-recession farming yielded better results than irrigated agriculture and was better for the environment.

This finding influenced decisions made by these countries and affiliated NGOs to manage the system with a controlled release from the Manatali Dam in Mali in order to reproduce as nearly as possible the pre-dam flow system. Horowitz's long-term field research demonstrated that seasonal flooding would provide economic, environmental, and sociocultural benefits for nearly one million small producers.

Recognized by national governments, NGOs, and development funding agencies, the work of Horowitz and his IDA colleagues on the Senegal River Basin Monitoring Activity (SRBMA) was a break—through in

Three Gorges Damn

Visible from space, China's Three Gorges hydroelectric dam is the world's biggest and most powerful hydroelectric dam. About 2,300 metres long and 185 metres high, it controls the Yangtze, the world's third largest river After fifteen years of construction with a price tag of US$22 billion, it became operational in 2009. The dam was built to provide a clean energy alternative to coal and to control flooding along the Yangtze River. However, it has been controversial since its inception, flooding ancient archaeological and cultural sites, displacing more than 1.4 million people, and causing significant ecological changes, including risks of landslides that threaten some 4 million people. Not one social scientist was consulted in the planning and assessment phase of the Three Gorges Dam.

Source: Earth Observatory - NASA

(Continued)

(*Continued*)

the concepts of resettlement and river management, and it continues to influence development policy. Prior to the IDA's work in West Africa, no hydroelectric dam had ever been managed with a controlled flood. Since then, the IDA has been asked to help apply the SRMBA model to other parts of the world, including the lower Zam-bezi River in Mozambique and the Mekong River in Laos, Cambodia, and Vietnam.

Adapted from W. Young, ed., "Kimball Award Winner," Anthropology News *41, no. 8 (2000): 29, with update based on personal communication with IDA, November 2003.*

The Anthropologist's World

Sustainable Archaeology: What Is the Future for Our Past?

Neil Ferris and Rhonda Nelson

The primary directive of archaeology is to make interpretations about the past based on the material culture that is recovered from excavation. Have you ever wondered what happens to all those artifacts and raw data after they've been excavated?

In 1975 the Ontario Heritage Act legislated that any alteration or removal of archaeological evidence from its original context would require an individual to hold a licence issued by the Minister of Tourism and Culture. This legislation, in association with initiatives introduced in the 1990s to the Planning Act and the Environmental Assessment Act, motivated a surge in commercial archaeology in Ontario. As this kind of development-motivated archaeology expanded in the decades that followed, so too did the material cultural that was collected. Museums and universities, already reaching their storage capacity for archaeological collections derived from excavations conducted throughout the 20th century, had no excess space available to house or keep up with the pace of incoming collections. As licensees under the Ontario Heritage Act were responsible for the curation and stewardship of artifacts and data that resulted from their excavations, collections tended to be stored in disparate locations under a variety of different conditions. Data collection methods were not standardized and varied widely. The result has been a wealth of accumulated archaeologicalmaterial and knowledge, but a limited capacity for researchers, First Nations communities, and the interested public to access and interpret it

In 2009 the Canadian Foundation for Innovation and the Ontario Ministry of Research and Innovation awarded to Dr. Neal Ferris at the University of Western Ontario and Dr. Aubrey Cannon at McMaster University a multimillion-dollar grant to amend this inaccessibility issue in southern Ontario. These partnered institutions are renovating and constructing new space for the curation of archaeological collections and developing innovative, state-of-the-art laboratories for materials analysis. The guiding premise of the project is to facilitate communication and the dissemination of research among researchers and commercial archaeologists,

First Nations, and others with an interest in this archaeological record. The artifact repositories will be connected and interoperable via standardized data collection protocols and a shared relational database management system. This will allow digital data of the entire compiled record of thousands of archaeological excavations across Ontario to be instantly accessible anywhere. The ultimate aim is to shift practice toward a sustainable archaeology that constantly reuses existing data and that integrates archaeological and non-archaeological interests in the record. Digital archiving, relational database design, and interoperability are the future of archaeological collections management—and accessible research-in Canada, as we join the ranks of similar initiatives already underway in the Britain, the United States, and Europe.

Private archaeological firms bid on these contracts. These contracts range from the "clearance" of just one field to the clearance of an entire stretch of land intended for a highway or other large project. Thus, salvage archaeological excavations can be vast and prolonged, or tiny and achieved in one afternoon, with a single arrowhead the sole discovery.

The CRM industry employs almost 70 percent of North American archaeologists. Most of the projects undertaken by CRM archaeologists are small-scale clearance or salvage digs. Usually, small parcels of recently ploughed land are "walked," and any surface finds, whether fragments of pottery, tools, or bones, are marked with small flags. If concentrations of artifacts or specific features are revealed, these may require further investigation. If so, test pits may be dug to determine the presence or absence of substantial archaeological material. Should this phase reveal features or artifact spreads indicating substantial archaeological material, the archaeological team may excavate a trench. If there is further evidence, a full scale excavation may be ordered.

The contributions of salvage archaeologists working in the private sphere are many. First, the developers of a specific site receive (usually) clearance to go ahead and undertake their work with the assurance that they will not be destroying a valuable part of the area's heritage. Second, the general public is served, because rare or important archaeological sites are preserved or fully excavated, thus contributing to our knowledge of the past. Third, students often gain valuable experience (which is hard to come by) working as field hands and gaining expertise, as well as employment skills suited to archaeological work. Practical, or salvage, archaeology is therefore an important component of the applied anthropological world.

11.4.1   Other Domains of Applied Anthropology

There is a vast and often bewildering variety of domains in which anthropologists can apply their skills. These domains are too many to adequately address here. There are anthropologists working in pure statistical analysis, in gerontology studies, in land claims involving Aboriginal peoples—the list is almost endless. Note also that there are many areas in which different *types* of anthropologists work together. Many projects employ more than one type of anthropologist at a given time. We examine some of these areas next.

11.4.1.1 Development Anthropology and Mega projects

Some applied anthropologists work on megaprojects. These include large under-takings, such as the construction of highways, dams, industrial refineries, or power stations, which can require many applied anthropologists. Usually, such projects require anthropologists from multiple subfields as well as input from other specialists such as geographers, geologists, and sociologists. For instance, the construction of a highway can impact a broad area containing many different cultures, landscapes, rivers, flora, and fauna. Therefore, specialists in all of these areas may be employed to undertake impact assessment studies.

A department of natural resources or a First Nation band council may hire anthropologists to undertake an impact assessment study. In this capacity, anthropological teams may advise on resource use and land management. This may involve expertise in woodlands, watersheds, and the cultural interactions between humans and these resources. Many of the skills required for such a broad knowledge base are taught in cultural ecology, which is the subfield of anthropology that studies interactions between humans and their environments. For the anthropologist, knowledge of past environmental conditions is often helpful in understanding current use of resources, as well as in predicting possible future scenarios. Anthropology is well suited to this form of prediction and analysis, given its focus on areas as diverse as past human adaptive strategies and in-depth understandings of soil morphology. In this way, knowledge about the collapse of the classic Maya or of the annual floods of the Nile in ancient Egypt can actually be of practical modern use. Such was the case some time ago with the Mackenzie Valley Pipeline and with the James Bay Agreement; both these projects stand as testament to the input that anthropologists can have on megaprojects, through their involvement with policy makers and Aboriginal peoples.[29]

11.4.1.2 Museum Anthropology

One of the oldest types of applied anthropology is museum anthropology. Many anthropology departments (especially in Europe) offer graduate degrees in museum curation (or "museology"). The links between museums and anthropology are many, for a deep knowledge of cultures and their pasts is essential to the museum world. Students enrolled in museology programs are taught the techniques of preserving, displaying, maintaining, and understanding the provenance of ancient and contemporary artifacts. One recent development is worth noting. In British Columbia, Michael Ames, curator of the Museum of Anthropology (MOA) has launched a project to deschool museums. This is considered a form of "advocacy anthropology," and involves doing away with the stuffy academic aura associated with museums and offering instead an interactive and participatory approach.

In summary, some applied anthropological domains are oriented toward a singular skill, such as museum studies or linguistics; others are the domain of multiple anthropologists oriented toward many different types of anthropological expertise. Some applied realms, such as museology and ethnography, have been part of anthropology since the very beginning; others, such as cultural ecology and corporate anthropology, are quite new to anthropology and the applied domain.

11.5   The Future of Applied Anthropology

Many anthropologists—and anthropological texts—discuss the future with a mix of trepidation and excitement. Some are pessimistic about and fearful of the growing homogeneity fostered by increasing globalization. Others argue that cultures have always been "altered," but nevertheless adapt and survive. They see the future with much more enthusiasm, contending that despite increased globalization, people and cultures interpret and use the idioms of the globalizing world in their own distinctive ways. Thus, as we have seen in this text, the way a bottle of pop is perceived in one culture may not be how it is perceived in another. Similarly, that technology is used and "situated" in a particular way in one culture does nor necessarily mean it will be so used or situated in another.

The role of the applied anthropologist in the future—in this brave new world of increased technological capacity and instantaneous communication—is destined be an important one and is likely to witness much growth. This growth will likely be the result of continued poverty, disasters, and other conditions that require the presence of many different anthropologists, among them environmental specialists, impact assessment teams, and health care workers. Medical anthropologists continue to find work in government (sponsored projects of inoculation and other major health drives). Also, applied anthropologists with expertise in health will continue to participate in large- and small-scale NGO-sponsored projects. The field of development anthropology is also quite likely to witness sustained growth, as major projects such as oilfields, nuclear power plants, highways, and hydroelectric projects are increasingly undertaken in the developed and the developing worlds.

One crucial issue for both academic and applied anthropology is the future of anthropological education. Many argue that there is a need for institutions to tailor anthropological education more toward practical issues. Advocates of practical anthropology point to the often paltry number of courses that are geared specifically toward applied issues. Health is one such example; there is a need for more courses that deal with the medical side of anthropology *and* with the social aspects of health issues. Another area of future expansion in applied anthropology will surely be related to the needs of indigenous peoples around the world. Canada needs more Aboriginal people trained in the methods of applied anthropology, more Aboriginal museum curators and archaeologists, and more courses that relate to cultural sensitivity in Aboriginal health issues. Some progress has been made in this regard, with heritage sires such as Head-Smashed-In Buffalo Jump in Alberta and Wanuskewin Heritage Park in Saskatchewan both being managed by Native Canadians. In this vein, Eldon Yellowhorn, an archaeology professor at Simon Fraser University, has become president of the Canadian Archaeological Association. Overall, it appears that anthropology will undergo a profound shift in the coming decades. with more applied courses and more and more anthropology students entering the professional world, using anthropology's training in a practical manner. Meanwhile, the number of academic anthropologists hired full-time by universities is likely to keep diminishing as anthropology becomes more and more an applied skill.

11.6 Conclusion

Applied anthropology as a discipline has carved out a place for itself as a relevant, much needed component in public policy, program development, program evaluation, interventions, and a number of other areas critical to the health of the public sphere. Still, in order to establish themselves as an important voice in such issues, anthropologists must compete with professionals from a number of other disciplines. Students of applied anthropology, then, must be keenly cognizant of the shifting functions and possibilities of their field and must be readily able to articulate the many services it has to offer a changing world.[31]

The student of anthropology has many possible future worlds awaiting her. There exist a vast array of exciting fields in which to work and conduct research. The scale of employment in applied anthropology has both broadened and increased, offering many career chances both inside and outside academe. Graduates with advanced anthropology degrees can enter, and have entered, careers that focus on applying anthropological knowledge. Anthropology students can be found in a variety of industries, ranging from corporate business and marketing to medical organizations, hydro projects, and cultural resource management. Within these areas and many others, anthropologists can make a difference, bringing their analytical and problem-solving skills to bear on issues such as human rights, dispute settlement, and environmental justice.

Our discussion of the history of applied anthropology revealed that it is not a new field of inquiry; it has, in fact, been present in one form or another since the founding days of anthropology. In this chapter we have focused on some of the ways that anthropologists can apply their training to non-traditional fields. We have seen that this path can lead to some rather startling outcomes. An applied anthropologist can take on a major international corporate company, and eventually win. The work of an applied anthropologist can take him to the White House, or take her to the killing fields of the world, working as a forensic anthropologist or archaeologist. Applied anthropology can enrich our understanding of the world's cultural diversity, or warn us of the threatened extinction of peoples, languages, and species. It can also lead to abuses, to the misappropriation and misuse of anthropological data, and to violations of anthropological principles. (These problems also exist in academic anthropology.) Generally, though, applied anthropology offers students a way to learn about cultures and provides them with careers in diverse fields. Applied anthropology offers students and professional anthropologists opportunities to put their specialized learning to good use and to become anthropologists at work.

Chapter Summary

1. What is applied anthropology?

Applied anthropology is the putting into practice, outside of the academic setting, of anthropological skills and resources. Applied anthropology has always been a part of anthropology, but has become much more prevalent over the past few decades. As disease and poverty increase and as more and more major development projects are undertaken (mainly in the developing world) the need for applied anthropologists has grown.

2. How did applied anthropology develop?

The domains of applied anthropology are myriad. Anthropologists of all types are employed in a very diverse set of employment areas. Some of these areas, such as medical anthropology or forensic anthropology, involve the anthropologist in political and social situations that can be contentious. Some areas of applied anthropology draw upon specific skill sets, such as the employment of archaeologists in CRM projects and linguists in translation areas. Other areas require diverse anthropological skills and team work. University courses in anthropology can be linked to a variety of future careers in applied anthropology. All of these areas require a thorough understanding and grounding in the basic theories, terms, and constructs of anthropology.

3. What are some of the challenges facing the applied anthropologist?

Applied anthropologists have been engaged with important social issues during the past few decades. The work of an applied anthropologist can result in conflict with major corporations or with local communities. The decisions that they make and the work that they do can have a profound impact on the peoples and societies in which they work. Whether in teams or as individuals, applied anthropologists can make a difference, and their research and findings can have important ramifications for individuals and groups alike.

4. What does the future hold for applied anthropology?

The future of applied anthropology is rather bright. There is a growing recognition that many large projects and developments do require anthropological expertise. Some have questioned whether this will place stress on the original goals of anthropology; others argue that the world is rapidly changing and that anthropologists, and the institutions that teach anthropology, must adapt to current circumstances and embrace the idea that more and more anthropologists will be employed in the practical realm.

Questions for Critical Thought

1. What are some of the differences between applied and academic anthropology?

2. What are some of the problems that face an applied anthropologist?

3. What will an anthropology student need to focus on to become an applied anthropologist? What career choices are open to students of anthropology?

4. Does the application of anthropological skills to practical areas clash with the historical goals of anthropology?

5. What areas of applied anthropology will likely grow in the near future, and why?

Internet Resources

Society for Applied Anthropology

http://www.sfaa.net

The home page for the Society for Applied Anthropology provides access to publications of the society, meeting reports, and general news on applied anthropology.

COPAA (Consortium of Practicing and Applied Anthropology Programs)

http://www.copaa.info

An American consortium of university departments and programs designed to advance the practice of applied anthropology.

American Anthropological Association

http://www.aaanet.org

Home page of the American Anthropological Association.

Notes

1. B. Malinowski, "Practical Anthropology," *Africa: Journal of the International African Institute* 2, no. 1 (January 1929): 22–38 at 22.

2. H. Schoolcraft and S. Eastman, *Historical and Statistical Information Respecting the History, Condition, and Prospects of the Indian Tribes of the United States* (Philadelphia: Lippincott, Grambo, 1851).

3. Ruth Benedict, *The Chrysanthemum and the Sword: Patterns of Japaense Culture* (New York: Mariner, 1989).

4. G.E. Lowe, "The Camelot Affair," *Bulletin of Atomic Scientists* 22, no. 5 (1966).

5. D. Jenness, "Eskimo Administration II: Canada," Technical Paper no. 14 (Montreal: Arctic Institute of North America, 1964), 58.

6. A.M. Ervin and L. Holyoak, "Applied Anthropology in Canada: Historical Foundations, Contemporary Practice, and Policy Potentials," *NAPA Bulletin* 25, no. 1 (2006): 134–55.

7. E.J. Hedican, *Applied Anthropology in Canada: Understanding Aboriginal Issues* (Toronto: University of Toronto Press, 2008).

8. Canadian Anthropology Society (CASCA), "Prix Weaver-Tremblay Award 2008," *Newsletter* 2, no. 2 (Fall 2008).

9. M. Dorerri and J. Burrell, "Gray Spaces and Endless Negotiations: Forensic Anthropology and Human Rights," in *Anthropology Put to Work*. ed. L. Field and R.G. Fox (Oxford: Berg, 2007), 45–64 at 46.

10. O. Beattie and J. Geiger, *Frozen in Time: The Fate of the Franklin Expedition* (London: Bloomsbury Publishing, 1987).

11. O. Beattie and j. Geiger, *Dead Silence: The Greatest Mystery in Arctic Discovery* (Toronto: Penguin, 1993).

12. Kingsolver, "'Thinking and Acting Ethically in Anthropology," in Thinking Anthropologically, ed. P.K. Salzman and P.C. Rice (Upper Saddle River: Pearson-Prentice HaJJ, 2008), 68–75.

13. G. Graffam, "*Design Anthropology Meets Marketing*," Anthropolog1ca 52 (2010): 155–64.

14. B. Burkhalter, "If Only They Would Listen: The Anthropology of Business and the Business of Anthropology," *in Classics of Practicing Anthropology*, 1978–1998, ed. P.J. Higgins and J.A. Paredes (Oklahoma City: Society for Applied Anthropology, 2000), 77–86.

15. D. Rohde, "Army Enlists Anthropology in War Zones," *New York Times*, October 5, 2007, http://www .nytimes.com/ 2007/ I 0/ 05/ world/ asia/ 05afgba n. html?_r=2&pagewanted=alL, accessed August 11, 2011.

16. Ibid.

17. P.A. Omidian, "Living and Working in a War Zone: An Applied Anthropologist in Afghanistan," *Practicing Anthropology* 31 (2009): 4–11.

18. http://aaanewsinfo.blogspoc.com.

19. A. Chung, "U.S. Army Recruiting Anthropologists," *Toronto Star*, November 25, 2007, http://www.thestar.com/ News/article/279646, accessed August 11, 2011.

20. B. Johnson, 2000. "Human Rights and the Environment," in *Classics of Practicing Anthropology*, 1978-1998, ed. P.J. Higgins and J.A. Paredes (Oklahoma City: Society for Applied Anthropology, 2000), 223–30 at 225–26.

21. H. Rosenberg. "From Trash to Treasure," in *Artiwlating Hidden Histories*, ed. J. Schneider and R. Rapp (Berkeley: University of California Press, 1997), 190–204.

22. L. Gibbs, *Dying from Dioxin: A Citizen's Guide to Reclaiming Our Health and Rebuilding Democracy* (Boston: South End Press, 1995); L.M. Gibbs. Love Canal: The Story Continues (Gabriola Island: New Society, 1998).

23. M. Barlow and E. May, *Frederick Street: Life and Death on Canada 's Love Canal* (Toronto: HarperCollins, 2000); C. Perkel, Well of Lies: Tl1e Walkerton Water Tragedy (Toronto: McClelland and Stewart, 2002).

24. P. Block, "Doing Cultural Anthropology and Disability Studies in Rehabilitation Training and Research Contexts," in *Anthropology Put to Work*, ed. L. Field and R.G. Fox (Oxford: Berg, 2007), 85–101 at 87.

25. Ibid.

26. L. Kilmurray and N. Faba, *Access to Academic Materials for Post-Secondary Students with Print Disabilities* (Ottawa: National Educational Association of Disabled Students, 2005), 234.

27. Ibid.

28. C. Renfrew and P. Bahn, *Archaeology: Theories, Methods, and Practice* (London: Thames and Hudson, 1996), 524.

29. N. Dyck and J.B. Waldram, eds., *Anthropology, Public Policy, and Native Peoples in Canada* (Monrreal and Kingston: McGill–Queen's Unjversity Press, 1993).

30. Ervin and Holyoak, "Applied Anthropology in Canada."

31. S. Keida, "Recent Changes and Trends in the Practice of Applied Anthropology," *NAPA Bulletin* 29 (2008): 14–28 at 26.

Key Terms

applied anthropology   Consulting work undertaken by anthropologists relating to practical problems.

Department of Indian Affairs   A department of the Government of Canada with responsibility for policies relating to Aboriginal peoples in Canada.

forensic anthropology   The examination of human skeletal remains. Part of physical anthropology, this field often works with law enforcement agencies to determine the identity of unidentified bones.

forensic archaeologist   An archaeologist who controls a site, recording the position of all relevant finds and recovering any clues associated with the remains.

medical anthropology   The subfield of cultural anthropology that analyses how cultures and societies are organized around issues of health and related issues.

environmental justice   A social movement in which citizen activists organize to defend against environmental threats to community health and well-being.

salvage archaeology   The collection of archaeological data and materials from any given site deemed to be in danger of destruction, as from new construction or weather damage.

cultural resource management (CRM)   The practice of managing cultural resources, such as arts and heritage. It incorporates cultural herit age management, which is concerned with traditional and historic culture and the material culture of archaeology.

Conclusion

It is hoped that this book has demonstrated some of the fascinating practices of the world's cultures and the institutions and customs that each possesses. Exposure to this variety helps to reveal to us our own culture in clearer detail. Through a grounding in anthropological data and theory we can learn that the particular manner in which we conduct our daily lives, our fashions, institutions, rules, and regulations, are just that; particular. They are particular to our own culture; products of histories and traditions bequeathed to us by our ancestors. Cultural practices are reviewed, changed, modified, abandoned, or preserved according to our choices. Other peoples in other places have their own historical trajectories, their own ways of doing things. We have seen some of the great diversity of cultural practices throughout this textbook and noted that anthropological inquiry shows that people do what works for them. Whether this is killing chickens to determine the presence of witchcraft, calling our mothers' sisters "mothers" or burying our dead with unused and beautifully made tools, these customs make sense of the world to the people who continue to follow them. Such practices are rarely maladaptive; they work for the people who undertake them, and they enable the continuance of social norms and institutions. There is no right and no wrong way to do culture. We have attempted to convey in this book a well-grounded examination of the four fields of anthropology. We have covered these fields in a manner that is both inclusive, and, by necessity, also quite selective. Each of the fields we have addressed also contains a multitude of subfields and specialized research areas that the student of anthropology may be exposed to in future studies. In this text, a balanced view of the major approaches and theories in anthropology has been presented. It is hoped that this will serves readers well, that it will inspire them to continue to pursue anthropological knowledge and to understand the pleasures, responsibilities, and fascination of the anthropological world.

This textbook has covered a broad array of topics and yet it has just scratched the surface of the fascinating and diverse world of anthropological interests. Anthropology, as we have seen, is the social science which attempts to penetrate and understand the wonderful world of culture and cultures. In endeavoring to portray some of this diversity, our chapters have discussed the ways in which anthropologists have studied human societies. The history of anthropological inquiry has demonstrated the dedicated and rigorous scholarship that researchers in diverse subfields have undertaken. From the evolution of

Homo sapiens and our first use of tools, to the emergence of language, kinship networks, and subsistence strategies, we have examined the myriad forms that cultural practices take. This conclusion turns an eye to the future of anthropology, arguing for its continued relevance in today's globalized world. The long history of anthropological research has demonstrated the absolute need for us to know ourselves and understand the patterns that human cultures enact. Anthropological knowledge contributes to society in many ways, not least to help us understand our past and our present, but also to face the challenges of modern life. Knowing ourselves helps us to contextualize human societies, to understand peace, war, trade, egalitarianism, capitalism, ethnocentrism, and spirituality. Perhaps most important of all, anthropology tells us that our story as a species, our stories as cultures are the source of our humanity and our hope for the future.

Anthropology, like culture itself, has a past, present, and future. Also, like culture, it faces change, revisionism, resistance, criticism, and renewal. What will anthropology look like in the future? What issues will anthropology face and what subject matter might attract the interest of anthropologists? What tools and theories will anthropologists use to study the diverse field of human culture? To begin to answer these questions we shall first examine what the future may hold in store for our species, *Homo sapiens*.

1   The future of humanity

While anthropology is not a panacea for the world's problems, nor, situationally, even as important as knowing how to gather edible plants in the Amazon, hunt in the Arctic, or reduce our carbon footprint in megacities, it can contribute to solving and limiting some major problems that exist today. Climate change, global warming, and population growth are all issues that concern anthropologists and other researchers. Specifically, from the anthropological viewpoint, these challenges threaten to disrupt, destroy, and alter ancient and modern cultures and societies and exacerbate many of the challenges that have always been present. Understanding population demographics, migration, assimilation, and culture change will become more and more valuable as tools for coping with these future challenges. The scope of anthropological expertise can contribute to debates and solutions in regard to such recent developments, and in particular to globalization.

2   Globalization and anthropology

Globalization is one of the major events in the history of our species. Along with the advent of bipedality and the agrarian and industrial revolutions, the emergence of globalization and its attendant Internet explosion has been and remains a momentous event. Anthropologists naturally take the long view of these massive social changes and the forces that cause them. After the sustained voyages between Europe and the Americas in the late fifteenth and sixteenth centuries, and at the time when the continents of Africa and Asia were becoming better known to Europeans, it was the early anthropologists who brought back riches from these faraway places—not the gold, spices, and other resources sought by conquistadors or missionaries, but the knowledge of other peoples and how they lived their lives. Some of these early attempts at understanding, many of which we now recognize as colonial or deeply misguided in other ways did broaden the horizons of humanity, opening up new worlds. Cultures and peoples that were virtually unknown to each other suddenly loomed large in people's minds and world views. After the so-called discovery of these new continents, after the annihilation, slavery, despair, and disease brought on by the processes of "discovery," the intervening centuries saw the world first expand and then shrink as whole continents were mapped, documented, counted, and in many cases "conquered" and exploited. By the twentieth century, scholars recognized that the peoples of the world were more connected than at any time in the past. A World Systems Theory emerged, in which anthropologists, sociologists, and economists all sought to understand the new patterns of international cultural exchange and commerce that had emerged. In the twenty-first century, the term globalization is now, well, a global term. However, it hides more than it reveals, since we have in many ways lived in a globalized world since the at least seventeenth century. What is different now is the pace of exchange, the presence of the Internet, borderless, cheap travel, and the seemingly unstoppable force of change. Globalization is defined as the growing interdependence of the world's populations, economies, and cultures, occurring through the processes of cross-border trade in technology, goods and services, and increased flows of investment, people, and information. Globalization may not be permanent, but it is currently having a vast impact on the way culture is understood and studied. Mass displacements and movements of people have resulted in many nation states becoming heterogeneous. Some, like Canada, embrace multiculturalism as a state policy. Others, like New Zealand, tend toward biculturalism. Much of Europe, which for many centuries was mostly homogenous, is now a collection of heterogeneous peoples and cultures. Massive growth in population, continued conflict, and large-scale migration have resulted in the majority of people now residing in cities. The process of globalization is studied by sociologists, economists, political scientists, and many others. In anthropology, however, we are not just limited to analyzing the penetration of market forces or the upward mobility of immigrants and similar interesting topics. We are interested in all of these in terms of what they imply for the study of humanity in all its cultural and social manifestations. The impact of globalization on some cultures has been extensive. The meetings of cultures and the intermixing of ethnic groups have resulted in new material for anthropology to study, but also, on the negative side, have resulted in the loss of many languages and the undermining of once traditional methods and practices. The large-scale abandonment of rural villages and the emigration of young people undermines the future of some cultures, destroys some languages, and lessens the cultural vivacity of once thriving smaller societies. Added to this, climate change and global warming have negatively impacted cultures around the world. Islands in the Pacific and Inuit communities in the Arctic, for example, are struggling to adapt to changed environmental circumstances. Their way of life, whether based around the winter hunt or seasonal voyages is threatened. What can anthropology offer in these changed global circumstances?

Anthropologists can document the last vestiges of various threatened cultures and practices, yet anthropology has much more to offer than this. It can be a bulwark against the rampant exploitation of poorer communities and it can be an activist voice, documenting human rights abuses or dangerous safety practices by large corporations operating in poor developing countries. Anthropology plays these roles, and they are valuable. It educates and lobbies—whether through academia or through engaged-public anthropology. It brings people together. Some anthropologists have helped to promote the development of craft cooperatives in Nunavut or Mesoamerica in their attempts to gain a foothold in the international market for their products. Likewise, anthropologists have played a very constructive role in collaborating with small communities or indigenous nations to set up larger organizations and international fora so that their voices can carry further. Human rights abuses have been documented and anthropology also educates and helps to combat extremism and racism. The exposure to anthropological knowledge and practice can help reduce conflict, racism, and ethnocentrism. Thus, knowledge of cultural anthropology, or the prehistory of a given people, can make a difference in reducing misunderstandings and ignorance.

What of culture change? Anthropologists have long created terms, concepts, and theories to classify and understand culture change. We speak of syncretism: the blending or selective borrowing of culture traits. We account for culture change through concepts such as ethnogenesis: the birth of new ethnicities, through assimilation, innovation, diffusion, revolution, acculturation, and other constructs. These have been applied to understanding the changes to cultures that anthropologists have documented and studied. In the current climate of rapid globalization, it is increasingly important for anthropology to document and try to understand these changes and the forces that instigate them. What impacts will things like syncretism and ethnogenesis have on language, the preservation of a past, the repatriation of heritage artifacts, or indigenous land claims? When there is great flux, great movements of peoples, and increased and instant communication, cultures will change, adopt, and adapt.

In linguistic anthropology there are exciting new challenges for anthropology and its students. The consolidation of globalization and the mass movements of peoples have resulted in much mingling of languages. Learning a second or third language, long practiced in many parts of the world, has become now a necessity for many in the academic, business, and political communities. The result is an increase in the appreciation of language, of its central role in culture, and its importance to ethnic and national identity. Multiculturalism and its attendant needs results in the need for learning, translation, and in a broader appreciation of the way educators approach language. In all this, linguistic anthropology has much to add. Recurrent and ongoing research seeks to link the Basque language to the Indo European super language-family. Certain Mayan glyphs remain undeciphered. Megalithic art still fascinates both the archaeologists and the linguists but remains enigmatic. On a sadder note, the documentation of lost and almost-extinct languages has been a major source of stress and academic focus for linguistic anthropologists. In short, linguistic anthropology remains a staple of the anthropological world, one that contributes much knowledge, provides us with warnings on disappearing languages and continues to be applied in numerous fields of communication.

In cultural anthropology, the future promises to be one of intense study and new material to encounter. New research includes the reassessment of kinship studies. New reproductive techniques, new forms of recognized marriage, adoption, kin-reckoning, and issues surrounding single and same-sex parents and other family structures have opened up new vistas for cultural anthropologists. Cultural anthropology is vast and diverse, as we have seen in this book. It remains always in flux, with little unifying unanimity regarding theoretical approaches and even subject matter. National traditions of practicing cultural anthropology still abound, and what is considered its domain of study differs from place to place. In England it is still referred to as social anthropology, in other places as sociocultural anthropology, and in North America simply cultural anthropology. However, in a field that covers so many areas of human behavior, it could hardly be otherwise.

Physical anthropology casts its wide net over many fields. Paleoanthropologists are engaged in the reconstruction of human phylogeny, tracing the footsteps, often literally, of our forebears. There have been many outstanding discoveries just in the past few years. Upper paleolithic figurines were discovered in the Swabian Alps in 2009, dated to some 40,000 years ago. *Homo denisovans* and *Homo floresiensis*, two startlingly new members of the genus *Homo*, have been discovered in the past decade alone. In November 2017, a team from the Max Planck Institute for Evolutionary Anthropology in Leipzig undertook genetic analysis of soil samples scraped from a cave floor which revealed the presence of neanderthals through that most definitive of biological markers: their DNA. The ability to discover DNA without discovering fossils is an extraordinary achievement indeed. In 2019, an international team working in Ethiopia announced the discovery of stone tools that push back their earliest known manufacturer from 2.58 million years to roughly 2.8 million years ago. Along with the introduction of LiDAR in archaeology, these technological developments promise to uncover more and more about the distant past.

In archaeology too there are promising developments and continuing research that will continue to enlighten the human story. Archaeology is in fact a growth industry, particularly in Western Europe and North America, where cultural resource management (salvage archaeology) is a significant employer. New sites are discovered weekly, as towns grow and highways are built, revealing more and more of the past. Archaeology is topical in film, literature, and the news. Archaeological finds are exhibited, go on tour, are analyzed and reinterpreted. The discovery of new settlements deep in Amazonia or Inca mummies high in the Andes Mountains are cause for great public excitement and academic delight. Newer technologies, although their use in archaeology is debated, are helping to reveal more and more of the past each year. Within the discipline, contentious issues and great intellectual battles still take place. Theoretical questions are still very much debated: should structuralist theory be reborn or jettisoned? Can postprocessualism be merged with symbolic interactionism? These debates, although sometimes conducted in arcane language, do improve our knowledge of both the past and the processes of theoretical development. Archaeology is also very relevant to current environmental concerns. Climate change has had a large impact on archaeology. Many coastal sites worldwide are threatened and in need of urgent mitigation. Understanding of past climate change and its effect on people as diverse as the Maya, Polynesians, and Australian Aboriginal peoples is actively sought by environmentalists, town-planners, and many others. Whether excavating the remains of our ancient relatives and constructing a timeline of human physical and cultural evolution, or debating the merits of postmodernist theory, archaeology still strives to get to the bottom of things.

3 A world without anthropology?

A world in which we lose touch with *Homo habilis*, where we forget millions of years of mutations and adaptations which made us upright and talking creatures, is a lesser and more disconnected world. Knowing *Homo sapiens*, having the "ology" of the "Anthropos," is essential. Appreciating the sometimes beautiful, sometimes terrible effects of natural selection makes us more fully human. Anthropology fills in the "blank spaces of prehistory." It also clarifies our current practices and sets them in a cultural context, often one with a lengthy pedigree. Anthropology fills our minds with the very, very, slow accretions that made up the Grand Canyon, or the sudden deluges that washed out ancient hominid base-camps, leaving us their bones and tools to marvel at. It tells us that the people of the Yucatan Peninsula, as they go about their daily lives today, walk over the bones of their Mayan ancestors, whose ground-breaking agricultural techniques such as floating islands and chinampas paved the way for the modern people and their communities. North Americans know, or can know, that the indigenous people around them came from Siberia some 17,000 years ago, or "time immemorial" for them, hunted woolly mammoth and giant mastodons created beautiful and stunning artworks, and have thriving, complex and varied cultures that continue to evolve today. Memories of European settlements, whether L'Anse Aux Meadow or the more long-lived Quebec City or Plymouth, linger on today. They linger in architecture, in artifacts excavated, examined, and painstakingly catalogued by anthropologists. Under the ground, or in upstanding (and outstanding) monuments, resides the strata of our past practices. These inform our ways of life today. Above the ground the genetic continuity of a people, borne through time as Francophones, Cree, American or Maya, is dressed in the particular and specific robes of culture. Anthropologists bear witness to all of this, they recreate and interpret pasts, they attend to present cultural constructions, they observe and document the ways of the peoples of the earth.

It is hoped that this textbook has equipped the reader and the student of anthropology with the tools to understand anthropology and the cultural world around them. Education and knowledge are likened to a cloud, one that diminishes, changes shape, expands, alters its direction, but nonetheless persists through time. It is hope that this book and the knowledge of anthropology can contribute to the continuance of that cloud of knowledge and insight. Anthropology remains vibrant in the world today and is thriving at an institutional level, though it is funded much less than law or business studies—due in part to a modern focus in some countries for sciences that produce IT experts, lawyers or stockbrokers. While its value may be less readily translated into dollars and profits, it is of enormous value to society, and an important investment. Anthropology is a practice and set of discourses that we cannot do without.

CPSIA information can be obtained
at www.ICGtesting.com
Printed in the USA
FSHW011020130819